Infinispan Data Grid Platform Definitive Guide

Master Infinispan to create scalable and high-performance applications

Wagner Roberto dos Santos

BIRMINGHAM - MUMBAI

Infinispan Data Grid Platform Definitive Guide

First published: May 2015

Production reference: 1250515

Published by Packt Publishing Ltd.
Livery Place
35 Livery Street
Birmingham B3 2PB, UK.

ISBN 978-1-78216-997-0

www.packtpub.com

Credits

Author
Wagner Roberto dos Santos

Reviewers
Ben D. Cotton III
Gustavo Fernandes
Zdenek Henek
Andrii Kravets
Ugo Landini
Marko Lukša

Commissioning Editor
Usha Iyer

Acquisition Editor
Usha Iyer

Content Development Editor
Rohit Kumar Singh

Technical Editor
Bharat Patil

Copy Editors
Merilyn Pereira
Laxmi Subramanian

Project Coordinator
Mary Alex

Proofreaders
Stephen Copestake
Safis Editing

Indexer
Rekha Nair

Graphics
Jason Monteiro

Production Coordinator
Manu Joseph

Cover Work
Manu Joseph

About the Author

Wagner Roberto dos Santos is an Italian Brazilian software architect living in Dublin, Ireland. He has more than 14 years of professional IT experience in software development, architecture, and Agile methodologies.

He is specialized in Java Enterprise technologies, and has deep knowledge of new emerging technologies such as cloud computing, NoSQL, and big data. As an architect, he supports teams in designing and developing scalable and maintainable solutions, following best practices, design patterns, and Domain-Driven Design practices.

As an agile coach, he supports teams in the adoption of Agile methodologies, such as Scrum, extreme programming, and Kanban, to make faster and better software deliveries to demanding time scales.

Until last year, Wagner was an MBA professor of distributed computing and Java Enterprise Development at FIAP and was also an instructor of several Agile and Java courses at Globalcode, a well-known Brazilian educational center specialized in software development.

Wagner contributes actively to the Agile and Java communities in Brazil. He is a member of SOUJava and speaks regularly at conferences such as The Developers Conference and Campus Party. He is also the former lead editor of the Architecture Queue at InfoQ Brasil and writes regularly for IT magazines, such as Mundo Java and Java Magazine.

Acknowledgments

I would like to thank, absolutely foremost, God and his son Jesus Christ for giving me the incredible opportunity to write this book because without him, nothing is possible.

Thanks to JBoss and all members of the Infinispan development team—Manik Surtani, Galder Zamarreño, Mircea Markus, Sanne Grinovero, Vladimir Blagojevic, Pedro Ruivo, Navin Surtani, and Bela Ban—for building such a great product. Special thanks to Manik Surtani and Pete Muir who reviewed the outline and provided useful suggestions; they have made all the difference. They asked me to include the Ticket Monster application in Chapter 6, which was developed by Red Hat/JBoss developers. I think it was an extraordinary idea and I would like to thank them all; they have done a wonderful job with this application.

I would also like to thank Mohammad Rizvi, Pramila Balan, Amey Sawant, Arshad Sopariwala, Priyanka Goel, Ritika Dewani, Rohit Kumar Singh, Bharat Patil, and Priya Singh from Packt Publishing for trusting in me to write this book and for the support and effort you put into this project. Thank you!

Thanks to my technical reviewers, Ugo Landini, Marko Luksa, Gustavo Fernandes, Andrii Kravets, Ben Cotton, and Zdenek Henek. Their insightful and valuable comments really improved the book.

And special thanks to my family—my wife, Marcia, supported me throughout this time and my little daughter, Maria Luiza, who couldn't play with her daddy as much as she wanted to.

About the Reviewers

Ben D. Cotton III is an IT consultant at J.P. Morgan Chase, currently using Java data grid technology on a UHPC Linux platform to render and aggregate real-time liquidity risk. He is a Java community process member presently sitting on two active JCP expert groups defining Java standard APIs for Caching (JSR-107) and distributed data grids (JSR-347). Ben graduated from Rutgers University in May 1985 with a BS in computer science. He spent his first 11 years at AT&T Bell Laboratories writing C++ code supporting numerous proprietary telecommunications network analytics and provisioning protocols, and he spent the last 14 years writing Java code supporting low-latency and transactional fixed income/derivatives, electronic trading, clearing, pricing, and risk systems.

Gustavo Fernandes is a developer, consultant, trainer, and architect with a background in server-side software, ranging from JEE to system integration and, more recently, free text and semantic search, big data, NoSQL, and devops/automation tools.

Throughout his career, he devoted many years developing open source-based solutions and products for a wide range of customers from different industries, including finance, betting, social media, telco, and e-commerce.

He's worked in several countries in South America and Europe, he is an occasional speaker at conferences, and he writes a blog and articles. He enjoys contributing to open source projects and when not writing code, and he likes traveling to see the world.

He currently works at Red Hat as part of the Infinispan team.

Zdenek Henek lives in the Czech Republic in Zidlochovice. He is a husband and a father. He enjoys software development, solving problems, and playing chess.

Andrii Kravets is a highly motivated, Agile-minded engineer with more than 5 years of experience in software development and software project management, who wants to make the world better. He has a lot of experience with high-loaded distributed projects, big data, JVM languages, and web architecture. He is a co-founder of Mriya Ideas Lab.

Ugo Landini takes the sentence "The only difference between men and boys is the cost of their toys" very seriously. He works as a software architect at Red Hat. He dedicates the rest of his time to what's new in the IT field and is strongly convinced that sharing knowledge is not only a must but also an opportunity for personal growth. A cofounder of the JUG Roma, Ugo is an Apache committer, develops games for mobile devices, and is convinced he can still play a decent football game (soccer for American people). He is also a cofounder and the chair of the technical committee at Codemotion.

I would like to thank Monica , Diego, and Luca, the most beautiful things that have happened to me.

Marko Lukša is a software engineer, currently working as a member of the Cloud Enablement team at Red Hat. He has been using Infinispan extensively as part of his work on project CapeDwarf, the open source implementation of the Google App Engine API. He has also contributed to Infinispan — mostly to its grid file system. Before joining Red Hat, he worked at various companies delivering different software solutions in healthcare, telecommunications, and hotel and restaurant management. He currently resides in Ljubljana, Slovenia.

www.PacktPub.com

Support files, eBooks, discount offers, and more

For support files and downloads related to your book, please visit www.PacktPub.com.

Did you know that Packt offers eBook versions of every book published, with PDF and ePub files available? You can upgrade to the eBook version at www.PacktPub.com and as a print book customer, you are entitled to a discount on the eBook copy. Get in touch with us at service@packtpub.com for more details.

At www.PacktPub.com, you can also read a collection of free technical articles, sign up for a range of free newsletters and receive exclusive discounts and offers on Packt books and eBooks.

https://www2.packtpub.com/books/subscription/packtlib

Do you need instant solutions to your IT questions? PacktLib is Packt's online digital book library. Here, you can search, access, and read Packt's entire library of books.

Why subscribe?

- Fully searchable across every book published by Packt
- Copy and paste, print, and bookmark content
- On demand and accessible via a web browser

Free access for Packt account holders

If you have an account with Packt at www.PacktPub.com, you can use this to access PacktLib today and view 9 entirely free books. Simply use your login credentials for immediate access.

Table of Contents

Preface   ix

Chapter 1: Getting Started   1

  Introducing the Infinispan data grid   2

  Infinispan and JSR 107 – Java Temporary Caching API   5

  Getting started with Infinispan   5

    Installing Infinispan   6

    Looking inside the box   6

    Using Maven   9

  Running the sample application   11

  Creating your first project   15

    Creating a Maven project manually   20

  Building Infinispan from source   21

    Setting up the environment   22

  Contributing to the project   25

  Summary   27

Chapter 2: Barriers to Scaling Data   29

  Understanding performance and scalability   30

  Improving performance using Infinispan   31

    An introduction to performance tuning   33

    Infinispan and performance   35

  Improving scalability   36

    Vertical scalability   37

    Horizontal scalability   38

    Design tradeoffs   39

  Points to consider about relational databases   39

    Distributed transactions and ACID   40

    CAP theorem   43

BASE	45
Infinispan, CAP, and BASE	46
Scaling out your database	**47**
Scaling options	47
Master-Slave replication	48
Active/Passive configuration	49
Database clustering	49
Database sharding	50
Infinispan and network partitions	55
Configuring partition handling	57
Infinispan and high availability	58
Summary	**58**
Chapter 3: Using the APIs	**59**
Infinispan architecture	**60**
Anatomy of an Infinispan clustered cache	**60**
The embedded (P2P) mode	61
The client/server mode	62
The cache container	63
Default cache	63
Naming your caches	64
Configuring an Infinispan cache	**67**
Declarative configuration on Infinispan 6.0.x	68
Global configuration (globalType)	70
Configuration settings	74
Declarative configuration on Infinispan 7.0.x	77
Understanding the JGroups element	78
Configuring the threads subsystem	78
Configuring the cache-container element	80
Programmatic configuration	82
Infinispan APIs	**85**
Learning the cache API	86
Understanding cache evictions	88
Configuring cache expiration	92
Eviction v/s Expiration	95
Persisting data in Infinispan	**96**
Configuring a cache loader	98
Filesystem-based cache loaders	98
JDBC-based cache loaders	99
JPA cache store	100
Selecting a JDBC cache loader	102
Using passivation in your application	103

Writing event listeners and notifications   **105**
The listener API   105
    Cluster listeners in Infinispan 7.0   106
Listening to cache-level events   107
Writing cache manager-level events   111
Registering event listeners   113
    Configuring logging in Infinispan   114
Introducing JSR-107 – The Java Caching API   **115**
Summary   **119**

Chapter 4: Infinispan Topologies   **121**
Clustering modes   **121**
The local mode   122
The invalidation mode   124
The replicated mode   126
    Understanding synchronous and asynchronous replication   127
The distribution mode   135
    Server Hinting   143
L1 caching   144
Summary   **147**

Chapter 5: Data Access Patterns   **149**
Data access patterns   **149**
Understanding and configuring second-level cache in Hibernate with Infinispan   **150**
Introducing first-level and second-level caching   150
    Configuring Infinispan as Hibernate second-level cache   152
Implementing the cache-aside programming pattern   **155**
Reading and writing through cache   **156**
Writing behind caching   **158**
The Unscheduled Write-behind strategy   159
The Scheduled Write-behind strategy   160
Summary   **161**

Chapter 6: Case Study – The TicketMonster Application   **163**
The JBoss developer framework   **164**
Installing and running the TicketMonster application   **165**
Project structure   166
    In Eclipse   167
    In IntelliJ   168
The TicketMonster application use cases   **169**
Administrators use cases   175
    Building the administration UI using JBoss Forge   177

Architecture and design of TicketMonster	**181**
The TicketMonster domain model	184
Utility classes in TicketMonster	185
The service layer of TicketMonster	186
Scaling TicketMonster	**189**
Clustered Web servers versus stateful session	190
Which pattern to use?	192
Adding Infinispan to TicketMonster	**193**
Configuring the infrastructure	196
Using caches for seat reservations	198
Implementing shopping carts	201
Summary	**213**
Chapter 7: Understanding Transactions and Concurrency	**215**
Transaction fundamentals	**216**
Java Transaction API	**217**
Transactional modes	**221**
Non-transactional data access	222
Transactional models	**222**
Optimistic transaction	223
Pessimistic transaction	225
Choosing the better transaction model	226
Batch mode	**226**
Transaction recovery	**229**
Integrating with Transaction Manager	232
Locking and concurrency control	**232**
Multiversion concurrency control	236
Configuring isolation levels in Infinispan	236
Implicit and explicit locking	242
Lock timeouts	243
Deadlock detection	244
Data versioning	246
Summary	**247**
Chapter 8: Managing and Monitoring Infinispan	**249**
An overview of monitoring and managing with Java	**249**
Monitoring and managing Java applications with JMX	250
Interacting with Infinispan via JMX	**252**
The CacheManager level	252
The cache level	254
Monitoring Infinispan with JConsole	255

Monitoring Infinispan with VisualVM   258
Infinispan's MBeans   262
Other management tools   **266**
Introducing RHQ   266
Installing and configuring RHQ   268
Monitoring Infinispan   274
Summary   **280**
Chapter 9: Server Modules   **281**
Client/Server access   **281**
Introduction to server modules   **282**
Starting the server   283
Configuration   284
Customizing the endpoint and Infinispan subsystem   284
Enabling protocol interoperability   287
Infinispan REST server   **288**
Introduction to the REST server   288
Configuring the Infinispan REST server on earlier versions   289
Introducing the REST API   290
Using HTTP request headers for GET and HEAD operations   293
Using HTTP request headers for POST and PUT operations   293
Client side code   295
cURL   295
Testing REST services with RESTClient   296
Consuming RESTful web services with Java   297
Using the Hot Rod server   **303**
Hot Rod clients   304
Using the Hot Rod Java Client   305
Starting a RemoteCacheManager   305
Configuring authentication for your Hot Rod application   308
Introducing the SASL framework   308
Supported SASL mechanisms   309
Configuring authorization policies   310
Infinispan memcached server   **318**
The memcached protocol   319
Connecting the Infinispan memcached server by using a Java Client   323
The Infinispan WebSocket server   **325**
Introducing WebSocket   325
Overview of the WebSocket API   326
WebSocket in Java   327
Using the Infinispan JavaScript API   327
Introducing the command line interface (CLI)   **329**
Starting the command line interface   330

Using Infinispan CLI commands   331
  Defining data types and time values   332
  Basic commands   333
  Manipulating caches   334
  Managing caches   335
  Managing transactions   336
  rollback   337
  Batching   337
  Getting statistics and system information   338
Summary   **339**
Chapter 10: Getting Started with Hibernate OGM   **341**
Introducing Hibernate OGM   **341**
  Hibernate OGM features   343
  Hibernate OGM architecture   343
  Understanding how the mappings work   345
Installing and using Hibernate OGM   **350**
  Creating a Hibernate OGM project using Maven   351
    Configuring the persistence unit   353
    Configuring Infinispan caches for Hibernate OGM   357
    Creating the domain model   360
Summary   **366**
Chapter 11: An Introduction to JGroups   **367**
Introduction to group communication   **367**
Understanding the JGroups project   **369**
The JGroups architecture   **370**
Customizing JGroups settings on Infinispan   **372**
  An Overview of protocols used by JGroups   375
    Transportation   375
    Membership discovery   378
    Merging   382
    Failure detection   382
    Reliable transmission   384
    Fragmentation of large messages   385
    Ordering protocols   386
    Group membership   386
    State transfer   387
    Security   388
    Flow control   389
    Message stability   389
Summary   **390**

Chapter 12: Advanced Topics   391
Cross-site replication   392
Configuring cross-site replication   393
Cross-site replication and transactions   397
Cross-site replication with non-transactional caches   398
Cross-site replication with transactional caches   398
Taking a site offline and online again   399
Integrating Infinispan with CDI   399
An introduction to CDI   399
Setting up CDI support in your Maven POM   400
Injecting an Infinispan cache into your Beans   401
Customizing the default configuration   403
Remote cache integration   405
JBoss AS7 configured Cache   406
Integrating with JCache annotations   407
Using the Map/Reduce API   410
An introduction to Map/Reduce   410
Map/Reduce in the Infinispan platform   411
Sample application – find a destination   413
Improving the serialization process using externalizers   418
Introducing the Infinispan externalizer API   419
Creating advanced externalizers   421
Summary   424
Index   427

Preface

Relational database solutions have dominated the IT industry since the '80s. Over the last decade, relational databases have been losing its preference and importance for NoSQL databases and in-memory data grids.

There are many reasons involved in the decay of popularity, such as the fixed schema model, difficulties in scaling, and the centralized design that requires a heavy disk I/O for high write workloads.

Now, with the advent of big data and cloud computing technologies, enterprise systems have to deal with large data sets pushing pushing its products to a new level, allowing businesses to reduce costs and distribute their data across multiple channels and applications.

Infinispan is an in-memory data grid and can help solve these challenges. It supports dynamic scalability and provides excellent performance for applications that require exposing and distributing data. Infinispan is an open source Java application that exposes a `Cache` interface that extends the `java.util.Map` interface, which can optionally distribute the cache data across a cluster.

This book will cover all aspects about Infinispan, from installation to tuning tips, and important concepts related to Distributed Transactions, Session Management, Map/Reduce, Topologies, and Data Access Patterns.

What this book covers

Chapter 1, *Getting Started*, introduces Infinispan and discusses the concept of data grid and its background. You will learn how to prepare the perfect environment to create an application using Infinispan and some valuable tips on how to contribute to the project.

Chapter 2, Barriers to Scaling Data, describes common approaches that are used to overcome obstacles such as performance, scalability, and high availability. It also talks about how these solutions can be improved using Infinispan and why the reader should use Infinispan and its benefits.

Chapter 3, Using the APIs, covers the core aspects of Infinispan. You will learn the basic concepts of the Infinispan API, such as how to use the core API to store, retrieve, and remove data from it. It also covers configuration.

Chapter 4, Infinispan Topologies, covers various cache topologies supported by Infinispan and provides guidance on when to use each one and how to configure them.

Chapter 5, Data Access Patterns, presents some caching access patterns and their advantages and disadvantages.

Chapter 6, Case Study – The TicketMonster Application, introduces the Ticket Monster application to show how to put into practice the strategies and concepts you learned in the previous chapters.

Chapter 7, Understanding Transactions and Concurrency, introduces important concepts about transactions and how you work with transactions with Infinispan.

Chapter 8, Managing and Monitoring Infinispan, dives into management and monitoring Infinispan details. It shows you how to enable JMX to collect runtime information and how to manage multiple Infinispan instances spread across different servers using RHQ.

Chapter 9, Server Modules, teaches you about Infinispan modules, which allow you to access an Infinispan data grid from remote clients and from platforms and languages other than Java.

Chapter 10, Getting Started with Hibernate OGM, discusses Hibernate Object/Grid Mapper (OGM) and presents the Hibernate OGM architecture, its current features, and how to integrate Hibernate OGM with Infinispan.

Chapter 11, An Introduction to JGroups, shows that Infinispan uses JGroups as a network transport. In this chapter, we will see more details on JGroups and how it relates to Infinispan.

Chapter 12, Advanced Topics, discusses Infinispan advanced topics, such as cross-site replication, CDI, the Infinispan MapReduce framework, and how to plug Infinispan with user defined externalizers.

What you need for this book

To follow and run the example code covered in this book, you will need a computer with OpenJDK 1.6.0/Sun JDK 1.6.0 or above installed.

Furthermore, you will also need a Java Integrated Development Environment (IDE) such as IntelliJ or Eclipse, an Apache Maven 3 framework, JBoss Application Server 1.7, a MySQL Community Server and RHQ Server 4.9.

Who this book is for

Infinispan Data Grid Platform Definitive Guide is intended for those who want to learn how to build extremely scalable applications, providing a highly available key/value data store.

You will learn how to use Infinispan as a distributed cache, putting it in front of a database or a NoSQL store or any part of your system that is a bottleneck to improve performance and avoid data "traffic jams".

The book is easy to read and previous coding experience with Infinispan is not required. It is aimed at Java Enterprise Developers with a solid knowledge of Java.

Conventions

In this book, you will find a number of text styles that distinguish between different kinds of information. Here are some examples of these styles and an explanation of their meaning.

Code words in text, database table names, folder names, filenames, file extensions, pathnames, dummy URLs, user input, and Twitter handles are shown as follows: "We can include other contexts through the use of the `include` directive."

A block of code is set as follows:

```
// cache operations
String key = "20130801";
String tempData = "Children are great comfort in your old age,
  and they help you to reach it faster too";
tempCache.put(key, tempData);
String otherTempData = tempCache.get(key);
assert (otherTempData.equals(tempData));
tempCache.remove(key);
assert ( tempCache.get(key) == null);
```

New terms and **important words** are shown in bold. Words that you see on the screen, for example, in menus or dialog boxes, appear in the text like this: "To install the plugin, open the **Preferences** window, go the **Plugins** option, and click in the **Browse Repositories** button."

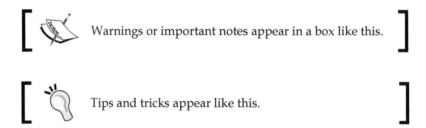

> Warnings or important notes appear in a box like this.

> Tips and tricks appear like this.

Reader feedback

Feedback from our readers is always welcome. Let us know what you think about this book—what you liked or disliked. Reader feedback is important for us as it helps us develop titles that you will really get the most out of.

To send us general feedback, simply e-mail feedback@packtpub.com, and mention the book's title in the subject of your message.

If there is a topic that you have expertise in and you are interested in either writing or contributing to a book, see our author guide at www.packtpub.com/authors.

Customer support

Now that you are the proud owner of a Packt book, we have a number of things to help you to get the most from your purchase.

Downloading the example code

You can download the example code files from your account at http://www.packtpub.com for all the Packt Publishing books you have purchased. If you purchased this book elsewhere, you can visit http://www.packtpub.com/support and register to have the files e-mailed directly to you.

Errata

Although we have taken every care to ensure the accuracy of our content, mistakes do happen. If you find a mistake in one of our books—maybe a mistake in the text or the code—we would be grateful if you could report this to us. By doing so, you can save other readers from frustration and help us improve subsequent versions of this book. If you find any errata, please report them by visiting http://www.packtpub.com/submit-errata, selecting your book, clicking on the **Errata Submission Form** link, and entering the details of your errata. Once your errata are verified, your submission will be accepted and the errata will be uploaded to our website or added to any list of existing errata under the Errata section of that title.

To view the previously submitted errata, go to https://www.packtpub.com/books/content/support and enter the name of the book in the search field. The required information will appear under the **Errata** section.

Piracy

Piracy of copyrighted material on the Internet is an ongoing problem across all media. At Packt, we take the protection of our copyright and licenses very seriously. If you come across any illegal copies of our works in any form on the Internet, please provide us with the location address or website name immediately so that we can pursue a remedy.

Please contact us at copyright@packtpub.com with a link to the suspected pirated material.

We appreciate your help in protecting our authors and our ability to bring you valuable content.

Questions

If you have a problem with any aspect of this book, you can contact us at questions@packtpub.com, and we will do our best to address the problem.

 All the source code used in this book, for both Infinispan version 6.0.2 and 7.* is available for download at https://github.com/wagnerrobsan/infinispan-guide.

1
Getting Started

With the advent of Cloud technology, many paradigms started to change, like the way the industry tackles issues related data security and user privacy. Even the most conservative and traditional organizations have been forced to start adapting to this new technology, and are trying to use one of the many existent cloud platforms.

There are numerous benefits offered by cloud computing, both to end users and companies of all sizes and shapes. For small companies, they are a good option because it can minimize licensing software, and for big companies that want to expand their business, cloud computing can help improve accessibility without the need to spend too much money on hardware.

Moving to the field of data, a few years ago, managers and even developers assumed that nearly all data should be stored in a Relational Database Management System (RDBMS). Some years ago, it was unthinkable to run a production system that kept all of its data within memory, but now, due to the continuous decline in the prices of RAM, modern in-memory products are emerging such as big data analytics tools (in-memory computation) and in-memory data grids. One such in-memory data grid system is Infinispan.

Infinispan is an open source data grid platform distributed by JBoss, written in Java; it exposes a JSR-107 compatible cache interface in which you can store objects.

This first chapter launches you on a tour of this technology by focusing on fundamentals.

In this chapter, we will cover the following topics:

- Introducing the Infinispan data grid
- Infinispan and JSR 107 – Java Temporary Caching API
- Getting started with Infinispan
- Running the sample application

- Creating your first project
- Building Infinispan from source
- Contributing to the project

Introducing the Infinispan data grid

Generally, data grids are considered an evolution of distributed caches. As the name implies, a distributed cache is characterized by the usage of multiple servers to host cached data, so that it can grow in size and in capacity. A distributed cache solution is mainly used to store temporary application data, such as web session data.

There are several benefits to using an in-memory data grid like Infinispan; a good and simple example is database offloading. Database offloading is the process of removing or reducing the database load, mainframes, and shared or partner services.

As mentioned in the introduction, Cloud platforms are also changing the way we store and distribute our data. A common solution adopted on cloud architectures is to expose the data through REST services.

In these cloud architectures, applications that expose the business data via REST services to clients normally decompose the system into layers, in order to separate the user interface from the business logic, as illustrated in the following image:

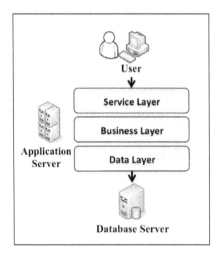

In the image, you can see how the data layer fits in a layered application. In our example, the data layer hides the implementation details to the database. We can consider that the database is a single repository of data, which is accessed at first by a few clients. However, that's the scenario if you're on a cloud environment, things can change fast.

From the performance point of view, retrieving data for every request from one single repository can be expensive, both in terms of time and hardware cost.

Also, you may need to provide access to your data for many clients' social media and mobile device integration, which can decrease the performance of your services, thereby impacting user experience.

This scenario can be a good example of offloading; in our scenario, we designed our database to provide a certain amount of data via REST services, which does not only impact the response time of the database request, but can also impact the whole infrastructure where the data is being transmitted.

Infinispan can work well in very demanding environments, as in this scenario. Thoughtful use of a distributed caching to offload the network and database can really improve performance. For instance, when a client makes a web method call to the service layer, which in turn performs several calls to the database, you could cache the query results in an Infinispan cache. Then, the next time this client needs to make the same Web method call, the service layer gets that data from the cache instead. This step can really improve overall performance because the application does not have to make an expensive database call. An Infinispan cache, in this scenario, can also reduce the pressure on the service layer, because data in an Infinispan cache can be distributed among all nodes of the cluster.

The following figure presents the same architecture as included in the first image, but now with an Infinispan cache:

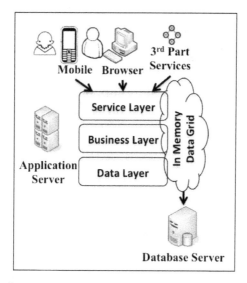

At the same time, Infinispan can also power embedded applications, be used as a JPA/ Hibernate second-level cache provider, or as a highly available key/value data store.

The scenario we presented previously is one of the two possible ways you can interact with Infinispan. We are using Infinispan in the embedded mode, which initiates the Infinispan data grid within the same JVM as the application.

The other way is the client/server mode, where you have an Infinispan data grid instance running in a separated server, which delivers and manages the grid content to be consumed by the client, including non-java clients, such as C++, Python, and .NET.

 We will cover Infinispan Server in detail in *Chapter 9, Server Modules*.

Infinispan also provides an extremely low latency access to the cache, and high availability of the application data, by keeping the data in the memory and distributing it to several nodes of the grid, which makes your application able to load terabytes of data into memory. However, it not only provides a new attempt to use the main memory as a storage area instead of a disk, (Infinispan perform much faster than disk-based databases) but it also provides features such as:

- Data partitioning across a cluster
- Work with domain objects rather than only bytes, arrays, or strings
- Synchronous and asynchronous operations throughout
- Distributed ACID transactions
- Data distribution through the use of a consistent hash algorithm to determine where keys should be located in the cluster
- Write-through/behind cache store support
- Eviction support
- Elastic scaling
- Multiple access protocols
- Support for compute grids
- Persisting state to configurable cache stores

We will cover all these features in detail throughout this chapter.

From a Java developer perspective, an Infinispan cache can be seen as a distributed key-value object store similar in its interface to a typical concurrent hash map, in a way that it can have any application domain object as either a value or a key.

Infinispan and JSR 107 – Java Temporary Caching API

The Java specification request 107 (JSR 107: JCACHE - Java Temporary Caching API) has been created to define a temporary caching API for the Java platform and presents a Map-like API. As in a regular `java.util.Map`, data is stored as values by keys.

> **Java Specification Request (JSR)** is a formal document that describes a proposal for a new feature or change in the Java Platform.
>
> This process is defined by the **Java Community Process (JCP)**, which is responsible for approving and developing the standard technical specifications for the Java technology.
>
> Any organization or individual can sign up to become a JCP member and then participate on the expert group of a JSR or even submit their own JSR proposals.

With JCACHE, you can store and retrieve your objects, control how values expire from the cache, inspect the contents of the cache, and get statistics about the cache. JCACHE also provides support for optional runtime cache annotations, support for transactions, and listeners to add custom behavior when setting and deleting values.

The primary programming artifact is the `javax.cache.Cache` interface, with some modifications for distributed environments.

Infinispan exposes a JSR-107 compatible cache interface in which you can store data, and enhances it by providing additional APIs and features.

Getting started with Infinispan

Let's see how to get started in the easiest way using Infinispan in the embedded mode. If you haven't done so already, the first thing you'll need to do is install Infinispan. To do so, you have two options. You can download the latest release from the Infinispan website. At the time of this writing, the page to download Infinispan was located at `http://infinispan.org/download/`, but this might change. If it does, you can find its new location by searching for Infinispan using your favorite search engine.

The second option is if you are using Maven/Gradle. You can download the binaries from the **JBoss.org Maven Repository**, as we will see in the upcoming section.

Installing Infinispan

Installing Infinispan is straightforward. In-keeping with the tradition of many open source tools, there are no fancy installers. Just download the latest version (version 7.1 at the time of this writing) from the previously mentioned Infinispan website and extract the package into a directory of your choice. The Infinispan website looks like this:

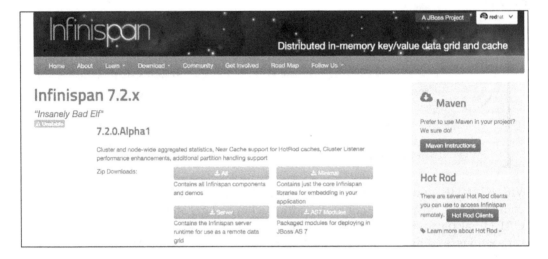

Looking inside the box

Once you download the zip file and extract it, you will find the following folder structure:

In the root folder, in our example `infinispan-7.1.1.Final-all.zip`, you can find the following files:

- The `infinispan-embedded.jar` file, which is the main library of the framework, contains everything you need to create a local or clustered cache. From Infinispan 7, this package includes all required dependencies such as the `JGroups`, `JCache`, and `JBoss Marshalling` classes. So you don't have to include these additional libraries in your classpath.

- The `infinispan-embedded-query.jar` file, which you'll need to include in your application if you want to provide query capabilities to your cache.

- The `infinispan-cli.jar` file, which you can execute using the `ispn-cli.sh` script to open a command-line interface. You can use this to interact with the data within the caches and some internal components.

Along with these JAR files, in the root folder, you will also find some README files and the following directories:

- `bin`: This folder contains a few batch scripts to run different Infinispan demos, like the `runEC2Demo** scripts` file, whose purpose is to show how Infinispan can easily run on an Amazon EC2 instance. It also contains scripts to manage your data grid using different flavors of clients, such as a Ruby and Python REST client. The scripts are as follows:

    ◦ A script to execute the command-line interface (`ispn-cli.sh/bat`)

    ◦ A lucene directory demo (`runLuceneDemo.sh`)

    ◦ `runWordCountDemo.sh` and `runPiApproximationDemo.sh` for a Map/Reduce task computation

    ◦ And finally, a `runGuiDemo.sh/.bat` script, which opens a nice swing app that starts Infinispan in a standalone JVM process that you can use to test your settings and your installation

- `configs`: This folder contains some sample configuration files. The `config-samples/sample.xml` file contains some configuration examples on how to use different features of Infinispan, such as transactions and cache loaders and you can find several examples of different cache configurations for different setups. The `distributed-udp.xml` file creates a cache that uses UDP as a transport protocol and `distributed-ec2.xml` for Amazon environments, both via `JGroups`.

 We are going to read more about JGroups in *Chapter 11, An Introduction to JGroups*.

- `demos`: This contains the JAR and WAR files for the sample applications.

- `docs`: The distribution comes with a rich API documentation, which contains the `Javadoc` files for the API (`api` folder) and some HTML pages that describe the configuration schemas.

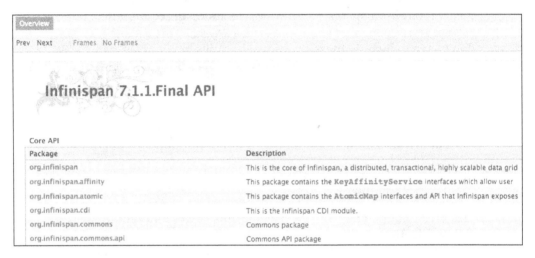

It also provides an `index.html` page with a link to the above-mentioned javadoc and configuration schemas for configuration files, and a link to an HTML document that describes the available JMX MBeans exposed by Infinispan.

You will learn more about configuring Infinispan in *Chapter 3, Using the APIs*.

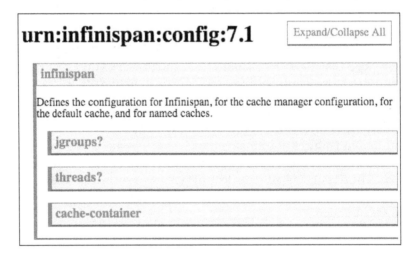

The other folders present are as follows:

- `lib`: This folder contains all the dependencies including the libraries used by the modules.

- `licenses`: The licenses directory contains the licenses for some of the other libraries shipped with the distributions that are not covered by the LGPL-2.1 license.

  All dependencies of Infinispan are available under the LGPL or a compatible license (such as the Apache License 2); a full dependency report can be found in every Infinispan JAR.

- `modules`: This directory contains a number of optional modules, such as the Infinispan spring, Infinispan tree, and the REST module that allows you to extend Infinispan functionalities.

- `rhq-plugin`: Infinispan provides a plugin if you are monitoring your systems with JBoss RHQ. You can read more about monitoring Infinispan in *Chapter 8, Managing and Monitoring Infinispan*.

- `schema`: This folder contains the XML schemas for the Infinispan configuration files, such as the `infinispan-config-7.1.xsd` and `infinispan-spring-7.1.xsd` files and several `infinispan-cachestore-*.xml` files to be used in different cache store configuration.

If you wish to use one or more of these modules, you will also need the module's jar file and all of its dependencies (listed in the corresponding `runtime-classpath.txt` file) to be on your classpath.

Using Maven

If you're a Maven user, Infinispan builds are also published to the JBoss.org Maven repository, which allows you to access the Infinispan builds with Apache Maven, Apache Ivy, or Apache Ant with Maven Ant Tasks. To accomplish this task, perform the following steps:

1. You have to include the following Infinispan dependency to your project's `pom.xml`:

```
<dependency>
    <groupId>org.infinispan</groupId>
    <artifactId>infinispan-core</artifactId>
    <version>${infinispan.version}</version>
</dependency>
```

2. It's optional, but if you want, it's recommended that you enable the JBoss Repository, so that you can import the dependencies directly from the `jboss.org` repository. To configure, add the following profile configuration to your Maven settings, located in your `.m2` directory, giving the new repository its own ID and URL, making modifications to the `settings.xml` file:

```xml
<profiles>
  <profile>
    <!-- Repository is active unless explicitly disabled
      e.g. -P!jboss-public-repository -->
    <activation>
      <property>
        <name>jboss-public-repository</name>
        <value>!false</value>
      </property>
    </activation>
    <repositories>
      <repository>
        <id>jboss-public-repository-group</id>
        <name>JBoss Public Maven Repository Group</name>
        <url>http://repository.jboss.org/nexus/content/
          groups/public</url>
        <layout>default</layout>
        <releases>
          <enabled>true</enabled>
          <updatePolicy>never</updatePolicy>
        </releases>
        <snapshots>
          <enabled>false</enabled>
          <updatePolicy>never</updatePolicy>
        </snapshots>
      </repository>
    </repositories>
    <pluginRepositories>
      <pluginRepository>
        <id>jboss-public-repository-group</id>
        <name>JBoss Public Maven Repository Group</name>
        <url>http://repository.jboss.org/nexus/
          content/groups/public</url>
        <layout>default</layout>
```

```
<releases>
  <enabled>true</enabled>
  <updatePolicy>never</updatePolicy>
</releases>
<snapshots>
  <enabled>true</enabled>
  <updatePolicy>never</updatePolicy>
</snapshots>
            </pluginRepository>
          </pluginRepositories>
      </profile>
  </profiles>
```

This piece of configuration in your `pom.xml` file will be active by default during the build process and will add the JBoss Repository to a profile. With this profile activated, Maven will be able to download dependencies from the JBoss repository during the build.

 If, for some reason, you want to disable the JBoss Repository, you can use the maven command line tool to deactivate this profile for a specific build, using the maven standard command:

mvn -P!jboss-public-repository install

3. If you want to know more details about how to customize the Maven settings, take a look at the Maven Settings Reference at `http://maven.apache.org/settings.html`.

Running the sample application

To get a feel of how Infinispan looks, we are going to execute a Swing GUI demo that ships with Infinispan and can be used to test its basic caching functionalities, either as a standalone server or as a clustered server.

It's a good way to test our environment without the need to write a single line of code. Perform the following steps:

1. First, open the `bin` folder and execute the `runGuiDemo.sh` script (adjust to `runGuiDemo.bat` if you are using a windows development environment) by executing the following command:

    ./runGuiDemo.sh

2. If everything went well, the following screen should be displayed:

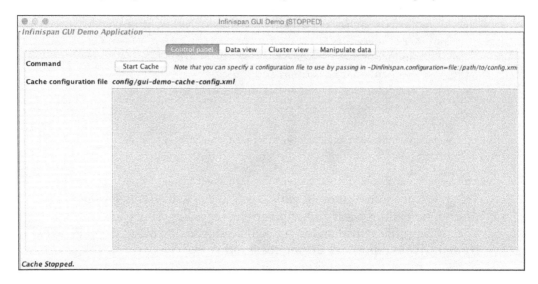

3. To start the cache, press the **Start Cache** button, which will instantiate a cache:

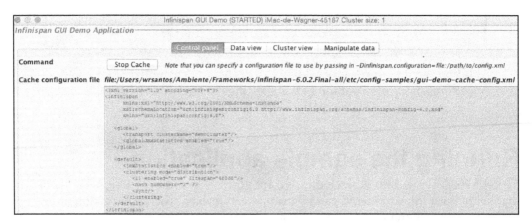

Note that the **GUI Demo** highlights the path to the configuration file used for initialization and presents its content in the text area.

This demo application provides a very useful way to quickly test your own configuration files; to do so, execute the script passing your configuration's file directory as a JVM parameter beginning with the file protocol:

```
./runGuiDemo.sh file:/devenv/infinispan/configs/
    config-samples/sample.xml
```

4. The most attentive readers will probably notice that now the toolbar is activated. Move to the Manipulate data tab; in this tab, you can perform CRUD operations on the cache, including a button to generate from 1 to 1000 random entries in the cache.

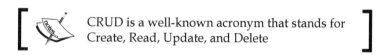 CRUD is a well-known acronym that stands for Create, Read, Update, and Delete

5. In the following example, we will add a sample entry in the cache by filling the **Key** and **Value** textboxes and hitting the **Go** button, which is shown in the following screenshot;

Infinispan GUI Demo (STARTED) iMac-de-Wagner-34222 Cluster size: 2

Infinispan GUI Demo Application

Control panel   Data view   Cluster view   Manipulate data

Single entry manipulator

Key	101	⦿ Put Entry
Value	Infinispan–Definitive Guide	◯ Get Entry
Lifespan (millis)	-1	◯ Remove Entry
MaxIdle (millis)	-1	Go

Random data generator

Max entries   [slider]   Generate 50 Random Entries

Clear cache

Clear cache

Cache Running.

Option **Lifespan (millis)** sets the lifespan of the cache entry, in milliseconds.

MaxIdle (millis) sets the max idle of the cache entry, also in milliseconds.

All these parameters can be set in the `configuration.xml` file.

6. Once added, the application will switch automatically to the **Data view** tab, which will display all entries contained in the cache, as shown in the following screenshot:

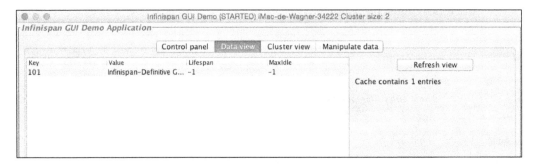

7. To test the cluster capabilities of Infinispan, let's open another command prompt and repeat the steps above, only changing the values in step 4. In both applications, move to the **Data view** tab, as shown in the following screenshot:

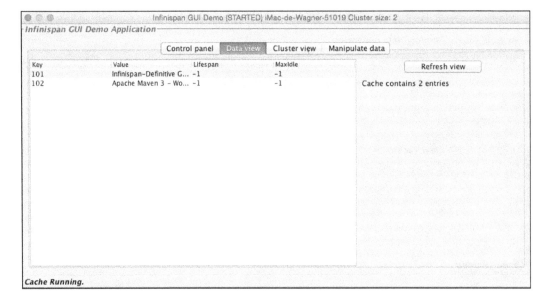

You can see that both applications now have the same data.

If one of the applications shows different values, hit the **Refresh view** button.

Invoking the `runGuiDemo` script a few more times will create GUI frames, and you'll be able to start a new cache instance in each JVMs.

8. Finally, in both applications, move to the **Cluster view** tab, as shown in the following screenshot:

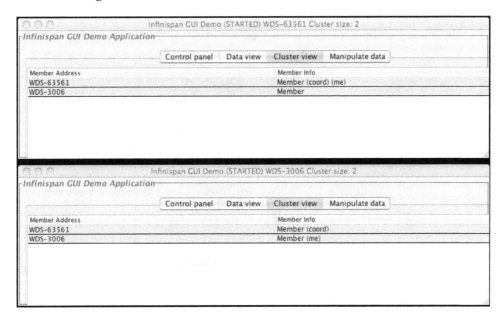

As you can see, despite the fact that the GUI Demo applications are running in the same environment, they are running on different JVMs and we can see that the caches have discovered each other and formed a cluster.

Creating your first project

To create our first Infinispan project we are going to use Eclipse with a specific Maven archetype to create the skeleton of our project.

Maven provides a useful mechanism called Maven Archetypes that you can use to define a template for project creation; the archetype can create the skeleton of a project with the right structure and dependencies.

Infinispan currently provides two archetypes that we can use to create a skeleton project, which includes everything you need to start to use Infinispan. The archetype also generates a sample code and a `pom.xml` file with all required dependencies.

To create an Infinispan project using the Maven template inside Eclipse, you will have to add the Infinispan archetype. To do so perform the following steps:

1. Navigate to **File | New | Project**. In the dialog box that opens, select the existing Maven projects option inside the `Maven` folder.

2. Select your project location and press the **Next** button in the dialog that will appear.

3. On the screen that comes up next, hit the **Add Archetype** button, as shown in the following screenshot:

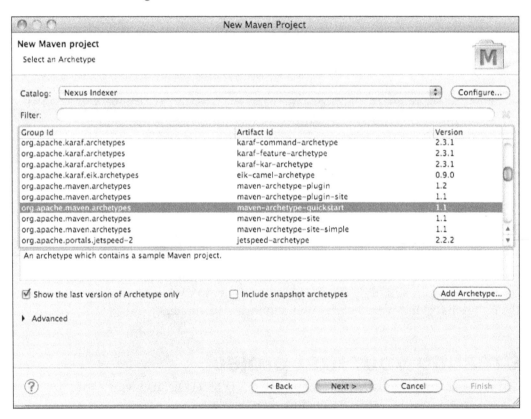

4. A new dialog box will appear asking you to add the new Archetype; include the information for the new project archetype, as in the following screenshot and press **OK**:

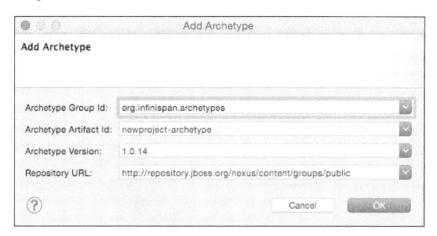

5. The new archetype should now be available in the list. Select it and confirm by pressing the **Next** button, as shown in the following screenshot;

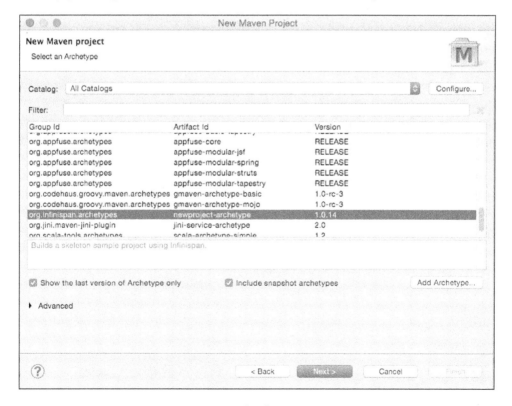

6. You will be prompted to enter some information to create the project; in this example, enter the **Group ID** (`com.packtpub`) and the **Artifact ID** (`infinispan-sample`), for the rest, keep the default values as they are.

7. You should then be taken back to the Project Explorer where you can see your new project created.

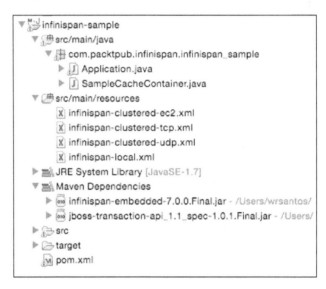

8. The first thing to notice is the `pom.xml` file, which includes the necessary dependencies, such as the infinispan-embedded module (see the following code), which provides the basic functionalities:

```
<dependencies>
    <dependency>
        <groupId>org.infinispan</groupId>
        <artifactId>infinispan-embedded</artifactId>
        <version>${version.infinispan}</version>
    </dependency>
</dependencies>
```

This also includes plugins to enforce the correct versions of Java and Maven, the JBoss public repository configuration, and a profile to run the sample application created.

9. In the structure of the project, you can find two classes for the sample application: SampleCacheContainer.java and Application.java. The SampleCacheContainer class contains all the logic to create and configure an embedded cache manager. The sample application ships with four different Infinispan files, to test different configurations.

10. The Application class is responsible for actually starting the program, and it executes four distinct operations. This example is demonstrated as follows:

   ° It presents a simple example of how to use Infinispan API, the cache stores and replaces arbitrary strings.

   ° This demonstrates how you can use Infinispan to store an entry with a lifespan.

   ° This demonstrates asynchronous operations, where writes can be done in a non-blocking fashion.

   ° This demonstrates how to register listeners.

 All features presented in this demo will be explained in the upcoming chapters.

11. The following code is an extract from the main method Application class:

```
public static void main(String[] args) throws Exception {
    System.out.println("\n\n\n    *****************************
*   \n\n\n");
    System.out.println("Hello.  This is a sample application
making use of Infinispan.");
    Application a = new Application();
    a.basicUse();
    a.lifespans();
    a.asyncOperations();
    a.registeringListeners();
    System.out.println("Sample complete.");
    System.out.println("\n\n\n    *****************************
*   \n\n\n");
}
```

12. Examine the source code to figure out what its doing and execute the `Application` class. The `Application` class will execute and print the four operations on your prompt, which is shown in the following screenshot:

```
Hello.  This is a sample application making use of Infinispan.

1.  Demonstrating basic usage of Infinispan.  This cache stores arbitrary Strings.
Mai 18, 2015 1:58:19 AM org.infinispan.factories.GlobalComponentRegistry start
INFO: ISPN000128: Infinispan version: Infinispan 'Guinness' 7.0.0.Final
  Storing value 'World' under key 'Hello'
  Done.  Saw old value as 'null'
  Replacing 'World' with 'Mars'.
  Successful? true

2.  Demonstrating usage of Infinispan with expirable entries.
  Storing key 'RHT' for 10 seconds.
  Checking for existence of key.  Is it there? true
  Sleeping for 10 seconds...
  Checking for existence of key.  Is it there? false

3.  Demonstrating asynchronous operations - where writes can be done in a non-blocking fashion.
  Put #1
  Put #1
  Put #1
  Checking future...
  Checking future...
  Checking future...
  Everything stored!

4.  Demonstrating use of listeners.
  Attaching listener
  Put #1
Thread main has modified an entry in the cache named another under key 1!
Thread main has modified an entry in the cache named another under key 1!
  Put #2
Thread main has modified an entry in the cache named another under key 2!
Thread main has modified an entry in the cache named another under key 2!
  Put #3
Thread main has modified an entry in the cache named another under key 3!
Thread main has modified an entry in the cache named another under key 3!
Sample complete.
```

Creating a Maven project manually

You have also the option to create an Infinispan manually using the same archetype that was used before. To do so, perform the following steps:

1. To create a new project manually, open a terminal prompt and navigate to the directory you want to create the project then type the following command:

```
mvn archetype:generate \
    -DarchetypeGroupId=org.infinispan.archetypes \
    -DarchetypeArtifactId=newproject-archetype \
    -DarchetypeVersion=1.0.14 \
    -DarchetypeRepository=http://repository.jboss.org/
      nexus/content/groups/public
```

2. To execute the application, type the following command in the same folder you created the project in:

```
mvn install -Prun
```

That's all! The application will execute and print the four operations on your prompt.

Building Infinispan from source

Infinispan uses Maven as a build tool. The following steps describe the sequence of tasks to build Infinispan from the source code:

1. You will need a copy of the Infinispan sources, which can be downloaded from Github, but it's important to note that the git version of Infinispan might contain unreleased and unstable changes, it's intended for developers and contributors.

2. To get the source from Github, first of all, you must have a git client to clone the repository. To clone the Infinispan from Github, you can execute the following command:

```
git clone https://github.com/infinispan/infinispan.git
```

3. If everything went well, you should see a new folder called Infinispan with the following folder structure:

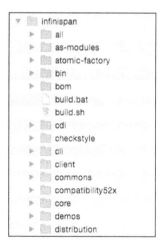

4. But first, since Infinispan is a very big multi-modular project, we will probably run into an `OutOfMemoryError` exception when building it. To prevent the error, we must instruct Maven to use more memory by setting the `MAVEN_OPTS` environment variable to increase the memory of the JVM executing the following command:

```
export MAVEN_OPTS='-Xmx512m -XX:MaxPermSize=128m'
```

5. On Windows, use:

```
set MAVEN_OPTS=-Xmx512m -XX:MaxPermSize=128m
```

6. Now, we can finally build Infinispan using the following command:

```
mvn clean package install -DskipTests
```

This command will first clean out any old build and binary and then it will package the module as a JAR file, and insert them into the target folder.

The `DskipTests` parameter will prevent the unit tests from being run and finally, the install command installs the artifacts in your local repo for use by other projects/modules, including inter-module dependencies within the same project.

The next step is to open the source code with your preferred IDE that provides basic support to Apache Maven such as Eclipse, IntelliJ IDEA, and Netbeans.

Here, we are going to present how to setup IntelliJ IDEA.

Setting up the environment

Assuming that you have downloaded and compiled the source code, let's import the Infinispan project to IntelliJ IDE. Perform the following steps:

1. If no project is currently open in your IntelliJ (I'm using IntelliJ IDEA 14.0.3), click on **Import Project** and change the directory to the location where you cloned Infinispan.

2. Automatically, IntelliJ will detect the `pom.xml` file in the infinispan root folder and import the Maven project. Select all the projects you want to import and press **Next**.

3. At the end of the import process, IntelliJ will open all projects, as you can see in the following image:

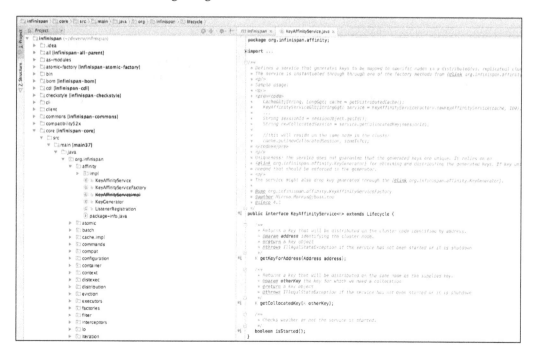

4. Before starting to code, on IntelliJ, you will need to set up a specific feature introduced in Infinispan 5, which uses annotation processing as part of the compilation, to allow log messages to be internationalized. To change IntelliJ, open the **Preferences** window and go to **Compiler | Annotation Processor** and select the **Enable annotation processing** option. In the **Annotation Processors** option, add a new **Processor FQ Name** by pressing the plus button and insert `org.jboss.logging.LoggingToolsProcessor`.

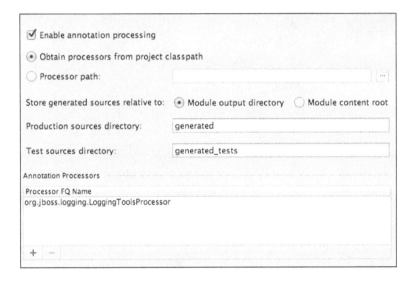

5. Infinispan also requires the IntelliJ Scala plugin to work. To install the plugin, open the **Preferences** window, go the **Plugins** option, and click in the **Browse Repositories** button. In the **Browse Repositories** pane, search for the **Scala** plugin and click on **Install plugin**.

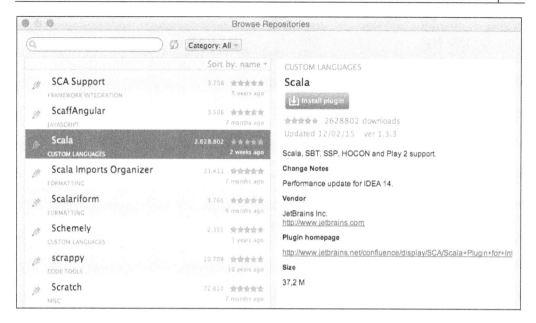

6. You will need to restart the IDE for the plugin installation to take effect.

You can also download the code style file used by the Infinispan team and import it into IntelliJ IDEA. To download the JAR file, click on the following link:

```
https://github.com/infinispan/infinispan/blob/master/
ide-settings/intellij/IntelliJ_IDEA_Code_Style.
jar?raw=true
```

Contributing to the project

What do people such as Linus Torvalds, Ward Cunningham, and Richard Stallman all have in common?

If you are just a little interested in software development, you may have heard about one of them. Even if you haven't heard of them, surely you are very likely to know about some of their creations: Linux, Wiki, and the GNU System.

They are all famous and successful software developers and all of them contribute to open source software. So what? You might be thinking, "Why should I contribute to open source software (OSS) projects?"

If you followed the last step and downloaded the source code, open it on IntelliJ or in your favorite IDE, I would like to share two important thoughts on this and maybe inspire you to participate, which are as follows:

- It's a great opportunity to learn and collaborate with really smart people and experts of the open source community you want to join
- It's also the best way to improve your resume; today more and more employers of developers are looking towards community contributors, blog writers, discussion lists, and committers on an OSS project

There are probably many software developers that would like to start contributing but don't know where to start. If you develop software for a while using open source projects, you'll probably face a bug and maybe have to fix it, whether you are a member of the project or not.

If you could fix a bug, why not make that your contribution? Now, try the following steps:

1. Download and build the source code.
2. Join the discussion list.
3. See how the Issue Management Tool works and ask for access.
4. Find a bug. You can find your own bug or access the Issue Management Tool and pick one.
5. Reproduce the error in your environment.
6. Create unit tests and fix the bug.
7. Make and submit the patch.
8. Communicate with other developers.
9. Welcome to the team!

For more information about how to contribute to Infinispan, please click on the following link:
`http://infinispan.org/docs/7.0.x/contributing/contributing.html`

Summary

In this chapter, we've taken an introductory look at Infinispan's defining characteristics and major features.

At this point, you have the source code ready to go and a new sample project created and running. You should also probably be thinking about how to spend some time contributing to open source software.

You've worked with the Infinispan GUI demo to insert and retrieve some data, and you're ready to take a step back and get the big picture on Infinispan before really diving into the details.

In the next chapter, you will discover common approaches used to overcome obstacles, such as performance, scalability, and high availability. It also covers how these solutions can be improved using Infinispan.

2
Barriers to Scaling Data

In addition to the functional requirements of any application, a good architect must satisfy the quality attributes requirements, also known as non-functional requirements. It's his/her duty to step up and understand the problems related to one of these non-functional requirements, before attempting to solve them.

When designing an application to fit any of the non-functional requirements, you will need to understand and make trade-offs between these requirements. But, that's not the only problem; today, a vast array of platforms, languages, and tools are available to build high-end applications that support large-scale business needs and appeal to a large number of people. While building an application is a relatively straightforward task for an application developer, building an application that can scale and scale well is often quite difficult. Infinispan specially addresses performance and scalability requirements.

In this chapter, we are going to explain how Infinispan can be used to either completely eliminate or significantly reduce some of these problems, and briefly discuss and analyze the following subjects:

- Difference between performance and scalability
- Improving the performance of your application
- Techniques to improve the scalability of the system
- Points to consider about relational databases
- Distributed transactions and eventually consistent transactions
- Infinispan, CAP, and Base

To begin, let's see the key differences between performance and scalability and vertical and horizontal scaling.

Understanding performance and scalability

As a web application grows and gains popularity, more and more users use it. Depending on the success of your application, it probably won't scale at the same speed as new users adopt your application.

The problem is not only a problem because of the increased number of users; due to the relative success of your application, users will naturally ask for new features, increasing the interaction with these users and your application.

Most scaling and performance problems don't give an advanced warning; they just suddenly appear one day. If you don't have a plan to scale your application, you'll probably have to work hard just to keep it responsive.

The truth is that most developers don't design the application to scale during the initial stages of development, arguing that performance and scalability should be deferred until the application is in production.

However, what is the difference between performance and scalability. The difference is described as follows:

- By definition, the performance requirement is an indication of how your application responds to execute actions in a given period. It refers to the experience of an individual user.

- Servicing a single user request might involve data access, web server page generation, an external web service access, parsing data, and the delivery of HTML and all its content, such as JS, CSS, and image files, over an Internet connection; and finally, the web browser still needs to assemble and render the page. Each of these steps takes time.

- The elapsed time necessary to complete all these steps limits overall performance. For interactive web applications, the most important of the performance-related measurements is response time.

- The scalability requirement is the ability to maintain the same quality of service, as it increases the load on the system without changing it, but improves the current hardware conditions by using some of the techniques we are going to show you in the upcoming sections.

- We can consider a system scalable if, as the load increases, the system continues to respond within the acceptable/business limits.

Let's say that for a given request, you have, in normal conditions, a response time between two and five seconds; to be considerably scalable, your system has to maintain the performance of less than a five-second response time, even if the system load increases. To understand scalability, we must first understand the real capacity of a system by pushing it to its boundaries, which is defined as the maximum number of users or processes a system can perform with, without losing the quality of service. We can determine that the system has reached its limit if our system is no longer responding the way the business expects.

To learn more about the boundaries of the system, every architect should be aware of some basic benchmarking principles. Since they're broadly useful, they can help you to:

- Measure how a system performs. It will be very important for you to understand what changes can be helpful.

- Validate your system's scalability by performing load tests to analyze how your application behaves with a higher load, with a load that your production systems are not used to, such as an increase in the number of simultaneous users.

- Estimate your infrastructure capacity through benchmarks, and determine how much hardware, network, and other resources you'll need.

Improving performance using Infinispan

Normally, we measure the performance requirements in terms of latency, which is the response time for a given transaction per user. For example, the time an e-commerce website takes to process the order, after the customer clicks on the **Buy** button for the checkout screen to appear, is the response time for the checkout page.

Typically, you would test this operation multiple times and note the average response time. We have to note that different operations on the e-commerce website, such as adding items to a cart, search for new products, and checkout order, might have different response time values.

In addition to response time, performance can also be based on transaction throughput, which is the number of events that take place within a given time period, usually one second.

Still, in the e-commerce example, you can get the total transaction time for the user (in this case, the transaction time to buy something in the website), by adding the time for searching items, adding items to a cart, and checking out to get the total transaction time. However, it's important to notice, this will not determine how long a user will have to wait every time, and the response time varies depending on the load on the website.

The term throughput usually means the same thing as transactions. Throughput is the number of transactions that can occur in a given period of time. The throughput is usually measured in **transactions per second (tps)**.

Both for measurements purposes as well as for rapid response to changing conditions, you want your architecture to be designed so you can easily split it into parts that perform discrete tasks. In an ideal world, each component of the backend should have a single job to do and at the same time, its effectiveness on each job should be easy to measure.

For instance, let's imagine our e-commerce website as a database-driven web application just starting on its path towards world domination. For a startup company, it's not difficult to start such a business having a web server and a database residing on the same hardware server. This means, all the parts share the same hardware resources.

However, by splitting the architecture into different hardware components, as depicted in the following figure, it's easier to understand the capacity demands, as the resources on each server are now dedicated to each piece of the architecture. It also means you can measure each server and its resource demands more distinctly.

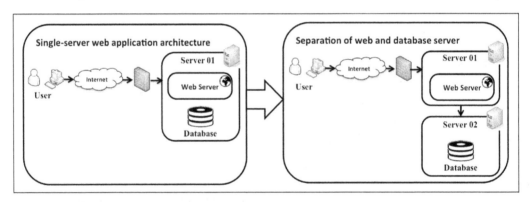

With this new architecture, you can answer a few questions that you couldn't before, focusing on each part of your architecture, such as:

- How can the increased number of requests in your web server affect CPU and RAM usage?
- How do increases in database queries-per-second affect CPU and RAM usage?

An introduction to performance tuning

Performance tuning can turn into a big project, so it is essential to provide a baseline that you can compare against new versions of the software on performance. To create a baseline, you usually create and execute a set of tests in order to use the results as a basis for comparison for the following tests and adjustments to the system.

After you've defined your performance goals, you can use a variety of tools to put a load on the system and check for bottlenecks. This can be done at the unit level, with tools such as **JUnitPerf**, **httperf**, or a home-grown harness.

Apache JMeter, **The Grinder**, **Pounder**, **ftptt**, and **OpenWebLoad** are more examples of the many open source performance and load test tools available at the time of this writing. Some of these, such as JMeter, can be used on a variety of server types, from **Simple Object Access Protocol (SOAP)** to **Lightweight Directory Access Protocol (LDAP)** to POP3 mail.

In the following figure, you can see a sample report from JMeter-Plugins with different information such as **Active Threads over Time**, **Response Times Over Time**, and **Transactions per Second**:

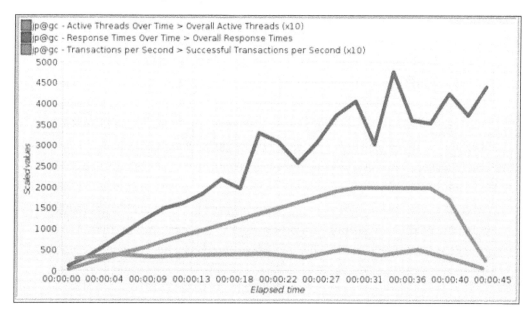

You can use these tools to look for performance bottlenecks, or tools like JProfiler or VisualVM to look for application bottlenecks and memory leaks, and JConsole to analyze database usage. The following figure shows the JVM Monitor on the VisualVM tool:

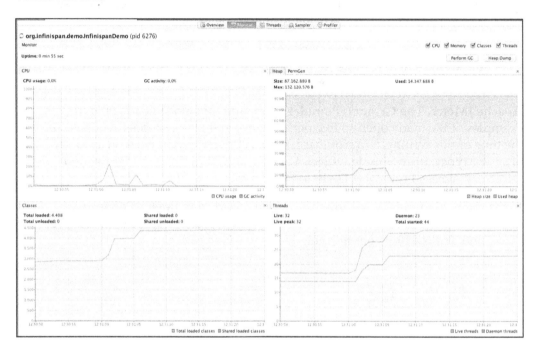

VisualVM is an open source graphical tool that began development in 2007. VisualVM was introduced in the Java 6 Update 7 JDK and is considered the second generation of the JConsole tool. VisualVM integrates several existing JDK software tools and lightweight memory monitoring tools, such as JConsole, along with adding profiling capabilities found in the popular NetBeans Profiler.

VisualVM is designed for both production and development environments and further enhances the capabilities of monitoring and performance analysis for the Java SE platform, which is shown in the following screenshot:

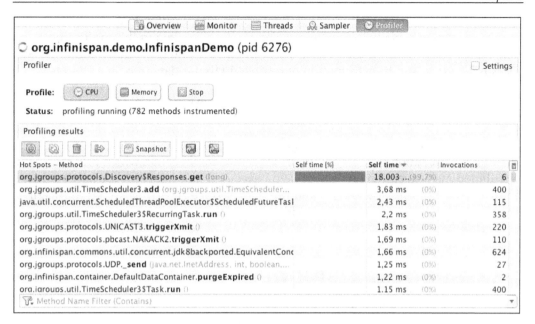

The objective of using a profiling tool or instrumenting your code, is to identify the performance bottlenecks in your application, and to address those specifically.

This performance bottlenecks can often be caused by external components. For instance, if a database call from your web application takes a long time, you could explore whether the SQL query can be made more efficient, use a database stored procedure call, tune database parameters, and so on.

Infinispan and performance

As you can see, separating the web server from the database server into different machines can improve monitoring and performance issues. On the other hand, separating our parts across distinct physical infrastructures will make you pay a network latency penalty, depending on where the server performing it is located. The farther away your web server is located from your database server, the greater will be the latency.

Typically, a transaction needs to be operated on a database. And I have seen some applications that for a single transaction, the system generates multiple database operations increasing the bandwidth usage and latency issue.

You could use Infinispan between the database and application to reduce the number of requests made to the database by caching the data in the application tier, avoiding disk I/O on the database server, parsing and execution planning for SQL Queries, and transformation of retrieved tabular data into Java Objects.

Infinispan also has a very nice feature called the L1 cache (or near cache), to prevent unnecessary remote calls.

Another Infinispan feature that can significantly improve performance is the Distributed Execution framework (*Chapter 12, Advanced Topics*), which provides distributed task execution; instead of being executed in local, JVMs are executed on entire clusters of Infinispan nodes and the Map Reduce APIs (*Chapter 12, Advanced Topics*), which allows transparent distributed processing of very large datasets over data grids.

Improving scalability

As we have seen, for a system to be considerably scalable, it must still perform well under increasing load. A good scalable system would also reduce the need of having to redesign the system in front of this kind of scalability problem, which we can convert into business gains, avoiding possible financial loss to the company or decreasing the customer's confidence.

To know the scalability of your system, you must first understand its capacity, which is defined as the maximum number of processes or users a system can handle without losing capacity.

The question now is "How do we scale?" There are two ways to improve scalability: scaling vertically (scale up) and scaling horizontally (scale out).

 In the following section, we assume we are scaling a distributed multi-tier web application, though the principles are also more generally applicable.

Vertical scalability

Scaling up or vertical scaling refers to resource maximization of a single unit, in order to expand its ability to handle increasing load. In hardware terms, it means adding more processing power to an existing server system, such as processors, memory, and disks. Sometimes, replacing an existing server with a completely new but more capable system is also considered vertical scaling.

Let's consider the following server, where we are going to use vertical scaling by upgrading the physical machine, adding more CPU, memory, and disks:

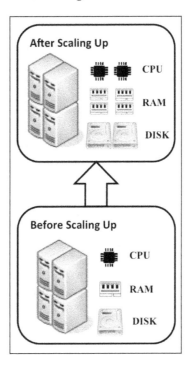

Vertically scaling is by far the easiest method of scaling; you can achieve vertical scaling by moving your application to a better computer or improve the current one. Vertical scaling works reasonably well but has important limitations. The most apparent limitation is outgrowing the capacity of an optimized system available. Another important limitation is the price that you'll have to pay to upgrade your hardware; as you get more hardware, the more expensive it gets, because it usually requires purchasing the next bigger system.

Finally, vertical scaling often creates vendor lock-in, as stipulated, a hardware does not support applications with different components attached, further adding to costs.

Horizontal scalability

Horizontal scaling offers more flexibility over vertical scaling, but it also introduces more complexity in your architecture by adding additional runtime server instances to host the software system, such as additional application server instances. Compared to vertical scaling, horizontal scaling does not have the physical limitation imposed by an individual server's hardware system. The following figure shows horizontal scalability:

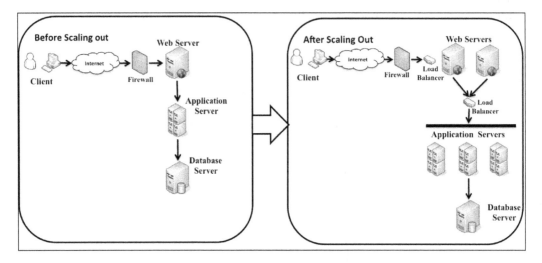

In scenario 2 of the figure, to scale out our solution, first we introduced redundancy to our system architecture, putting in place two machines into a cluster for our web servers and three machines into a cluster for our application servers. This configuration enables you to manage all these machines as a single cluster.

We have also implemented load balancing to redirect the request to one of servers. The advantage of load balancing is that it lets you distribute the workload across several smaller machines instead of using one large machine (as in Scenario 1) to handle all the incoming requests. This typically results in lower costs and better use of computing resources. Load balancing addresses architectural concerns, such as throughput and scalability.

> Load balancing is a feature that allows server systems to redirect a request to one of several servers based on a predetermined load-balancing algorithm, such as round robin, first available, least-loaded, or weighted algorithm.

Design tradeoffs

However, there are disadvantages to horizontal scaling as well; having your architecture running on multiple machines and still appearing to be on one system is more difficult than vertical scaling. Increasing the number of units means that more resources need to be invested in their maintenance. Also, the code of the application itself needs to be modified to allow parallelism and distribution of work among various units. In some cases, this task is not trivial and scaling horizontally might be a tough task.

Modern applications maintain state, which means that they remember you did the last request, as part of the session. The stateful nature of the application also means that if the server holding that state goes down, the entire user state is lost.

The key to efficiently utilizing resources is to try to make each of the nodes stateless and autonomous, but we have to recall that stateless nodes do not imply a stateless application.

In an ideal world, you should be able to move the state out of any component, since requiring a component to store the session state between service calls can have a drastic impact on scalability; instead, each method call should be independent and store the associated state outside the component, for instance, in the cache memory of the service or in a storage service. The state should be available when required across method calls. The problem is that the state is generally stored inside a relational database, which is the most difficult and expensive resource in our architecture to scale.

Points to consider about relational databases

A **Database Management System (DBMS)** is a set of programs that is used to store and manipulate data. Relational databases have become overwhelmingly popular over the last four decades. Much of this success is due to the Structured Query Language (SQL), which is feature-rich and uses a simple, declarative syntax.

SQL was first officially adopted as an ANSI standard in 1986; since that time, it's gone through several revisions and has also been extended with vendor proprietary syntax such as Microsoft's T-SQL and Oracle's PL/SQL, to provide additional implementation-specific features.

In the early days, before the advent of modern web development, most development projects were standalone data centric applications, where generally the data model or entity-relationship model was usually the most important artifact for an information system (a rule that still stands today).

An entity-relationship model (ERM) is an abstract conceptual data model used in software engineering to represent structured data.

As mentioned earlier, most of the scalability problems start to occur when our relational applications become successful and usage goes up. Queries that used to be fast are now rather slow. The way databases gain consistency is typically through the use of transactions, which require locking some portion of the database so it's not available to other clients. This can become unsustainable under heavy loads, as the locks, meaning competing threads (users) start queuing up, waiting for a chance to manipulate the data.

Distributed transactions and ACID

A transaction is a group of operations (normally SQL queries) that are treated as a single unit of work. If the database engine can process all operations that are part of the transaction to the given database session, it does so. However, if for some reason any operation can't be performed, none of them are applied to the database. It's the famous all or nothing approach.

A key feature of transactions is the possibility to execute a sequence of operations in a temporary and separate space, allowing the programmer to rollback any changes that may have gone away during execution; if all operations have been executed successfully, the transaction can be committed.

A transaction can be considered reliable if the system implements the ACID properties. ACID stands for Atomicity, Consistency, Isolation, and Durability. These properties describe well-defined criteria that a system that provides transaction support must meet:

- **Atomicity**: This defines that a transaction will be considered as completed successfully only if all operations within a transaction are performed, so that the entire transaction is either committed or rolled back. When transactions are atomic, all changes are made (commit), or none (rollback).

- **Consistency**: This states that only valid and reliable data will be written to the data store. If during a transaction, the system identifies an operation or something that violates the consistency rules, the whole transaction will be invalidated and rolled back.

- **Isolation**: Isolation keeps transactions separated from each other during the transaction duration, which ensures that transactions are processed independently, in parallel without any interference. However, Isolation does not ensure the correct order of transactions.

- **Durability**: Once committed, a transaction's changes are permanent. Durability guarantees that the system can keep a track of pending change and recover from unexpected interruptions.

Hence, even if the database server shuts down unexpectedly during a transaction, it should be able to return to a consistent state after initialization. The system can achieve this by storing uncommitted transactions in a transaction log, so that when the database reboots, it automatically starts to examine the transaction log for the completed transactions that had not been committed and applies them.

Some durability strategies provide a stronger safety guarantee than others, and nothing is ever 100 percent durable.

The classic example to illustrate ACID applicability is a transfer of funds between two bank accounts, the bank must ensure the transaction atomicity while debiting one account and crediting another; banks must ensure that they do not lose your money.

It is generally quite difficult to guarantee these ACID properties with application logic; most of the problems start when you attempt to distribute your relational database, by scaling it horizontally. As explained earlier in this chapter, in distributed transactions, your transaction is not operating inside a single table, but is spread across multiple nodes. So you'll need a transaction manager to orchestrate the transaction across the nodes, in order to ensure the ACID properties of transactions.

A well know practice to ensure the atomicity of a transaction that accesses multiple resource managers is the idea of a two-phase commit (also known as 2PC), a standard protocol for making the commit and rollback process atomic.

In 2PC, we have the following actors:

- **Coordinator**: This is responsible to coordinate commitment between multiple hosts
- **Participant**: This is the resource participant of the transaction

Generally, there are two distinct phases to ensure that either all the participants committed or rolled back their changes. The phases are as follows:

- **Prepare phase**: The coordinator inquires whether all participants are prepared to commit changes. It sends a Request-to-Prepare message to each participant and waits for all participants to vote, which can be prepared (ready to commit), no (for any reason) or the participant may delay indefinitely.
- **Commit phase**: All participants are asked to commit changes.

The following diagram presents the components interacting in each phase:

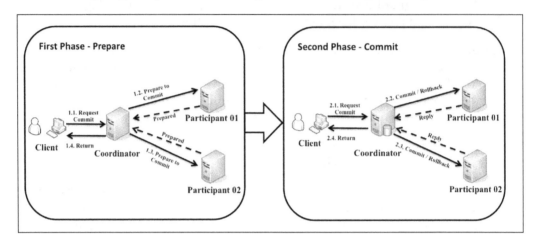

As you can imagine, two-phase commit locks all associate resources during the transaction time, so it's a useful practice only for operations that you can complete very quickly.

2PC introduces some issues for application developers that include loss of availability and higher latency during partial failures. There could be some cases where your application will require coordination across multiple hosts; coordinating several different but related tasks can take hours to update. This can happen during communication with many hosts, where uncertainty periods are unavoidable (a coordinator is never uncertain). If one of the participants fails or loses the communication with the coordinator while it's uncertain, at recovery, it must take a decision. Neither of these is desirable. But, if you really necessitate scaling your database past a single machine, you have to work in a way that your application complies with the ACID properties. No matter how many database machines you have, atomicity is still required in transactions as if you were working on a single node.

Nowadays, in modern and highly scalable architectures, it's quite difficult to find systems using distributed transactions with 2PC, because it's hard to keep the consistency of the entity. When you decide to distribute your data, depending on the case, we can be talking about changing a distributed object on multiple nodes.

To maintain consistency, the 2PC coordinator must lock all data sources during transaction and wait until the transaction is resolved, which creates a very tight dependency between the physical devices (coordinator and the nodes) and a higher contention. A highly distributed system must consider that messages sent between nodes can be lost, a node can crash, and the network can fail, among other possibilities.

So, many solutions are giving up a strong consistency for a better throughput, by designing idempotent capabilities in their products.

 Idempotent is a mathematical term that in computer science states that an operation can be executed once or multiple times without a change in result.

In practical terms, it means that if the sender of the message does not receive an acknowledgement, he will send the message again, which can make the target system receive the same message multiple times.

Idempotence comes in place if the original message was already processed by the target system and it receives a second request for the same messages. An idempotent operation must ensure that a repeated request has already been processed and will not have any effect beyond the original request. In this solution, the locking mechanism is replaced by a system that guarantees that messages will be processed at least once.

CAP theorem

In 2000, the computer scientist Dr. Eric A. Brewer posited his CAP theorem at the Symposium on the **Principles of Distributed Computing** (**PODC**), and was formally proved to be true by Seth Gilbert and Nancy Lynch of MIT in 2002 using an asynchronous network model, rendering it a theorem. He first presented the CAP theorem in the context of a web service.

The CAP theorem describes some strategies to distribute the application logic across the network and was introduced as a trade-off between consistency, availability, and partition tolerance, which are as follows:

- **Consistency**: This states that only valid and reliable data will be written to the data, and even with concurrent updates, all clients will see the same set of data.

- **Availability**: All requests must have a response about whether it was successful or it failed.

- **Partition Tolerance**: This refers to the underlying system and not to the service. It states that operations will complete, even if individual components are unavailable.

Brewer's theorem states that you can only guarantee two of consistency, availability, and partition tolerance at the same time.

Therefore, only CP systems (consistent and partition tolerant, but not highly available), AP systems (highly available and partition tolerant, but not consistent), or CA systems (consistent and highly available, but not partition tolerant) are possible.

You have to choose between two of these three characteristics because of this sliding mutual dependency. The more consistency you demand from your system, for example, the less partition tolerant you're likely to be able to make it, unless you make some concessions around availability.

Another example is an ordinary web application with any relational database design that needs to be scaled. A reasonable solution horizontal scaling strategy is based on data partitioning; therefore, you would be required to decide between consistency and availability.

For a system to achieve data consistency and availability (usually through transaction protocols), it has to be intolerant to network partitions. But, for larger distributed scale systems, network partitions are essential, thus consistency and availability cannot be achieved at the same time. Forcing you to choose between relaxing consistencies to keep it highly available or giving up high availability to prioritize consistency.

Because only two of the three requirements can be met simultaneously in a distributed environment, the CAP theorem is often visualized as a triangle in which a specific application can be classified in one of the edges.

The following figure visually illustrates the CAP theorem:

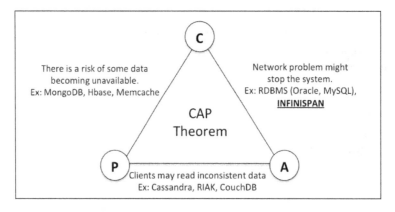

It's easy to ensure consistency when data is on a single node, but once it's distributed, we have to consider partition tolerance. If your data is distributed over several nodes, you might run the risk of losing communication between one of the nodes, which can impact consistency and data integrity. If an application does not guarantee immediate consistency with the use of locks or a similar mechanism, it is said to be eventually consistent.

BASE

If ACID is desirable in traditional database systems and provides the consistency choice for partitioned databases, BASE is diametrically opposed to ACID, because it promotes availability over consistency.

BASE stands for **Basic Available, Soft State, Eventual Consistency** and embraces the fact that consistency cannot be achieved. The description of BASE is as follows:

- **Basically Available**: The system will respond even with stale data.
- **Soft State**: State might not be consistent and could be corrected.
- **Eventually Consistent**: It allows a delay before the result of an operation propagates completely through the system. A system providing eventual consistency guarantees that replicas would eventually converge to an identical content. This means that there are no guarantees about the freshness of data returned by a read operation.

Eventual Consistency can be implemented with two steps:

- When all writes to one node eventually propagate to all replicas.
- When new writing operations arrive in one node, they are written to a log file and applied to all replicas respecting the order, which can be easily done with timestamps and undoing optimistic writes.

In this approach, if all clients stop issuing write operations, then all replicas will eventually converge to the same values. The following figure shows the difference between a traditional 2PC system and a BASE consistency model:

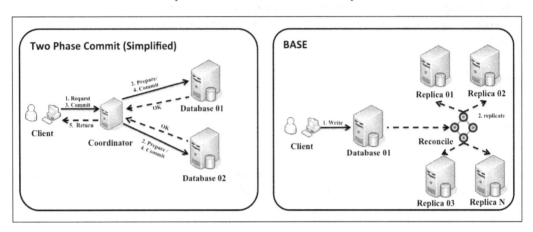

In the 2PC approach, to commit to **Database 01** and **Database 02**, the **Client** depends on the availability of both databases (high coupling) and there is latency on both paths.

In the **BASE** approach, the **Client** depends only on the **Database 01**; after the commit, a reconcile operation is made asynchronously, providing latency tolerance.

 For more details about BASE and ACID, read the white paper *Cluster-Based Scalable Network Services* by *Fox, Gribble, Chawathe, Brewer, and Gauthier* at `http://www.cs.berkeley.edu/~brewer/cs262b/TACC.pdf`.

Infinispan, CAP, and BASE

As we could see, the CAP theorem proposed by Eric Brewer and later proved by Seth Gilbert and Nancy Lynch, shows that when you choose to horizontally scale your application, you have to settle on only two of its three properties Consistency, Availability, and Partition-tolerance.

Infinispan chooses to follow ACID principles as far as possible, which leads Infinispan to operate in a traditional "Strong Consistent" model facilitated by its built-in support for transactions.

Infinispan can be configured to use and to participate in the Java Transaction API – JTA compliant transactions. See *Chapter 9, Server Modules* for more details.

Alternatively, BASE essentially embraces the fact that true consistency cannot be achieved in the real world; while an ACID system ensures consistency after each operation, a BASE ensures an eventual consistency. In other words, a BASE system guarantees consistency after a reasonable time span.

Today, Infinispan does not have support for eventual consistency: however an eventually consistent mode embracing BASE is planned on the roadmap.

Scaling out your database

Most problems related to scalability appear out of nowhere without giving advance notice. If you did not design your application to scale, once these kinds of problems appear, you will probably need to invest a lot of time just to keep your system responsive.

You can decide to scale your database for a variety of reasons, such as to support a higher volume of users or provide a better performance experience for them, store a larger volume of data, and improve the current system availability through geographic dispersion.

Obviously, there is a high cost to scale your database that you should consider, such as cost of hardware (adding or upgrading of servers) and cost with maintenance.

Scaling options

Your approach to scaling your database is a critical design consideration. Options for scaling a database can be separated into vertical and horizontal. As you can see, scaling vertically generally describes adding capacity to existing database instance(s) without increasing the number of servers or database instances.

Horizontal scaling, on the other hand, involves adding additional servers and can be the right solution. It can be done with a variety of approaches such as Master-Slave replication, Database Clustering, and Database Sharding. In general cases, when you scale your application, you can also choose to combine these two basic choices: scale up (vertically) and scale out (horizontally)

We will discuss the pros and cons of each in the upcoming section.

Master-Slave replication

Master-Slave replication is a basic form of replication; in this structure, you have a single master database server replicating to one or more slaves asynchronously.

The following diagram shows the database and replication service topology for a typical master-slave cluster:

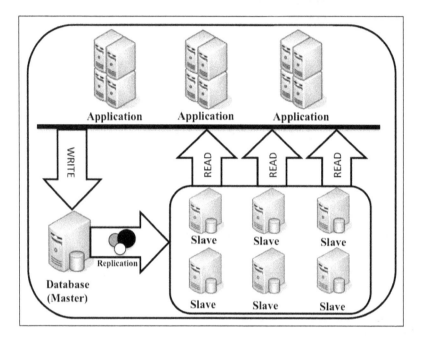

Master-Slave replication can be helpful for many reasons; the most important is the ability to scale up your application distributing the data. Another very important aspect is that it also provides a smart way to backup your data and a way to analyze it without using the master database.

Under a simple setup for write operations, your applications will write to the master database instance, and then the written data will be replicated to the slaves. On the other hand, read operations are routed to the slave instances. Consequently, your database slave can fail without impacting your application. To recover, you just have to start up a new database slave and point it to the master; if the master node fails, it is a little more complicated, but you can recover the database promoting a slave instance to the database master.

The advantage of having such a configuration is the unlimited number of slave instances that can be added. It's a good option for applications required to perform many read operations, because it addresses the I/O bottlenecks issue quite nicely.

The main trade-off related to this configuration lies in replication; as it is asynchronous, instances are not guaranteed to be in sync. In other words, the process that performs the replication from the master to the slave is not atomic with respect to the original transaction. Just because a transaction commits with success in the master node, it does not mean the transaction will be replicated successfully to any slaves.

Hence, there will be a time during replication when the data is not the same across all the database replicas, which means that you can have data inconsistency.

Active/Passive configuration

A similar configuration to the Master-Slave replication is the Active/Passive configuration. The main difference from the Master-Slave replication is that the Active/Passive configuration provides a fully redundant instance of each node. This configuration is also known as **Site Backup**, so as the name states, the passive node should only be used when its associated primary node (active node) fails. You can see how this configuration works in the following figure:

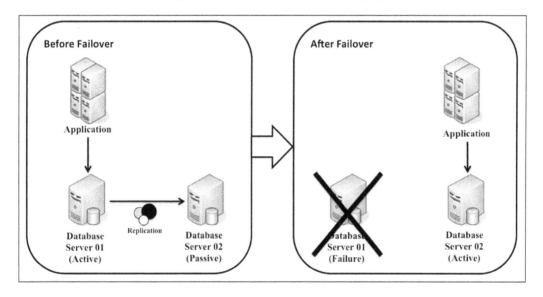

Database clustering

The database cluster configuration to scale out a database, also known as shared everything, consists of several hosts on a local area network configured to appear as a single server. It works on the principle that you have one array of disks, typically a **Storage Area Network (SAN)** or **Network Attached Storage (NAS)**, that holds all of the data in that database.

The following figure shows database clustering:

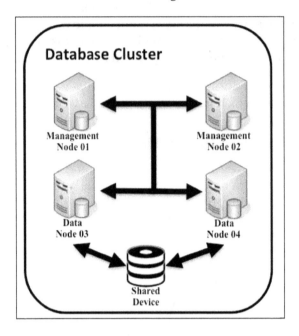

In a shared everything architecture, as the name itself indicates, not only the disks are shared, but they also share memory among a group of nodes in the cluster. Since all resources are shared, all cluster nodes can serve any request, which makes it a great strategy for availability.

 A variation on clustering is federation—that is, accessing remote servers as though they're local, which transparently maps multiple autonomous database systems into a single federated database.

Database sharding

Database sharding is a concept that has been gaining popularity over the past few years. Due to the large adoption of web solutions, especially **Software as a Service (SaaS)** solutions, we have seen a huge growth in the number of transactions where, as a consequence, many business application databases have been moved from giga to tera to peta scales.

There are actually different ways to implement sharding. The basic idea behind it is that you can partition the data (equivalent of horizontally scaling) in a way that means you can replicate all of the data across multiple database nodes in a cluster, so as to ensure the scalability of the architecture. Each individual partition is referred to as a database shard.

Database sharding is an approach adopted by some of the major Internet players such as Amazon, eBay, Facebook, and Google, which support billions of queries a day; it's recommended when your application database is dealing with high transactions and a high volume of data and you require a fast response from the database.

Generally, to implement database sharding, we have to split the database schema. Just to exemplify, let's take as an example, a new e-commerce application with a centralized database, as shown the following figure:

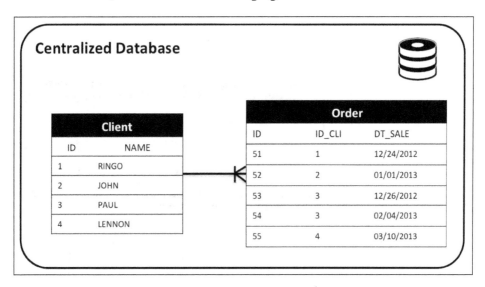

In the following sections, through this simple example, I will present two well-known ways to partition your database—vertical partitioning and horizontal partitioning:

- **Vertical Partitioning**: Vertical partitioning is most commonly used. We have to make the partition based on business concepts. It's important to keep the model strictly consistent with these bounds, which requires decomposing the schema into tables grouped by functionality.

In our earlier example, let's suppose that the web application was a huge success; as a consequence of these positive results, the load on the database server starts to degrade performance. As an initial solution, the database administrator decided to perform vertical partitioning deciding to include the client table into a different schema and the order table into another. Also, since the order table is heavily used, the database administrator splits the table by columns to make the order table faster, which is more appropriate for a table that has some columns that are rarely used.

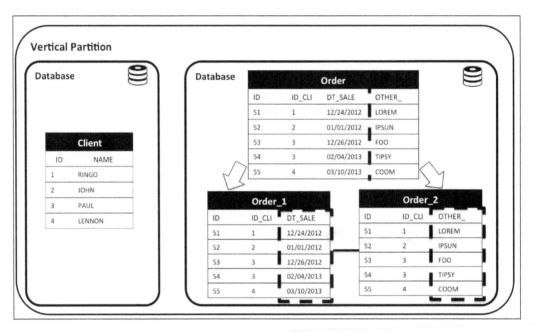

The major issue related to this approach is the existing limitation related to the number of functional areas you can identify; if you choose to split your table by columns, each record in a table will just represent partial information.

Another point is related to database constraints; if you want to separate the database by different schemas, database constraints naturally create a coupling of the schema, which will require moving data constraints out of the database and control it in the application level.

And at last, once you reach the capacity of any vertical partition, you will either need to scale up or partition data horizontally.

- **Horizontal Partitioning**: Now we are really talking about sharding — the concept of horizontal partitioning refers to the idea of distributing all records in a table on multiple machines, splitting the table by rows. At the end of this process, you will have the exact same schema in all database shards and unlike vertical partition, each record will represent the full information.

  Horizontal partitioning enforces a "share nothing" architecture, where each node is independent and shares no data with the other participant nodes of the cluster, (hence the term share nothing) which give us the ability to scale our architecture without any limits.

  When introducing horizontal partitioning, you will need to define the rule on how to divide the tables. There are some methods for deciding how to shard your data, and it's important to understand characteristics of your application, such as table volumes, key distribution, transaction rates, and so on.

The basic methods for determining shard structure are as follows:

- **Key-based or range partitioning**: This is the most easiest and common option to map to map the data to the given sharding. In this approach, you find a key in your data that will evenly distribute it across shards, where part of the data itself is used to split the data falling within a range to be accessed to one of the shards that stores it, , as in the following example, where we are mapping the customers ranging from 01 to 10.000.000 to the correct Shard, as you can see in the following example:

  - Shard #01: CustomerId 1 to 10.000.000
  - Shard #02: CustomerId 10.000.001 to 20.000.000
  - Shard #03: CustomerId >= 20.000.001

- **Hash partitioning**: An alternative for key-based or range partition is the Hash Partition. The basic idea is using a hash algorithm with the modulus operator. A simple example: assuming there are four partitions the hash function could return from 0 to 3:

  ```
  int _shardId = getCustomerId() % NUMBER_OF_SHARDS;
  ```

  The downside of this approach is that if you add new shards, you must redistribute data between them.

- **Directory-based partitioning**: In this approach, one of the nodes in the cluster acts as a master table, and is used to lookup which node has the data you're trying to access. One of the nodes will contain an index of the partitioned dimensions and their shard locations, which lets you move data between shards. For instance, for each customer ID you have to associate a shard ID in a table.

The trade-off to use this method is that it can become quite heavy and expensive (due to successive reads to the database table). So, it's recommended to replicate the table, otherwise you will have a single point of failure.

In addition to the database shards, a good practice is to create a root database to keep all the tables that represent the global information, such as the domain information that are difficult to change (such as Profession, Region, ZIP Code, and so on), system settings, and metadata. This kind of table/information should not be split. So, a good practice is keeping them in their original database. On the other hand, you will have to replicate these root tables' data between all the shards.

Coming back to our earlier ecommerce example, the database administrator realized that vertical partition was not enough, so he/she decided to partition it horizontally, splitting the tables following a key based strategy.

At the end, the database looks like the following figure:

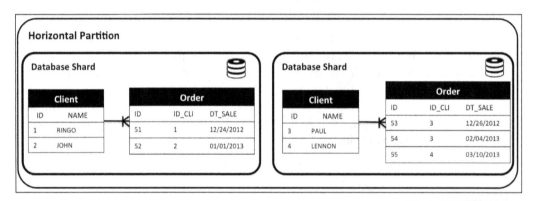

Unfortunately, not everything is as one always hopes, so you have to consider some issues before introducing sharding, such as:

- The application must be designed from the outset to manage sharding to avoid migrating existing data to new partitions.

- The application must be adapted to take into account the distribution, especially to avoid inter-shard queries because the cost of accessing multiple remote nodes is very high.

- The atomicity (the A in ACID) is frequently limited in order to avoid updates involving several shards. It will require distributed transactions across multiple machines, which will affect performance.

- Implementing sharding will certainly impact your code. You will need to figure out which database to connect to.

- A simple change in the schema must be replicated across all shards.

- For best performance, make sure that all the data from a shard can be held in the RAM.

So, to conclude this topic, the next figure presents, in a graphic way, the difference between **Shared Everything Architecture** (for Database clustering) and **Shared Nothing Architecture** (for Database sharding):

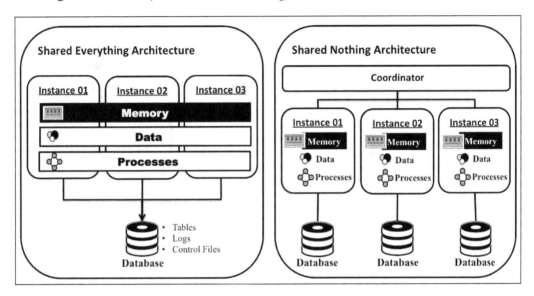

Infinispan and network partitions

Infinispan 7 introduces partition-handling support, which is an important feature that helps prevent a well-known problem in distributed computing—the Network Partition also known as Brain Split.

A split-brain is a scenario where a failure of a network links to one or multiple nodes and creates two or more separated clusters. This situation can make these fragmented clusters become unaware of each other.

During these cases, each network partition will create its own JGroups view, and determine, via a **Failure Detection** protocol (**FD**), whether members of the cluster are alive. If a node is not available, JGroups will exclude this node from the other partitions using the **Group Membership** protocol (**GMS**).

 Read more about JGroups in *Chapter 12, Advanced Topics*.

In a scenario without partition handling, each partition would continue to work as an independent grid, and clients will be able to perform reading/writing operations from different partitions and consequently see different versions of the same cache entry.

The following diagram illustrates the split-brain condition:

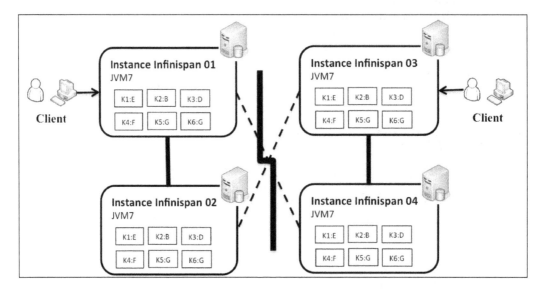

The golden question here is: What will happen if we have different versions of a cache entry in our cache nodes after the network failure is fixed, and the two clusters start to exchange data again? If our clusters merge into one node again, what should we do or what happens if each partition could write different values to the same cache entry in the cache?

Considering the CAP theorem, in a configuration with partition-handling disabled, you would probably be sacrificing data consistency for availability, which is not a good thing if your application requires a high consistency because your cache clients can read and write inconsistent data.

On the other hand, with partition-handling enabled, Infinispan will preserve the data consistency and the cache, but at the cost of sacrificing availability in the presence of partitions. If it detects a partition, Infinispan will freeze the rebalance of the entries (in the distribution mode) and will check if it should enter into the degraded mode.

The degraded mode happens when a segment loses all its owner nodes or the partition doesn't contain the majority of the nodes.

Configuring partition handling

We are going to see how configuration works using the APIs in the next chapter, but for further reference, we are now going to show you how to enable partition-handling.

Basically, you can configure an Infinispan cache with a programmatic API or via XML.

If you have no earlier experience with Infinispan, we suggest you read *Chapter 3, Using the APIs*.

By default, partition handling is disabled, but it may change in the future. In order to enable partition handling for you cache, you will need to include the following line to your XML configuration.

For configuring in Infinispan 7 add the following lines:

```
<distributed-cache name="adistCache">
    <partition-handling enabled="true"/>
</distributed-cache>
```

This configuration works only for distributed caches, otherwise it's ignored.

If you prefer, you can also create it programmatically, using the following code:

```
ConfigurationBuilder cc = new ConfigurationBuilder();
cc.clustering().
    partitionHandling().
    enabled(true);
```

Note: There are plans to add JMX monitoring operations in order to forcefully migrate a cluster form the degraded or unavailable state back to available, at the cost of consistency.

Infinispan and high availability

Infinispan can provide high availability. In a clustered environment, you can configure Infinispan to replicate every new object to all nodes (Infinispan instances), which will result in simply maintaining a copy of each object in every node, so that if one of the nodes fails, state is not lost.

But, what is usually good for high availability (such as in this case) is not necessarily good for scalability, because if you want to keep 100 percent of your objects replicated to all nodes, for large clusters, you can be sure it will not scale well.

If you are looking for scalability, you can configure Infinispan to distribute the objects across the nodes in the grid, as opposed to replication, which isn't scalable. In this configuration, Infinispan will not store each cache entry on all the nodes, but will only store a fixed number of replicas for each cache entry by making use of a consistent hash algorithm.

 Consistent hashing is a mapping schema for key-value stores, which maps hashed keys to physical nodes. We are going to discuss cache topologies and Consistent hashing in *Chapter 4, Infinispan Topologies* and *Chapter 5, Data Access Patterns*.

If you are using master-slave replication or clustering to scale out your database, Infinispan could effectively eliminate or reduce the need for these options, providing a distributed cache to avoid database access.

Summary

In this chapter, we've taken you on a tour of scalability, analyzing the challenges and issues related to scalability. We explored what scalability and performance is, their differences, and how they are implemented.

We also looked at some scalability options, such as options to scale out databases, caching, load balancing, and performance optimization—key techniques that are used to scale any application. With a special focus on how it's related to Infinispan, and how we can achieve quality attributes such as high availability, scalability, and performance.

In the next chapter, let's get our hands dirty and learn the core aspects of Infinispan, and also learn the Infinispan API basic concepts.

3
Using the APIs

In the previous chapter, you saw the basics of performance, scalability, and how to solve some of these problems using different techniques.

This chapter provides an overview of the architecture of Infinispan. It explains the terminology of the main components and the main APIs, which we will first cover the basics of by looking at some of the foundational interfaces and classes in Infinispan.

To begin with, we are going to be covering the basic concepts required to understand how Infinispan is structured and how applications can use it.

In this chapter, we briefly discuss and analyze the following subjects:

- Infinispan architecture
- Anatomy of an Infinispan clustered cache
- Configuring an Infinispan cache
- Learning the cache API
- Cache store and cache loaders
- Listeners and notifications
- JSR-107 — the Java caching API

Infinispan architecture

We will start this topic with an overview of Infinispan from the user's perspective, which is shown in the next image, with the elements that a user can interact directly with. An end user application (for instance, a web browser) can interact with the data grid by using a cache interface.

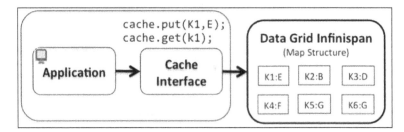

We use the term grid to refer to a part of Infinispan infrastructure for coordinated resource sharing that store and manage map-based caches that contain the grid's data. The key abstraction introduced by a map-based cache is that it can be partitioned. This means, it can be split into parts that can be spread over multiple instances in different containers.

The next figure exposes the next level of detail by introducing the map-based cache and partitioning concepts:

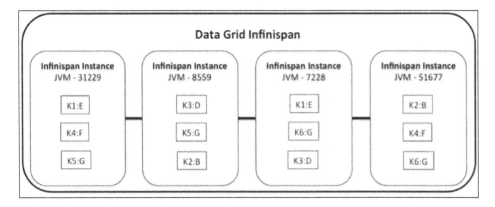

Anatomy of an Infinispan clustered cache

There are two ways you can interact with Infinispan. The first use is in embedded mode, which is the easiest way to start with and to figure things out. The embedded mode initiates an Infinispan instance within the same JVM as the application.

The other way is the client/server mode, where you have an Infinispan data grid instance running in a separated process. Since it is remote, you and multiple applications are able to connect through client connectors.

The embedded (P2P) mode

In this mode, Infinispan runs embedded in the same JVM as the application logic, where each JVM that is part of the cluster will run an individual Infinispan instance.

This mode is perfect if you are running your application in a large cluster, it lets your Infinispan data grid scale linearly with growth, since you can increase your grid by adding new node instances to your cluster, where each of these servers add their Virtual Memory (Heap) to form a data grid, which makes this the perfect solution for service providers, such as (SaaS) and Cloud computing.

Infinispan is this scalable because internally it uses Peer-to-Peer (P2P) communication, which eliminates the need of a centralized coordinator of instances. In some cases, a centralized coordinator might become a major problem in enterprise applications, to be a single point of failure. In a P2P architecture, cluster nodes send **Remote Procedure Calls** (**RPC**) messages to neighbor nodes, in a similar way to a local invocation.

Peer-to-Peer systems are application layer networks, which enable networked hosts to share resources in a distributed manner.

This option is recommended if you are building an application that requires being cluster-aware, or if you need an in-memory distributed cache to confront a database or some other expensive data source, as shown in the following figure;

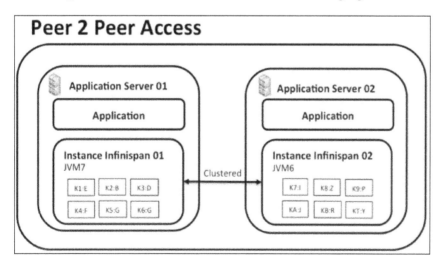

The client/server mode

For cases where you need to provide external access to the grid, you can make use of the client/server mode. The client/server mode describes the relationship between the Infinispan data grid with one or more nodes, providing data to one or more clients. You can also consider using Infinispan in the client/server mode for security reasons, or if you want to provide the data for other applications that are different from Java to consume.

In these cases, Infinispan contains special modules that provide access beyond the JVM to external clients that are not Java-based.

All these modules follow the same structure; a server-side application creates an instance of Infinispan responsible for controlling the state of the objects in each of the nodes that are part of the grid.

Infinispan also provides client components necessary to access the data grid using the specific protocol.

For instance, in the following diagram, we have the **Server Modules REST** and **Memcached**; the first client application is using the **REST HTTP** protocol and the second one is using any **Memcached** client to access the data grid:

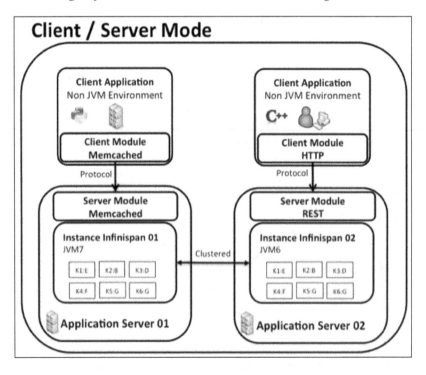

Infinispan provides several modules ready to use on a JBoss Container, which can be connected to different clients over a range of protocols, such as Memcached, Hot Rod, and REST. We are going to cover all of these endpoints in *Chapter 9, Server Modules*.

The cache container

Infinispan provides the EmbeddedCacheManager interface, a special class that works as a factory to obtain an instance of a cache, and the starting point to obtain an instance of a cache by using one of the overloaded getCache() methods.

You can construct a CacheManager using one of its constructors, which optionally takes in a specified path to an XML compliant configuration file or a Configuration object.

The class DefaultCacheManager implements the EmbeddedCacheManager interface and the Lifecycle interface, responsible for the lifecycle of the CacheManager class. It has two methods start() and stop(). Before you create any cache instance, you have to start the CacheManager class, the default constructor creates and starts a new default instance of the CacheManager.

Infinispan also provides the stop() method on the CacheManager class, that should be called before the application terminates. This method ensures proper cleanup of all caches managed by the CacheManager.

Default cache

In a clustered environment, Infinispan can be configured to provide shared settings for all caches created by the same CacheManager.

You can define shared settings through a default cache configuration, so that it can be reused and available for any instance in the data grid. These settings include JMX configuration, network, transport and replication settings, eviction process, marshalling, and serialization characteristics.

You can also define specific characteristics of your cache, such as clustering modes, transaction and locking support, eviction and expiration settings, and cache store and loader settings, among others. To retrieve a default cache, you can call the getCache() method from the CacheManager class.

Changes to your default cache configuration will apply to every instance that is part of the grid, unless explicitly overridden.

Since an XML configuration file is required, you can provide the following code as the minimum code required:

```
<infinispan>
</infinispan>
```

> The Infinispan configuration file can be used to configure all aspects of the cache, such as clustering, persistence, communication, monitoring and security, and so on. We will see more about configuration later in this chapter, in the *Configuring an Infinispan cache* section.

Naming your caches

As you can see in the previous code example, like everything in Infinispan, a named cache does not need to be declared in the configuration. If undefined, since named caches have the same XML configuration as the default cache, they are automatically configured in a manner identical to the default cache. To retrieve a named cache you can call the `CacheManager.getCache(String name)` method. But, note that the cache indicated by the name attribute must exist, and the value must be unique for every named cache specified.

It's possible to override the default settings and configure a specific cache to meet your application's requirements by specifying a configuration declaratively, providing your own XML file or programmatically by using the configuration API.

For the declarative configuration, you will have to load the configuration file before creating any cache instance, which is not necessary if you choose to configure the cache programmatically.

Therefore, as mentioned, all named caches inherit all the defined settings from the default cache; you can add or change a specific behavior by changing the settings.

In the same Infinispan grid, you can have as many as you want different named caches under the same CacheManager. And Infinispan allows different named caches to have identical keys. This feature provides a way of multi-tenancy for your cache store.

> Multi-tenancy is a well-known architecture in SaaS applications, where multiple customers of the same application share the same instance provided by the software to store their data. Each customer in a multitenant architecture is known as a tenant.

This can be very useful if you want to run a Software as a Service(SaaS) application. In a SaaS model, cloud applications can be offered as services to many organizations. For providers of these services, it is essential that the computational resources offered be widely shared.

According to Gartner's definition:

SaaS is a software distribution model in which applications are hosted, owned, delivered, and managed remotely by one or more providers. It is a software that is rented rather than purchased on a pay-for-use basis or as a subscription based on use metrics.

The following figure shows a graphical representation of an interaction of different clients with a default cache and named caches.

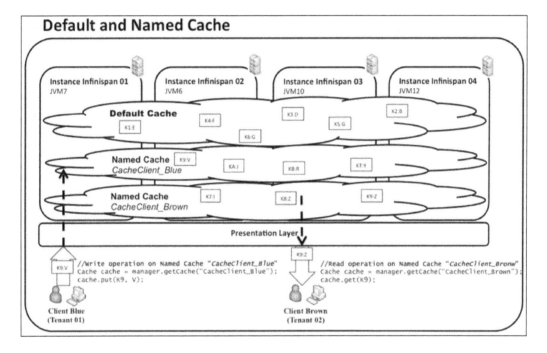

The following code is a simple declarative Infinispan 6.0.* configuration example of individually configured namedCaches:

```
<namedCache name="CacheClient_Blue">
  <clustering mode="invalidation">
    <sync replTimeout="20000"/>
  </clustering>
</namedCache>

<namedCache name=" CacheClient_Brown">
```

```
    <clustering mode="replication">
      <async asyncMarshalling="true"/>
    </clustering>
  </namedCache>
```

 Note that any of the elements appearing in a namedCache section can also appear in the default section as a template.

The following code shows the same example now with Infinispan 7.0.*:

```
<invalidation-cache name="CacheClient_Blue" mode="SYNC"
  remote-timeout="20000"/>
<replicated-cache name="CacheClient_Brown" mode="ASYNC"
  async-marshalling="true"/>
```

The following is the same configuration example, but programmatically configured:

```
EmbeddedCacheManager manager = new DefaultCacheManager(new
  GlobalConfigurationBuilder().transport().defaultTransport().
build());
  public Cache<String, String> getInvalidationCacheForClient(String
    name){
    Configuration config = new ConfigurationBuilder()
        .clustering()
        .cacheMode(CacheMode.INVALIDATION_SYNC)
        .sync().replTimeout(20000)
        .build();
        manager.defineConfiguration(name, config);
    return manager.getCache(name);
}

public Cache<String, String> getReplicationCacheForClient(String name)
{
    Configuration config = new ConfigurationBuilder()
        .clustering()
        .cacheMode(CacheMode.REPL_ASYNC)
        .async().asyncMarshalling(true)
        .build();
        manager.defineConfiguration(name, config);
    return manager.getCache(name);
}
```

The programmatic configuration API was not changed in Infinispan 7.0.*.

To retrieve a named cache, you repeat the same steps you performed to call a default cache; the only difference is that you have to use an overloaded `getCache()` method in which you specify the named cache you want by passing the cache name:

```
Cache<String, String> blueCache =
  getInvalidationCacheForClient("CacheClient_Blue");

Cache<String, String> brownCache =
  getReplicationCacheForClient("CacheClient_Brown");
```

Configuring an Infinispan cache

As you will see in the upcoming chapters, Infinispan is designed to operate in many different environments in a number of ways and provide a broad range of configuration parameters such as Cache Modes, Transactions, Listeners, Expiration, and many others. Fortunately, most have sensible default values, and so you can even run your applications using zero configuration, as we did in the previous section *Anatomy of an Infinispan clustered cache*.

Cache instances can be retrieved using an appropriate CacheManager, which represents a collection of caches. Thus, if you want to create a better and improved cache for Infinispan, you have to understand how this configuration works. There are two approaches you can use to configure Infinispan, An Infinispan cache may be configured declaratively using an XML configuration file, or programmatically via the fluent configuration API.

The configuration file conforms to the XML Schema, which you can find in the following directory `$INFINISPAN_HOME/etc/schema`. All the settings that you can configure declaratively can also be performed programmatically through a Builder class.

Generally, the XML approach is better for defining your configuration, for the following reasons:

- This configuration is the most common approach, as it relies on an XML file, which is parsed when Infinispan starts.

- It is easy if you have your entire configuration in one place.

- Since you can see your entire configuration in one place, it becomes easier to validate and tune your configuration. You could do all this in code, but it would not be visible to those interested in knowing how it's configured.

- Cache configuration can be changed at the time of deployment.

- Infinispan will verify the configuration file at startup, rather than an unexpected runtime exception.

At the time of writing, the current Infinispan version was 7.0.x, which revamped the Infinispan embedded configuration, making it more aligned with the server module configuration.

We will learn more about server modules in *Chapter 9, Server Modules*.

The Infinispan server is based on the JBoss AS 7.2, which is completely different compared to the Infinispan 6.0.x configuration schema. It must be configured using the same configuration schema with some minor differences, such as the addition of the JGroups, Infinispan, and Endpoint subsystems.

In the next section, we will present an analysis on how to configure an Infinispan cache with versions 6.0.x and 7.0.x.

Declarative configuration on Infinispan 6.0.x

We'll now look at some of the configuration options available in the Infinispan configuration file. The Infinispan element is the root element and defines the configuration for Infinispan and for the cache manager configuration, which can optionally contain three elements **global**, **default**, and **namedCache**.

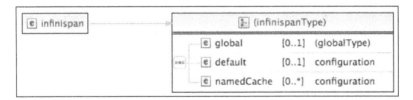

These elements are defined as follows:

- **global**: As the name implies, global configuration is the global settings shared among all cache instances; changes to these setting will globally affect the behavior of all cache instances created by a single CacheManager

- **default**: This specifies the default configuration for all named caches belonging to this cache manager

- **namedCache**: This specifies the configuration for a named cache. All settings contained within a **namedCache** element will override the default configuration

The most attentive readers will notice that in the last image, both **default** and **namedCache** elements share the same XML type configuration. The following figure shows both the **globalType** and **configuration** types:

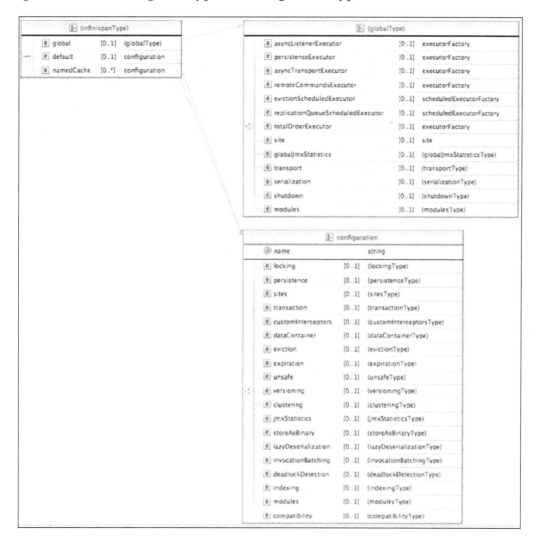

Global configuration (globalType)

In the global section, you can define the settings related to controlling thread pools, total order executor service, configuration for cross-site replication, serialization, and elements to configure transport used for network communications, among others.

The following table reviews them with a short description for each:

Element	Description
`asyncListenerExecutor`	The asynchronous listener executor section is used to configure the service responsible to notify the asynchronous listeners. It will only be useful if you have attached an asynchronous listener to it. You can learn more about Listeners and Notification in this chapter.
`asyncTransportExecutor`	The asynchronous transport executor section is used to configure the asynchronous settings on the transport, including marshalling operations and `async` operations of the Cache, such as `putAsync()`. It is only useful if you intend to use the asynchronous cache API or have configured your cluster to use asynchronous communications.
`remoteCommandsExecutor`	The remote commands execute section is used to configure the executor service to execute remote commands. To disable the remote command execution, set the `factory` to `org.infinispan.executors.WithinThreadExecutorFactory`. This will configure the executor to execute the tasks in the caller thread.
`evictionScheduledExecutor`	Define the settings for the scheduled eviction service, that will run periodically the eviction process. It's useful if you have eviction enabled and wish to customize the executor used by the eviction process.

Element	Description
`replicationQueue ScheduledExecutor`	This is used to configure scheduled executors, which will be responsible for flushing replication queues. Note that this option will have an effect only when the `useReplQueue` attribute is true and asynchronous clustering is enabled.
	This is useful if you have enabled a replication queue and wish to fine-tune the scheduled thread that flushes such batch RPCs.
	More about replication is explained in *Chapter 4, Infinispan Topologies*.
`totalOrderExecutor`	The configuration for the total order executor service is used to validate concurrently non-conflicting transactions. More details about Total Order and Transactions are provided in *Chapter 7, Understanding Transactions and Concurrency*.
`site`	This is the configuration for the cross-site replication. More details on cross-site replication are provided in *Chapter 11, JGroups*.
`globalJmxStatistics`	This setting enables statistics collection and reporting via JMX for all caches managed by this cache manager.
`transport`	This configures the transport used for network communications across the cluster. If the transport is omitted, there is no way to create distributed or clustered caches.
	You can read more about this in *Chapter 11, An Introduction to JGroups*.
`serialization`	This configures the serialization and marshalling settings.
`shutdown`	This element specifies the actions should be taken in the cache when the JVM shuts down.
`modules`	This element provides new options to configure additional modules.

The following example shows an extensive and complete example of a global configuration that uses most of the elements and attributes aforementioned:

```
<global>

<!-- Configuring the executor service in the global section to emit
notifications to asynchronous listeners. -->

  <asyncListenerExecutorfactory=
    "org.infinispan.executors.DefaultExecutorFactory">
    <properties>
      <property name="maxThreads" value="20" />
      <property name="queueSize" value="10000" />
      <property name="threadNamePrefix"
        value="AsyncListenerThread" />
    </properties>
  </asyncListenerExecutor>

<!-- Configuring the asynchronous transport executor for asynchronous
work on the Transport. -->

  <asyncTransportExecutorfactory=
    "org.infinispan.executors.DefaultExecutorFactory">
    <properties>
      <property name="maxThreads" value="25" />
      <property name="queueSize" value="10000" />
      <property name="threadNamePrefix"
        value="AsyncSerializationThread" />
    </properties>
  </asyncTransportExecutor>

<!-- Configuring the Executor Service to execute remote commands -->
  <remoteCommandsExecutorfactory=
    "org.infinispan.executors.DefaultExecutorFactory">
    <properties>
      <property name="maxThreads" value="50" />
      <property name="coreThreads" value="5" />
      <property name="keepAliveTime" value="15000" />
      <property name="threadNamePrefix" value="RemoteCommandThread" />
    </properties>
  </remoteCommandsExecutor>

<!-- Changing the Thread name prefix of the executor used by the
eviction process. -->
```

```
  <evictionScheduledExecutorfactory=
    "org.infinispan.executors.DefaultScheduledExecutorFactory">
    <properties>
      <property name="threadNamePrefix" value="EvictionThread" />
    </properties>
  </evictionScheduledExecutor>

<!-- Changing the Thread name prefix of the scheduled executor that
will be used to flush the replication queues periodically. -->
  <replicationQueueScheduledExecutorfactory=
    "org.infinispan.executors.DefaultScheduledExecutorFactory">
    <properties>
      <property name="threadNamePrefix"
        value="ReplicationQueueThread" />
    </properties>
  </replicationQueueScheduledExecutor>

<!-- Configuring the number of threads, queue size and thread name
prefix of the total order executor service. -->
  <totalOrderExecutorfactory=
    "org.infinispan.executors.DefaultExecutorFactory">
    <properties>
      <property name="threadNamePrefix"
        value="TotalOrderValidatorThread" />
      <property name="coreThreads" value="1" />
      <property name="maxThreads" value="16" />
      <property name="queueSize" value="0" />
      <property name="keepAliveTime" value="1000" />
    </properties>
  </totalOrderExecutor>

<!-- Changing transport settings. -->
  <transport clusterName="infinispan-cluster"
    distributedSyncTimeout="50000" nodeName="PacketPub"
      machineId="m1" rackId="r1" siteId="s1">
    <properties>
      <property name="configurationFile"
        value="jgroups-udp.xml" />
    </properties>
  </transport>

<!-- Changing serialization and marshalling settings adding a custom
externalizer class. -->
  <serializationmarshallerClass=
    "org.infinispan.marshall.VersionAwareMarshaller"
      version="1.0">
```

```
  <advancedExternalizers>
    <advancedExternalizer id="1528"
      externalizerClass="Ticket$TicketExternalizer" />
  </advancedExternalizers>
</serialization>

<!-- Enabling the global JMX statistics for the given cache manager
and customizing the jmx domain name. -->
  <globalJmxStatistics enabled="true"
    jmxDomain="PacketDomain"mBeanServerLookup=
      "org.infinispan.jmx.JBossMBeanServerLookup"
        allowDuplicateDomains="true" />

<shutdown hookBehavior="DEFAULT" />
```

Configuration settings

Both the **default** and **namedCache** sections share the same type definition (configuration) that will be either used for all caches (**default**), or for a specific cache (**namedCache**).

You can use the elements that are described in the following table to define different configurations:

Element	Description
locking	This defines the concurrency level for lock containers, isolation level, lock acquisition time and concurrency behavior of the cache.
persistence	This is the configuration for cache loaders and stores.
	You'll learn more about cache loaders and cache stores in this chapter.
sites	This is the cache configuration for the cross-site replication. It can be used to configure a backup cache for a remote grid.
	More about cross-site replication is explained in *Chapter 11, An Introduction to JGroups*.
transaction	This allows you to define the transactional settings of the cache. More about transactions and concurrency is explained in *Chapter 6, Case Study – The TicketMonster Application*.
customInterceptors	This configures custom interceptors for a given cache. We will see Interceptors and Integration with CDI in *Chapter 12, Advanced Topics*.
dataContainer	This controls the internal data structure for the cache.
eviction	This defines the eviction characteristics for the cache.

Element	Description
expiration	The expiration tag allows you to define the expiration settings for entries in the cache.
unsafe	Use this with care; this is recommended only in certain circumstances. The unsafe tag contains the unreliableReturnValues Boolean attribute, which can improve the performance by breaking the map contract.
versioning	This controls the versioning for entries in the cache. We are going to talk about data versioning in detail in *Chapter 7, Understanding Transactions and Concurrency*.
clustering	The clustering tag allows you to specify the cluster settings of the cache, such as synchronization characteristics, transfer state when a new cache joins or leaves the cluster, and so on.
jmxStatistics	This setting enables statistics collection and reporting via JMX.
storeAsBinary	This setting is often used in a clustered mode and allows you to specify whether keys and values of the cache entries will be serialized and stored in binary format or stored as references. You can decide to store, as binary only, the keys, the values, or both by changing the attributes to storeKeysAsBinary and storeValuesAsBinary. It stores the entries as binary, as a consequence, we will have an impact in the serialization process, that will happen at an earlier time. But further, it can improve the throughput of a system through lazy deserialization.
invocationBatching	This enables invocation batching for the cache. It defaults to false.
deadlockDetection	This configures deadlock detection.
indexing	This allows you to enable indexing of the cache entries for searching. It is disabled by default.
compatibility	This enables the compatibility mode for embedded and remote endpoints that shares cached data.

Let's have a look at the default configuration in the following example:

```
<default>
  <locking concurrencyLevel="100" lockAcquisitionTimeout="1000" />
  <transaction transactionMode="NON_TRANSACTIONAL"
    reaperWakeUpInterval="123" completedTxTimeout="3123" />
  <jmxStatistics enabled="false" />
<!--
```

A common use of the `dataContainer` element is for equivalence; it contains the attributes `keyEquivalence` and `valueEquivalence` that can be used to customize the way Infinispan compares cached keys. For instance, when you want to store an array in an Infinispan cache, the default implementation of `equals()` and `hashcode()` might produce undesirable results, since you probably want this function to be calculated based on the contents of the arrays and not in the object reference.

Starting with Infinispan 5.3, Infinispan users can use the new `Equivalence<T>` interface to provide their own implementation for both keys and values.

Infinispan provides two implementations, which are `org.infinispan.commons.equivalence.ByteArrayEquivalence` to compare unsigned byte arrays and the default option `org.infinispan.commons.equivalence.AnyServerEquivalence` that can support multiple different types, which delegates the call to the `equals()` and `hashCode()` methods to the objects themselves.

There are two examples of configuration files. One with the `AnyServerEquivalence` configuration file is as follows:

```
<dataContainerkeyEquivalence=
  "org.jboss.as.clustering.infinispan.equivalence.
    AnyServerEquivalence"
      valueEquivalence="org.jboss.as.clustering.infinispan.
        equivalence.AnyServerEquivalence" />
```

And the other with the `ByteArrayEquivalence` configuration file is as follows:

```
<dataContainerkeyEquivalence=
  "org.infinispan.commons.equivalence.ByteArrayEquivalence"
      valueEquivalence="org.infinispan.commons.equivalence.
        ByteArrayEquivalence" />
```

To create an Infinispan cache declaratively with an XML file, create a `CacheContainer` instance passing the path/name of the configuration file or a stream containing the configuration file's contents to the constructor.

The following example shows how to create a `CacheContainer` class with the name of the XML configuration file, to use it as a template for all caches in the classpath at `src/com/packetpub/infinispan/chapter3/infinispan-eviction.xml`:

```
String config = "resources/infinispan-eviction.xml";
CacheContainer container = new DefaultCacheManager(config);
```

Declarative configuration on Infinispan 7.0.x

As mentioned, the central motivation for completely rebuilding the current XML schema-based configuration files was to make the declarative configuration more aligned with the server module configuration.

The `<infinispan>` root element is still present in the Infinispan 7.0 new XML schema file; however, the global, default and namedCache sub-elements from Infinsipan 6.0.x were removed, because in the server module the semantics of the default cache of a cache containers are slightly different. That's the same with global configuration, where mostly all of the services in the server module are auto-injected behind the scenes.

The new `<infinispan>` sub-elements are defined as follows:

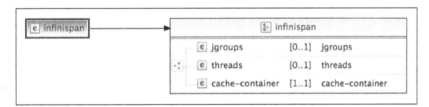

- **jgroups**: The transport protocol stack configurations are defined within this section using JGroups
- **threads**: This defines the threading subsystem, which can be used by Infinispan cache containers to declare and reference manageable thread pools and resources
- **cache-container**: This specifies the cache container configuration

Understanding the JGroups element

As the name implies, the `jgroups` element deals with transport configuration. It lets you define an individual JGroups stack. These configuration settings are in a file containing its definition, which can be referenced in the element stack-file, which is as follows:

```
<jgroups>
  <stack-file name="udp" path="jgroups-udp.xml"/>
  <stack-file name="tcp" path="jgroups-tcp.xml"/>
</jgroups>
```

The above configuration uses two `jgroups` files, which can be referenced by the `transport stack` attribute contained within the `cache-container` element.

Configuring the threads subsystem

The `thread` element is used to define thread executors and manage thread pools and resources.

The thread subsystem is an essential part of Infinispan used to perform a collection of tasks in parallel. Infinispan provides a number of useful thread pools, which become more relevant in multi-core architectures.

There are few sub-elements that should be configured in the thread subsystem to support thread pool management. First, we must define a `<thread-factory>` element, which will be used to create new threads when needed.

It implements the `java.util.concurrent.ThreadFactory` class, and we also need to add a name for the created bean; optionally, we can define the name of the thread group (group-name attribute), a pattern to create names for threads (thread-name-pattern attribute), and specify the thread priority of created threads, by using the priority attribute.

The following sample defines a `thread-factory` called `infinispan-factory`:

```
<threads>
  <thread-factory name="infinispan-factory"
    group-name="infinispan" thread-name-pattern="%G %i"
      priority="5"/>

    <blocking-bounded-queue-thread-pool name="infinispan-listener"
      thread-factory="infinispan-factory" core-threads="1"
        max-threads="1" queue-length="0" keepalive-time="0" />
```

```
<blocking-bounded-queue-thread-pool name=
    "infinispan-transport" thread-factory="infinispan-factory"
      core-threads="5" max-threads="10" queue-length="100"
        keepalive-time="10000" />

<cached-thread-pool name="infinispan-cached"
    thread-factory="infinispan-factory" />

<scheduled-thread-pool name="infinispan-eviction"
    thread-factory="infinispan-factory" />

<scheduled-thread-pool name="infinispan-repl-queue"
    thread-factory="infinispan-factory" />

</threads>
```

Infinispan ships with three useful thread pool executors you can use out of box, which are as follows:

Element	Description
`blocking-bounded-queue-thread-pool`	This defines a thread pool executor with a bounded queue where, threads submitting tasks might get blocked unless a free thread were there to handle them.
	The thread pool can work on several tasks in parallel, limited by the `max-threads` attribute. If the number of running threads is equal to this attribute, the task will be placed in a queue.
	To avoid creating a huge queue and a possible out of memory problem, you can use the `queue-length` attribute to define the queue length attribute. You can also define other attributes such as:
	• name: This determines the name of the bean
	• `core-threads`: This defines the number of threads to keep in the pool.
	• `keepalive-time`: This specifies the maximum amount of time pool threads will remain running when idle. If not specified, threads will stop only when the executor is shut down.
	• `thread-factory`: This determines the name of the thread factory, which actually creates worker threads.

Element	Description
cached-thread-pool	This defines a thread pool executor that creates new threads as needed, but if available, it will return the previously constructed threads from the cache; otherwise, a new thread will be created and included in the pool. Other attributes are as follows: • name: This determines the name of the bean • thread-factory: This determines the name of the thread factory, which actually creates worker threads
scheduled-thread-pool	This defines a thread pool executor that creates a single-threaded executor, which can schedule the execution of tasks to be executed periodically or after a specific delay. Other attributes are as follows: • name: This determines the name of the bean • thread-factory: This determines the name of the thread factory, which actually creates worker threads

We are not going to spend much time going over these in detail, as their purpose is fairly obvious and you can clear any doubts by consulting the API documentation. Anyway, we will cover a broad range of the configuration options in the following chapters and sections.

Configuring the cache-container element

The cache-container element must appear once, which means that you can define a single cache manager that comprises one or more caches under the same cache container.

The <cache-container> element contains several attributes, which are as follows:

- name: The name attribute can be use to define the unique name of the cache container.
- default-cache: This defines the default cache to be used for this cache container.
- listener-executor: This defines the executor used for asynchronous cache listener notifications
- eviction-executor: This defines the scheduled executor used for evictions.

- `replication-queue-executor`: This defines the scheduled executor responsible for managing and executing tasks to handle asynchronous operations used by the asynchronous replication queue.

- `persistence-executor`: When interacting with a persistent store, you can use this attribute to configure the executor service.

- `statistics`: This is a Boolean attribute that enables or disables a collection of statistics for the cache container; for best performance keep it disabled.

- `shutdown-hook`: Infinispan attaches a shutdown hook to the cache. You can use this attribute to define the behavior of the JVM when it begins its shutdown. The possible values are DEFAULT, REGISTER, and DONT_REGISTER.

The following `cache-container` configuration was extracted from the `sample.xml` file:

```
<cache-container name="SampleCacheManager" statistics="true"
   default-cache="the-default-cache" shutdown-hook="DEFAULT">
```

Within the `cache-container` element you also have other important elements, such as the `transport` element, which lets you override the transport settings for the cache container. In the next example, we are making a reference to the `tcp` (`jgroups`) stack file:

```
<transport stack="tcp" cluster="infinispan-cluster"
   node-name="Node-A" machine="m1" rack="r1" site="LON" />
```

We also have the serialization element, used to customize the way data is serialized and deserialized by the cache container. In the next example, it shows how you can specify custom advanced-externalizer for custom user types:

```
<serialization
  marshaller="org.infinispan.marshall.core.
    VersionAwareMarshaller" version="1.0">
  <!-- AdvancedExternalizer defined as inner static class, with
    id set via XML configuration -->
  <advanced-externalizer id="1234"
    class="org.infinispan.marshall.
      AdvancedExternalizerTest$IdViaConfigObj$Externalizer"/>
  <!-- AdvancedExternalizer defined as inner static class,
    with id set via annotation -->
  <advanced-externalizer
    class="org.infinispan.marshall.
      AdvancedExternalizerTest$IdViaAnnotationObj$Externalizer"/>
  <!-- AdvancedExternalizer defined as inner static class,
    with id set both via XML config and annotation -->
```

```
<advanced-externalizer id="3456"
  class="org.infinispan.marshall.
    AdvancedExternalizerTest$IdViaBothObj$Externalizer"/>
</serialization>
```

We will see more about externalizers in
Chapter 12, Advanced Topics.

The following code snippet shows how to use the `jmx` attribute to customize the domain name, where all the information collected by JMX will be shown:

```
<jmx domain="org.infinispan" />
```

From Infinispan 7.0, it's possible to configure security settings for your cache container (global) or per-cache. The following code snippet shows an example of the `security` element in the cache container:

```
<security>
  <authorization
    mapper="com.packtpubl.infinispan.sec.InfRoleMapper">
    <role name="admin" permissions="ALL" />
    <role name="reader" permissions="READ" />
  </authorization>
</security>
```

We will learn more about security in the *Chapter 9, Server Modules*, and *Chapter 12, Advanced Topics.*

The remaining elements `local-cache`, `replicated-cache`, `invalidation-cache`, and `distributed-cache` are used to define the topology of your grid. We will address all cache topologies in *Chapter 4, Infinispan Topologies.*

Programmatic configuration

There are times when we would like to configure our application at runtime without using a configuration file. In order to achieve this, we can use the Infinispan's configuration API that was shipped with Infinispan. The API can be used to configure every single aspect of Infinispan declarative configuration. Also, if you already have a cache configuration in your `config` file, you will be able to merge the configuration you created at runtime or update it.

To represent the global and the `default/namedCache` configuration section that we have in the configuration file, Infinispan provides the `org.infinispan.` `configuration.global.GlobalConfiguration` and `org.infinispan.` `configuration.cache.Configuration` classes, respectively.

In order to use the configuration API to create a configuration object, you will need to create a `ConfigurationBuilder` class, which is the main class to build a runtime configuration. Each feature in Infinispan, such as the JMX Statistics, for example, can be configured through specialized builder classes, which implement the `Builder` interface.

The use of these builders are very intuitive and easy, and assists the developer to chain method calls to set configuration options, in order to make the coding process more efficient and also improve the readability of the configuration.

The following diagram shows the classes that compose the `ConfigurationBuilder` API:

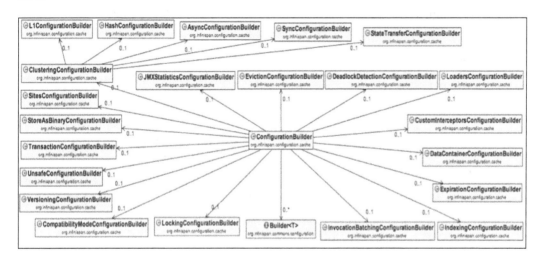

The `ConfigurationBuilder` class is located in the `org.infinispan.` `configuration.cache` package.

In the same way, we have a builder class for configuration settings; you also have a `GlobalConfigurationBuilder` class for configuring global settings that are shared among all cache instances.

Regardless of whether you opt to configure your cache declaratively or programmatically, you have the same options in both approaches. Neither of the two approaches is better than the other; which one you decide to use will depend on the requirements of your application, but if you are writing an application from scratch and you don't know exactly how it's going to work out, it may be preferable to start with an XML configuration file and adjust it in runtime to suit your needs.

The following code sample shows how to create an EmbeddedCacheManager object using a predefined XML configuration file and obtaining the default cache from it:

```
EmbeddedCacheManager manager = new
  DefaultCacheManager("my-config-file.xml");
Cache defaultCache = manager.getCache();
```

Let's assume that a new cache is to be configured programmatically for finer control, without any configuration file. First, a fresh instance of a Configuration object is created using the ConfigurationBuilder helper object.

Then, we configure it to gather statistics to be reported via JMX. Finally, the configuration is defined/registered within a manager:

```
Configuration c = new ConfigurationBuilder()
  .jmxStatistics().enable()
    .build();
    String statisticsCacheName = "statisticsCache";
    manager.defineConfiguration(statisticsCacheName, c);
    Cache<String, String> cache =
      manager.getCache(statisticsCacheName);
```

If you do not wish to start your cache with an XML configuration file, you can create a cache using the ConfigurationBuilder API:

```
GlobalConfiguration globalConfig = new
  GlobalConfigurationBuilder().globalJmxStatistics().build();
  Configuration config = new
    ConfigurationBuilder().eviction().maxEntries(20000)
      .strategy(EvictionStrategy.LIRS)
        .expiration().wakeUpInterval(5000L).maxIdle(120000L)
          .build();
  CacheContainer container = new
    DefaultCacheManager(globalConfig, config);
```

 The ConfigurationBuilder API assumes that you will always end with a build() method being called to build the instance.

Infinispan 5.1 introduced a fluent configuration API and a new XML configuration parser. These were, however, limited to the configuration of the core elements of Infinispan, relying on key/value properties for configuring any additional modules in a way that all modules could define their own builders and parsers. To learn more, visit `https://developer.jboss.org/wiki/ExtendingInfinispansConfiguration`.

Infinispan APIs

Infinispan provides the following APIs to access the grid:

- **Cache API**: This is Infinispan's primary API to access the grid, it's located in the `org.infinispan` package.

- **TreeCache API**: Infinispan provides the `org.infinispan.tree.TreeCache` interface to provide compatibility with JBoss Cache. It can be used for caching data organized as tree-like structures, like a filesystem tree.

  To create an instance of `TreeCache`, you will need a factory class called `org.infinispan.tree.TreeCacheFactory`. Define the tree structure using the `org.infinispan.tree.Node` interface, by defining a root node and a collection of node objects that contain the key and value data.

  You can find a simple example of the `TreeCache` API using the Infinispan configuration API here:

```
EmbeddedCacheManager manager = new
  DefaultCacheManager("sample.xml");
TreeCache<String, String> tc = new
  TreeCacheFactory().createTreeCache(manager.<String,
    String>getCache("TreeCache"));
tc.put("/books/packt/infinispan/guide", "ISBN",
  "1782169970");
tc.put("/books/packt/infinispan/guide", "Author", "Wagner
  R. Santos");
tc.put("/books/packt/infinispan/guide", "ReleaseYear",
  "2014");
assertEquals("1782169970",
  tc.get("/books/packt/infinispan/guide", "ISBN"));
assertEquals("Wagner R. Santos",
  tc.get("/books/packt/infinispan/guide", "Author"));
assertEquals("2014",
  tc.get("/books/packt/infinispan/guide", "ReleaseYear"));
tc.remove("/books/packt/infinispan/guide", "ReleaseYear");
assertNull(tc.get("/books/packt/infinispan/guide",
  "ReleaseYear"));
```

A very important configuration to notice, is that in order to use the TreeCache API, you must first enable batching to your cache. Please see the following Infinispan 7 configuration to create a basic TreeCache:

```
<local-cache name="TreeCache">
  <transaction mode="BATCH" locking="PESSIMISTIC" />
</local-cache>
```

There are other ways to manipulate data in a tree cache. For more details about the TreeCache API, visit the following link:

http://infinispan.org/docs/7.2.x/user_guide/
user_guide.html#_tree_api_module

- **JCache API**: Infinispan provides an implementation of JCache API (JSR-107), a Java Caching API that provides applications with the caching functionality, in particular, the ability to cache Java objects.

Learning the cache API

Infinispan provides a simple cache API using the org.infinispan.Cache interface, which extends java.util.concurrent.ConcurrentMap. So, if you know how to work with a Map interface from the Java Collections API, you will be very familiar with the Infinispan cache API.

A Cache provides a highly concurrent, optionally distributed data structure with additional features such as:

- Eviction and expiration support to prevent OutOfMemoryErrors
- JTA transaction compatibility
- Event notification via the Listeners
- Persistence of entries to a CacheStore, to maintain copies that would withstand server failure or restarts

The next figure shows the class diagram of the Cache API

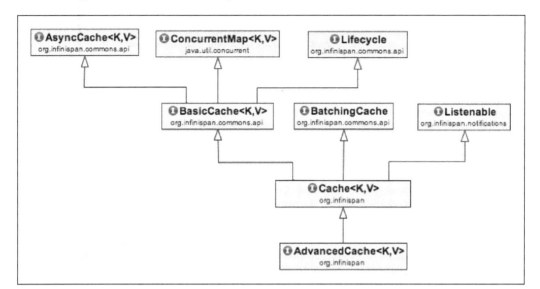

The **Cache** is the central interface of Infinispan, and exposes simple methods for adding, retrieving, and removing entries, including atomic mechanisms exposed by the JDK's **ConcurrentMap** interface. So , because of that, the Infinispan Cache doesn't accept null values, but it allows you to store, retrieve, and remove values in the cache, the same way you usually do with a map structure.

Many different threads or processes can get a **Cache** instance that operates on the same Infinispan data grid.

As you will see in the next chapter, how entries are stored depends on the cache mode in use, which defines whether an entry can be replicated, invalidated, or distributed to a remote node.

In the preceding image, we can see that **Cache** extends the `org.infinispan.commons.api.Lifecycle` interface, which defines the lifecycle of components. It also extends the `org.infinispan.commons.api.AsyncCache` interface, which includes support for async remote operations.

Note that all methods of the `AsyncCache` interface such as `getAsync()`, `putAsync()`, `removeAsyn()` return a `NotifyingFuture` interface, which is a sub-interface of future and allows observers to be notified by listeners when the future completes.

So, these services were designed for use on a clustered cache.

The `org.infinispan.commons.api.BatchingCache` interface is implemented by all caches that support batching.

We will talk more about batching API in the *Chapter 7, Understanding Transactions and Concurrency*.

Understanding cache evictions

Before we start to talk about eviction and expiration, it is important to note that expiration and eviction are completely different of each order.

Infinispan uses a part of the application's memory to cache data and we can face scenarios, where the total amount of data held in a cache is greater than the available amount of memory. So, in order to not run out of memory and always maintain the memory capacity available for new entries on each cache host, Infinispan supports eviction, which is a special thread responsible that is used to remove (evict) entries from the cache in order to make room for new entries.

The algorithm that determines which entry should be evicted is called eviction policy; currently, Infinispan supports multiple eviction policies ,which are as follows;

- **LRU**: LRU or Least Recently Used, discards the least recently used items first, although easy to understand, in some cases the performance is below expectations in weak access locality. Entries frequently accessed can be unfortunately replaced.

- **LIRS**: This is the default eviction algorithm. LIRS or Low Inter-reference Recency Set is basically a page replacement algorithm that performs better than the LRU and similar replacement algorithms. Eviction in the LIRS algorithm depends on history information access about cache data to evaluate **Inter-Reference Recency (IRR)**, to make a replacement decision.

- **NONE**: When set on, the eviction thread process will be disabled.
- **UNORDERED**: A deprecated eviction strategy.

After the release of Infinispan 6.0, LIRS became the new default eviction policy, since it's a new algorithm, I will give a brief overview about how it works.

As mentioned, eviction in the LIRS algorithm makes use of recency to evaluate IRR to take a replacement decision. Infinispan uses recent IRR by maintaining information of the recorded history of the number of cache entries accessed between the last two consecutive accesses to the same cache entry.

Recency refers to the number of other cache entries manipulated in the last consecutive operations over the same cache entry.

Additionally, LIRS keeps track of cache elements that are present in two different cache entry blocks, called **low IRR** (also known as **LIR**) and **high IRR** (also known as **HIR**). While the LIR area holds hot entries, the HIR area holds recently accessed entries, which might get promoted to the LIR area.

The LIRS eviction algorithm will evict elements with a high IRR from the cache and keep entries that have a low IRR in the cache as much as possible.

If within an LIR queue, the recency of the cache entries starts to increase in front of the cache entries of an HIR queue. This in turn, starts to get accessed at a smaller recency in comparison to the LIR queue, Infinispan will probably switch the status of the two LIR/HIR queues.

As a consequence, regardless of its recency, cache entries in the HIR queue may be evicted, even if the cache entry was recently accessed. The following diagram illustrates an example of how it works:

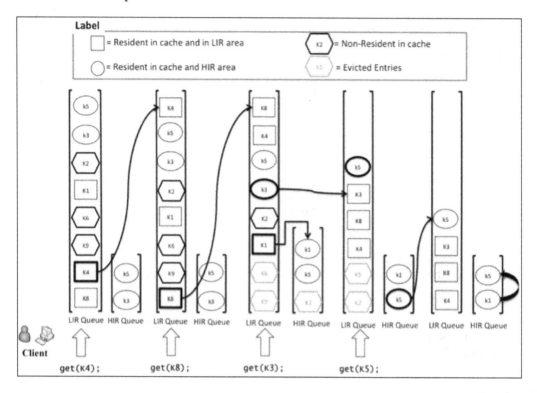

Another important aspect about eviction in Infinispan is that if you use eviction together with a cache store, you will not lose an evicted entry permanently, since the eviction process only remove entries from the heap memory, with the cache loader option, an evicted entry will be persisted to the underlying cache store, which can be retrieved from the cache store later for any further usage.

> Passivation is a feature often used in conjunction with eviction, in order to keep only a single copy of a cache entry, either in the cache memory or in a cache store, but not both.
>
> We will see Cache Loaders and Passivation in the next section.

Infinispan doesn't run a cluster-wide eviction process, because it runs the process on each node. The eviction process considers the `maxEntries` attribute of the `<eviction>` element as a threshold.

And it is responsible to execute the eviction thread, that will analyze the cache contents based on the configuration, before start the eviction process.

You can configure Infinispan to evict data from your cache either programmatically or via the configuration file.

Eviction can be configured using the `<eviction />` element in your `<default />` or `<namedCache />` configuration sections or using the `EvictionConfigurationBuilder` API programmatic approach.

The `<eviction/>` element contains two attributes `maxEntries`, which defines the maximum number of entries in a cache instance; `strategy`, to define the algorithm our cache should use to determine which entry should be evicted; and `threadPolicy`, to specify a threading policy for eviction. For `threadPolicy`, you have two distinct approaches, the `piggyback` and `default` approach using a dedicated `EvictionManager` thread.

The piggyback eviction thread policy, as its name implies, performs eviction by piggybacking on user threads that are accessing the data container.

 Piggybacking is a technique applied in the network layer, which evolves a bi-directional data transmission from receiver to emitter, where the receiver confirms, by sending an acknowledge (ACK) signal to the sender, that the message was received successfully.

In order to turn eviction on via the configuration file, it is required to change the eviction element by populating the `maxEntries` attribute to a number higher than zero. But, before you change it, you have to consider the amount of available memory, to not run the risk of getting an `OutOfMemory` exception. An example of eviction in Infinispan 6 can be seen in the following code:

```
<namedCache name="EvictionCache">
  <evictionmaxEntries="2000"
    strategy="LIRS"
      threadPolicy="PIGGYBACK"/>
</namedCache>
```

This code is written in Infinispan 7 as follows:

```
<local-cache name="EvictionCache">
  <evictionmax-entries="2000"
    strategy="LIRS"
      thread-policy="PIGGYBACK"/>
</local-cache>
```

In this example, we defined the named cache `EvictionCache`, which can handle 2000 entries before beginning the eviction process; we are using the LIRS strategy and the `PIGGYBACK` thread policy.

 Since you can only set the number of `maxEntries`, and there is no way to set the maximum size of the cache, you have to know the average size of your individual elements to know how many entries your RAM can hold.

Configuring cache expiration

While eviction removes cache entries when the number of entries reaches a certain level, cache Expiration allows Infinispan to remove entries from the cache automatically after specified period of time. When using an overload method of the `put()` or `putAll()` methods, which takes a `TimeUnit` enum, that can be defined for one specific cache entry, that based on the configuration, defines the amount of time a cache entry can live in the cache. All cache data that exceed the specified period of time will be removed from the cache.

On the other hand, simply using the `put(key, value)` method would create a cache entry that would probably live forever in the cache, until it's removed by someone else and evicted from the memory by an eviction process.

Along with `lifespan`, you can set the `maxIdle` attribute to determine how long a cache entry will remain in the cache before expiration. You can use `lifespans` or `maxIdles` in any possible combination.

The following is a configuration of a sample named cache, which defines that our cache can hold an object for a maximum of 10 seconds (`lifespan`) and up to three idle seconds (`maxIdle`).

For Infinispan 6 the code is as follows:

```
<namedCache name="ExpirationCache">
  <expirationlifespan="10000"
    maxIdle="3000"/>
</namedCache>
```

For Infinispan 7 the code is as follows:

```
<local-cache name="ExpirationCache">
  <expirationlifespan="10000"
    max-idle="3000"/>
</local-cache>
```

To test the preceding configuration, let's create a simple test case with the following code:

```
String config = "src/com/packetpub/infinispan/chapter3/
  infinispan-eviction.xml";
CacheContainer container = new DefaultCacheManager(config);
Cache<String, String> cache = container.
  getCache("ExpirationCache ");
System.out.println("*********************************************
  *");
System.out.println("Expiration Test by maximum idle time
  (maxIdle)");
cache.put("key_01", "Key 01 Value");
System.out.println("Key01 = " + cache.get("key_01"));
Thread.sleep(3000);
System.out.println("Key01 " + cache.get("key_01"));

System.out.println("*********************************************
  ");
System.out.println("Expiration Test by lifespan (lifespan)");
cache.put("key_01", "Key 01 Another Value");
for (int i = 1; i <= 10; i++) {
  Thread.sleep(1000);
  System.out.println(i + " second(s) >> Object on key_01 = "
    + cache.get("key_01"));
}
System.out.println("*********************************************
  ");
```

After we execute the code, we should see the following output:

```
Console ⊠  Problems  @ Javadoc  Declaration
EvictionTest [Java Application] /Library/Java/JavaVirtualMachines/jdk1.7.0_45.jdk/Contents/Home/bin/java (10/01/2014 17:54:13)
log4j:WARN No appenders could be found for logger (org.jboss.logging).
log4j:WARN Please initialize the log4j system properly.
log4j:WARN See http://logging.apache.org/log4j/1.2/faq.html#noconfig for more info.
***********************************************
Expiration Test by maximum idle time (maxIdle)
Key01 = Key 01 Value
Key01 null
***********************************************
Expiration Test by lifespan (lifespan)
1 second(s) >> Object on key_01 = Key 01 Another Value
2 second(s) >> Object on key_01 = Key 01 Another Value
3 second(s) >> Object on key_01 = Key 01 Another Value
4 second(s) >> Object on key_01 = Key 01 Another Value
5 second(s) >> Object on key_01 = Key 01 Another Value
6 second(s) >> Object on key_01 = Key 01 Another Value
7 second(s) >> Object on key_01 = Key 01 Another Value
8 second(s) >> Object on key_01 = Key 01 Another Value
9 second(s) >> Object on key_01 = Key 01 Another Value
10 second(s) >> Object on key_01 = null
***********************************************
```

In our test case, we created a `CacheManager` interface, passing the previous configuration file in the constructor to retrieve an `ExpirationCache` from it.

Next, we put a new entry with the `key_01` entry in the cache and we put the thread to sleep for 3 seconds, to exceed the maximum idle time a cache entry can be maintained in the cache.

From the output, we can see the `key_01` entry was removed from the cache.

Now, the next entry allows us to see how expiration works by lifespan, we added another entry `key_01` and after each second, we printed the value inside a loop. Again, from the output, we can see that after 10 seconds `key_01` was removed from the cache.

The next table describes the attributes of the `<expiration>` element:

Attribute	Type	Default	Description
wakeUpInterval (ISPN 6) interval (ISPN 7)	long	1000	This defines, in milliseconds, an interval for which Infinispan will sleep before looking for expired entries in order to purge them from the memory and cache stores. To disable the periodic eviction process, you can set it to -1.
Lifespan (ISPN 6 and 7)	Long	-1	This defines, in milliseconds, the maximum lifespan of a cache entry, that when expired, Infinispan will automatically remove the cache entry cluster-wide. The default value -1 disables the lifespan and the entries will never expire. Note that you can override this value for each entry by using the Cache API.

Attribute	Type	Default	Description
maxIdle (ISPN 6) max-idle (ISPN 7)	Long	-1	This defines, in milliseconds, the maximum idle time a cache entry can be in the cache. When the time exceeds, the entry will expire cluster-wide. The default value -1 disables the maxIdle and the entries will never expire. Note that you can override this value for each entry by using the Cache API.
reaperEnabled (only ISPN 6)	boolean	true	When enabled, a background reaper thread is initialized to test cache entries eligible for expiration.

Eviction v/s Expiration

You can use both the Eviction and Expiration features to avoid OutOfMemory exceptions, in order to keep, in the cache, only really necessary entries for your application, so it's quite important to understand the differences between these two functionalities.

With eviction you can define the right eviction policy for your application, by setting the maximum number of entries (through maxEntries) you can have in the cache.

If this limit is exceeded, Infinispan will execute the eviction strategy (LRU, LIRS, and so on) defined for the cache and remove the entries according to the chosen strategy.

In order not to lose your data during the eviction process, you can configure it to work with passivation, which will be responsible to evict the entries from the cache to a cache store.

For Expiration, on the other hand, you have to define the criteria and for how long you want to keep the entries in the cache. You can define how much time an entry can stay in the cache, changing the maximum lifespan. Or you can change the maximum idle time, which specifies the maximum idle time a cache entry can stay in the cache.

And at last, unlike eviction, when removed, expired entries are not passivated like evicted entries, even if passivation is enabled. They are removed globally from the grid, from memory and cache stores.

Persisting data in Infinispan

Infinispan can use a CacheLoader interface to save the in-memory cache data to a persistent cache store, such as a database or text file. And during initialization, CacheLoader can pre-load the cache using data from the persistent cache store.

The following figure shows an Infinispan instance using a backend store:

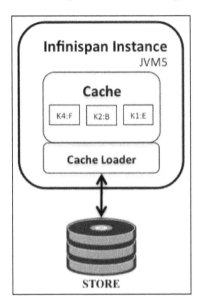

The entries are fetched from the store lazily, when the get() operation can't find the value in the cache the cache loader enters in action. The object returned by CacheLoader will be stored into the cache and reused as a response to the get() request.

Once the entry is in the memory available for modifications, the underlying cache store is notified about any changes in the cache entry, so that the entries are properly synchronized in the persistent store.

Starting with Version 6.0 and up, Infinispan has changed the way data is persisted, so if you stored data in an earlier version (using Infinispan 4.x or 5.x), you must perform a data migration. Otherwise, Infinispan won't be able to read persisted data on the previous versions.

For rolling upgrades of Infinispan, please visit http://infinispan. org/docs/6.0.x/user_guide/user_guide.html#_Rolling_ chapter.

For simplicity purposes, Infinispan follows the same interface of JCache, with two separated interfaces CacheLoader<K,V> and CacheWriter<K,V> and convenient methods to integrate with different external resources.

 If you are a store provider, it's recommended to implement both interfaces CacheWriter<K,V> and CacheLoader<K,V> for reading and writing operations.

You can also use the interfaces AdvancedCacheLoader<K,V> and AdvancedCacheWriter<K,V> to provide advanced functionality and methods, to allow parallel iteration over the cache entries and methods for bulk operations when persisting or loading data from/to an external storage, as shown in the following diagram:

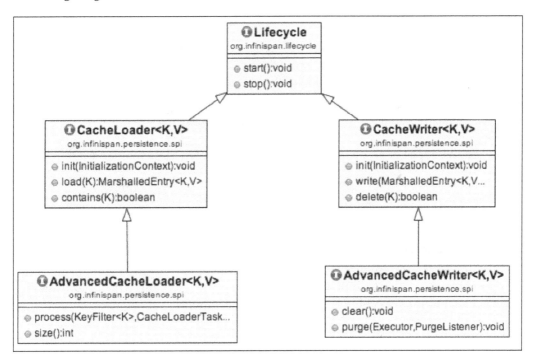

You can associate a cache loader with an individual cache, for instance, you can have many named caches under the same cache manager, where each named cache might have a different cache store configuration.

It's important to note that Infinispan is not an **Object/Relational Mapping (ORM)**, so it doesn't know where the data came from. Infinispan cannot invalidate data that is pulled from a data store automatically. The application or mapper must provide this function and manage the data stored in Infinispan.

Configuring a cache loader

To configure a cache loader and store, declaratively, Infinispan specifies a `persistence` element, which can enclose multiple different `store` elements in a chain. The drawback of multiple cache loaders, is that during read operations, the cache loader is invoked to bring in the data from the data store; if they are more than one data stores defined in the configuration file, Infinispan will invoke all `CacheLoaders` and read them until it finds a valid element of data.

During write operations, Infinispan will update and write all cache loaders, except if the cache loader is using the `ignoreModifications` attribute set to `true`, in this case the changes will not be written to the cache store.

You can opt from among several available cache store implementations by setting the appropriate class attribute in your cache loader definition.

There are two types of cache loaders available, which are filesystem and JDBC-based.

Currently, Infinispan comes shipped with the following Cache Loaders implementations , which are described in the following section.

Filesystem-based cache loaders

Infinispan ships with a file cache store that utilizes the filesystem as a data store. It requires a `location` attribute within the `singleFile` element, which indicates the directory Infinispan will use to create the data store.

For Infinispan 6, the code is as follows:

```
<persistence passivation="true">
<singleFileshared="false"
  preload="false"
    fetchPersistentState="false"
      purgeOnStartup="false"
        location="/tmp/cache/backup">
</singleFile>
</persistence>
```

For Infinispan 7, the code is as follows:

```
<persistence passivation="true">
  <file-store path="/tmp/cache/backup" max-entries="10000"/>
</persistence>
```

In our example, we are using a brand new filesystem-based cache store called `SingleFileStore`; it was introduced with Infinispan 6.0 to replace the `FileCacheStore` implementation, which didn't perform as expected. Due to the large number of files created, this version keeps all cache data in a single file.

This implementation doesn't need extra dependencies and also performs much better by keeping an index of keys and position of their values in the file in the memory; in some cases, it even outperforms the LevelDB-based JNI cache store.

This offers great speed improvements but results in extra memory consumption. To limit this, the cache store's maximum size can be set, but this will only work as expected in a very limited set of use cases.

In Infinispan 7.0, as you can see in the previous example, we are using the `path` attribute of the `file-store` element to define the path where the file will be created and the `max-entries` attribute to specify the maximum number of entries Infinispan can keep in the file store.

JDBC-based cache loaders

The other available type of cache loader is the JDBC-based cache loader that will store or load the cache state from a relational database using JDBC.

Infinispan provides three types of JDBC cache loaders based on the type of key your cache will persist. They are as follows:

- `JdbcBinaryCacheStore`: This cache store uses the hash value returned by the `hashCode` method of the entry key to determine which row in the table it will be stored in, and also has the benefit that it can store any type of key. If you have a hashcode collision with one or more cache objects with the same hashcode, Infinispan will not overwrite them, but will instead store them all in the same table row.

- `JdbcStringBasedCacheStore`: This is the implementation that stores the entries in a database. In contrast to the `JdbcBinaryCacheStore`, this cache store will store each entry within a row in the table (rather than grouping multiple entries into a row). This assures a finer-grained granularity for all operations and better performance. In order to be able to store non-string keys, it relies on a `Key2StringMapper`, which defines the logic of mapping a key object to a string. Infinispan provides a default implementation called `DefaultKey2StringMapper` to handle primitive types.

- `JdbcMixedCacheStore`: This is a hybrid implementation that combines functionality of both `JdbcBinaryCacheStore` or `JdbcStringBasedCacheStore` cache stores. For a single `<persistence>` section in your configuration file, you can have a definition of both cache stores, and based on the key type, in runtime, Infinispan will delegate to the most suitable one.

JPA cache store

The **Java Persistence API (JPA)** is the standard API that allows the mapping of Java objects to relational databases (ORM) and enterprise Java persistence. The JPA specification describes several metadata annotations to define the mapping between Java objects and a relational database table and the **Java Persistence Query Language (JPQL)**.

 In *Chapter 10, Getting Started with Hibernate OGM*, we will present the Hibernate OGM, a framework that provides JPA support for Infinispan and other NoSQL data stores.

This was introduced in version 5.3.0 of Infinispan as a JPA cache loader implementation that allows you to interact with any database supported by it. The JPA cache store allows you to store cache entries in the database using proper schema, so that other applications can read the persisted data as well.

To create a JPA cache store, add the following dependency to your `pom.xml` file:

```
<dependency>
  <groupId>org.infinispan</groupId>
  <artifactId>infinispan-cachestore-jpa</artifactId>
  <version>7.0.2.Final</version>
</dependency>
```

To demonstrate how it works, let's examine a simple example using a persistence unit `userDBPersistenceUnit` and a JPA entity `User`:

```
@Entity
public class User implements Serializable {
    @Id
    private String username;
    private String firstName;
    private String lastName;

    ...

}
```

Then you can configure, declaratively, a cache `usersJPACache` to use the JPA cache store, so that when you put data into the cache, the data would be persisted into the database based on the JPA configuration.

For Infinispan 6, the code is as follows:

```
<namedCache name="usersJPACache">
    <loaders passivation="false" shared="true" preload="true">
        <jpaStore
            persistenceUnitName="userDBPersistenceUnit"
            entityClassName="org.packetpub.domain.User"
        />
    </loaders>
</namedCache>
```

For Infinispan 7, the code is as follows:

```
<local-cache name="JPA-Cache">
    <persistence passivation="false">
        <jpa-store xmlns="urn:infinispan:config:store:jpa:7.0"
            shared="false" preload="true"
            persistence-unit="com.packtpub.infinispan.
userDBPersistenceUnit"
            entity-class="org.packetpub.domain.User"
            batch-size="1">
        </jpa-store>
    </persistence>
</local-cache>
```

Otherwise, if your prefer, you can create it programmatically, as follows:

```
Configuration cacheConfig = new ConfigurationBuilder().loaders()
            .addLoader(JpaCacheStoreConfigurationBuilder.class)
            .persistenceUnitName("userDBPersistenceUnit")
```

```
                    .entityClass(User.class)
                    .build();
     cacheManager.defineCache("usersJPACache", cacheConfig);

     Cache<String, User> usersCache =
        cacheManager.getCache("usersJPACache ");
     usersCache.put("wds", new User(...));
```

Normally, a single Infinispan cache can store multiple types of key/value pairs, for example:

```
     Cache<String, User> usersCache = cacheManager.getCache("myCache");
     usersCache.put("raytsang", new User());
     Cache<Integer, Teacher> teachersCache =
        cacheManager.getCache("myCache");
     teachersCache.put(1, new Teacher());
     Cache<String, User> usersCache =
        cacheManager.getCache("myJPACache"); // configured for User entity
     class
     usersCache.put("raytsang", new User());
     Cache<Integer, Teacher> teachersCache =
        cacheManager.getCache("myJPACache"); // cannot do this when this
           cache is configured to use a JPA cache store
     teachersCache.put(1, new Teacher());
```

 It's important to note that, when a cache is configured to use a JPA cache store, that cache would only be able to store *one* type of data.

Selecting a JDBC cache loader

For simplicity reasons, when you are responsible for the key types of your cache objects, it is preferable to use the `JdbcStringBasedCacheStore` cache store, as it offers better throughput under heavy load.

If, for some reason, you are not responsible for the key types of your cache objects or you can't use `Key2StringMapper` to map the keys of your objects to string objects, it's preferable to use either the `JdbcBinaryCacheStore` or `JdbcMixedCacheStore` cache store.

 For a complete list of cache store implementations, please visit the following link at `http://infinispan.org/cache-store-implementations/`.

Using passivation in your application

Passivation is a feature used to reduce cache memory usage, where Infinispan removes an entry from the cache while preserving its state on a secondary data store on eviction, which can later be reloaded.

While passivated, the cache entries are not in memory and are not immediately available for client requests, as they are when in the cache. When a client requests a passivated entry that is in the store, Infinispan executes a reversal process, known as activation. In both passivation and activation processes, the cache loader is always used to read and write data from the cache store.

 Passivation is only performed on entries that have been evicted.

To enable `passivation` you need to set the `passivation` attribute in the `persistence` element to `true`. If `passivation` is active and you have multiple cache loaders configured, Infinispan will use only the first one and ignore the others.

Let's see a simple configuration using a `SingleFileCacheStore` loader.

For Infinispan 7, the code is as follows:

```
<namedCache name="EvictionAndPassivationCache">
  <eviction maxEntries="10" strategy="LRU"/>
  <expiration wakeUpInterval="500"
    lifespan="60000" maxIdle="1000"/>
  <persistence passivation="true">
    <store class="
      org.infinispan.persistence.file.SingleFileStore">
      <properties>
        <property name="location" value="/tmp/cache/backup"/>
      </properties>
    </store>
  </persistence>
</namedCache>
```

For Infinispan 7, the code is as follows:

```
<local-cache name="EvictionAndPassivationCache">
  <eviction max-entries="10" strategy="LRU" />
  <expiration interval="500" lifespan="60000" max-idle="1000" />
  <persistence passivation="true">
    <file-store path="/tmp/cache/backup" />
  </persistence>
</local-cache>
```

If we use `evictionAndPassivationCache` that we defined in our last configuration example, Infinispan will create a new file under the directory `/tmp/cache/backup` named `evictionAndPassivationCache.dat` with all entries passivated or evicted from the cache. The code for it is as follows:

```
public void passivationAndEvictionTest(){
  Cache<String, String> cache =
    container.getCache("EvictionAndPassivationCache");
  for (int i = 1; i < 10; i++) {
    cache.put("key_"+i, "Key "+i+" Value");
  }
}
```

If we execute the previous code, a new directory and a cache file will be created. For each entry in the cache, the loader will generate a new line in the file. The output of the program looks like this:

```
WDS:~ wsantos$ ls -ll  /tmp/cache/backup/
total 8
-rw-r--r--  1 wsantos  wheel  1234  9 Set 00:45
  evictionAndPassivationCache.dat
```

In addition to the aforementioned options for configuring a JDBC cache loader, there are also many cache stores, as follows:

- `CloudCacheStore` class to work with cloud storage, such as the Amazon S3 (Simple Storage Service) and Rackspace services. All this with the use of JClouds, a cloud agnostic library for the JVM that provides a toolkit for developers to connect several cloud providers.

- `ClusterCacheLoader`, a cache loader implementation designed to retrieve data from other nodes participating in the cluster.

- `LevelDB` is a key/value storage written by Google that can be considered an embedded database, which provides a mapping for keys and values. Currently, LevelDB uses a Java implementation, but in the future, it may also be possible to use a JNI implementation.

 The **Java Native Interface (JNI)** is an interface part of the Java SDK. JNI allows that Java code that is running in a virtual machine (JVM) to interact with native code and libraries written in other languages, for instance C and C++.

- `RemoteCacheStore` is a cache loader implementation that is suitable when you want to store your cache data in a remote Infinispan cluster. It internally uses the HotRod client/server architecture to communicate with the remote cluster.

We will see more details about Hot Rod and other server modules in *Chapter 9, Server Modules*.

- And lastly, Infinispan provides the class `CassandraCacheStore`, a Cache Loader option for the popular Apache Cassandra database, and MongoDB cache store, both of which are cache stores for well-known NoSQL solutions.

Writing event listeners and notifications

It is often useful for the application be aware of some events that occur inside the grid. It provides a better separation of responsibilities and allows developers to implement more generic features and the extension of built-in functionality. Infinispan provides an event notification system for this purpose; this mechanism allows you to register listeners to detect when events take place.

The listener API

Cache-level events such as entries being added, removed, or modified in a specific cache, can trigger a notification that is dispatched to listeners registered to one single cache.

By default, Infinispan will synchronously dispatch the notification to the method object.

Notifications are by default, dispatched synchronously. That is, your `callback` function will be called in the same thread that is emitting the event. This means that your listener should try to perform quick tasks to avoid blocking the original caller's thread.

If you do need to perform such tasks, `@Listener` contains an optional `sync` attribute, which indicates whether the invocation of the listener method annotated with `@Listener` happens synchronously in the caller's thread or not. If you set `sync` to `false`, then invocations are made asynchronously in a different thread without blocking the caller's thread.

```
@Listener(sync=false)
public class MyAsynchronousListener { .... }
```

Asynchronous thread pool

To tune the thread pool used to dispatch such asynchronous notifications, use the `<asyncListenerExecutor />` XML element in your configuration file.

Cache listeners implement the `Listenable` interface. Both `Cache` and `CacheManager` interfaces extend `Listenable`.

To be useful, a listener class should expose one or more listener methods, which will be invoked when events happen. A `listener` method is a public method with no return type and any arbitrary name, and takes in a single parameter representing the event type, or something that the event type can be assigned to. The same listener method can be annotated with more than one annotation.

As mentioned before, there are two levels of events—events that occur on the cache interface, represented by annotations in the `org.infinispan.notifications.cachelistener.annotation` package, and events that occur on the `CacheManager` interface, represented by annotations in the `org.infinispan.notifications.cachemanagerlistener.annotation` package.

Cluster listeners in Infinispan 7.0

Prior to Infinispan 7.0, even in a distributed cache, listeners were guaranteed to be notified of events only on the node where data resides. Now, in Infinispan 7.0, support for clustered listeners was introduced, which allows the event to be propagated remotely in a distributed cache configuration.

To enable a clustered listener, all you need to do is set the `clustered property` of the `@Listener` annotation to `yes`:

```
@Listener(clustered=yes)
public class MyClusteredListener { .... }
```

This simple use case will enable a single clustered listener to receive any write notification (today limited to the `CacheEntryCreatedEvent`, `CacheEntryModifiedEvent`, and `CacheEntryRemovedEvent` events).

The big difference between a local and a cluster listener is that while a local listener is notified before the operation is completed and after the entry is updated, a cluster listener is notified only once, when the operation is completed.

During transactions, cluster listeners are slightly different, because in transactional caches a local listener can be notified when a transaction begins and after a `commit` / `rollback` operation, while a cluster listener will be notified only after a `commit` or `rollback` operation.

Listening to cache-level events

Cache-level events such as entries being added, removed, or modified in a specific cache, can trigger a notification that is dispatched to listeners registered to one single cache.

All events implement an `Event` interface, which each of the event handling methods accept as an argument, and then carry detailed information about the event that occurred, such as the type of event represented by this instance, a reference to a cache that event occurred on, and it also provides a method `isPre()`, which indicates whether the callback is before (`true`) or after (`false`) the event takes place.

 Please note that cache-related events are triggered twice by Infinispan, once before and once after the event happens.

The following table presents annotations and the associate event defined for cache-level events:

Annotation	Event	Description
CacheEntryCreated	CacheEntry CreatedEvent	A cache entry was created.
CacheEntryModified	CacheEntry ModifiedEvent	A cache entry was modified.
CacheEntryRemoved	CacheEntry RemovedEvent	A cache entry was removed.
CacheEntryVisited	CacheEntry VisitedEvent	A cache entry was visited.
CacheEntryLoaded	CacheEntry LoadedEvent	A cache entry was loaded.
CacheEntryInvalidated	CacheEntry InvalidatedEvent	A cache entry was invalidated by a remote cache, only if the cache mode is INVALIDATION_SYNC or INVALIDATION_ASYNC.
CacheEntriesEvicted	CacheEntries EvictedEvent	Cache entries were evicted.
CacheEntryActivated	CacheEntry ActivatedEvent	A cache entry was activated.

Annotation	Event	Description
`CacheEntryPassivated`	`CacheEntry PassivatedEvent`	One or more cache entries were passivated.
`TransactionRegistered`	`Transaction RegisteredEvent`	The cache has started to participate in a transaction.
`TransactionCompleted`	`Transaction CompletedEvent`	The cache has completed its participation in a transaction.
`DataRehashed`	`DataRehashedEvent`	This occurs when a rehash starts or ends. This is only fired if in a `CacheMode. DIST_SYNC` or `CacheMode.DIST_ASYNC` configured cache.
		`DataRehashedEvent` includes special methods such as `getConsistentHashAtStart()` and `getConsistentHashAtEnd()` that return the associated `ConsistentHash` instance when the rehash process starts or ends.
		Note that the `getConsistentHashAtStart()` and `getConsistentHashAtEnd()` may return different values in the pre-event notification and in the postevent notification. For instance, the end CH in the prenotification may be a union of the start and end CHs in the postnotification.
`TopologyChanged`	`TopologyChangedEvent`	This annotation should be used on methods that need to be notified when the `ConsistentHash` implementation in use by the `DistributionManager` changes due to a change in cluster topology. Only fired if the cache mode is `DIST_SYNC` or `DIST_ASYNC`.

Multiple methods can be annotated to receive the same type of event, and if a method is using a super type, it can be annotated to receive multiple events.

The following example defines a cache level listener that logs all available cache events. Note that in the `entryManipulated()` method, we are passing the super type `CacheEntryEvent` while calling this method:

```
@Listener
public class CacheLevelLoggingListener {
  private Log log =
    LogFactory.getLog(CacheLevelLoggingListener.class);
  private ConcurrentMap<GlobalTransaction, Queue<Event>>
    transactions = new ConcurrentHashMap<GlobalTransaction,
      Queue<Event>>();
```

```
/*
We are logging information when a cache entry is added to the
  cache.*/
  @CacheEntryCreated
  public void entryAdd(CacheEntryCreatedEvent<String, String>
    event) {
    if (!event.isPre()) // Message is only logged after operation
      succeeded
      log.infof("[Event %s] Cache entry %s added in cache %s",
        event.getType(), event.getKey(), event.getCache());
    }
/*
In this method we are using annotations to be notified when a cache
entry is visitor, modified, loaded, invalidated or removed.
*/
  @CacheEntryVisited
  @CacheEntryModified
  @CacheEntryLoaded
  @CacheEntryInvalidated
  @CacheEntryRemoved
  public void entryManipulated(CacheEntryEvent<?, ?> event) {
    log.infof("[Event %s] Cache entry %s manipulated in cache %s",
      event.getType(), event.getKey(), event.getCache());
    }

/*
  We are logging information when a cache entry is evicted from the
cache.
*/
  @CacheEntriesEvicted
  public void entriesEvicted(CacheEntriesEvictedEvent<?, ?> event)
  {
    for (Entry<?, ?> entry : event.getEntries().entrySet()) {
      log.infof("[Event CACHE_EVICTION] Cache entry %s evicted",
        entry.getKey());
    }
  }

/*
  We are logging information when a cache entry is evicted from the
cache.
*/
  @CacheEntryPassivated
  @CacheEntryActivated
  public void entryPassivationActivation(Event<?, ?> event) {
```

```
      switch (event.getType()) {
        case CACHE_ENTRY_PASSIVATED:
          log.info("Cache Passivated.  Details = " + event);
          break;
        case CACHE_ENTRY_ACTIVATED:
          log.info("Cache Activated.  Details = " + event);
          break;
      }
    }

  /*
    Method to logging information when a transaction is registered.
  */
    @TransactionRegistered
    public void transactionRegistered(TransactionRegisteredEvent<?,
      ?> event) {
      log.infof("[Event %s] Transaction '{%s}' registered",
        event.getType(), event.getGlobalTransaction().getId());
      transactions.put(event.getGlobalTransaction(), new
        ConcurrentLinkedQueue<Event>());
    }

  /*
    Method to logging information when a transaction is completed.
  */
    @TransactionCompleted
    public void transactionCompleted(TransactionCompletedEvent<?,?>
      event){
      Queue<Event> events =
        transactions.get(event.getGlobalTransaction());
      transactions.remove(event.getGlobalTransaction());
      log.infof("[Event %s] Transaction '{%s}' completed",
        event.getType(), event.getGlobalTransaction().getId());
      if (event.isTransactionSuccessful()) {
        for (Event e : events) {
          log.info("Event " + e);
        }
      }
    }

  /*
    Method to logging information when the data is rehashed.
  */
    @DataRehashed
```

```
public void dataRehashed(DataRehashedEvent<?, ?> event) {
  log.infof("[Event %s] Data rehashed. Consistent hash before
    the rebalance start: %s. Consistent hash at the end of the
      rebalance: %s",
  event.getType(), event.getConsistentHashAtStart(),
    event.getConsistentHashAtEnd());
}

/*
  Method to logging information when the ConsistentHash implementation
in use by the DistributionManager.
*/
  @TopologyChanged
  public void topologyChanged(TopologyChangedEvent<?, ?> event) {
    log.infof("[Event %s] Cache entry Topology Changed. New
      Topology ID: %s", event.getType(),
        event.getNewTopologyId());
  }
}
```

Writing cache manager-level events

On the other hand, cache manager-level events are higher events triggered by a cache manager action. These events are global and affect all caches maintained by the CacheManager across the cluster. For example, the notification system can trigger an event when the cache manager starts or stops a cache. The following table shows the four annotations and the associated events that you can use in your listener classes:

Annotation	Event	Description
CacheStarted	CacheStartedEvent	A cache was started.
CacheStopped	CacheStoppedEvent	A cache was stopped.
ViewChanged	ViewChangedEvent	A view change event was detected. This annotation should be used on methods that need to be notified when the cache is used in a cluster and the cluster topology changes (that is, a member joins or leaves the cluster).

Annotation	Event	Description
Merged	MergedEvent	This annotation should be used on methods that need to be notified when the cache is used in a cluster and the cluster topology experiences a merge event after a cluster split.

Now, let's create another cache listener that will be notified by the cache manager when the state changes:

```
@Listener
public class CacheManagerLevelLoggingListener {
  private Log log = LogFactory.getLog(CacheLevelLoggingListener.
class);

  @CacheStarted
  @CacheStopped
  public void notificationforStartOrStop(Event event) {
    switch (event.getType()) {
      case CACHE_STARTED:
        log.infof("[Event %s] Cache started.", event.getType());
        break;
      case CACHE_STOPPED:
        log.infof("[Event %s] Cache stopped.", event.getType());
        break;
    }
  }

  @ViewChanged
  public void viewChanged(ViewChangedEvent event) {
    log.infof("[Event %s] View change event. isMergeView? %s.
      Local Address: &s. JGroups View ID: %s. Old Members: %s,
        NewMembers: %s", event.getType(), event.isMergeView(),
          event.getLocalAddress(), event.getOldMembers(),
            event.getNewMembers());
  }

  @Merged
  public void merged(MergeEvent event) {
    log.infof("[Event %s] Merge event. isMergeView? %s. Local
      Address: &s. Subgroups Merged: %s. JGroups View ID: %s. Old
        Members: %s, New Members: %s", event.getType(),
          event.isMergeView(), event.getLocalAddress(),
            event.getSubgroupsMerged(), event.getOldMembers(),
              event.getNewMembers());
  }
}
```

Registering event listeners

The org.infinispan.notifications.Listenable interface provides the method addListener() that registers the specified listener on the Cache or CacheManager it's called on.

The process described above can be written in the following format in the method setUpBeforeClass():

```
static DefaultCacheManager cacheManager;
static Cache<String, String> cache;

@BeforeClass
public static void setUpBeforeClass() throws Exception {
  String config = "resource/infinispan-eviction.xml";
  CacheLevelLoggingListener cacheListener = new
    CacheLevelLoggingListener();
  CacheManagerLevelLoggingListener cacheManagerListener = new
    CacheManagerLevelLoggingListener();
  cacheManager = new DefaultCacheManager(config);
  // Add a listener to the cache manager component
  cacheManager.addListener(cacheManagerListener);
  cache = cacheManager.getCache("ExpirationCache");
  // Add a listener to the cache component
  cache.addListener(cacheListener);
  cacheManager.start();
}
/* Simple test methods to triggers some events */
@Test
 public void testEntryAdd() {
  for (int x = 0; x < 100; x++)
    cache.put("key" + x, "Value " + x);
}

@Test
public void testEntryManipulated() throws InterruptedException {
  //Wait 5 seconds
  Thread.sleep(5000);
  cache.remove("key0");
  cache.put("key10", "Value 174", 5, TimeUnit.SECONDS);
  cache.put("Key01", "Value 01");
}

@Test
public void testEntriesEvicted() {
```

```
    cache.evict("key15");
    assertNull(cache.get("key15"));
    assertNull(cache.get("key1"));
}


@AfterClass
public static void testCacheManagerNotification() {
    cacheManager.stop();
}
```

When you run the previous example, you should see the following output:

As you can see, the events were captured by the listener registered in the `Cache` and `CacheManager` instance.

Configuring logging in Infinispan

Now that you have learned most of Infinispan APIs, it's time to show you how to configure `Log4j` in the Infinispan application.

Infinispan 6 provides the `LogFactory` classes to create `Log` instances and the `Log` class, which are Infinispan's log abstraction layer on top of JBoss Logging.

In our previous code, we used a `Log` interface to generate log messages, which are as follows:

```
private Log log =
   LogFactory.getLog(CacheLevelLoggingListener.class);
```

The previous code will get an instance of `Log`, which can be used to generate log messages either via JBoss Logging, or if not present, the built-in JDK logger.

Now, you will need to create a `log4j.properties` file in order to configure `Log4J` for your application. You can find a simple example of a `Log4J` file below, remember to include it in your `CLASSPATH` variable:

```
### direct log messages to stdout ###
log4j.appender.stdout=org.apache.log4j.ConsoleAppender
log4j.appender.stdout.Target=System.out
log4j.appender.stdout.layout=org.apache.log4j.PatternLayout
log4j.appender.stdout.layout.ConversionPattern=%d{ABSOLUTE} (%t) %5p
%c{1}:%L - %m%n
### direct messages to file infinispan.log ###
log4j.appender.file=org.apache.log4j.FileAppender
log4j.appender.file.File=infinispan.log
log4j.appender.file.layout=org.apache.log4j.PatternLayout
log4j.appender.file.layout.ConversionPattern=%d{ABSOLUTE} (%t) %5p
%c{1}:%L - %m%n
### set log levels - for more verbose logging change 'info' to 'debug'
###
log4j.rootLogger=info, file, stdout
log4j.logger.org.jboss=info
log4j.logger.org.infinispan=info
```

Using a similar configuration for your log, you can centralize the logging information from all the nodes into the same log file, which can be very handy when debugging an Infinispan application.

Introducing JSR-107 – The Java Caching API

Starting with version 5.3, Infinispan has provided a preview implementation of JCache API (JSR-107) via the `javax.cache` package.

 The final version of the JSR 107: JCACHE – Java Temporary Caching API was released on April 18th, 2014.

JCache specification standardizes in-process caching of Java objects, allowing developers to focus on application development, and removing the burden of implementing caches themselves from the application programmer.

JCache JSR 107 is specification that defines a distributed cache with an interface similar to `java.util.ConncurrentHashMap`, and cache features such as data validation, locking, eviction, and management. As well as providing the basic put and get methods, the API offers a pluggable `CacheLoader` interface so that users can add custom loaders for whatever data sources they are using.

In addition, part of the JCache specification defines a set of annotations, which are designed to solve common caching use cases. In order to use these annotations in an application, Infinispan includes integration with CDI in the `infinispan-cdi` module to process these annotations and intercept calls to annotated application objects.

These annotations provide value by intercepting method calls invoked on your CDI beans and performing storage and retrieval tasks in Infinispan as a side-effect.

In order to start using the Infinispan JCache implementation, a single dependency needs to be added to the Maven `pom.xml` file:

```
<dependency>
    <groupId>org.infinispan</groupId>
    <artifactId>infinispan-jcache</artifactId>
    <version>7.1.1.Final</version>
</dependency>
```

The Java Caching API defines five core interfaces:

- **CachingProvider**: A CacheProvider defines the mechanism to establish, configure, acquire, manage, and control zero or more `CacheManagers`.

- **CacheManager**: A CacheManager provides a means of establishing, configuring, acquiring, closing, and destroying uniquely named Caches. They are a core concept of the Java Caching API. They provide developers with the means to interact with caches, enable and disable statistics gathering for caches, and acquire a `UserTransaction` for managed caches (if supported by the cache provider), among other functionalities.

- **Cache**: A Cache is a map-like data structure that provides temporary storage of application data.

- **Cache.Entry**: A Cache.Entry is a single key-value pair stored by a Cache.

- **ExpiryPolicy**: ExpiryPolicy defines functions to determine when cache entries will expire based on creation, access, and modification operations.

Let's see a simple example to illustrate how this works. First, in our example it obtains the single `CachingProvider` visible to the default `ClassLoader`, (in Infinispan, `org.infinispan.jcache.JCachingProvider`).

And then, we call the `getCacheManager()` that requests a CacheManager configured according to the identified URI and scoped by `ClassLoaders`.

The meaning and semantics of the URI used to identify a CacheManager is defined by `CachingProvider` implementations. For applications to remain implementation-independent, they should avoid attempting to create URIs and instead use the URI returned by `getDefaultURI()`.

```
// resolve a cache manager
CachingProvider cachingProvider = Caching.getCachingProvider();
CacheManager cacheManager = cachingProvider.getCacheManager();
```

To simplify the configuration, JCache provides an easy-to-use API based on the concept of a fluent interface. The class `javax.cache.configuration.MutableConfiguration` exposes functions for cache management and statistics through the `javax.cache.configuration.Configuration` interface.

In our next example, we configure our cache to store the entry by reference, calling the method `setStoreByValue()`; if `true`, as its name states, JCache will use a store-by-value semantic.

We also configured our cache with an expiry policy of 30 minutes, all values put with that instance use the same expiration policy, and finally turn on the statistics gathering. Lets have a look at the following code:

```
// configure the cache
MutableConfiguration<String, String> config = new
    MutableConfiguration<String, String>();
config.setStoreByValue(false)
    .setTypes(String.class, String.class)
    .setExpiryPolicyFactory(AccessedExpiryPolicy.factoryOf
      (Duration.THIRTY_MINUTES))
    .setStatisticsEnabled(true);
```

Now that we have a configuration, let's create a named cache at runtime. If a cache with the specified name is not known to the CacheManager, a `CacheException` is thrown.

Next, we call the `getCache()` method, which looks up a `Cache` using its name and more arguments to define the expected class of the key and another expected class of the value:

```
// create the cache
cacheManager.createCache("_TempCache", config);
// get the cache
Cache<String, String> tempCache =
    cacheManager.getCache("_TempCache", String.class, String.class);
```

Lastly, we perform some put, get, and remove operations. The `Cache` behaves like a map; you store keys and values using the `put()` method, and retrieve values using the `get()` method. You can use any serializable object for either the key or the value. The `remove()` method removes a value from the cache, which will evict it immediately.

You can also put multiple values calling the `putAll()` method with a Map as its argument:

```
// cache operations
String key = "20130801";
String tempData = "Children are great comfort in your old age,
    and they help you to reach it faster too";
tempCache.put(key, tempData);
String otherTempData = tempCache.get(key);
assert (otherTempData.equals(tempData));
tempCache.remove(key);
assert( tempCache.get(key) == null);
```

Like Infinispan, JCache provides a convenient mechanism for registering notifications on cache events. The `javax.cache.event` package contains classes and interfaces for event processing.

By now, transactions are an optional requirement of this specification. Transactions have the meaning provided by the JTA specification.

> For more information about the JCache, visit
> http://jcp.org/en/jsr/detail?id=107.

In *Chapter 12*, *Advanced Topics*, we will come back to this subject and have another look at the integration between JCache and CDI.

Summary

During this chapter we got an overview of how Infinispan works in an embedded or client/server mode and, the differences between default and named cache.

You learned how to perform simple operations on the data within the cache and how to configure an Infinispan cache, whether its declaratively or programmatically. We also covered important features and aspects, such as Eviction, Expiration, cache stores, and Passivation.

We saw how event listeners and the notifications mechanism work, the annotations used for registration, and some code.

We also talked about the JSR-107 — The Java Caching API, also known as JCache, and how it works in practice with Infinispan.

In the next chapter, we will look at many different topologies that Infinispan supports, and data access patterns, to better understand where the data physically resides and how it is accessed in a distributed environment.

Infinispan Topologies

In the previous chapter, you have seen how to use the Cache API and how to configure Infinispan, whether it is declaratively or programmatically. In this chapter, you will explore different ways to design and implement your cache solution, according to the different caching requirements an application might have. Some application might require only basic caching capabilities, others may need only transactional requirements and a cache that handles both read/write operations, and some others may only need a distributed second level cache for an ORM framework.

In order to address these different requirements, Infinispan provides support for a rich set of configuration options, where you can decide for different cache topologies. To begin with, we will cover the internal details of different cache topologies and their respective advantages and disadvantages of each approach.

In this chapter, we will discuss the following topics:

- Clustering modes
- Consistent hashing and virtual nodes
- Caching access patterns
- Configuring second-level cache in Hibernate with Infinispan

Clustering modes

Different applications might have different requirements for interacting with the grid, some applications might require on-demand loading from an external data source; others use it for read-mostly purposes; some can need transactional support others need a data grid that handles both write and read operations. Infinispan can be configured to behave in different ways, depending upon how it is configured. These ways are called **Caching Modes**, and determine which strategy will be used to manage Infinispan objects within machines that are designated as the cluster members.

Infinispan uses the JGroups library to provide network communication capabilities. JGroups is a toolkit for reliable group communication and provides many useful features and enables cluster node discovery, point-to-point and point-to-multipoint communication, failure detection, and data transfer between cluster nodes.

You will learn more about JGroups in *Chapter 11, An Introduction to JGroups*.

 JGroups is a toolkit written in Java that provides reliable communication via multicast, and includes a flexible protocol stack with several protocols.

You can configure Infinispan to either be only on local JVM or clustered. However, as you could see in the first chapter, its major benefit is the use in cluster mode, where all nodes act as a single cache, providing a large amount of memory heap.

If in a cluster, the cache can be configured for full replication, where all new entries and changes are replicated to all the grid participants, or it can be configured to invalidate changes across the grid or finally, it can be configured for distribution on mode, where instead of full replication, you can specify how many replicas of an entry the cluster will have, allowing fault-tolerant properties to exist.

We will see all of them in detail in the upcoming sections.

The local mode

The simplest way to work with Infinispan is in a local mode, where Infinispan will consider only the local JVM to cache objects, obviously, it's not a real data grid, since you cannot replicate or distribute the data to other nodes.

Local caches won't communicate or join with other instances in a cluster. In this mode, Infinispan doesn't require a JGroups channel; however, the dependency on the library is still standing.

In local mode, your application will be limited by the maximum size of your JVM heap. The following diagram shows a graphical representation of an interaction with a local cache:

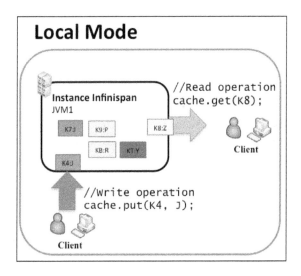

The following code shows a method that returns an `EmbeddedCacheManager` object configured to local mode:

```
public EmbeddedCacheManager getCacheManager(){
  GlobalConfiguration glob = new GlobalConfigurationBuilder()
    .nonClusteredDefault()
      .build(); // Builds the GlobalConfiguration object

  Configuration loc = new ConfigurationBuilder()
    .clustering().cacheMode(CacheMode.LOCAL)
      .eviction().maxEntries(400).strategy(EvictionStrategy.LIRS)
        .build();

    return new DefaultCacheManager(glob, loc, true);
}
```

 To create a local cache, it's not necessary to create a `Configuration` or `GlobalConfiguration` class. You can create a local cache by default, by creating a `DefaultCacheManager` class calling the no-argument constructor, as shown in the following example code:

```
return new DefaultCacheManager();
```

The following is a sample configuration file configured to provide a local cache in an Infinispan 6 application:

```
<clustering mode="local" />
```

If you're using Infinispan 7, the configuration should look like this:

```
<local-cache name="DefaultLocalCache" />
```

The invalidation mode

Invalidation means that you don't want to replicate or distribute cached data but only want to inform other nodes that form the grid that under specific addresses, a specific object or data should be evicted because it's stale. This means that every time an object undergoes some sort of change in a cache, Infinispan broadcasts it to the cluster, stating that the changed object is stale in other instances and should be evicted from the cache memory.

The effect of this is that your cluster will consist of several standalone local mode caches that are network-aware, and will be able to invalidate stale data even if the modifications that make data stale occur remotely.

The benefit of invalidation is that network traffic is reduced, as the invalidation messages are quite small compared to actually replicating updated data. Another benefit is that other caches that take part of the grid look up modified data only when needed, in a lazy manner.

The tradeoff for this caching mode is that if an object in the cache changes frequently, it is not suitable for invalidation mode, because the cost associated with overhead from the cache invalidation messages on the network may outweigh this cache mode benefits. The next diagram shows how it works:

Invalidation Mode

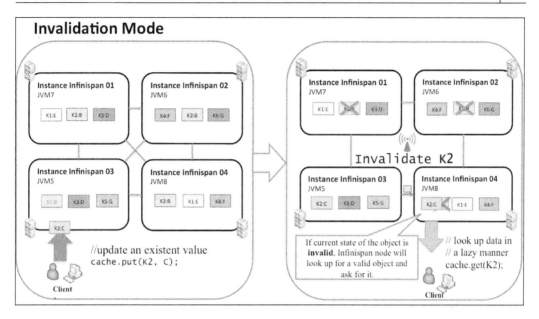

The following sample was extracted from the `sample.xml` file of Infinispan 6 and 7 distributions, and presents a cache configured with cache invalidation instead of using state transfer to retrieve data on startup. It is configured with a cluster cache loader that allows it to query the cluster for data, if not present locally.

This type of cache loader is particularly interesting for scenarios where state transfer is a lengthy process, in other words, in scenarios where you have many large objects stored in the cache, such as a binary object.

For Infinispan 6, the code is as follows:

```
<namedCache name="invalidatedWithClusterCacheLoaderCache">
  <clustering mode="invalidation">
    <sync replTimeout="20000" />
  </clustering>

  <persistence>
    <store class="ClusterLoader" preload="false">
      <properties>
        <property name="remoteCallTimeout" value="20000" />
      </properties>
    </store>
  </persistence>
</namedCache>
```

Note that in the `<store>` element we specified `ClusterLoader` in the class element that corresponds to the `org.infinispan.persistence.cluster.CacheLoader` class. This class is a cache loader that search for values in other cluster members. The `remoteCallTimeout` property is required and will define the amount of time in milliseconds that this thread will wait for results before returning a null.

For Infinispan 7, the code is as follows:

```
<invalidation-cache name="invalidatedWithClusterCacheLoaderCache"
  mode="SYNC" remote-timeout="20000">
  <persistence>
    <cluster-loader remote-timeout="20000" preload="false" />
  </persistence>
</invalidation-cache>
```

The Infinispan 7 configuration version creates the same `invalidatedWithClusterCacheLoaderCache` cache, but now without the need to include properties, once the `cluster-loader` element contains the `remote-timeout` and `preload` attributes.

The replicated mode

Replication is the simplest clustered mode and comprises of one or more cache instances that replicate its data to all cluster nodes; in the end, all cluster nodes will end up with the same data.

In TCP, connections occur point to point, and as the cluster size increases, the application performance can be seriously compromised. In order to mitigate this problem, you can configure Infinispan to use a UDP multicast to perform peer discovery and transport, which to a certain extent, improves the performance of large clusters, broadcasting a message or data to multiple destination nodes simultaneously in a single transmission.

Even though replication mode provides a simple and quick way to share the state of objects across the grid, this strategy has a good performance only in small clusters, due to the number of replication messages that need to be sent among the server.

On the other hand, every change to an object in the grid requires pushing the new version of the object to all other Infinispan instances inside the grid, which can increase utilization of network resources and reduce bandwidth.

In TCP, connections occur point to point, and as the cluster size increases, the application performance can be seriously compromised. In order to mitigate this problem, you can configure Infinispan to use UDP multicast to perform peer discovery, which improves to a certain extent, the performance of large clusters, broadcasting a message or data to multiple destination nodes simultaneously in a single transmission.

The following image shows the difference between TDP and UDP in a graphical way:

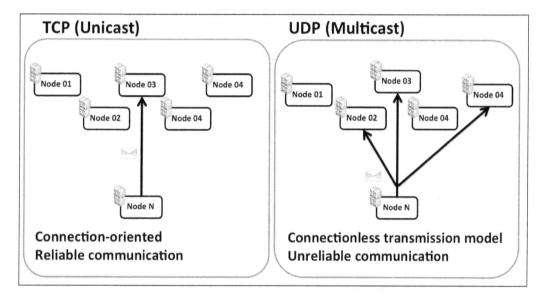

Understanding synchronous and asynchronous replication

There are two kinds of replication techniques you can configure Infinispan when it is replicating modified objects to another instance (JVM): synchronous replication and asynchronous replication.

Before we start the following section, as mentioned in the last chapter, Infinispan also provides an asynchronous API. But we are presenting here replication techniques, which has nothing to do with the asynchronous API.

The asynchronous API is a non-blocking API, which means the cache will not block your application thread. The API provides the same cache operations, however using an async version, such as `putAsync(Object, Object)` and `getAsync(K key)`.

The synchronous replication

Essentially, synchronous replication writes the data to all nodes in a cluster before returning to the caller. In doing this, the data remains completely current and identical. The main advantage of synchronous replication is that it reduces the chances of data loss by accident. The downside is that synchronous replication requires low-latency communication, because requires that all instances of the grid acknowledges the receipt of the object, where a put () call will not return to its client (caller) before performing the required changes on all the nodes.

The following diagram presents a simplified view of a synchronous replication configuration:

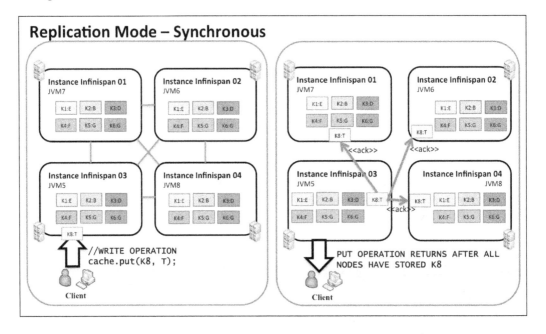

The following is a code snippet for both Infinispan versions (6.0 and 7.0) that creates an Infinispan cache with replication mode, inside it we have a state transfer element, which contains the definition of how a state is transferred from one node to other when an instance joins or leaves the grid.

For Infinispan 6, the code is as follows:

```
<clustering mode="replicationCache">
  <stateTransfer chunkSize="0" fetchInMemoryState="true"
    timeout="240000" />
  <sync replTimeout="20000" />
</clustering>
```

If the `<sync>` tag is configured, all communications will be synchronous in that whenever a node sends a message to the grid, Infinispan will block that thread until it completes the operation. The `<sync>` option is mutually exclusive with the `<async>` configuration. Sync has only one attribute, which is `replTimeout`, a timeout used to wait for the return of a remote call. If the specified time expires, the operation is aborted and an exception is thrown. In our sample, we set it up to wait 20 seconds (defaults to 15 seconds).

For Infinispan 7, the code is as follows:

```
<replicated-cache name="replicationCache" mode="SYNC"
  remote-timeout="20000">
  <state-transfer enabled="false" timeout="240000"
    chunk-size="0" />
</replicated-cache>
```

The Infinispan 7 version is similar to the previous version, except by the use of an additional `<sync>` element. In Infinispan 7, you can use the `mode` attribute to enable a synchronous (SYNC) or asynchronous (ASYNC) cache.

The following table describes the attributes of the state transfer element:

Attribute	Type	Default	Description
chunkSize (ISPN 6) chunk-size (ISPN 7)	int	10000	If set with a value greater than 0, defines that the state will be transferred in batches of cache entries defined in the attribute. Otherwise, the state will be transferred in one go, which is not recommended.
fetchInMemoryState (only on ISPN 6)	boolean	true	If set to true, the cache will preload data, which means that during the startup of the cache, Infinispan will request for state, although it will impact startup time. Defaults to true if the cache is replicated/distributed, otherwise false.

awaitInitialTransfer (ISPN 6) await-initial-transfer (ISPN 7)	boolean	true	This option only works on distributed or replicated caches. If set to true, in the first call to CacheManager.getCache(), Infinispan will block and wait for new nodes to join and complete the grid. And if fetchInMemoryState attribute is enabled, it will also wait to complete receive state from neighboring caches. Please note that the usage of this setting won't have any impact on your application, it will only avoid an extra remote call, because the key cannot be available locally.
timeout (ISPN 6 and ISPN 7)	long	240000 (ISPN 6) 60000 (ISPN 7)	Specifies in milliseconds the maximum amount of time, Infinispan can wait for state from other instances in the grid, before abort the cache operation and throw an exception, default value is 4 minutes.

The asynchronous replication

The other kind of replication technique, as we said earlier, is the asynchronous replication, which also writes data to all nodes in a cluster, generally faster than synchronous replication, because there is no caller blocking. Elements are accumulated in a queue and sent asynchronously to all target nodes in the grid, which can be configured to execute replication after a defined period of time has elapsed, or after a defined number of elements have been queued.

In fact, when Infinispan instances are clustered, you can configure to propagate the cache data to other nodes asynchronously or synchronously. In a synchronous cache, the sender of the message will be waiting for replies from the receiver(s).

But if the cache is asynchronous, the sender will not wait for replies from the other members of the grid.

Since it performs replication in the background asynchronously at scheduled intervals to all nodes in the grid, the put() call returns immediately, even if replication to other nodes isn't complete yet.

However, with this process there is a delay when data is replicated from one node to another, so we run the risk of possible data loss of latest operations if the node instance on which operation was performed fails while replicating the accumulated elements to the grid. Another problem is data consistency; the source and the rest of the grid may not have identical data all the time.

In the next diagram, we can see an asynchronous replication configuration at work:

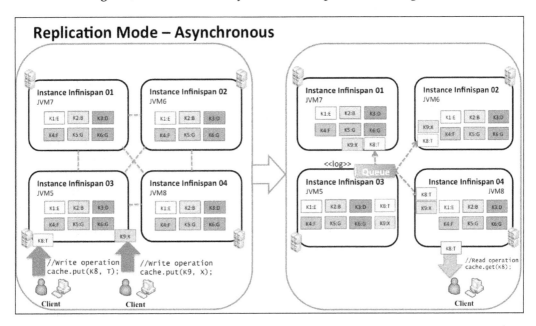

With asynchronous mode, the application will favor speed over consistency, thus increasing performance.

You can create an asynchronous replication cache in the same way you did to create a synchronous replication cache, the difference is that you have to include the `<async>` under the `<clustering>` tag in configuration file for Infinispan 6:

```
<clustering mode="replication">
  <async/>
</clustering>
```

If you are using Infinispan 7, you have to change the `mode` attribute to `ASYNC` as shown in the following code:

```
<replicated-cache name="asyncQueueCache" mode="ASYNC" />
```

When you enable asynchronous replication to your cache, Infinispan will start the JGroups layer to use asynchronous communication, which means that JGroups will send packets to the other nodes in the cluster, without waiting for a reply (ACK) from the receiver.

Infinispan provides some additional configuration options that may interest you. The following table defines the possible attributes that can be used in conjunction with the asynchronous mode:

Attribute	Type	Default	Description
`asyncMarshalling` (ISPN 6) `async-marshalling` (ISPN 7)	`boolean`	`False`	If this is set to `true`, the marshaling process will be asynchronous, which means that the caller will not wait for an acknowledgment and return even faster. The drawback of enabling this option is that it can lead to reordering of messages.
`replQueueClass` (only in ISPN 6)	`String`	`org.infinispan. remoting. Replication QueueImpl`	This is the name of the replication queue class in use.
`replQueueInterval` (ISPN 6) `queue-flush-interval` (ISPN 7)	`long`	`5000`	This attribute controls the interval of time the asynchronous thread will run in order to flush the replication queue. It defaults to 5 seconds.

Attribute	Type	Default	Description
replQueue MaxElements (ISPN 6) queue-size (ISPN 7)	long	1000	This attribute can be used to define the maximum number of elements a queue can handle before flushing it out. It defaults to 1,000 elements.
useReplQueue (only in ISPN 6)	boolean	false	If this is set to true, it will enable a queue to send out all dependent async communications periodically, just like a batch.

The asynchronous marshalling

In our last sample configuration, we didn't used the attribute asyncMarshalling, with asynchronous marshalling enabled, which indicates that in addition to the separate thread (asynchronous) used by JGroups to send asynchronous messages, as soon as Infinispan identifies that a new cache entry must be replicated, Infinispan will submit a request to the async transport executor that will be responsible for communicating with the underlying JGroups layer. This means it's not a guarantee that Infinispan requests will reach the JGroups layer in the same order that they were called in, which could lead to data consistency issues. That's because requests can return back to the caller faster with asynchronous marshaling enabled.

The next diagram presents a possible scenario with async marshalling that can result in data inconsistency. The client requests two operations—first they call the **put(K8, T)** method and then removes the cache entry for the same key **cache.remove(K8)**. Note that operations can be replicated out of order to other nodes.

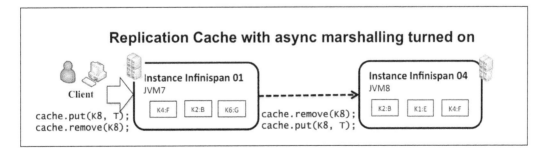

So, if your application performs several modifications on the same cache entry, you should consider that asynchronous marshalling from your cache is never turned on. The value is false by default.

The following example shows how to enable asynchronous marshaling by using Infinispan 6:

```
<namedCache name="noAsyncMarshllingCache">
  <clustering mode="replication">
    <async asyncMarshalling="false"/>
  </clustering>
</namedCache>
```

Next, an example by using Infinispan 7:

```
<replicated-cache name="noAsyncMarshllingCache"
  mode="ASYNC" async-marshalling="false"/>
```

The replication queue

As the name states, the replication queue aims to provide a mechanism to batch the cache operations and send them as a single operation. Without a replication queue, each cache operation is sent one by one as individual operations.

As a result, with a replication queue in place, the performance of an application can improve the overall performance compared to applications without an enabled replication queue.

An example of how to turn on the replication in Infinispan 6 can be seen as follows:

```
<clustering mode="replication">
  <async useReplQueue="true" replQueueInterval="10000"
    replQueueMaxElements="400"/>
</clustering>
```

And the same cache configuration in Infinispan 7, is as follows:

```
<replicated-cache name="asyncQueueCache" mode="ASYNC"
  queue-interval="100" queue-size="200"/>
```

The replication queue is flushed periodically, which can cause some problems in a large grid. Because depending on the queue interval and size defined in the configuration, the replication or distribution process to refresh the data in the affected nodes might take longer than usual to complete.

However, if the replication queue is turned off, the caches will update the affected nodes immediately and consequently, it will take less data to get the other nodes.

The distribution mode

While considering all the other strategies, we can say that distribution mode is the real grid. The key point of distribution mode is that it provides you with linear write scalability, which means that you can scale out your data grid to the maximum capability of your cluster size. The distribution strategy is designed for larger in-memory data grid clusters and it's the most scalable data grid topology. Distribution strategy improves the application's performance dramatically and outperforms the replication mode on traditional networks.

Because unlike the replicated mode, which simply replicates all the data to all cluster nodes, in the distribution mode, updated objects are not replicated to all nodes in the cluster, it ensures that a given number of copies of the cache entry defined by the user (we'll see the numOwners property), exist within the grid to provide durability and fault tolerance, which can improve the overall scalability of the application.

In the distribution mode, you can define, via configuration, the number of replicas that are available for a given data grid.

Before we go further on how Infinispan handles distribution, let's consider that the classical model of distribution uses a load balancer to direct traffic across multiple servers, which is generally based on a static formula (such as hash or round robin) that assigns each incoming piece of data to a node. This allocation depends on the number of resources available, and when adding or removing nodes from the cluster, it still requires a substantial effort to rebalance the grid again, when the number of nodes changes, which leads us to the following questions:

- How to distribute the objects evenly between different instances
- How to ensure this distribution is not too sensitive to dynamic addition or removal of instances

One possible solution to address these problems is the use of a consistent hash algorithm. Consistent hashing is basically a mapping schema for key-value store, which maps hashed keys into fixed segments, and segments are mapped to physical nodes, depending on the topology.

Infinispan uses a consistent hash algorithm to read/write an entry in a cluster. This technique is deterministic, fast, and does not rely on any additional metadata or cluster-wide broadcasts to locate data. This reduces the cost of performing reads and writes on any given member in the cluster and improves redundancy, because in case of node failure, it's not necessary to replicate the ownership information.

You can define the number of segments by changing the numSegments (ISPN 6) / segments (ISPN 7) attributes. However, it's not possible to change the number of segments at runtime; to do so, you'll need to restart the system.

It's important to note that the cache object will not necessarily stay in the same node, where the put operation has been done.

The following diagram shows a data grid configured to distribute two copies on the grid:

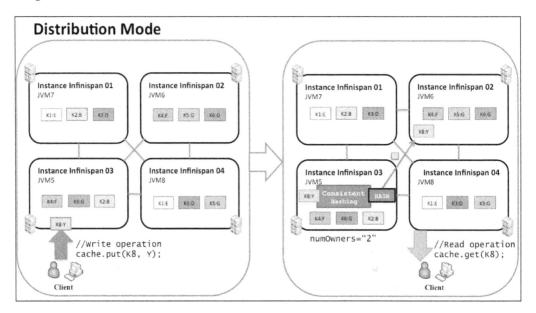

The following is a sample distribution configuration in Infinispan 6:

```
<clustering mode="distCache">
  <sync replTimeout="60000"/>
  <hash numOwners="2" numSegments="80" capacityFactor="2"
    factory="org.infinispan.distribution.ch.
      SyncConsistentHashFactory"/>
</clustering>
```

This code is written in Infinispan 7, as follows:

```
<distributed-cache name="distCache"
                   mode="SYNC"
                   owners="2"
                   segments="80"
                   capacity-factor="2" />
```

This configuration creates a cache that uses synchronous calls to send off information on the network.

You must have noticed that in the Infinispan 6 version, under *Clustering modes* we have included the hash element with a few attributes. This section lets you to fine-tune the internal rehash characteristics.

 The <hash> section must only be used with the distribution cache mode.

If you are using Infinispan 7, you can find the same attributes in the distributed-cache element. The next table presents the available attributes in the hash (Infinispan 6) or distributed-cache (Infinispan 7) elements, which you can use for fine-tuning the rehashing characteristics of your cache:

Attribute	Type	Default	Description
factory (only on ISPN 6)	String		This is the factory class that you want to use to generate the consistent hash. It must implement org. infinispan.distribution. ch.ConsistentHashFactory.
hashFunctionClass (only on ISPN 6)	String		This is a class that implements the org.infinispan.commons.hash. Hash interface, which contains the function that calculates and spreads a hash code for a given object.
numOwners (ISPN 6) owners (ISPN 7)	int	2	This is the number of replicas Infinispan can replicate on the grid for each cache entry.
numSegments (ISPN 6) segments (ISPN 7)	int	60 (ISPN 6) 80 (ISPN 7)	This defines the total number of hash space segments that the instance can have per cluster. The recommended value for this setting is 10 * max_ cluster_size. We will see this in more detail in the next section.

Attribute	Type	Default	Description
capacityFactor (ISPN 6) capacity-factor (ISPN 7)	float	1	You can use the capacityFactor setting to define on each cache node if it can take a higher (for instance, 2x or more entries than a regular node) or a lower proportion (0.5x entries than a regular node) of the entries in the cache that will reside on the local node.
			Note that it's only a suggestion; there is no guarantee that this number will be respected. In fact, depending on the ConsistentHashFactory implementation, this setting can be completely ignored.
			In some cases, it is recommended to set the capacity factor to 0 (zero). This setting can be especially useful in scenarios where one or more nodes are too short-lived to be useful as data owners, and the client cannot use a remote protocol (such as Hot Rod), because they need the transactions.
			Setting the capacity factor to 0 can also be useful with cross-site replication, if you want to keep the site master responsible for forwarding messages between sites and not handle user requests.

Infinispan also provides a Grouping API with the hashing functionality, which allows you to co-locate a group of entries onto a particular node. We will see more about Grouping APIs in *Chapter 12, Advanced Topics*.

In consistent hashing, let's call the number range of our hash function as a hashing wheel..

Now, for each node in the system, we can assign a random value, which represents its position on the wheel. The basic idea is to map the cache and objects into the same hash space by using the same hash function.

In release 5.0, Infinispan changed its current consistent hash function to use `MurmurHash3` for better performance. `MurmurHash3` is a new noncryptographic hash function based on an algorithm called MurmurHash, published by Austin Appleby. This demonstrated a better performance in a random distribution of regular keys than other popular hash functions.

For example, let's suppose we have three different server nodes, where after assigning different values to it we hash them into 64-bit numbers, in order to stick them on the wheel.

Now, we do the same for each object of the cache, that is, hash these elements and put them into points on the hash wheel. The following diagram shows these two steps:

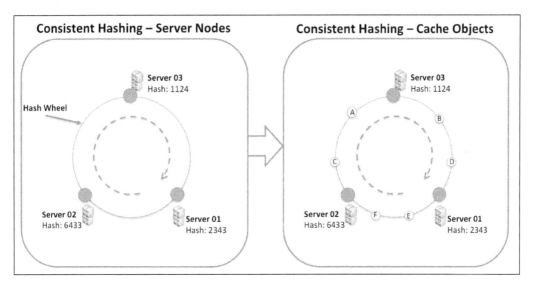

For every new entry in the cache, as we said, Infinispan will use a consistent hash in order to stick it on the wheel. An example is shown in the next diagram:

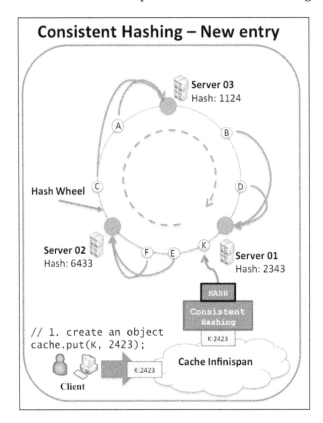

In the diagram, you can see how a put () operation works in the cache and how it finds which cache to place the new entry on. To find the server, the node moves clockwise around the ring until it finds the right node. The first node it finds will be the primary owner of that key. So, in the preceding diagram, the **Server 01** store keys in range {B, D}, **Server 02** store keys in range {K, F, E} and objects {C, A} belong to **Server 03**.

While this has a positive impact on network traffic, on the other hand, it means that some nodes can occupy a larger space portion on the ring space than others, which combined with potential irregularities in the hash functions can lead to poor distribution of data in the cluster.

Another point we have to understand is that there is no hard-and-fast rule on how Infinispan maps the segments to owners. So, when removing or adding a new node to the grid, it is desirable to have an automatic rebalance, where the hashing algorithm will try to balance the segments allocated to each neighboring servers. This is so that, in the end, all the servers in the cluster can have an equal amount of data. As the new host can only take a small set of data of an existing range, as it relies on the hash code of an entry's key, at the end, our strategy can lead again to a poor distribution of data in the cluster. So in Infinispan, the consistent hashing algorithm is optimized to minimize the number of segments to move during rebalance (after a node joins or leaves the grid).

For instance, consider Server 03 of the preceding diagram is down, the objects A and C would now belong to cache node A, and all the other object mappings remain the same. If the distance between two different node caches is random, we will probably have a very nonuniform and bad distribution of our objects between caches, as shown in the following diagram:

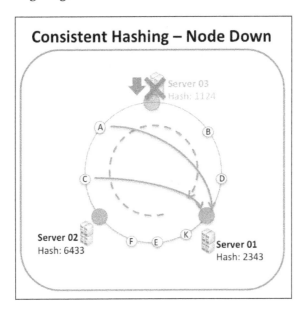

It could be even worse, if, in the preceding diagram, **Server 02** is more powerful than **Server 01**. The same thing happens when we have to add a new host, to keep your cluster nodes balanced. The right thing to do is to have the new host take an equal portion of data from each cluster node.

You can define the number of hash space segments an instance should manage. An example of the configuration in Infinispan 6 is done via the number of segments attribute in the hash element:

```
<clustering mode="distribution">
  <sync/>
  <hash numOwners="2" numSegments="20" />
</clustering>
```

The following is an example in Infinispan 7:

```
<distributed-cache name="distributedCache"
                   mode="SYNC"
                   owners="2"
                   segments="20" />
```

The numSegments/segments parameter defines the total number of segments the instance can have in the cluster.

To perform the same configuration programmatically, add the following code:

```
public EmbeddedCacheManager getCacheContainer() {
    Configuration config = new ConfigurationBuilder()
                .clustering().cacheMode(CacheMode.DIST_SYNC)
                .hash().numOwners(4).numSegments(20)
                .build();
    return new DefaultCacheManager(configuration);
}
```

 There is a method called numVirtualNodes, which was deprecated in the Infinispan version 6.0 release and was replaced by the numSegments method.

The hashing algorithm in Infinispan is customizable, and in fact there are five implementations that ship with Infinispan, by default:

- org.infinispan.distribution.ch.DefaultConsistentHashFactory: As the name states, this is the default hashing algorithm. It achieves a uniform distribution. The downside of this algorithm is the order that cache joins the grid and impacts the mapping of segments to nodes. As a consequence, Infinispan cannot guarantee that the key's owner will be the same in all the caches.

- `org.infinispan.distribution.ch.TopologyAwareConsistentHashFac tory`: This is a specialization of the default algorithm. The topology-aware algorithm will make use of the Server Hinting properties (see the next subtopic) when enabled and will try to spread each segment's copies across all the possible nodes.

- `org.infinispan.distribution.ch.SyncConsistentHashFactory`: This algorithm is similar to consistent hashing and addresses the weakness of the default algorithm. Basically, if the clustering is symmetric, Infinispan guarantees that cache with the same members will always have the same consistent hash, which means that Infinispan will always assign a key to the same node. However, the algorithm has some weak spots, namely the load distribution is less even, and it can potentially move more segments than necessary during a rebalance.

- `org.infinispan.distribution.ch.TopologyAwareSyncConsiste ntHashFactory`: This is similar to the `SyncConsistentHashFactory` algorithm, but it will make use of the topology information defined in `TransportConfiguration` (See the next subtopic, *Server Hinting*).

- `org.infinispan.distribution.ch.ReplicatedConsistentHashFact ory`: This algorithm should never be used in a distributed cache. It's used internally to implement replicated caches.

You can find an example on how to change the consistent hash algorithm in Infinispan 7, which is as follows:

```
<distributed-cache name="distributedCache"
                   mode="SYNC"
                   owners="4"
                   segments="2"
                   async-marshalling="false"
                   consistent-hash-factory=
                   "org.infinispan.distribution.ch.impl.
                   SyncConsistentHashFactory">
```

Server Hinting

Server Hinting is a mechanism implemented to be used only on caches with distributed mode, to ensure that Infinispan will not store backups of cache data on a node in the same machine, rack, or data center.

You can configure server hinting in the `transport` element (Infinispan 6/7) that is used to configure and refine details of the transport that will be used in the network communication across the grid.

Let's look at the configuration now. The following code presents a sample transport configuration, that's using some hints configured in the `transport` element:

```
<transport
    cluster = "Infinispan Cluster"
    machine = "ubuntu.server.01"
    rack = "r101"
    site = "IE-DUB" />
```

The preceding sample code configures the following topology hints:

- **machine**: This is quite a useful property, to nominate multiple JVM instances running on the same node, or even multiple virtual hosts on the same physical host.

- **rack**: This is useful in larger clusters, with nodes that take more than one rack. This attribute defines the ID rack where this node runs. This setting prevents that backups from occupying the same rack.

- **site**: This is used to give a name (or ID) of the site that this instance is running.

All of the preceding elements are optional, and if not provided, Infinispan cannot guarantee that there is no way for Infinispan to know if he's storing backups in instances that are running in the same environment (machine, rack or site).

L1 caching

Imagine the situation, where you have a data grid in distribution mode, and a client begins to read a key K8 many times on the same node, but this node is not the owner of K8—another member in the cluster owns it. Each `get(K8)` will be a remote operation, creating multiple network trips.

If you face such a situation, where there is a cache that is the read most, then you should consider creating an L1 cache. L1 cache (or Level 1 cache) can hold remote cache entries for a short time after they are initially accessed from a remote source, thus preventing additional remote fetch operations every time you need to use the same entries. When you enable L1 caching, by default, the maximum lifespan for an entry in the cache is 600,000 milliseconds.

If you're using the Hot Rod server (see *Chapter 9, Server Modules*), the Java Hot Rod client on Infinispan 7.0 can be configured to use a nearby cache.

For more information visit `https://github.com/infinispan/infinispan/wiki/Near-Caching`.

If an update is made to an entry in the L1 cache, Infinispan invalidates L1 cache entries using an invalidation strategy. The advantage of using such a configuration is that you can have a fast response time because all access to the data is local. Looking for the data in the L1 cache first saves a trip to the grid of servers, thus making even the remote data locally accessible.

Here is the minimum configuration you will need in order to enable L1 Caching.

For Infinispan 6, add the following code:

```
<L1 enabled = "true" />
```

You can configure it yourself using the following settings:

Attribute	Type	Default	Description
enabled	boolean	true	This is the Boolean attribute that can be used to enable or disable the L1 cache.
lifespan	long	600000	This is the maximum period of time an entry can be placed in the L1 cache.
onRehash	boolean	true	If this is set to true, all the entries moved to other nodes due to a rehash operation, will be moved to the L1 cache rather than being removed from the node completely.
invalidation Threshold	int	0	By default (the value is set to 0), Infinispan uses multicast to perform L1 invalidation operations. If the threshold is set to -1, Infinispan will make use of a web of unicasts to perform these invalidations.

In Infinispan 7, L1 caching is enabled by default, so to disable L1 caching, you have to set the `l1-lifespan` attribute to 0 of the cache configuration to zero. For instance:

```
<distributed-cache name="distributedCacheWithouL1" mode="SYNC"
owners="3" l1-lifespan="0" />
```

The `l1-lifespan` attribute defines the maximum period of time (in milliseconds), an entry can be placed in the L1 cache. You can also configure the `l1-cleanup-interval` attribute that defines the cleanup task interval. This configuration defines how long Infinispan will wait before pruning the L1 data, the default value is 10 minutes.

You can see an example using this attribute right below.

The following diagram shows the sequences involved in L1 caching:

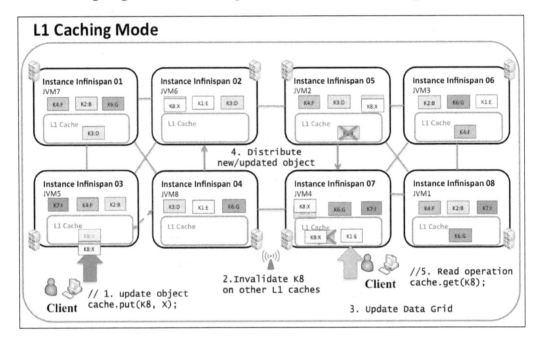

However, all these benefits don't come free. When using the L1 cache, you should consider issues such as more cached data in the JVM heap, which can increase consumption of the JVM heap memory to some degree. If you have too many write operations or entries are updated frequently, then an invalidation message needs to be multicast (or unicast if invalidationThreshold is set to -1) to ensure all the nodes with the entry in the L1 cache invalidates the entry.

The following is a sample declarative distribution configuration with L1 caching:

- For Infinispan 6, it is as follows:

```
<namedCache name="cacheDistWithL1">
  <clustering mode="dist">
    <async/>
    <hash numOwners="2" />
    <l1 enabled="true" lifespan="1000000"
      invalidationThreshold="1"/>
  </clustering>
</namedCache>
```

- For Infinispan 7, it is as follows:

```
<distributed-cache name="cacheDistiWithL1"
      mode="ASYNC"
      owners="2"
      l1-lifespan="600000"
      l1-cleanup-interval="1200">
```

The invalidation threshold attribute was removed from L1 caching configuration in Infinispan 7.

Next, we have a sample code showing how to configure it programmatically, via the builder-style API:

```
GlobalConfiguration glob = new GlobalConfigurationBuilder()
                            .transport().
                              defaultTransport()
                            .build();

Configuration config = new ConfigurationBuilder()
            .clustering()
            .cacheMode(CacheMode.DIST_ASYNC)
            .l1().enable().lifespan(1000000)
            .hash().numOwners(2)
            .build();

return new DefaultCacheManager(glob, config);
```

Summary

During this chapter, we got an overview about the several cache topologies Infinispan provides.

You can use the replication mode to provide fast access to the cache data, because clients will be able to read the information quickly, with the data available on each node of the grid. However, for each data manipulation, the updated cache will send its new state to the other members of the cluster, which can be an expensive operation and add some overhead to your network.

In invalidation mode, the updated cache will send a message to the other members of the cluster stating that a particular piece of data has been modified. After receiving this message, the other nodes will remove this data from their local cache.

If you decide for a local-mode cache, the updated cache is not aware there are other nodes running in the cluster, and will not attempt to exchange data with them. However, a local-mode cache is a drop-in replacement for a Java Map, with the added values of supporting expiration, eviction, persistence, and all features offered by Infinispan.

And finally, the distribution mode represents the real data grid. This mode allows Infinispan to scale linearly, so if you want to add more nodes, in this mode the grid will automatically rebalance the cache data among them. Distribution makes use of a consistent hash algorithm to determine which node and segment a cache entry should be stored in. For an advanced distributed cache, you have the option to enable L1 caching to prevent expensive and repeated remote calls during execution of GET operations.

In the next chapter, we are going to cover some key guidelines and design patterns to design the data layer of an application.

5

Data Access Patterns

In the previous chapter, we got an overview of the several cache topologies Infinispan provides.

This chapter will describe the key guidelines and design patterns we will need in order to design the data layer of an application. It will also describe how to configure Infinispan to use Hibernate second-level cache with Infinispan.

In this chapter, we will discuss the following topics:

- Data access patterns
- Understanding and configuring second-level cache in Hibernate with Infinispan
- Implementing the cache-aside programming pattern
- Reading and writing through cache
- Writing behind cache

Data access patterns

Infinispan can play a vital role in maximizing performance; however, while the nature of caching depends on your applications' requirements, you can employ common caching strategies to avoid running the risk of reducing performance by choosing an inappropriate pattern. In the rest of this chapter, we will cover some caching access patterns and their advantages and disadvantages. Each of these patterns is independent from the others. You can mix and match them to build as comprehensive a data grid solution as your applications require.

Understanding and configuring second-level cache in Hibernate with Infinispan

Nowadays, web applications face many problems in performance due to database traffic. One of the great advantages of using an **Object/Relational Mapping (ORM)** solution like Hibernate or JPA is the ability to reduce or even eliminate multiple round trips to the database. However, to take advantage of this benefit, it's quite important to design a good model. With well-known ORM solutions like Hibernate and JPA, you can define your model on top of an existent database schema, or let the ORM engine generate the database model from your object model.

On the opposite side, if you design a bad model, your Hibernate/JPA application may produce the opposite effect and create more requests to the database and increase I/O workload against the database.

Anyway, if you are looking to gain good performance, some techniques are necessary to keep your application at top performance. One of the best techniques is optimize the performance of your application by improving the database access by introducing a cache solution. By storing the data needed to meet customer requests in a cache, you can drastically reduce the time required to access an object that was previously in a database and it can also reduce the network traffic.

However, in this case, the cache stores only the data related to the current running application, so it must be cleared from time to time, whenever the application changes state.

Both JPA and Hibernate support two different levels of caching; they are the first-level and second-level caching. So, let's start with a brief explanation.

Introducing first-level and second-level caching

The first-level cache is the session cache. For instance, on Hibernate, the cache is managed by the framework, so the first-level cache is enabled by default in Hibernate, where the objects are cached in the session cache and they will be available in the memory while the session is still valid on the server side.

The second-level cache is an optional cache; Hibernate's second-level cache is associated with the `SessionFactory` object, and during a transaction will load these objects at the session factory level, which will make these cached objects available to the whole application.

This configuration enables the cached objects to be accessed at the application level, from the memory, which reduces the number of SQL queries/statements an application requires in order to access an object.

Objects found in the second-level cache are returned to the user running the query; whereas, if an object is not found in the cache, a database query will be fired.

In Hibernate, the interface `org.hibernate.cache.CacheProvider` is provided to handle the cache implementation, which allows the second-level cache to be implemented via any third party cache implementation, such as Ehcache and Infinispan.

There is also another cache called query cache, which is used to store the results of a query related to a combination of parameters. Therefore, it is only useful for queries that are run frequently with the same parameters.

JPA caching is slightly different from Hibernate caching; the persistent context works as the first-level cache in JPA.

The second-level cache was introduced in JPA 2.0, which is a local store of entity data managed by the persistence provider. In order to share the state of an entity, you have to enable it, and you will be able to access the shared entities with the help of the entity manager factory across all persistence contexts.

The following diagram illustrates the scopes to which both caches are related:

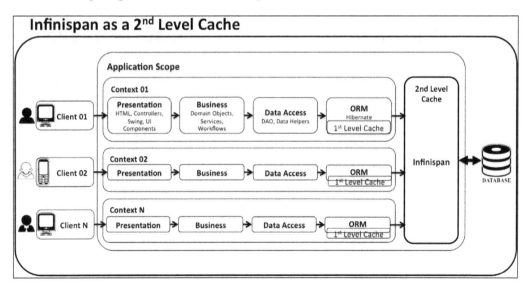

The recommended clustering mode when Infinispan is being used as a second-level cache for Hibernate is the invalidation mode.

Before you configure a second-level cache, it's important to understand some basic concepts. The second-level cache can handle the following four types of data:

- **Entities**: This is the data type most frequently cached in the second-level cache.
- **Collections**: This refers to cached entities that have one or more of its attributes defined as a collection of another entity.
- **Query results**: Specific to Hibernate, you can cache query results in the second-level cache. The HQL statement and its parameter values are also cached along with the PKs (primary keys) of all entities that make up the result set.
- **Timestamps**: Hibernate stores the timestamp of the most recent query executions in the second-level cache for each query result.

In order to properly handle each type of data, you have different caching semantics. Hibernate's second-level cache must implement the interface `org.hibernate.cache.RegionFactory`, which defines methods for each of these types and allows Hibernate to notify the caching integration layer about which type of data is being cached. The `org.hibernate.cache.infinispan.InfinispanRegionFactory` class is a class inside Infinispan that provides an implementation of the `RegionFactory` interface, supplying a way to build second-level cache regions.

Configuring Infinispan as Hibernate second-level cache

As you can see, Hibernate and Infinispan provide an excellent way to use an Infinispan cache and take advantage of its benefits.

Once you've made proper decisions regarding the type of data, you will cache and decide which topology you want to use. You will have to configure the setup based on your selected options.

In JBoss 7, Infinispan is the default second-level cache, even for non-clustered use. Infinispan replaced the JBoss cache, which requires some changes in the `persistence.xml` file. The following steps need to be performed to configure Infinispan as hibernate second-level cache:

1. The first step is to activate JPA or Hibernate second-level cache with query result caching. Add one of the following code snippets to configure your application:

```
<!-- If using JPA, add to your persistence.xml -->
<property name="hibernate.cache.use_second_level_cache"
  value="true" />
<property name="hibernate.cache.use_query_cache"
  value="true" />
<!-- If using Hibernate, add to your hibernate.cfg.xml -->
<property
  name="hibernate.cache.use_second_level_cache">true
</property>
<property name="hibernate.cache.use_query_cache">true
</property>
```

2. Now for the second step, configure the cache region factory; you can opt for one of the following configurations, based on the framework you've selected:

> If your Infinispan `CacheManager` instance is bound to the JNDI tree, you will have to include the `JndiInfinispanRegionFactory` class, a `RegionFactory` class specific for Infinispan caches, which can find its `CacheManager` in JNDI, and the JNDI name of the cache manager.

```
<!-- If using JPA, add to your persistence.xml -->
<property name="hibernate.cache.region.factory_class"
  value="org.hibernate.cache.infinispan.
    JndiInfinispanRegionFactory" />
<property name="hibernate.cache.infinispan.cachemanager"
  value="java:CacheManager" />


<!-- If using Hibernate, add to your hibernate.cfg.xml -->
<property
  name="hibernate.cache.region.factory_class">
    org.hibernate.cache.infinispan.
      JndiInfinispanRegionFactory</property>
<property
  name="hibernate.cache.infinispan.cachemanager">
    java:CacheManager/entity</property>
```

JBoss application server and Infinispan

The JBoss AS Versions 6 and 7 provide an Infinispan cache manager that can be used by all services, so when you define the configuration, to enable and use Infinispan as the second-level cache in your application, you will need only to use the JNDI name assigned to the Infinispan cache manager that will manage the second-level cache.

The containers will lookup the Cache Manager under the `java:CacheManager/entity` JNDI name. Normally, if you are configuring Infinispan as a second-level cache for an application server other than JBoss AS, you would be able to deploy your own cache manager with your configuration and bind the cache manager to the JNDI of your selected application server.

If you're running a JPA/Hibernate and an Infinispan application on a standalone mode or within a non-JBoss application server, as we said earlier, the cache region factory that you will need to select is the **InfinispanRegionFactory** option, because that's the `RegionFactory` implementation that make use of a Infinispan cache to store the data:

```
<!-- If using JPA, add to your persistence.xml -->
<property name="hibernate.cache.region.factory_class" value="org.
hibernate.cache.infinispan.InfinispanRegionFactory"/>
<!-- If using Hibernate, add to your hibernate.cfg.xml -->
<property
  name="hibernate.cache.region.factory_class">org.hibernate.cache.
    infinispan.InfinispanRegionFactory</property>
```

This will be all the configuration you need to set up a JPA/Hibernate application in order to use Infinispan as a cache provider (using the default settings). Anyway, you will still need to define which entities or queries you want to cache.

The default configuration presented here should suit most of the needs and scenarios; however, if you're looking for a different configuration, please check the online documentation at `http://infinispan.org/docs/7.0.x/user_guide/user_guide.html#_using_infinispan_as_jpa_hibernate_second_level_cache_provider`.

Implementing the cache-aside programming pattern

Perhaps the most common caching pattern in use today is cache-aside. In this strategy, an application populates a cache lazily, as applications request data, and as the system runs, the cache client gradually populates the cache to contain most of the data that it refers to frequently.

In this pattern, the cache doesn't interact with the database; it is kept aside as a more scalable in-memory data store.

 Infinispan will always attempt to load data from CacheStore or CacheLoader. We are talking about a situation where the data comes from an external data store, such as a database.

Consider a simple `Reference Data Service` example, which will be used to store and retrieve reference data, as the meaning of a given code. For instance, for the code M, the service will return `Male` for the meaning. A basic implementation is shown in the following listing:

```
public class ReferenceCodeService {
  private final Cache<String, String> cache;
  private IDataStore dataStore;
  public ReferenceCodeService() {
    Configuration config = new ConfigurationBuilder().clustering()
      .cacheMode(CacheMode.LOCAL).build();
    this.cache = new DefaultCacheManager(config).getCache();
    this.dataStore = RefCodeDataStore.getInstance();
  }

  public String get(String code) throws CodeDoesNotExistsException {
    String meaning;
    if ((meaning = cache.get(code)) != null) {
      return meaning;
    }

    if ((meaning = readDataFromDataStore(code)) != null) {
      cache.put(code, meaning);
    } else {
      throw new CodeDoesNotExistsException("Reference Code does
        not exists!");
    }
    return meaning;
  }
```

```
        public void put(String refCode, String meaning) {
          writeMessageToDataStore(refCode, meaning);
          cache.put(refCode, meaning);
        }

        private String readRefDataFromDataStore(String refCode) {
          String meaning = dataStore.getEntry(refCode);
          return meaning;
        }

        private void writeRefDataToDataStore(String refCode, String
          meaning) {
          dataStore.setEntry(refCode, meaning);
        }
      }
```

As you can see in the preceding code, when you call the put service, it will write the new reference code first to the data store (through the writeRefDataToDataStore method).

And the get service will first try to read data from the cache, and then if it doesn't exist, the service will try to read the reference code from the data store.

Reading and writing through cache

In this pattern, application treats the cache as the main data store for read and write operations. The cache is responsible for reading and writing to an underlying resource.

Read-Through looks like the structure of the cache-aside pattern for read operations, the difference is on how the system behaves in the data changes. After retrieving the data from a data store and when data is not found in the cache, the cache updates itself and returns the data to the calling application.

In the **Write-Through** mode, if the client change the cache content by invoking a write operation, for instance, using the put() or putAll() methods, Infinispan will not return the call to the client until Infinispan finishes updating the underlying cache store. This means that the client thread will be blocked until all updates are written to the cache store, which can result in a very expensive operation.

A graphical representation of this pattern is illustrated in the following diagram:

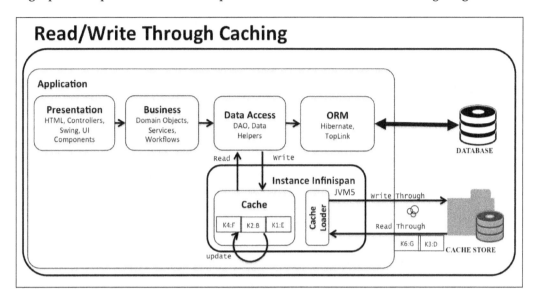

One of the benefits of this mode is that the cache and the cache store are kept in sync, which means that when you update a cache entry, Infinispan will update that entry in the cache store at the same time. Hence, we can guarantee that the cache store will always be consistent with the content in the cache. On the other hand, there is a trade-off here in performance; to keep this level of consistency, you will need to give some performance up, because the latency our system will have in order to access and update the cache store at the same time will have an impact on the overall duration of the cache operation.

Configuring a `writeThroughCache` store does not require any specific configuration, because by default, all cache stores are Write-Through, unless you configure it explicitly as a Write-behind cache, all cache stores are write-through.

You can find a sample configuration in XML of `writeThroughCache` named cache (unshared) with `SingleFileStore` for persistence in the following code:

Infinispan 6

```
<namedCache name="writeThroughCache">
  <persistence passivation="false">
  <store class="org.infinispan.persistence.file.SingleFileStore"
      fetchPersistentState="true" preload="false" shared="false"
        purgeOnStartup="false" ignoreModifications="false">
```

```
  <async />
   <properties>
     <property name="location" value="/tmp/cache/backup" />
   </properties>
   </store>
     </persistence>
   </namedCache>
```

We are not enabling passivation in this example, because with passivation, Infinispan will store the cache state to the file system only when data is evicted from the memory. And when the cache data is requested again, the entry is removed from the file system and loaded into the memory.

The shared attribute will make all instances in the grid share the same cache loader. The code for that is as follows:

Infinispan 7

```
<local-cache name="writeThroughToFile">
  <persistence passivation="false">
    <file-store path="/tmp/cache/backup" shared="false"
      preload="true" purge="true">
    <write-behind thread-pool-size="22" />
    </file-store>
    </persistence>
</local-cache>
```

In the preceding code, as you can see, a write-behind element was introduced to configure the cache store as write-behind.

Writing behind caching

Write-behind cache is a well know pattern, used in every CPU for code optimization. It's especially recommended for situations where it is expensive to save a cache object that is highly accessed.

A Write-behind cache, unlike a writeThroughCcache, performs all cache write operations on the cache to the backing store asynchronously. This means that all write operations in the given data store are not performed by the thread used by the client to interact with the cache, but by a different one.

The major advantage of this pattern is that performance and experience of using the cache are not affected by these asynchronous writes to the underlying store, which can substantially improve the performance in scenarios where values are constantly changing.

The following diagram shows how this pattern works:

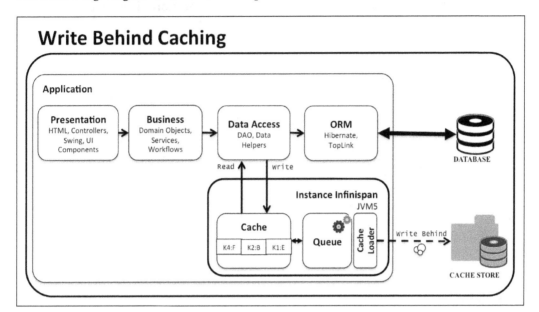

Besides all these advantages, you have to consider where to use this pattern; given the fact that changes are made asynchronously, there is a time window when your cache client can see stale data.

When you choose to use a Write-behind, there are two different strategies that you can choose to store data. They are the Scheduled and Unscheduled Write-behind strategy.

The Unscheduled Write-behind strategy

The Unscheduled strategy is supported from version 4.0. In this strategy, Infinispan stores the pending changes to the cache store parallelly as soon as possible. In practice, there are several threads looking for changes, when the thread detects a modification event and they're available, Infinispan applies the pendent changes to underlying cache stores.

This strategy is recommended for local caches or environments with low latency or low operation cost. A simple example: a cache with a local and unshared cache store mechanism (SingleFileStore), but in this case, our cache store must reside in the same place the cache is running.

With this simple configuration, we can reduce the risk of inconsistency to the maximum in the cached data and in the data in our cache store. The next example shows a sample configuration file that uses this strategy:

Infinispan 6

```
<namedCache name="writeBehindCache">
  <persistence>
  <store class="SingleFileStore" shared="true" preload="false">
  <async enabled="true" flushLockTimeout="15000"
threadPoolSize="10"/>
  <singleton enabled="true" pushStateWhenCoordinator="true"
    pushStateTimeout="20000"/>
  <properties>
  <property name="location" value="/tmp/cache/backup"/>
  </properties>
  </store>
    </persistence>
  </namedCache>
```

Infinispan 7

```
<persistence passivation="false">
  <file-store fetch-state="true"
      read-only="false"
      purge="false" path="/tmp/cache/backup" />
  <write-behind />
  </file-store>
</persistence>
```

The Scheduled Write-behind strategy

Currently, this strategy is not implemented in Infinispan, but it's planned for the next release. In this strategy, Infinispan maintains a queue of the data pending to be sent to the cache store and periodically stores these changes asynchronously after a configurable time, which could be defined after 10, 20, or 30 seconds, minutes, or even days.

This strategy, unlike the unscheduled strategy, is recommended for caches with high latency. Since changes are coalesced, if you have many operations by different clients to the same object, only the latest state is written. Which means that in this strategy, the higher the interval time is set to update the cache store, higher are the chances of inconsistencies in the data.

Summary

In this chapter, we presented some techniques based on standards data access patterns to leverage Infinispan usage.

In the next chapter, you'll find out more about interacting with data in the grid, and examine the Ticket Monster case study in order to know how to design a data grid application to take full advantage of Infinispan.

6
Case Study – The TicketMonster Application

In this chapter, you will learn how to implement Infinispan in a sample application called **Ticket Monster**, which illustrates the use of some of the strategies you learned in the last chapters.

The Ticket Monster application is a simple online ticketing broker providing access to events such as concerts and shows, with an online booking application. It is a moderately complex application that demonstrates how to build modern web applications that are optimized for mobile and desktop. It uses a mix of Java EE6 technologies such as JSF 2, JPA 2, CDI, and JAX-RS along with HTML5, jQuery Mobile, and GWT.

We will first present a version of Ticket Monster with a traditional database-driven architecture without Infinispan. In the second step, we will introduce new requirements related to performance and scalability thresholds in order to discuss the specific problems and study possible solutions, and finally introduce Infinispan to our architecture as a possible solution to solve our problem.

In this chapter, we will briefly discuss and analyze the following subjects:

- The JBoss developer framework
- Installing and running Ticket Monster
- Ticket Monster's application use cases
- Administrators use cases
- Architecture and design
- Scaling Ticket Monster
- Adding Infinispan to Ticket Monster

The JBoss developer framework

We cannot talk about Ticket Monster without talking about the **JBoss developer framework (JDF)**. JDF is a central documentation hub containing tools, examples, and documentation for developers to create rich applications using JBoss technology, which allows developers to focus on a single documentation resource instead of hunting down several individual guides for different parts.

The framework is made up of four components:

- **Quickstarts**: Provide templates and tutorials for small applications using one specific API or technology. Currently, there are hundreds of quickstarts and videos, ranging from JBoss Applications on Openshift to hybrid mobile tools to Hibernate OGM.

- **Examples**: The Ticket Monster application is part of JDF, as we will see throughout this chapter.

- **Migrations**: This provides guides for individuals looking to move to JBoss from another platform, such as Seam 2, Spring, and Spring mixed with Java EE 6 or Java EE 5.

- **JBoss stacks**: Also known as JBoss BOMs, JBoss Stacks allows you to easily choose and use a stack of JBoss runtimes, frameworks, and tools. BOMs start with Java EE 6, and build on that base API with JBoss extensions such as Hibernate (Search, Validator, and so on), Errai, and Arquillian.

Errai is a GWT-based framework to build rich web applications, which promote annotation-driven development.

Arquillian is a test framework that can be used to perform testing inside a remote or embedded container, and it's quite useful to validate the business rules in your application server. Arquillian integrates pretty well with various testing frameworks, such as JUnit and TestNG, allowing the use of IDE, Ant, and Maven test plugins.

If you would like to know more about these frameworks, please access the following links:

- **Errai**: http://www.jboss.org/errai
- **Arquillian**: http://arquillian.org/

Installing and running the TicketMonster application

In order to run Ticket Monster, you will need the following environment:

- Java Development Kit Version 6 or 7
- Eclipse (Java EE Developers edition) and JBoss Tools Plugin
- JBoss Enterprise Application Server 6 or JBoss AS 7
- Maven 3.0

 Ticket Monster is an open source application created with Java and JBoss technologies. You can learn more about it from the accompanying tutorial at http://www.jboss.org/jdf/examples/get-started/.

As we stated in the previous section, Ticket Monster is an example from JDF, so there are two ways you can follow this chapter.

In the first option, you can create the application from scratch and learn how to use several features of the Java EE 6, HTML5, and JBoss technologies. If you decide for this first option, at the end, you will have learned about a range of topics such as:

- Creating a Java EE 6 project using Maven
- Creating a JPA entity using JBoss Forge
- Using Hibernate tools
- Using CDI for integrating individual services
- Adding a JAX-RS endpoint
- Adding a jQuery Mobile client
- Creating single-page applications using HTML5, JavaScript, and JSON
- Adding GWT to your application
- Setting up server-client eventing using Errai CDI extension
- Testing GWT applications
- Creating a native application for Android and iOS with Apache Cordova

As you might realize, these topics are beyond the scope of this book and the information is provided for your reference only.

The second option is you can just follow this chapter and learn how Infinispan can fit in the Ticket Monster architecture.

Anyway, for a better comprehension of the application and the environment, we are going to analyze the application architecture, the use cases, and finally, understand how Infinispan can help you overcome particular challenges Ticket Monster can face.

Project structure

So the first thing you'll want to do is to get the source code of Ticket Monster to your local machine by cloning it from the Github repository:

```
git clone -b "2.0.9.Final"
    https://github.com/jboss-developer/ticket-monster.git
```

 You can download it or fork it on GitHub by navigating to the following link:

https://github.com/jboss-jdf/ticket-monster

Navigate to the root folder where Ticket Monster is stored and you'll find the following folders:

- `demo`: This includes sources of the TicketMonster application. You can build and run it! Just follow the instructions in the README file.

- `cordova`: This includes the sources of the TicketMonster Hybrid Mobile (Cordova) application.

- `dist`: This includes utility scripts for versioning and release. The `release.sh` script will update the version number, commit and tag, and publish to the JBoss Maven repository.

 You'll need access to some of these to perform releases.

- `tutorial`: This includes sources of the TicketMonster tutorial, which describe how it works, how it's designed, and outlines a series of steps for you to build it.

 To install and prepare the environment, take a look at the following tutorial:

http://www.jboss.org/tools/

Now, you can open the Ticket Monster project in your favorite IDE such as Eclipse or IntelliJ.

In Eclipse

To open the project in Eclipse, you will need the M2 plugin, as it allows a project to be imported using the Eclipse import wizard.

 M2Eclipse is an Eclipse plugin, which provides a first-class Apache Maven support in the Eclipse IDE. For more information, visit http://eclipse.org/m2e/.

Assuming you have already installed the M2Eclipse plugin in your Eclipse. Navigate to **Import | Maven | Existing Maven Projects** and click on the **Next** button. On the next page, specify the root directory ($PATH/ticket-monster/demo) to scan for projects, and then hit the **Refresh** button.

Now, you can check the demo project and press the **Finish** button to import it into the Eclipse workspace. At the end, your workspace should look like following figure:

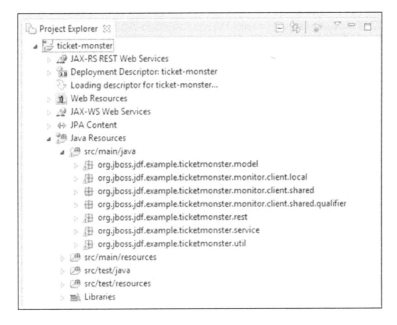

In IntelliJ

With IntelliJ, it's easier to open the Ticket Monster project, because it provides an excellent M2 integration and can automatically recognize any existing Apache Maven project. Perform the following steps in IntelliJ:

1. Open IntelliJ and click on the **Import** option, navigate to the project directory, and select the **demo** folder.

2. Select the **Import project from external model** option on IntelliJ, click on the **Maven** option, and press the **Next** button.

3. Choose the root directory for your project and click on **Next**.

4. IntelliJ will ask you to select a profile; select the **default** option, which will use the H2 database to store the application's data and click on **Next**. The following screenshot shows different profiles in **Import Project**:

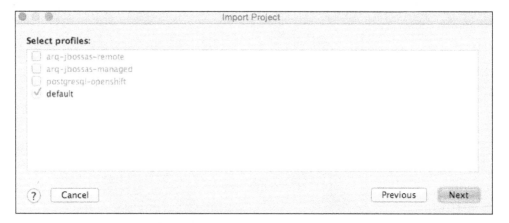

5. In this step, select the maven project (**ticket-monster:2.0.9.Final**) and click on **Next**.

6. Select an **SDK** and click on **Next** again. Finally, let the default project name choose a project file location to create the IntelliJ project and click on **Finish**.

7. IntelliJ will open the project. The IDE should look similar to the following screenshot:

Now that you are able to run Ticket Monster, let's understand the application use cases and how it works.

The TicketMonster application use cases

The end users of the application want to attend some cool events. They will try to find shows, create bookings, or cancel bookings. The use cases are as follows:

- Look for current events
- Look for venues
- Select shows (events taking place at specific venues) and choose a performance time
- Book tickets
- View current bookings
- Cancel bookings

The use cases are shown in the following diagram:

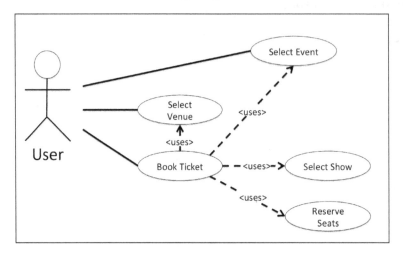

- **Look for current events**: In this use case, the user can look for current events available for booking. To visualize the current events on the main menu of Ticket Monster, select the **Events** option, which will open a menu with three different categories, such as **Concert**, **Theatre**, and **Sporting** on the left side of the page.

  To see the details of an event, just hover your mouse over the event and the information will be displayed as shown in the following screenshot:

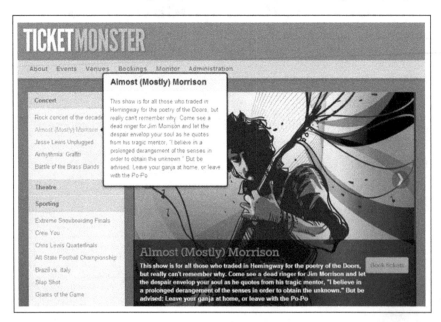

- **Look for venues**: Just like the previous use case, to look for venues, select the **Venues** option on the main menu, which will open up a menu with two different cities, **Sydney** and **Toronto** on the left side of the page, as shown in the following screenshot:

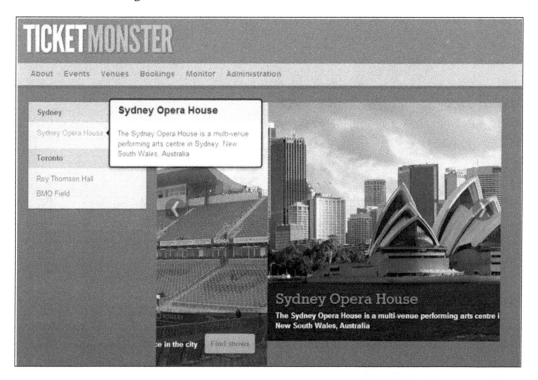

- **Select shows**: The user can select shows (events taking place at specific venues) and choose a performance time. You can do this in two different ways. The first option is selecting the desired event (as described in the *Look for current events* use case); a new panel will show you a pop-up list of venues you would like to attend.

Select a venue and a third panel will appear on the right part of the browser, asking you to select the date you want to attend the show on, which is shown in the following screenshot:

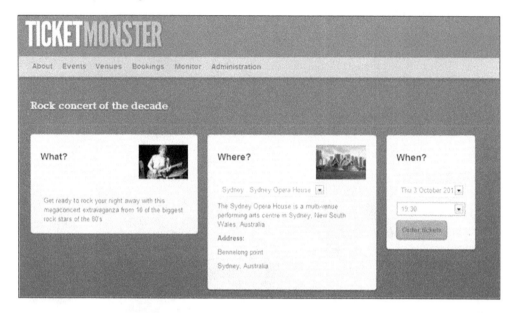

The second option is to select a venue (as described in *Look for Venues*) first, then, similar to the first option, a panel will be shown, asking the user to select an event. After selecting the desired event, the same panel asks when you want to attend the show will appear again, with all available dates, as shown in the following screenshot:

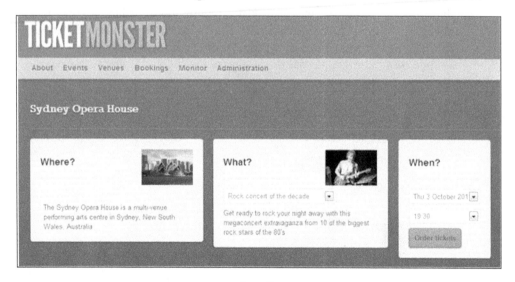

- **Book tickets**: After selecting the desired show (as described in *Select shows*), a new page will open, where you can select the section to watch the show and the number of tickets in the first pane.

  When you confirm the number of tickets, press the **Add Tickets** button. An order summary will be displayed in the right-hand panel. To checkout your tickets, enter a valid e-mail address and press the **Checkout** button, which is shown in the following screenshot:

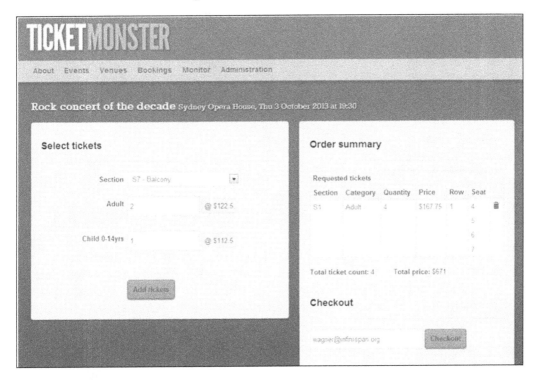

A new page will display the booking confirmation and all the important details regarding the event and number of tickets, as shown in the following screenshot:

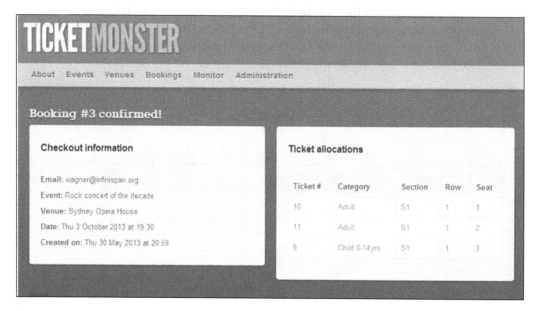

- **View current bookings**: The user can consult current bookings in the system and information such as booking number, purchaser, creation date, number of tickets, and total price. To visualize the current bookings on the main menu of Ticket Monster, select the **Bookings** option, as shown in the following screenshot:

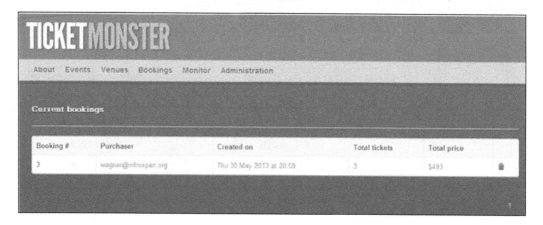

- Canceling bookings: Users can cancel the booking any time by deleting the selected booking in the booking page (as described in *View current bookings*).

Administrators use cases

Administrators are more concerned with the operation of the business. They will manage the master data, which includes information about venues, events and shows, and will want to see how many tickets have been sold.

These are shown in the following diagram:

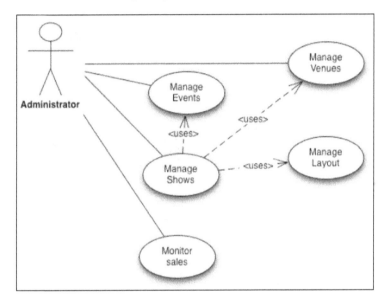

The use cases are as follows:

- Monitor tickets for current shows: A user can consult real-time information about ticket sales and attendance and he/she can execute a bot service that creates a bulk of bookings to test the system. To visualize the dashboard that can collect data and receive real-time updates and start a bot service, select the **Monitor** option, as shown in the following screenshot:

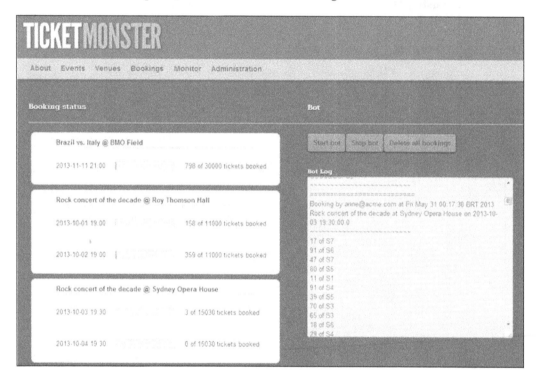

- Manage master data (Events, Shows, and Venues): An administrator can manage the master data such as Events, Shows, Menus, and Sections through a GUI.

  If you select the **Administration** option on the main menu, Ticket Monster will display the following page:

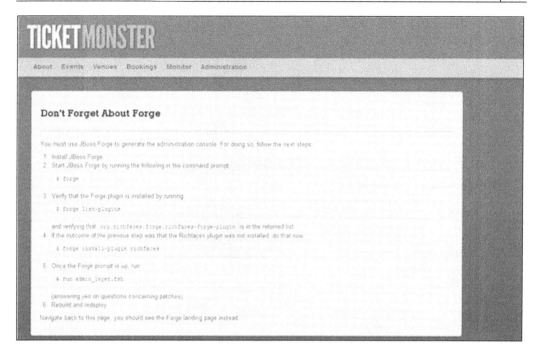

As you can see, the **Administration** module is not activated by default. In the upcoming section, you will learn how to activate it.

Building the administration UI using JBoss Forge

Now, it's time to build an administration GUI for the Ticket Monster application using JSF and RichFaces.

To generate the administration console, you must use JBoss Forge, a rapid application development framework for Java developers, similar to Spring Roo. The difference is that JBoss Forge is not tied to any specific framework, which enables setting up different flavors of Java EE applications, which can run on any container.

One of the best parts about the Forge framework is its feature called scaffolding. Scaffolding, as it's famously called in Ruby on Rails CakePHP, Spring Roo, and Groovy and Grails, provides a quick way to generate some of the major pieces of your application.

Forge's default UI scaffolding generates a pure Java EE application with a JavaServer Faces user interface. This UI includes support for basic database CRUD (Create, Read, Update, Delete) operations, as well as sophisticated pagination and search support.

The scaffolding uses pure JSF tags, with no runtime dependencies on any non-Java EE libraries.

 Forge is designed to be used on any kind of Maven project and provides an easy API to write plugins for any kind of technology that you might use in your projects.

JBoss Forge installation and setup

Perform the following steps:

1. To install JBoss Forge, you can download the latest stable version at `http://forge.jboss.org/`.

2. Unzip Forge into a folder on your hard disk and add $FORGE_HOME/bin to your path.

 Consider installing Git and Maven 3.0 or above (both optional), before installing Forge.

3. When you finish the preceding steps, open a Command Prompt and run forge (for Windows users, there is a .bat file available). This command will launch the Forge console, which is as follows:

```
Prompt de Comando - forge

       Forge »

JBoss Forge, version [ 1.3.0.Final ] - JBoss, by Red Hat, Inc. [ http://forge.jb
oss.org ]
[ticket-monster] demo $
```

Forge Plugin for Eclipse

JBoss Forge is also available as an Eclipse Plugin (it's an integrated part of JBoss Tools plugin).

The most convenient way to install JBoss Forge is by instructing Eclipse to fetch the plugin from the update site. To see the best update site to fit your needs, visit JBoss Tools page at `http://www.jboss.org/tools`.

 If you are using JBoss Enterprise Application Platform 6, Forge is available in JBoss Developer Studio 5.

If you are using Eclipse Juno, follow these instructions:

1. Start Eclipse.
2. Navigate to **Help | Install New Software** from the menu.
3. Click on the **Add** button to add a new repository.
4. Enter `JBoss Tools` as the name and `http://download.jboss.org/jbosstools/updates/stable/juno/` as the URL and click on **OK**.
5. If you want to install all plugins under JBoss Tools, select the item **Abridged JBoss Tools 4.0**, otherwise, in the text search, type `Forge`, make sure Forge Tools is selected and click on **Next**.
6. Read through the license agreement, select **I accept...** and click on **Next**.
7. Click on **Finish** to install JBoss Tools (or JBoss Forge).

At the end, Eclipse will prompt for restarting. Once restarted, switch to the Forge Console View, as shown in the following screenshot:

A new tab view will be available in Eclipse, press the start button to start the default Forge runtime, which is shown in the following screenshot:

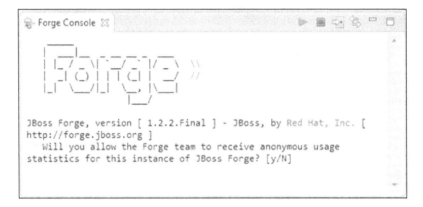

If you see an output like the preceding screenshot, follow the next steps as stated in the Administration page:

1. Verify that the Forge plugin is installed by running the following command line:

   ```
   $ forge list-plugins
   ```

   Verify that org.richfaces.forge.richfaces-forge-plugin is in the returned list.

2. If the outcome of the previous step was that the Richfaces plugin was not installed, do that now:

   ```
   $ forge install-plugin richfaces
   ```

3. Once the Forge prompt is up, run the following command:

   ```
   $ run admin_layer.fsh
   ```

   (answering yes on questions concerning patches)

4. Rebuild and redeploy.

When you come back to the Administration page, on the left side of the page, you will see a menu to manage the data employed by the main interface, as shown in the following screenshot:

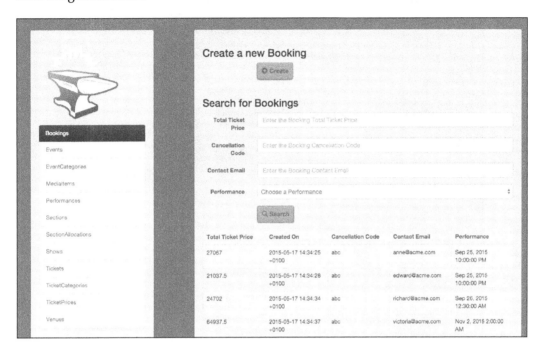

Architecture and design of TicketMonster

TicketMonster is a web application that incorporates several Java EE technologies. The application has two main user interfaces, a main interface for customers and an administration interface for people who maintain the system, both of which are packaged within a single WAR file.

The following figure depicts the application architecture summary:

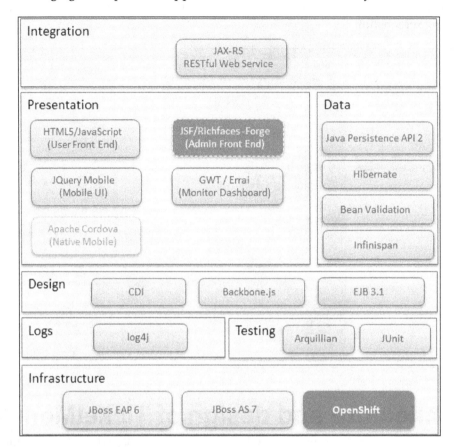

 TicketMonster added Infinispan support starting from version 2.1.0.

The business logic for customer interfaces is provided by services that implement the business logic of the application and expose them to the frontend.

The business logic and persistence layer are implemented using frameworks such as CDI, EJB 3.1, JAX-RS, and JPA 2. These services back the user-facing booking process, which is implemented by using HTML5 and JavaScript, with support for mobile devices through jQuery Mobile.

The business logic required to create bookings, shows, venues, and so on is provided by enterprise beans. The enterprise beans expose a REST interface and use the Java Persistence API to create and store the application's data in the database.

The administration site is centered around CRUD use cases, so instead of writing everything manually, the business layer and UI are generated by Forge, using EJB 3.1, CDI, and JSF. For a better user experience, the Richfaces UI components are used.

Monitoring sales requires staying in touch with the latest changes on the server side, so this part of the application is developed in GWT and showcases Errai's support for real-time updates via client-server CDI eventing.

The next figure shows how applications and the web service interact in a traditional architecture without Infinispan:

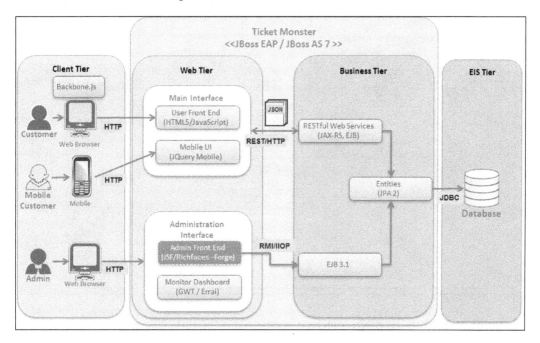

The architecture covered in this section without Infinispan (see the next diagram), is available in the release 2.0.9 of Ticket Monster. If you didn't follow the previous steps, you can download the source code from the following link:

`https://github.com/jboss-jdf/ticket-monster/archive/2.0.9.Final.zip`

The TicketMonster domain model

Based on the preceding use cases and requirements, we have defined the following model to represent the domain knowledge:

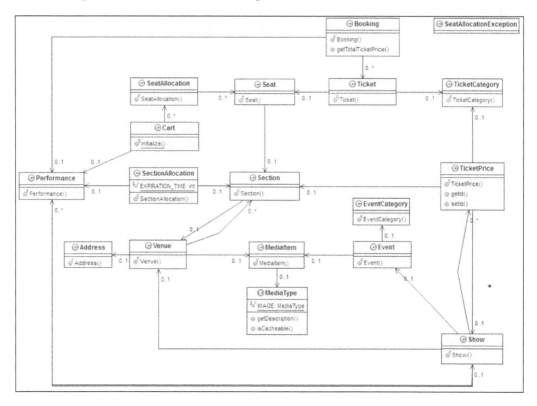

The entities used in the main interface encapsulate the data stored and manipulated by TicketMonster, and are located in the `org.jboss.jdf.example.TicketMonster.model` package.

TicketMonster contains 14 entities of varying complexity; we'll go deeper into domain model design and give an overview of these entities.

MediaType is an enumeration that describes the types of media this application can handle and render.

The entity `MediaItem` represents a reference to a media object, such as images, sound bites, video recordings, that can be used in the application. It defines attributes specific to media, this includes information such as the MediaType and the URL, to store in the database. The application will use this URL to access the media item.

Event, as its name indicates, represents an event, which may have multiple performances with different dates and venues. Event has a reference to `MediaItem`, as multiple events (or venues) could share the same media item. EventCategory represents the different categories of events (such as Concert, Theatre, Sporting, and so on).

The entity `Show` is an instance of an event taking place at a particular venue. A `Show` entity can have multiple performances. The entity `Performance` represents a single instance of a show.

`Venue` represents a single venue, the scene at which an event will take place, and has an `Address` attribute. A `Venue` layout may consist of multiple sections; in our model, , we are using the Section class to represent this information. And the `SectionAllocation` class represents the state of ticket allocation in a section, for a specific performance.

The entity `Ticket` represents a seat sold for a particular price. `TicketCategory` represents a lookup table containing the various ticket categories (such as Adult, Child, Pensioner, and so on).

`TicketPrice` contains the price categories; each category represents the price of a ticket in a particular section at a particular venue. This entity defines the attributes `Show`, to which this ticket price category belongs, `Section`, to which this ticket price category belongs, `TicketCategory`, which defines the price category of the ticket.

The entity `Cart` contains tickets that the user has reserved for purchase in this session.

Finally, the `Booking` entity stores a set of the `Tickets` entity purchased for a performance. This includes information such as the `Performance` entity of the show with which the booking is validated, the contact e-mail of the customer, and a cancellation code provided to the ticket booker to allow them to cancel a booking.

Utility classes in TicketMonster

TicketMonster provides a number of helper classes providing low-level utilities for the application; these classes are located in the `org.jboss.jdf.example.Ticket Monster.util` package. The helper classes contained in the package are as follows:

- `Base64.java`: This is an improved implementation class to encode and decode to and from BASE64 in full accordance with RFC 2045.

- `*CacheProducer.java`: This is the producer for the EmbeddedCacheManager instance used by the application. It defines the default configuration for caches.

- `CircularBuffer.java`: This implements a circular buffer to store the log messages generated by the Bot Service.

- `*DataDir.java`: This is an annotation to inject a `datadir` parameter.

- `ForwardingMap.java`: A map that forwards all its method calls another map.

- `MultivaluedHashMap.java`: A hash table-based implementation of the `MultivaluedMap` interface. This implementation provides all of the optional map operations.

- `Reflections.java`: These are utilities relating to the Java reflection.

- `Resources.java`: This class uses CDI to alias Java EE resources, such as the persistence context, to CDI beans.

 Classes `DataDir.java` and `CacheProducer.java` are not available in the first version (2.0.9.Final) presented in this chapter. `CacheProducer.java` was introduced in the version 2.1.0.Final and `DataDir.java` in the version 2.1.2.Final.

The service layer of TicketMonster

Now that we have defined our domain model and helper classes, we can move on to discuss how the service layer is constructed. The service layer is implemented by a number of classes, each with different responsibilities, and it allows the user to perform the following tasks:

- Manage venues
- Manage events
- Manage shows
- Manage media items
- Manage cart (add or remove tickets or create bookings)
- Manage seat allocation
- Monitor booking

Some of the services are intended to be consumed within the business layer of the application, while others provide an external interface as JAX-RS services.

The majority of services in the application are the JAX-RS web services. They are a critical part of the design, because they are used to provide communication with the HTML5 view layer. The JAX-RS services used in the main interface range from simple CRUD to processing bookings and media items, the REST services are located in the package `org.jboss.jdf.example.TicketMonster.rest`.

The services that are intended to be consumed within the business layer of the application are located in the `org.jboss.jdf.example.TicketMonster.service` package.

The services are consumed by various other layers of the application:

- The media management and ticket allocation services encapsulate complex functionality, which in turn is exposed externally by RESTful services that wrap them
- RESTful services are mainly used for consumption by the HTML5 view layer and the mobile application
- The ticket availability service is used by the Errai-based view layer

Since the business services of our application are exposed through the RESTful endpoint, the main interface should be flexible enough to be used with both desktop and mobile clients.

The next figure shows an example of how the web application and the web service `BookingService` interact. In the figure, notice that both `BookingService` and `SeatAllocationService` use the `EntityManager` entity, first to save the current state of a booking bean in the database and lastly, to lock the entity object `SeatAllocation` explicitly using the `lock()` method:

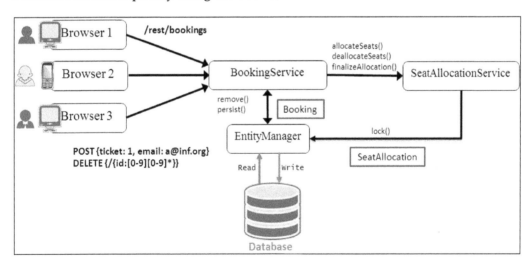

The main interface is built using HTML5, CSS, and JavaScript, and everything is retrieved within a single page load. Rather than refreshing the page every time, the user changes a view, the content of the page will be redrawn by manipulating the DOM in JavaScript. The application uses the REST services via AJAX calls to communicate and retrieve data from the server.

Because this is a moderately complex example, which involves multiple views and different types of data, TicketMonster uses a client-side MVC framework called Backbone.js to structure the application, which provides many advantages, such as:

- Routing support within the single page application
- Event-driven interaction between views and data
- Simplified CRUD invocations on RESTful services

The following figure presents Backbone architecture:

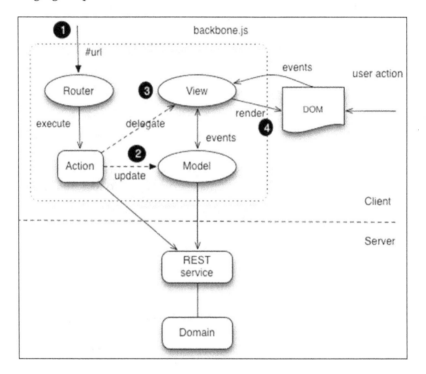

Backbone.js is a library that gives structure to web applications by providing models, collections, and views, all hooked up together with custom events. It connects your application to your backend via a RESTful JSON interface, and can automatically fetch and save data. The basic terminology about Backbone is the following:

- **Backbone Models**: These contain data for an application, as well as the logic around this data.

- **Backbone Views**: These are logical representations of user interface elements that can interact with data component, they don't contain the HTML markup for your application; they contain the logic behind the presentation of the model's data to the user.

- **Backbone Collections**: These are ordered sets of models. They can handle events that are fired as a result of a change to an individual member and can perform CRUD operations for syncing contents against RESTful services.

- **Backbone Events**: These are a basic inversion of control. Instead of having one function call another by name, the second function is registered as a handler to be called when a specific event occurs.

Scaling TicketMonster

After the release of the first version of TicketMonster, it was based on a traditional architecture. Let's imagine, that our application has grown enough to force changes in the current architecture. Due to the great growth of transactions in our system, TicketMonster starts decreasing the performance of the system.

In order to keep running TicketMonster without losing quality of service, we will need an environment that meets the following requirements:

- **High Concurrency**: During high season, weekends, special events, or show, tickets can be sold out in 5 minutes

- **High Volume**: Depending of the venue and show, we can have thousands of tickets

- **Location Awareness**: Shows can take place all around the world, and we'd like the data to be available in the same region as where the show will be taking place (such as concerts in London and New York)

Furthermore, with the imminent success of TicketMonster, our customers are asking us to add new features such as the ability to reserve seats temporarily.

Clustered Web servers versus stateful session

As we have seen in *Chapter 2, Barriers to Scaling Data*, system requirements describe the quality of service that a deployed system must provide to meet the business requirements that have been determined by business analysis.

In order to address the requirements above, we can scale the application up or down by simply adding new component instances as required, such as a load balancer to route each request to the application instance with the smallest load.

The distribution of requests over a number of servers imposes new processing demands to guarantee the consistency of information among them.

In our case, we would like to add the ability for users to reserve seats temporarily. To implement such functionality, we have to take into consideration that the service has to actually enquire and ensure availability.

For example, if we have different users that want to book a seat in the same section, we really need to ensure that they have exclusive access in order to make sure that they don't get the same ticket or access the same information.

Under these circumstances, we may have an extra overhead to ensure data consistency. Our application may grow to a point where adding servers may, in fact, make overall performance even worse.

We have to manage the distribution of requests in the presence of a Session State. Just to remember, since HTTP is a stateless protocol, each subsequent request to a website is treated as new by the web server. In a distributed architecture with multiple servers, each request for a page is independent of all others and may be directed to any host in a distributed server cluster.

To allow our users to temporarily reserve a seat, our application needs to keep all its state while waiting for a user to confirm the booking. So, if we want to provide high availability, we have to ask ourselves where to store the session state.

Martin Fowler, in his celebrated book *Patterns of Enterprise Application Architecture, Pearson*, talks about three patterns to store session state, they are Client Session State, Server Session State, and Database Session State, which are described as follows:

- **Client Session State**: Session data is stored on the client side. This can be done in some different ways; you can use HTTP cookies to store the session data, to encode data in an URL, to append some extra data on the end of each URL (URL Rewriting) or to serialize the data into hidden fields on a Web form.

- **Server Session State**: Session data is stored on the server in a serialized form. The developer just enables server sessions and creates a session for each user to store all the transient data. The data is typically stored in the server memory and is looked up on each web request via a session key.

  In Java, they are some well known implementations, such as Stateful Session Beans and Servlet Sessions (HttpSession).

- **Database Session State**: This is also a server-side storage, the session state is stored in a relational database and the server retrieves session information from the database.

The following table describes the advantages and disadvantages of each approach:

Pattern	Advantage	Disadvantages
Client Session State	This is resistant to server failures.	• **Performance**: View state is stored in client side (cookies); storing large values implies that for every request you have to transfer all the data the server uses for it • **Security**: The danger in keeping the user data in cookies is that sensitive information is automatically vulnerable to tampering
Server Session State	This is fast and easy to implement, given available support.	• **Overhead**: This requires additional configuration, in the case you want to support failover or an efficient clustering • **Cluster**: Not trivial to manage a session object in a cluster environment
Database Session State	With many servers, it's easier to keep the data consistence.	• Integrity: Difficult to ensure isolation between sessions • Overhead: Need to transform data • Exception Handling: Need to handle exceptions related to sessions

Which pattern to use?

Before choosing an option, we must understand the relationship between the various entities involved and the architecture of the server side as a whole.

Ticket Monster has basically two types of data:

- Master data
- Operational data

Master data comprises low concurrency information that changes infrequently, which is not affected by the services provided by Ticket Monster such as Events, Venues, Shows, and Performances.

Operational data, on the other hand, is the dynamic data that changes frequently, is highly concurrent, and contains all the information that is affected by the operations performed while providing services, such as seat allocation.

The identification of static and dynamic data is crucial for the distribution of the application. While static data can be easily replicated among the elements of a server cluster, each dynamic piece of data must be properly identified and any access to it must be properly controlled to avoid inconsistencies.

In the Ticket Monster application, we are going to discard the first option Client Session State, because, as we said before, in order to implement the ability for users to temporary reserve seats, we have to control the data in session. All that remains now are the other two options, Server Session State and Database Session State.

To implement the pattern Server Session State, we have to make use of web sessions to store orders. There are two kinds of sessions handled by a server cluster: sticky, and replicated sessions:

- Sticky sessions (also known as session affinity) enable the load balancer to route all requests that belongs to the same user's session to a specific application instance. The user state data will live on the server that owns that information during the whole session's life. Each cluster member doesn't have any knowledge of other members' session.

- Replicated sessions, as the name states, the session state is replicated to all of the other servers in the cluster whenever the session is modified.

The issue with the Sticky sessions comes in when the load balancer is forced to shift users to a different server. When that happens, all of the user's session data is lost. The effects of this will vary by application and what the user is doing at the time, but if session-failover is not implemented and the server goes offline, all users will lose their session.

Session-failover is a concept used in a high availability cluster where sessions are not lost when an application server goes offline, or is otherwise unreachable.

Regarding replicated sessions, the problem comes in the replication process, because it involves copying the session data over to all the servers in the cluster, which directly impacts the performance. The more servers you have in the cluster, the more overheads you will have. So, where should we store temporary data?

The third pattern Database Session State is similar to the Server Session State, the only difference being that it includes a database to persist the temporary data.

In our current architecture, we are exclusively using a database. To implement temporary reserve seats using this pattern, we have to consider how it would impact the performance of the application for the following reasons:

- Before making a temporary reservation, as a user, I would want to know how many seats are available. So in order to ensure availability, our code will have to generate multiple round trips to the database.

- The application will have exclusive access to the data of seats available; we really need to ensure that they have exclusive access, to make sure users don't get the same ticket or access the same information. To do that, we need a mechanism of pessimistic locking to ensure thread safety, which will ensure no one else will have access to a particular record.

As a consequence, distributed transactions (XA) with a pessimistic locking strategy configured in a highly concurrent application, will lead to multiple round trips to the database, will surely slow the data access, which will cause a number of scalability problems, and lead to an exponential increase in the network traffic and latency as well. In *Chapter 7, Understanding Transactions and Concurrency*, we will see in detail how it works. We will also outline completely some of the principal concepts of transactions.

Adding Infinispan to Ticket Monster

So, in front of these new requirements, we will introduce Infinispan for the new architecture, thus addressing the preceding concerns as follows:

- **High concurrency**: This enables in-memory data access and optimized locking

- **High volume**: The application can handle increasingly large data amounts by adding new data grid nodes

- **Location awareness**: A multi-node data grid can be configured so that data is stored on specific nodes. There are two ways to configure it, which are as follows:

  ° We have seen in *Chapter 4, Infinispan Topologies* and *Chapter 5, Data Access Patterns*, that there are two ways in which you can interact with Infinispan. One is in the embedded mode, where you start an Infinispan instance within your JVM.

  ° The other is the client/server mode, where you start a remote Infinispan instance and connect to it using a client connector.

For questions of simplicity and clarity, we will use the library access pattern, as in this particular case, we can benefit from the simpler setup. In any case, switching from one mode to the other is non-intrusive, the only major difference being the infrastructure setup.

The next figure shows an improved architecture that uses Infinispan:

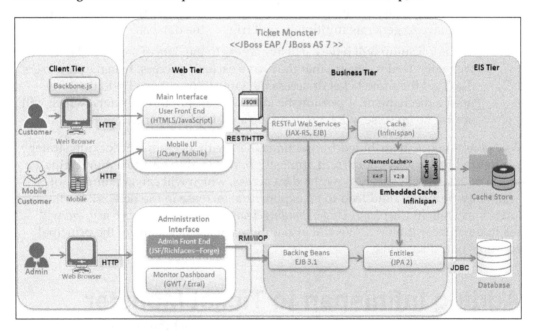

The version of Ticket Monster with Datagrid Support presented in this book is the version 2.1.3.Final, which can be found at `https://github.com/jboss-jdf/ticket-monster/archive/2.1.3.Final.zip`.

We will begin by adding the JBoss Developer Framework Bill of Materials (BOM) that describes the correct version for the Infinispan artifacts.

In order to use the BOM to add Java EE 6 stack to your application, you need to import it into to your dependency management. The code for dependency is as follows:

```
<project>
  <dependencyManagement>
    <dependencies>
      <dependency>
        <groupId>org.jboss.bom</groupId>
        <artifactId>jboss-javaee-6.0-with-tools</artifactId>
        <version>${jboss.bom.version}</version>
        <type>pom</type>
        <scope>import</scope>
      </dependency>
    </dependencies>
  </dependencyManagement>
</project>
```

Note that the `jboss-javaee-6.0-with-tools` stack also includes deployment and test tooling (example, Arquillian).

Next, we will include the infinispan-core library in the project:

```
<project>
  <dependencies>
    <dependency>
      <groupId>org.infinispan</groupId>
      <artifactId>infinispan-core</artifactId>
    </dependency>
  </dependencies>
</project>
```

Configuring the infrastructure

The first thing we have to do is set up the necessary infrastructure to interact with an Infinispan instance. So, to start, we will create a CDI producer method and a CDI disposer method for the Infinispan cache manager, where we define the global cache configuration and set up default options for the caches used in the application.

 CDI provides the @Produce annotation, which can be applied on methods or fields to specify a resource that can be injected.

Also, a CDI provides the @Disposes annotation, a mechanism that we can use on resources returned by a producer, which we might need to clean up.

The cache manager is unique for the application and to the data grid node, so we will create it as an application scoped bean. This new class will be located in the package `org.jboss.jdf.example.TicketMonster.util`. The code for this is as follows:

```
@ApplicationScoped
public class CacheProducer {
  @Inject @DataDir
  private String dataDir;
  @Produces
  @ApplicationScoped
  public EmbeddedCacheManager getCacheContainer() {
    GlobalConfiguration glob = new GlobalConfigurationBuilder()
    .nonClusteredDefault()
    .globalJmxStatistics().enable()
    .build();//Builds  the GlobalConfiguration object
      Configuration loc = new ConfigurationBuilder()
        .jmxStatistics().enable()
        .clustering().cacheMode(CacheMode.LOCAL)
        .transaction()
        .transactionMode(TransactionMode.TRANSACTIONAL)
        .transactionManagerLookup(new
          GenericTransactionManagerLookup())
        .lockingMode(LockingMode.PESSIMISTIC)
        .locking()
        .isolationLevel(IsolationLevel.REPEATABLE_READ)
        .eviction()
        .maxEntries(4)
        .strategy(EvictionStrategy.LIRS)
        .loaders()
        .passivation(false)
        .addFileCacheStore()
```

```
            .location(dataDir + File.separator +
              "Ticket Monster-CacheStore")     .purgeOnStartup(true)
            .build();
            return new DefaultCacheManager(glob, loc, true);
    }

    public void cleanUp(@Disposes EmbeddedCacheManager manager) {
        manager.stop();
    }
}
```

The CacheProducer class defines the default configuration for caches and we have to implement two methods to set up the basic Infinispan infrastructure. They are:

- **getCacheContainer()**: This is the method that encapsulates the information about how to connect to the Infinispan instance, which configures, builds, and returns an EmbeddedCache.

- **cleanUp()**:This is the method that stops the cache and clears all cache in-memory state.

The getCacheContainer() method uses the Infinispan's GlobalConfigurationBuilder class to build a default constructed GlobalConfiguration, calling the nonClusteredDefault() method to get you a configuration preconfigured for use in the LOCAL mode and globalJmxStatistics().enable() method to enable the JMS statistics.

Now, we have a fully configured default GlobalConfiguration to use. Next, using the same strategy, it starts by creating a ConfigurationBuilder class to build a configuration, enabling JMX Statistics, setting the cache mode to local (data is not replicated), setting up the cache to work in a transactional mode by using pessimistic locking.

Enabling eviction by limiting the maximum number of cache entries to four and setting the eviction strategy to LIRS. And next, we are disabling the passivation and adding a FileCacheStore class that is purged on startup.

And finally, build the DefaultCacheManager class by simply passing in the objects we just created. Now, we can inject the cache manager instance in various services that use the data grid, which will use it in turn to gain access to application cache.

Using caches for seat reservations

First, we are going to change the existing implementation of the
SeatAllocationService class to use the Infinispan data grid. Rather than
storing the seat allocations in a database, we will store them as data grid entries.

To introduce Infinispan in our current architecture, it will require some changes to
our existing classes.

For the Ticket Monster version with a database implementation, we are using the
properties of the SectionAllocation class to identify the entity that corresponds
to a given Section and Performance.

But to implement a new version using Infinispan, we will need to create a similar
class named SectionAllocationKey, that we are going to use as the key for the
cache. And we need to make sure that the equals() and hashCode() methods
are implemented correctly, as shown in the following code:

```java
public class SectionAllocationKey implements Serializable {
   private final Section section;
   private final Performance performance;
   private SectionAllocationKey(Section section, Performance
performance) {
      this.section = section;
      this.performance = performance;
   }

   public static SectionAllocationKey of (Section section, Performance
performance) {
      return new SectionAllocationKey(section, performance);
   }


   public Section getSection() {
      return section;
   }

   public Performance getPerformance() {
      return performance;
   }

   @Override
   public boolean equals(Object o) {
      if (this == o) return true;
         if (o == null || getClass() != o.getClass()) return false;

         SectionAllocationKey that = (SectionAllocationKey) o;
```

```
      if (performance != null ?
        !performance.equals(that.performance) :
          that.performance != null) return false;
          if (section != null ? !section.equals(that.section) :
            that.section != null) return false;

        return true;
    }

  @Override
  public int hashCode() {
    int result = section != null ? section.hashCode() : 0;
    result = 31 * result + (performance != null ?
      performance.hashCode() : 0);
    return result;
  }
}
```

Now, we can proceed with modifying the SeatAllocationService class. Since we are not persisting seat allocations in the database, we will remove the EntityManager reference and use a cache that has been acquired from the cache manager. We inject the cache manager instance produced previously and create a SeatAllocation specific cache in the constructor. The code for constructor is as follows:

```
public class SeatAllocationService {
public static final String ALLOCATIONS = "TICKET
  MONSTER_ALLOCATIONS";

private Cache<SectionAllocationKey, SectionAllocation> cache;

@Inject
public SeatAllocationService(EmbeddedCacheManager manager) {
  Configuration allocation = new ConfigurationBuilder()
  .transaction().transactionMode(TransactionMode.TRANSACTIONAL)
  .transactionManagerLookup(new JBossTransactionManagerLookup())
  .lockingMode(LockingMode.PESSIMISTIC)
  .loaders().addFileCacheStore().purgeOnStartup(true)
  .build();
  manager.defineConfiguration(ALLOCATIONS, allocation);
  this.cache = manager.getCache(ALLOCATIONS);
}

  public AllocatedSeats allocateSeats(Section section,
    Performance performance, int seatCount, boolean contiguous) {
    SectionAllocationKey sectionAllocationKey =
      SectionAllocationKey.of(section, performance);
    SectionAllocation allocation =
      getSectionAllocation(sectionAllocationKey);
    ArrayList<Seat> seats = allocation.allocateSeats(seatCount,
      contiguous);
```

```
    cache.replace(sectionAllocationKey, allocation);
    return new AllocatedSeats(allocation, seats);
}

public void deallocateSeats(Section section, Performance
  performance, List<Seat> seats) {
  SectionAllocationKey sectionAllocationKey =
    SectionAllocationKey.of(section, performance);
  SectionAllocation sectionAllocation =
    getSectionAllocation(sectionAllocationKey);
  for (Seat seat : seats) {
    if (!seat.getSection().equals(section)) {
      throw new SeatAllocationException("All seats must be in
        the same section!");
    }
  sectionAllocation.deallocate(seat);
  }
  cache.replace(sectionAllocationKey, sectionAllocation);
}

public void finalizeAllocation(AllocatedSeats allocatedSeats) {
  allocatedSeats.markOccupied();
}

public void finalizeAllocation(Performance performance,
  List<Seat> allocatedSeats) {
  SectionAllocation sectionAllocation = cache.get(
  SectionAllocationKey.of(allocatedSeats.get(0).getSection(),
    performance));
  sectionAllocation.markOccupied(allocatedSeats);
}
private SectionAllocation
  getSectionAllocation(SectionAllocationKey
    sectionAllocationKey) {
  SectionAllocation newAllocation = new
    SectionAllocation(sectionAllocationKey.getPerformance(),
      sectionAllocationKey.getSection());
  SectionAllocation sectionAllocation =
    cache.putIfAbsent(sectionAllocationKey,
      newAllocation);
  cache.getAdvancedCache().lock(sectionAllocationKey);
  return sectionAllocation ==
    null?newAllocation:sectionAllocation;
  }
}
```

As you can see, both the `deallocateSeats` and `allocateSeats` methods calls the
`replace` method in the `Cache` class. The method replaces the entry for a key only
if it is currently mapped to some value.

The getSectionAllocation() method retrieves a SectionAllocation instance for a given Performance and Section that is embedded in the SectionAllocationKey class. It executes the putIfAbsent method, which ensures that the specified key is not already associated with a value, and associates it with the given value.

On the next line, we call the getAdvancedCache() operation, which retrieves an instance of AdvancedCache, an advanced interface that exposes additional methods not available on Cache, to perform a lock in a given key across the cache nodes in our data grid in the end.

Implementing shopping carts

Once we have stored our allocation status in the data grid, we can move on to implementing a cart system for TicketMonster. Rather than composing the orders on the client and sending the entire order as a single request, users will be able to add and remove seats from their orders while they're shopping.

We will store the carts in the data grid, thus ensuring that they're accessible across the cluster, without the complications of using a web session.

The following diagram illustrates how the different classes interact within the new structure and the data grid:

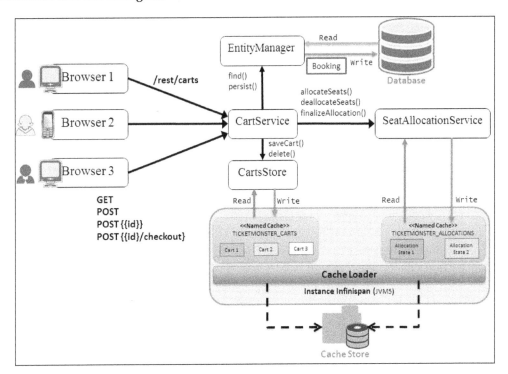

In the diagram, you can see that in this architecture, we are using two named caches, TICKET MONSTER_CART to store Cart objects and TICKET MONSTER_ALLOCATIONS to store SeatAllocation objects, both of them in separate named caches.

Let's start the implementation by creating the Cart class as follows:

```
public class Cart implements Serializable {

  private String id;
  private Performance performance;
  private ArrayList<SeatAllocation> seatAllocations = new
    ArrayList<SeatAllocation>();

  private Cart() {
  }

  private Cart(String id) {
    this.id = id;
  }

  public static Cart initialize() {
    return new Cart(UUID.randomUUID().toString());
  }

  public String getId() {
    return id;
  }

  public Performance getPerformance() {
    return performance;
  }

  public void setPerformance(Performance performance) {
    this.performance = performance;
  }

  public ArrayList<SeatAllocation> getSeatAllocations() {
    return seatAllocations;
  }
}
```

A `Cart` object contains a list of `SeatAllocation` classes for the corresponding seats of a particular `TicketRequest` class (which represents a number of seats requested for a particular performance), as shown in the following code:

```
public class SeatAllocation {

    private TicketRequest ticketRequest;
    private ArrayList<Seat> allocatedSeats;

    public SeatAllocation(TicketRequest ticketRequest, ArrayList<Seat>
allocatedSeats) {
        this.ticketRequest = ticketRequest;
        this.allocatedSeats = allocatedSeats;
    }

    public TicketRequest getTicketRequest() {
        return ticketRequest;
    }

    public ArrayList<Seat> getAllocatedSeats() {
        return allocatedSeats;
    }
}
```

We use this structure so that we can easily add or update seats to the cart when the client issues a new request.

We will update the `SectionAllocation` class, introducing an expiration time for each allocated seat. With this implementation, seats can have three different states:

- **Free**: The seat has not been allocated
- **Allocated permanently**: The seat has been sold and remains allocated until the ticket is canceled
- **Allocated temporarily**: The seat is allocated, but can be re-allocated after a specific time

So, when a cart expires and is removed from the cache, the seats it held become available again. With these changes, the updated implementation of the `SectionAllocation` class will be as follows:

```
@Entity
@Table(uniqueConstraints = @UniqueConstraint(columnNames = {
    "performance_id", "section_id" }))
public class SectionAllocation implements Serializable {
```

```
public static final int EXPIRATION_TIME = 60 * 1000;

@Id
@GeneratedValue(strategy = IDENTITY)
private Long id;

@SuppressWarnings("unused")
@Version
private long version;

@ManyToOne
NotNull
private Performance performance;

@ManyToOne
@NotNull
private Section section;

@Lob
private long allocated[][];

private int occupiedCount = 0;

public SectionAllocation() {
}

public SectionAllocation(Performance performance, Section
  section) {
  this.performance = performance;
  this.section = section;
  this.allocated = new long[section.getNumberOfRows()]
    [section.getRowCapacity()];
  for (long[] seatStates : allocated) {
    Arrays.fill(seatStates, 0L);
  }
}

@PostLoad
void initialize() {
  if (this.allocated == null) {
    this.allocated = new
      long[this.section.getNumberOfRows()]
        [this.section.getRowCapacity()];
    for (long[] seatStates : allocated) {
```

```
            Arrays.fill(seatStates, 01);
        }
    }
}

public boolean isAllocated(Seat s) {
    return allocated[s.getRowNumber() - 1][s.getNumber() - 1] !=
      0;
}

public ArrayList<Seat> allocateSeats(int seatCount, boolean
contiguous) {
    ArrayList<Seat> seats = new ArrayList<Seat>();

    for (int rowCounter = 0; rowCounter <
      section.getNumberOfRows(); rowCounter++) {
      if (contiguous) {
        int startSeat = findFreeGapStart(rowCounter, 0,
          seatCount);
        if (startSeat >= 0) {
          for (int i = 1; i <= seatCount; i++) {
            seats.add(new Seat(section, rowCounter + 1, startSeat
              + i));
          }
          break;
        }
      } else {
        int startSeat = findFreeGapStart(rowCounter, 0, 1);
        if (startSeat >= 0) {
          do {
            seats.add(new Seat(section, rowCounter + 1,
              startSeat + 1));
            startSeat = findFreeGapStart(rowCounter, startSeat,
              1);
            } while (startSeat >= 0 && seats.size() < seatCount);
          if (seats.size() == seatCount) {
          break;
          }
        }
      }
    }

    if (seats.size() == seatCount) {
      for (Seat seat : seats) {
```

```
          allocate(seat.getRowNumber() - 1, seat.getNumber() - 1, 1,
            expirationTimestamp());
        }
        return seats;
      } else {
        return new ArrayList<Seat>(0);
      }
    }

    public void markOccupied(List<Seat> seats) {
      for (Seat seat : seats) {
        allocate(seat.getRowNumber() - 1, seat.getNumber() - 1, 1, -
          1);
      }
    }

    private int findFreeGapStart(int row, int startSeat, int size) {

      long[] occupied = allocated[row];
      int candidateStart = -1;

      for (int i = startSeat; i < occupied.length; i++) {
        long currentTimestamp = System.currentTimeMillis();
        if (occupied[i] >= 0 && currentTimestamp > occupied[i]) {
          if (candidateStart == -1) {
            andidateStart = i;
          }
          if ((size == (i - candidateStart + 1))) {
            return candidateStart;
          }
        } else {
candidateStart = -1;
        }
      }
      return -1;
    }

  private void allocate(int row, int start, int size, long
    finalState)
      throws SeatAllocationException {
      long[] occupied = allocated[row];
      if (size <= 0) {
        throw new SeatAllocationException("Number of seats
          must be greater than zero");
      }
```

```
    if (start < 0 || start >= occupied.length) {
      throw new SeatAllocationException("Seat number must be
        betwen 1 and " + occupied.length);
    }
    if ((start + size) > occupied.length) {
      throw new SeatAllocationException("Cannot allocate
        seats above row capacity");
    }

    for (int i = start; i < (start + size); i++) {
      occupied[i] = finalState;
      occupiedCount++;
    }
  }

  public void deallocate(Seat seat) {
    if (!isAllocated(seat)) {
      throw new SeatAllocationException("Trying to deallocate
        an unallocated seat!");
    }
    this.allocated[seat.getRowNumber() - 1][seat.getNumber() - 1]
      = 0;
    occupiedCount--;
  }

  public int getOccupiedCount() {
    return occupiedCount;
  }

  public Performance getPerformance() {
    return performance;
  }

  public Section getSection() {
    return section;
  }

  public Long getId() {
    return id;
  }

  private long expirationTimestamp() {
    return System.currentTimeMillis() + EXPIRATION_TIME;
  }
}
```

Next, let's look at how to implement a cart store service for cart CRUD operations. Since users may open as many carts as they want, but not complete the purchase, we will store them as temporary entries with an expiration time, leaving the job of removing them automatically to the data grid middleware itself. Thus, you don't have to worry about cleaning up your data. The code for removing the temporary cart is as follows:

```java
public class CartStore {

    public static final String CARTS_CACHE =
        "TICKETMONSTER_CARTS";

    private final Cache<String, Cart> cartsCache;

    @Inject
    public CartStore(EmbeddedCacheManager manager) {
        this.cartsCache = manager.getCache(CARTS_CACHE);
    }

    public Cart getCart(String cartId) {
        return this.cartsCache.get(cartId);
    }

    public void saveCart(Cart cart) {
        this.cartsCache.put(cart.getId(), cart, 10, TimeUnit.MINUTES);
    }

    public void delete(Cart cart) {
        this.cartsCache.remove(cart.getId());
    }
}
```

Now, we can go on and implement the RESTful service for managing carts.

First, we will implement the CRUD operations—adding and reading carts, as a thin layer on top of the CartStore class. Because cart data is not tied to a web session, users can create as many carts as they want without having to worry about cleaning up the web session. Moreover, the web component of the application has a stateless architecture, which means that it can scale elastically across multiple machines—the responsibility of distributing data across nodes falls to the data grid itself.

To begin, we are going to create four operations, which are as follows:

- `openCart`: This method allows opening a cart by posting a simple JSON document that contains the reference to an existing performance to `http://localhost:8080/ticket-monster/rest/carts`.

- `getCart`: This method allows accessing the cart contents from a URL of the `http://localhost:8080/ticket-monster/rest/carts/{id}` form using the `GET` method. Thus, the carts themselves become web resources.

- `addTicketRequest`: This method adds the ability of adding or removing seats from a cart. This will be done as an additional RESTful endpoint, that allows user to post ticket (or seat) requests to an existing cart, at the `http://localhost:8080/ticket-monster/rest/carts/{id}` URL. Whenever such a `POST` request is received, the `CartService` class will delegate to the `SeatAllocationService` class, to adjust the current allocation, returning the cart contents (including the temporarily assigned seats) at the end.

- `createBookingFromCart`: At the end, when the user has finished reserving seats, they must complete the purchase, at the `http://localhost:8080/ticket-monster/rest/carts/{id}/checkout` URL. Posting the final purchase data (such as e-mail, and in the future, payment information) will trigger the checkout process, ticket allocation, and making the seat reservations permanent.

In true RESTful fashion, if the cart cannot be found, a `Resource Not Found` error will be thrown by the server.

Finally, with the proposed methods, let's look at the implementation of the `CartService` class:

```
@Path("/carts")
@Stateless
public class CartService {

    public static final String CARTS_CACHE = "CARTS";

    @Inject
    private CartStore cartStore;

    @Inject
    private EntityManager entityManager;

    @Inject
    private BookingService bookingService;
```

```
@Inject
private SeatAllocationService seatAllocationService;

@Inject @Created
private javax.enterprise.event.Event<Booking> newBookingEvent;


@POST
public Cart openCart(Map<String, String> data) {
  Cart cart = Cart.initialize();
  cart.setPerformance(entityManager.find(Performance.class,
    Long.parseLong(data.get("performance"))));
  cartStore.saveCart(cart);
  return cart;
}

@GET
@Path("/{id}")
public Cart getCart(String id) {
  return cartStore.getCart(id);
}

@POST
@Path("/{id}")
@Consumes(MediaType.APPLICATION_JSON)
public Cart addTicketRequest(@PathParam("id") String id,
  TicketReservationRequest... ticketRequests){
  Cart cart = cartStore.getCart(id);
  for (TicketReservationRequest ticketRequest : ticketRequests)
    {
      TicketPrice ticketPrice =
        entityManager.find(TicketPrice.class,
          ticketRequest.getTicketPrice());
      Iterator<SeatAllocation> iterator =
        cart.getSeatAllocations().iterator();
      while (iterator.hasNext()) {
        SeatAllocation seatAllocation = iterator.next();
          if
            (seatAllocation.getTicketRequest().getTicketPrice()
              .getId().equals(ticketRequest.getTicketPrice())) {
                seatAllocationService.deallocateSeats(ticketPrice.
getSection(),
                  cart.getPerformance(),
                    seatAllocation.getAllocatedSeats());
```

```
                              ticketRequest.setQuantity(ticketRequest.
getQuantity() +
                        seatAllocation.getTicketRequest().
getQuantity());
                      iterator.remove();
                }
            }
            if (ticketRequest.getQuantity() > 0 ) {
              AllocatedSeats allocatedSeats =

seatAllocationService.allocateSeats(ticketPrice.getSection(),
                  cart.getPerformance(),
                    ticketRequest.getQuantity(), true);
              cart.getSeatAllocations().add(new
                SeatAllocation(new TicketRequest(ticketPrice,
                  ticketRequest.getQuantity()),
                    allocatedSeats.getSeats()));
            }
        }
        return cart;
    }

    @SuppressWarnings("unchecked")
    @POST
    @Consumes(MediaType.APPLICATION_JSON)
    @Path("/{id}/checkout")
    public Response createBookingFromCart(@PathParam("id") String
      cartId, Map<String, String> data) {
      try {
        Cart cart = cartStore.getCart(cartId);
        Booking booking = new Booking();
        Booking.setContactEmail(data.get("email"));
        booking.setPerformance(cart.getPerformance());
        booking.setCancellationCode("abc");

        for (SeatAllocation seatAllocation :
          cart.getSeatAllocations()) {
          for (Seat seat : seatAllocation.getAllocatedSeats()) {
            TicketPrice ticketPrice =
              seatAllocation.getTicketRequest().getTicketPrice();
            booking.getTickets().add(new Ticket(seat,
              ticketPrice.getTicketCategory(),
                ticketPrice.getPrice()));
          }
```

```
                    seatAllocationService.finalizeAllocation(cart.
getPerformance(),
                    seatAllocation.getAllocatedSeats());
        }

        booking.setCancellationCode("abc");
        entityManager.persist(booking);
        cartStore.delete(cart);
        newBookingEvent.fire(booking);
        return
          Response.ok().entity(booking).type
            (MediaType.APPLICATION_JSON_TYPE).build();

    } catch (ConstraintViolationException e) {
      Map<String, Object> errors = new HashMap<String,
        Object>();
      List<String> errorMessages = new ArrayList<String>();
      for (ConstraintViolation<?> constraintViolation :
        e.getConstraintViolations()) {
        errorMessages.add(constraintViolation.getMessage());
        }
      errors.put("errors", errorMessages);
      throw new
        RestServiceException(Response.status
          (Response.Status.BAD_REQUEST).entity(errors).build());
    } catch (Exception e) {
      Map<String, Object> errors = new HashMap<String,
        Object>();
      errors.put("errors",
        Collections.singletonList(e.getMessage()));
      throw new
        RestServiceException(Response.status
          (Response.Status.BAD_REQUEST).entity(errors).build());
    }
  }
}
```

All that remains now is to modify the client side of the application to adapt the changes in the web service structure. During the ticket booking process, as tickets are added and removed from the cart, the CreateBookingView class will invoke the RESTful endpoints to allocate seats and will display the outcome to the user in updated TicketSummaryView. You will have to make changes in the create-booking.js and router.js JavaScript code.

Next, we need to update a few templates to account for the changes made to the code, such as displaying the seats in the ticket summary view; and finally, we have to update both the booking details' **view template** and the booking confirmation page.

Summary

In this chapter, you learned and analyzed the application Ticket Monster on two different application architectures and how to install the application locally.

We discussed and presented various types of classes and how they are separated in different layers. We have seen in detail the use cases for users and the administration profile, and how to use JBoss Forge to create the administration UI.

Then we moved on to discuss architecture and design in two different scenarios, a traditional architecture with a database approach, and another architecture contemplating Infinispan.

After that, we presented new requirements related to performance, where we discussed different solutions to scale the Ticket Monster application.

We discussed the issues in distributed web application, three patterns to store session state, and how to apply them to solve these issues.

Finally, we presented how to implement Infinispan involving the current architecture.

In the next chapter, you will learn in detail how transactions work and how they are managed and used with Infinispan.

7
Understanding Transactions and Concurrency

In the previous chapter, we introduced the Ticket Monster application to learn about JBoss Developer Framework and JBoss-related technology. We added some requirements in order to analyze how Infinispan can be used to improve scalability.

In this chapter, we will talk about transactions and how you can work with transactions with Infinispan. We'll discuss the following topics:

- Transaction fundamentals
- Java Transaction API
- Transaction models
- Locking and concurrency control

Designing your cache application and the transaction configuration that connects your application to a data store for optimal performance isn't easy. This chapter will help you identify the best concurrency model and help you determine how to better manage your transactions.

To begin with, we are going to be cover the basic concepts required to understand how Infinispan is structured and how applications can use it.

Transaction fundamentals

Before we start to learn how Infinispan deals with transactions, let's learn the basics about transactions in order to extract the best from this feature.

By definition, a transaction allows you to set the boundaries of a user-defined series of logically related read or write operations (`get()` or `put()`). All changes brought by a write operation (update, remove, or add an entry in the cache) are either undone or made permanent at the same time.

The processing of these transactions is divided into individual, atomic operations and might help you isolate one transaction from another transaction in a multiuser application. Each transaction at the end must complete the processing with success or failure as a complete unit, and a transaction should not complete the processing in an intermediate state.

To execute all your data grid operations inside a transaction, you have to mark the boundaries of that transaction. You must start the transaction and at some point commit the changes. Generally, you conclude a transaction with the **COMMIT** or **ROLLBACK** statements, to ensure that all or none of your changes are stored in the grid.

The commit processes writes the data into the cache and makes it visible to other users. Rolling back discards any changes that have been made to any cache entry since the beginning of the current transaction.

Let's exemplify this concept with the classical example of a bank transfer operation, in which a customer performs a transfer of $50,000 between accounts. The bank application needs to perform an operation that consists of three separate but related actions, as follows:

1. Debit the source account by the required amount of $50,000.
2. Credit the target account by the required amount of $50,000.
3. Write a log entry recording the transfer.

When viewed as three separate operations, it's not difficult to imagine a disaster. These operations should be performed as a unit. Imagine that for some reason the debit operation succeeds, and the bank's central server fails just after the debit operation, before the credit operation completes. This kind of error can cause a great deal of damage to the bank's image.

It is important to understand that transactions in Infinispan are not like transactions on a relational database product. Infinispan is an in-memory database, it utilizes volatile storage for in-memory data, which means that if the application goes down all the data cached in the memory is lost.

It's the responsibility of the cache to recreate data upon startup, either from backup nodes or from other persistent storage systems, if you have a cache loader/store configured.

Another important responsibility of the data grid is to protect your information and to guarantee that the data between different grid nodes must remain consistent, which is part of the ACID criteria commonly applied to transactional database management systems.

In a distributed environment, things get more complicated. Infinispan uses a two-phase commit (also known as 2PC) to manage all the cluster nodes that are participating in a distributed transaction. A well known practice to ensure the atomicity of a transaction that accesses multiple resource managers.

 We have covered about ACID and two-phase commit in *Chapter 2, Barriers to Scaling Data*.

Java Transaction API

Infinispan can be prepared to participate in JTA-compliant transactions.

JTA or the Java Transaction API, allows developers to demarcate transactions in a way that makes your code independent of the implementation details of the transaction manager.

With JTA, developers have to worry about getting their code up and running on the platform and using code that manages transactions rather than connections, such as JDBC. JTA exposes several interfaces such as `javax.transaction.UserTransaction`, where the developer can start the transaction with the `begin()` method and either the `commit()` or `rollback()` method to terminate the transaction and the `javax.transaction.TransactionManager` API to participate in the transaction lifecycle.

One of the responsibilities of the transaction manager when a transaction is about to be committed is to ensure that everything is committed or rolled back.

When more than one Infinispan instance is involved in the transaction, the management of the commit gets more complicated, an XA protocol with the two-phase commit is used. A basic difference with a normal distributed transaction is that an XA protocol includes an additional prepare phase that occurs just before the actual commit phase.

In computing, the **XA (eXtended Architecture)** standard is a specification published by the Open Group for Distributed Transaction Processing. The goal of XA is to allow multiple resources to be accessed in the same transaction, preserving the ACID properties across applications.

The JTA specification provides the **XAResource** interface, a Java mapping of the Open Group standard XA interface.

Before asking any of the instances to commit the changes, the transaction manager must first check with all the participants of the grid to prepare to commit. When one of the participant instances acknowledges that it is ready (or prepared) to commit the transaction, it is an indication that it can commit the transaction. If any of the participants fails to prepare, the transaction manager will rollback the whole transaction.

If all participants confirm the first phase (prepare), in the second phase, the transaction manager will ask all the resources to commit the transaction, which cannot fail otherwise, as we said, the transaction will be rolled back.

The transaction manager can coordinate a transaction that spans several resources.

Infinispan will perform the following operation for every transaction:

- Get the current transaction associated with the current thread
- If not already done, the transaction manager obtains and registers the XAResource with the transaction to receive notifications when a transaction is committing or is rolled back.

 To participate in a distributed transaction, you must enlist the XAResource instance with the Transaction object.

A `TransactionManager` object can be obtained from an `AdvancedCache` class using the `getTransactionManager()` method, which is as follows;

```
TransactionManager tm =
    cache.getAdvancedCache().getTransactionManager();
```

However, before you obtain a `TransactionManager` object, you have to specify the settings for a transaction either declaratively or programmatically. In either case, the result is the same.

If you want to use a configuration file, you can define the transactional characteristics of the cache through the `<transaction>` tag, under a cache configuration for a specific cache.

In Infinispan 6, you can include the `<transaction>` tag under a `<default>` tag in order to define default transactional behavior to all caches belonging to the cache manager.

The following example shows a simple transaction configuration. We are going to explain all aspects of these sample configurations in this chapter.

The code in Infinispan 6 is as follows:

```
<transaction transactionManagerLookupClass =
   "org.infinispan.transaction.lookup.
     GenericTransactionManagerLookup"
   cacheStopTimeout="30000"
   use1PcForAutoCommitTransactions="false"
   autoCommit="true"
   useSynchronization="false"
   transactionMode="TRANSACTIONAL"/>
```

This code is written in Infinispan 7, as follows:

```
<local-cache name="pessimisticCache">
   <transaction transaction-manager-lookup=
      "org.infinispan.transaction.lookup.
        GenericTransactionManagerLookup"
   stop-timeout="30000"
   auto-commit="true"
   locking="PESSIMISTIC"
   mode="NON_DURABLE_XA" />
</local-cache>
```

Otherwise, you can configure a transactional cache programmatically as well:.

```
Configuration config = new ConfigurationBuilder()
   .transaction()
     .transactionMode(TransactionMode.TRANSACTIONAL)
     .transactionManagerLookup(new
       GenericTransactionManagerLookup())
     .cacheStopTimeout(300001)
     .use1PcForAutoCommitTransactions(false)
     .autoCommit(true)
     .useSynchronization(false)
   .build();
```

The `cacheStopTimeOut` / `stop-timeout` attribute defines the amount of time the `TransactionManager` object is allowed to wait for any local or remote ongoing transaction to finish their job after a cache is stopped.

Another configuration option that we have used is the Synchronization, a mechanism that allows Infinispan to be notified before and after a transaction completes during the two-phase commit process.

By default, Infinispan registers itself as a participant in distributed transactions as a full XAResource. But, there can be some situations like when you use Infinispan as a second level cache in Hibernate, where it is not required to be a full XA resource in a transaction.

In these cases, you can register synchronization with the `TransactionManager` object by enabling transaction enlistment.

Using the Infinispan 6 configuration, you can enable the transaction enlistment using the `useSynchronization` attribute. To enable transaction enlistment using the Infinispan 7 declarative configuration, you'll have to set the transaction mode to `NON_XA`, as you can see in the following example:

```
<transaction mode="NON_XA" />
```

In order to look up a native transaction manager within your environment, Infinispan makes use of an implementation of the `TransactionManagerLookup` interface. The `transactionanagerLookupClass`/`transaction-manager-lookup` attribute configures the Transaction manager lookup directly using an instance of `TransactionManagerLookup`.

During the startup phase of the cache, it will create an instance of the `TransactionManagerLookup` interface and invoke the `getTransactionManager()` method, responsible for a reference to the JTA TransactionManager.

Currently, Infinispan provides four transactional manager lookup classes, as follows:

- **DummyTransactionManagerLookup**: A `TransactionManagerLookup` interface for testing, it is not recommended for use in the production environment and it has important limitations related to concurrent transactions and recovery.

- **JBossStandaloneJTAManagerLookup**: This is the recommended lookup class used in a standalone environment and it overcomes all limitations and deficiencies of the `DummyTransactionalManagerLookup` interface.

- **GenericTransactionManagerLookup**: This is the lookup class that tries to find the transaction manager in the most popular application servers. If the `TransactionManager` object is not found, it will use a `DummyTransactionManagerLookup` interface.

- **JBossTransactionManagerLookup**: If you are using Infinispan with JBoss Application Server, then this is your best option; it locates the transaction manager running within a JBoss AS instance.

Most cache operations within the scope of a JTA Transaction will propagate a runtime `CacheException` or any of its subclasses on failure, causing the transaction to be automatically marked for rollback for all application exceptions.

Transactional modes

The transaction mode attribute is slightly different in Infinispan 6 and 7. In Infinispan 6, the `transactionalMode` attribute configures whether the cache is transactional or not.

In the next example, we can see a sample configuration using Infinispan 6:

- `<transaction transactionMode="NON_TRANSACTIONAL"/>`
- `<transaction transactionMode="TRANSACTIONAL"/>`

Starting with Infinispan 5.1, you cannot mix transactional and non-transactional operations anymore; you have to decide which cache mode you want to use.

There are many reasons to follow this path, but one of the most important reasons is the clean semantics on how concurrency is managed between multiple requestors for the same cache entry. If we were allowed to mix transactional and non-transactional operations, we would run the risk of experiencing unexpected behavior, such as deadlocks, interacting with a transactional and non-transactional code.

In Infinispan 7, we have the mode attribute, which configures the transaction type for the cache to one of the following modes: NONE, BATCH, NON_XA, NON_DURABLE_XA, and FULL_XA.

The code in Infinispan 7 is as follows:

```
<transaction transaction-manager-lookup=
  "org.infinispan.transaction.lookup.
    GenericTransactionManagerLookup" mode="NON_XA"/>
```

Alternatively, you can configure a transactional cache programmatically:

```
Configuration c = new
  ConfigurationBuilder().transaction().transactionMode
    (TransactionMode.TRANSACTIONAL).build();
```

If unspecified, it defaults to NON_TRANSACTIONAL.

Non-transactional data access

Infinispan provides an autocommit mode on every new data grid access, by default. The autocommit mode is useful for an interactive data access, when you have a sequence of operations that you do not consider to be part of a transaction, for example, when you connect to your cache to get some values, and maybe even remove or add entries. The default autocommit mode on the cache is perfect for these scenarios – after all, you will probably not want to begin and end a transaction for every statement you write and perform in the grid.

Using the autocommit mode, a short transaction begins and ends for each operation you send to the grid. You're effectively non-transactional, because in this mode Infinispan cannot guarantee the atomicity or isolation properties for your session.

Infinispan provides an autocommit (ISPN 6) / autocommit (ISPN 7) attribute to assure backward compatibility with Infinispan 4.

On a transactional cache with auto commit enabled, any call performed outside a transaction's scope is transparently wrapped within a transaction. Before the call, Infinispan adds the logic for starting a transaction and performs a commit after the call.

In Infinispan 6, when using the autocommit mode, you can sacrifice data consistency for a better performance by using the use1PcForAutoCommitTransactions attribute on the <transaction> element. If you set it to true, Infinispan will commit the transaction in a single phase by reducing the number of operations from 2 to 1 Remote Procedure Calls (RPC).

Transactional models

A transactional cache in Infinispan supports two different transactional models, optimistic and pessimistic.

The optimistic model refers to an approach in which transactions are allowed to proceed, with conflicts resolved as late as possible, deferring lock acquisitions for the transaction, in order to prepare time.. The entry will not be immediately locked when it is accessed by a transaction, which means that the cache entries will be available to other transactions for concurrent access, opening up the possibility of conflicts.

At commit time, when the entry is about to be updated in the grid, Infinispan will compare the version of the current object to the version that was initially saved at the moment the entry was first requested in the transaction. If both versions differ from each other, Infinispan will consider that a conflict exists, and will mark the transaction for rollback. This avoids deadlocks, optimizes the lock acquisition time, and increases throughput significantly.

On the other hand, the pessimistic model refers to an approach in which potential conflicts are detected and resolved earlier. Cluster wide locks are acquired for every write operation and only released after the transaction commits.

Optimistic transaction

As we said, during optimistic transactions, locks are acquired during the prepare phase and are held until the time the transaction commits (or rollbacks).

Optimistic transactions are recommended when the probability of two different users change the same data in parallel is low.

The following diagram shows how the optimistic lock works:

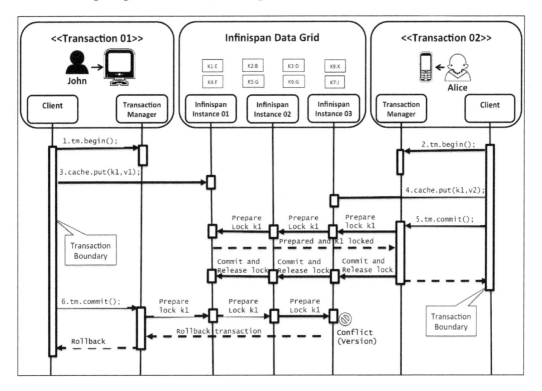

The diagram shows the users, **John** and **Alice**, issuing a put operation to the **k1** object in a different transaction context. We can see that **John** invoked the put() method first, but **Alice** performed a commit operation in her transaction (**Transaction 02**) before **John** saved his changes.

After invoking the commit operation, the Transaction Manager starts the prepare phase and locks the **k1** object, and at the end of the commit phase, it releases the lock, making the **k1** object stale to **John**. When he tries to commit his transaction, Infinispan identifies a conflict, throws an exception, and marks the transaction for rollback.

In Infinispan 6, optimistic transactions can be enabled specifying the lockingMode attribute in the configuration file, as you can see in the next example:

```
<namedCache name="transactionalOptimistic">
  <transaction transactionMode="TRANSACTIONAL"
    lockingMode="OPTIMISTIC"/>
</namedCache>
```

You can enable optimistic transactions, specifying the locking attribute within the <transaction> element. Check the following example for the Infinispan 7 configuration that creates a cache with an optimistic locking schema. The code in Infinispan 7 is as follows:

```
<local-cache name="transactionCache">
  <transaction transaction-manager-lookup=
    "org.infinispan.transaction.lookup.
JBossStandaloneJTAManagerLookup"
      mode="NON_XA" locking="OPTIMISTIC" />
</local-cache>
```

Otherwise, it can be programmatically configured as follows:

```
Configuration c = new
  ConfigurationBuilder().transaction().
    lockingMode(LockingMode.OPTIMISTIC).build();

assert c.transaction().lockingMode() == LockingMode.OPTIMISTIC;
```

Pessimistic transaction

Pessimistic transactions prevent that other concurrent transactions modifying the same entry. Infinispan obtains locks on entry keys at the time it is written. The following diagram shows how the pessimistic lock works:

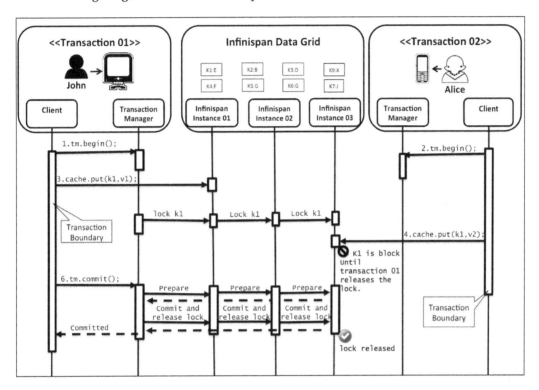

In our example, when the **cache.put(k1,v1)** method returns, the **k1** object will be automatically locked in the transaction, preventing concurrent transactions from updating it. Concurrent transactions are allowed only to read the **k1** object, but not update it, which is the case with Alice's transaction. The lock is released when the transaction completes via a commit or rollback operation.

You can enable or disable pessimistic transactions in the configuration file by changing the correspondent locking attribute.

The following sample code shows how to configure pessimistic locking with Infinispan 6:

```
<namedCache name="transactional"/>
  <transaction transactionMode="TRANSACTIONAL"
    lockingMode="PESSIMISTIC"/>
</namedCache>
```

Configure pessimistic locking with Infinispan 7 as follows:

```
<local-cache name="pessimisticCache">
  <transaction transaction-manager-lookup=
    "org.infinispan.transaction.lookup.
      JBossStandaloneJTAManagerLookup" locking="PESSIMISTIC"
        mode="NON_DURABLE_XA"/>
</local-cache>
```

Otherwise, it can be programmatically configured as follows:

```
Configuration c = new
  ConfigurationBuilder().transaction().lockingMode
    (LockingMode.PESSIMISTIC).build();
assert c.transaction().lockingMode() == LockingMode.PESSIMISTIC;
```

Choosing the better transaction model

As we saw, the pessimistic model will fail when it faces a conflict; while the optimistic model will give an opportunity to resolve the conflict at commit time.

In other words, optimistic transactions do not lock cache entries, two different transactions might change the same entry at the same time, and an eventual conflict will be detected during the second phase, if a second transaction attempts to flush or commit locked entry. This happens because optimistic transactions will rollback the transaction if the data has changed after the application reads the data, and before the application commits the transaction (`writeSkewCheck`).

Unlike optimistic transactions, pessimistic transactions generally lock the entry they act on, preventing other concurrent transactions from using it, which avoids conflicts between transactions, so maybe the pessimistic model is better for applications that have a high risk of contention. The disadvantage of pessimistic transactions is that they consume additional resources since the resource is locked for each write operation.

In most scenarios, optimistic transactions are more efficient and can be the best choice for most applications, since they offer higher performance, better scalability, and might reduce the risk of a deadlock.

Batch mode

Infinispan provides several methods of putting data in the cache, such as the standard map operations such as `cache.put(...)`, `cache.putAll(...)`, or `cache.putIfAbsent(...)` an overloaded form of `ConcurrentMap.putIfAbsent()`, which only stores the value if no value is stored under the same key.

However, these methods will result in a separate network call for each operation, which is not suitable for scenarios where large amounts of data must be loaded into the data store, especially for caches in replication mode. This is the case, for instance, building a mirror site or importing data to the cache when transaction control is not important.

For these cases, Infinispan provides the ability to batch multiple cache operations through the interface `org.infinispan.commons.api.BatchingCache` that provides the `startBatch()` method to start the batch process, and `endBatch(boolean)` to complete the process.

The Infinispan batching mode allows atomicity and other transactional characteristics, but doesn't provide full JTA or XA capabilities.

In the batching mode, all configuration options related to the transaction such as `syncRollbackPhase`, `syncCommitPhase`, `useEagerLocking`, and `eagerLockSingleNode` are applied as well. Internally, the batching process starts a JTA transaction using a simple internal TransactionManager implementation without recovery. And all the entries in that scope will be queued on the same instance and changes are batched together around the cluster in a part of the completion process, reducing replication overhead for each update in the batch.

 When you use the batch mode, there is no transaction manager defined.

By default, invocation batching is disabled; how to enable batch process declaratively is shown in the following example. Invocation batching configuration with Infinispan 6 can be done as follows:

```
<invocationBatching enabled="true" />
```

For Infinispan 7, we don't have more `<invocationBatching>` elements, so to enable invocation batching you have to specify the transaction mode to `BATCH`:

```
<transaction transaction-manager-lookup=
  "org.infinispan.transaction.lookup.
    JBossStandaloneJTAManagerLookup" mode="BATCH"
      locking="OPTIMISTIC"/>
```

Otherwise, it can be programmatically configured, on the `InvocationBatchingConfiguration` object:

```
conf.invocationBatching().setInvocationBatchingEnabled(true);
```

After this, configure your cache to use batching. Perhaps the easiest way to illustrate this is to demonstrate a simple scenario showing how to import a CSV file into Infinispan, in order to prepopulate a cache before the application makes use of it.

 CSV stands for **Comma Separated Values**.

First, we created a CSV file in the `resource` folder with the name `csv_guest_list.csv`, with the following content:

```
ID, first_name, last_name, document_number, birth_date

1,John, Wayne,832218,19801112

2,Eddy,Murphy,822712,19901003

3,Fred,Mercury,872211,19640321

4,Juliette,Lewis,862211,19720804

5,Kate,Moss,872911,19790413
```

The content of the CSV file is a guest list for a given event. Next, we created a POJO class `Guest` for the imported data and a utility class `GuestListImporter` to import CSV files.

Finally, we can use the batching process by calling `startBatch()` and `endBatch()`, as highlighted in the following example:

```
Cache<Integer, Guest> cache =
  container.getCache("batchingCacheWithEvictionAndPassivation");
List<Guest> guests = new
  GuestListImporter().parseGuestFile("guest_list.csv");
try{
    cache.startBatch();
    for(Guest guest : guests){
      // do some processing
      cache.put(guest.getId(), guest);
}
assertEquals(guests.size(), 5);
cache.endBatch(true);
}catch(Exception ex){
    cache.endBatch(false);
}
```

Note that the `endBatch()` method receives a Boolean parameter, which completes the batch if true; otherwise, it will discard all changes made in the batch.

Transaction recovery

Although XA transactions possess the ACID characteristics in order to guarantee the atomicity of operations, our system must be able to handle failures in order to guarantee the consistency of customer data, which can occur at any time due to unexpected server crash or network loss.

To guarantee transaction consistency, Infinispan supports transaction recovery, a well known feature of XA transactions, present in the specification published by the Open Group.

Let's suppose a situation where a customer buys from Ticket Monster, a ticket for a specific show, but we have to save the ticket in two different nodes in Infinispan. The Transaction Manager will be responsible for communicating with both resources that are in use.

When the transaction manager commits, in phase one, the transaction manager asks both resources to prepare the commit. Then both resources verifies they can persist the data and each resource sends an acknowledgement to the coordinator. In the second phase, when resources are requested to commit, for some reason one of the them fails to complete the commit operation, thus leaving the cache data in an inconsistent state.

In situations like this, Infinispan supports automatic transaction recovery coordinated by the Transaction Manager, to make sure data in both resources ends up being consistent.

The Transaction Manager works with Infinispan to determine any transaction in an in-doubt state that was prepared but not committed. If there are no left-pending transactions, it will proceed normally, otherwise, the Transaction Manager will request the Infinispan cluster to complete the commit or force the rollback to release any resource.

There are some cases where Infinispan will not be able to recover all transactions in an in-doubt state, and where recovery could not be complete, for these cases, Infinispan can list transactions that require a manual intervention.

As a system administrator, you can configure Infinispan to receive notifications about these cases that require manual intervention by e-mail or log alerts, which require some configuration on the transaction manager.

Infinispan provides **JMX** tooling to view any transactions that require manual intervention, which we will see in *Chapter 8, Managing and Monitoring Infinispan.*

The following diagram shows a graphical illustration of the concept, with a node failure in the originator:

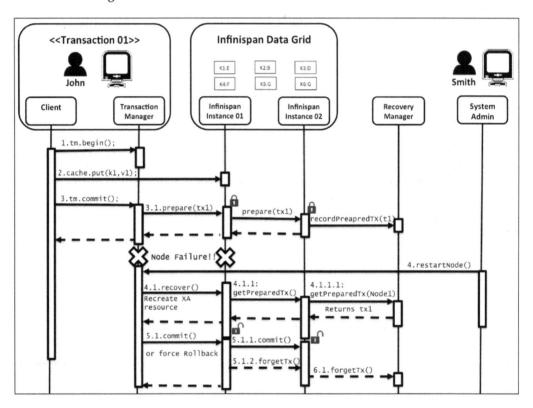

From the image you can see that the changed data is held by the **Recovery Manager** only for in-doubt transactions, being removed for successfully completed transactions after the commit or rollback phase is complete.

You can enable transaction recovery per cache level through XML configuration. If you are using Infinispan 6, you can enable transaction recovery by adding a `<recovery>` element, a child element of the `<transaction>` parent element, as follows:

```
<transaction transactionManagerLookupClass=
    "org.infinispan.transaction.lookup.
    GenericTransactionManagerLookup"
        transactionMode="TRANSACTIONAL">
```

```
<recovery enabled="true" recoveryInfoCacheName="recoveryCache"/>
</transaction>
```

 For recovery to work, the useSynchronization attribute must be set to false.

Enabling transaction recovery with Infinispan 7 is considerably easier than its predecessor; for the recovery to work, you must set the mode attribute to FULL_XA, because it only works if the transaction is registered as a full XA resource:

```
<replicated-cache name="transactionCacheWithRecoveryExample"
  mode="SYNC">
  <transaction transaction-manager-lookup=
    "org.infinispan.transaction.lookup.
      JBossStandaloneJTAManagerLookup" mode="FULL_XA"
        recovery-cache="recoveryCache" />
</replicated-cache>
<local-cache name="recoveryCache"/>
```

Alternatively, you can enable recovery programmatically on the RecoveryConfiguration class, as follows:

```
config = new ConfigurationBuilder()
  .transaction()
  .transactionMode(TransactionMode.TRANSACTIONAL)
  .transactionManagerLookup(new GenericTransactionManagerLookup())
  .recovery()
  .enable()
  .recoveryInfoCacheName("recoveryCache")
  .build();

//or just check its status
boolean isRecoveryEnabled = config.isTransactionRecoveryEnabled();
```

 In Infinispan 6, the <recovery> element defines the attributes enabled that you use to enable transaction recovery.

The recoveryInfoCacheName class in Infinispan 6 (recovery-cache in Infinispan 7) can be optionally set up to provide a name to the cache that will hold all recovery information, it's not mandatory, but if omitted, the cache's default name is __recoveryInfoCacheName__.

All in-doubt transaction data will be backed up at a local cache specified through the `recoveryInfoCacheName` configuration attribute, if available, which allows data to be evicted to the disk through the cache loader as normal cache, in case it gets too big.

Integrating with Transaction Manager

During recovery, the Transaction Manager communicates to all the resource managers that are participating in the transaction. But there can be some situations where we may need to run the recovery in a different process from the one running the transaction.

To retrieve the transactions that are currently in a prepared state, the Transaction Manager uses the `XAResource.recover` method on it. To obtain a reference to an Infinispan XAResource, the following API can be used to return the XAResource associated with this cache:

```
XAResource xar = cache.getAdvancedCache().getXAResource();
```

Besides the fact that the XA specification allows to run the recovery in a different process, today in Infinispan it's only possible to run the recovery process in the same process, where the Infinispan instance exists.

A future release is planned for Hot Rod clients to support transactions. We will see Hot Rod in action in *Chapter 9, Server Modules*.

Locking and concurrency control

As we have seen, we can have one or more clients participating on a transaction that issues read and write operations to a cache. When transactions execute concurrently on the same cache entry, the interleaved execution of their reads and writes by the cache can produce undesirable results. On the other hand, a good cache solution must guarantee consistency of data while allowing multiple transactions to read/write data concurrently.

Concurrency control is an activity that is important to avoid unexpected results; its primary goal is to ensure that all transactions will have the same effect as a serial one.

Traditionally, the problem of concurrency is solved providing transaction isolation, keeping a single version of the data and locking other requests to manage concurrency.

Locking is essential to avoid change collisions resulting from simultaneous updates to the same cache entry by two or more concurrent users.

If locking is not available and several users access a distributed cache concurrently, concurrency problems may occur if their transactions access the same data at the same time.

Concurrency problems include:

- **Dirty Reads**: This means that a client can read uncommitted changes made by another client, which is shown in the following figure:

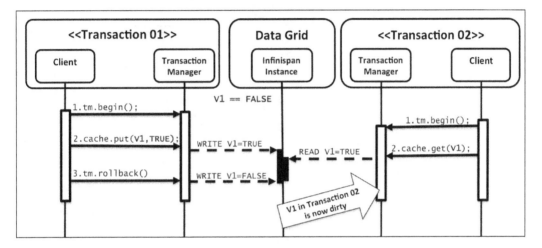

- **Non-Repeatable Reads**: A client gets a cache entry, another client changes the same cache entry and commits, and the first connection re-reads the same entry and gets the new result, which is shown in the following figure:

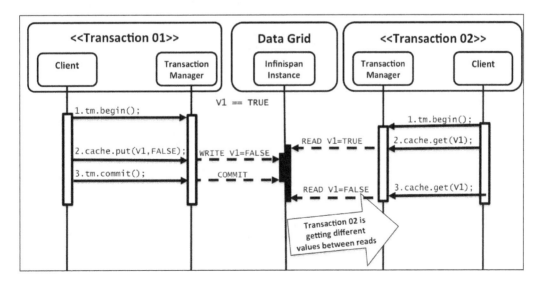

- **Phantom Reads**: It may happen when a client performs an insert or delete operation against an entry that belongs to a collection of entries being read by another transaction. Then the second client re-reads using the same condition and gets the new entry, which is shown in the following figure:

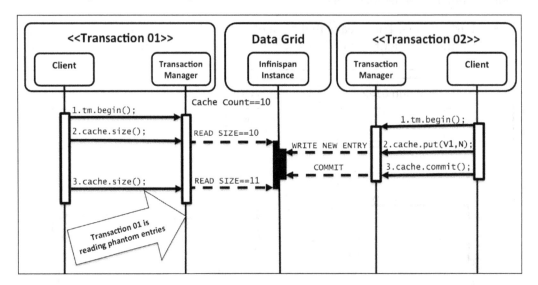

- **Lost Updates**: It may happen when two or more clients, during their individual transactions select the same entry and change their value. The transactions are independent and unaware of each other; lost updates might happen when the last update to the entry overwrites updates performed by other clients, which results in lost data, as shown in the following figure:

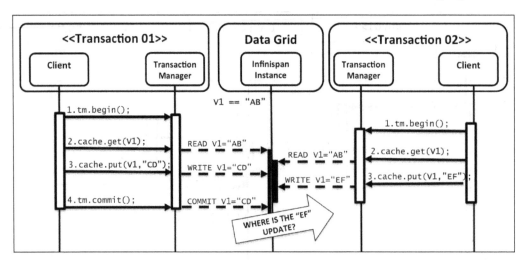

To overcome these phenomena, the **ANSI/ISO SQL** standard defines four levels of transaction isolation that will provide a different level of access control which may or may not be more restrictive.

As you can deduce by the ANSI/ISO standard, isolation levels have their origins in relational databases. The defined transaction isolation levels are:

- **READ COMMITTED**: This level means that the read operation can see only data committed before the operation began, because the read lock is released immediately after operation. But, during the write operation, the system keeps the lock until the transaction commits. Higher concurrency is possible when using this level. This mode prevents dirty reads but allows problems of lost updates, nonrepeatable reads, and phantom reads to occur.

- **READ UNCOMMITTED**: This level means that transaction isolation is disabled. This mode allows all aforementioned concurrency problems.

- **REPEATABLE READ**: This level means that every lock acquired during a transaction is held until the end of the transaction. This mode prevents the problem of non-repeatable reads, because once data has been written, no other transaction can read it, but it allows problems related to phantom reads to occur.

- **SERIALIZABLE**: This is the most restrictive isolation level. This level requires read and write locks to be released at the end of the transaction and does not allow the insertion of new entries into the range that is locked. This mode prevents all concurrency problems, but it can cause serialization failures.

> Please consult the `java.sql.Connection` API for more references.

As we have seen before, Infinispan uses the two-phase commit (2PC) protocol, in order to coordinate with all the processes that participate in a distributed transaction. However, there are also costs related to 2PC in a replicated cache. First, the cost associated to memory consumption by the replicated entries that can be reduced drastically by changing the cache mode to distribution. Also, the more objects you have in your data grid, the more and more expensive it becomes to ensure the consistency of these objects.

You might be saying that the distribution clustering mode can overcome these disadvantages, by configuring the Infinispan cache in such a way that each item is replicated in a limited number of nodes. But, in the distribution mode, we have an additional overhead associated with the coordination costs.

For these reasons, Infinispan has opted for relaxing consistency, ensuring weaker semantics in order to allow more efficient implementations.

Specifically, Infinispan supports the following isolation levels: read committed and Repeatable read. But remember, transactions in Infinispan are not like transactions in a relational database product.

In Infinispan, READ COMMITTED and REPEATABLE READ work slightly differently than databases. In READ COMMITTED, reads can happen anytime, while in REPEATABLE READ, once the data has been written to the cache, no other transaction can read it so there's no chance of later re-reading the data under the same key and getting back a completely different value.

Infinispan has only been able to provide all of this thanks to **Multi-Version Concurrency Control (MVCC)**, which is the subject of the next section.

Multiversion concurrency control

Infinispan implements a concurrency schema well known in relational databases called multi-version concurrency control (MVCC).

MVCC offers many advantages over Java synchronization and JDK locks for access to concurrent data. Infinispan can achieve an excellent performance by maintaining multiple versions of data instead of using any synchronization or locking for reader threads.

It allows readers to get consistent data without blocking writers. And allows writes to happen on copies of data, rather than on the data itself. Thus, even in the presence of a write, reads can still occur, and all read operations in Infinispan are non-blocking, improving the general performance of cache applications in a multiuser environment.

The Infinispan implementation of MVCC is well optimized for read operations, because for read operations, Infinispan does not acquire an explicit lock on the data being read. On the other had, to ensure one concurrent writer per entry, Infinispan acquires a lock for write operations, queuing up the changes to the entry.

Configuring isolation levels in Infinispan

You can configure the isolation levels by adding a `<locking>` configuration element, which lets you define the local, concurrency level, isolation level, lock acquisition timeout, and other characteristics of the cache.

Isolation levels define the level a reader can see of a concurrent write. Depending on the isolation level you choose, you will have a different behavior in how the state is committed back to the cache.

The default isolation level used by Infinispan is READ_COMMITTED, which also performs the best, and is generally good enough for most applications.

Let's take a look at a more detailed example that shows the difference between READ_COMMITTED and REPEATABLE_READ. With the read committed isolation level, during two consecutive read operations on the same key, if the key is updated by a third transaction, the second read will return the new value, which is shown in the following figure:

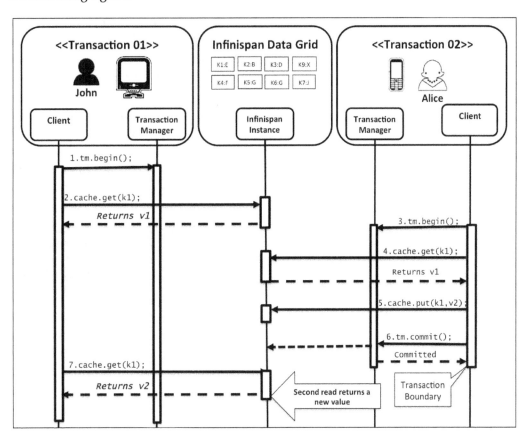

As you can see, in this diagram we are showing an example of a possible scenario with the READ COMMITED isolation level, and at the end of the diagram, in step 7 the second read returns a new value **v2**.

However, if we were using the REPEATABLE_READ isolation level, step 7 would still return **v1**. So, if you want to read the same entry multiple times within a transaction, we recommend you to use REPEATABLE_READ. The REPEATABLE_READ isolation level also allows for an additional safety check known as Write Skew Check.

In the classical literature, the term 'write skew' refers to an anomaly that can arise with **Snapshot Isolation (SI)**.

 Snapshot Isolation is a guarantee that a transaction will always read data from a snapshot of the cache store data as of the time the transaction started, which is called its Start-Timestamp.

In the context of Infinispan, you have seen that Infinispan is not implementing Snapshot Isolation, but rather an efficiently weaker consistency level. The key difference with respect to SI is that the grid is storing a single version of each entry, and there is no guarantee that the reads of a given transaction will return from the same snapshot.

Infinispan provides a reliable mechanism of data versioning to improve write skew checks when using optimistic transactions, REPEATABLE_READ, and a clustered cache. To enable write skew check, set the `<locking>` element's writeSkewCheck attribute to `true` in the config file. The following table describes the attributes of the `<locking>` element:

Attribute	Type	Default	Description
concurrencyLevel (ISPN 6) concurrency-level (ISPN 7)	int	32 (ISPN 6) 1000 (ISPN 7)	You can use this setting to specify a fixed concurrency level for lock containers. It defines the number of available concurrent threads you might have interacting with Infinispan.

Attribute	Type	Default	Description
isolationLevel (ISPN 6) isolation (ISPN 7)	REPEATABLE_ READ READ_ COMMITTED	READ_ COMMITTED	This defines the isolation level for the cache. As we said, Infinispan supports only the REPEATABLE_ READ and READ_ COMMITTED isolation levels.
lockAcquisitionTimeout(ISPN 6) acquire-timeout (ISPN 7)	long	10000 (ISPN 6) * 10 seconds 15000 (ISPN 7) * 15 seconds	This defines the maximum time (in milliseconds) to attempt a lock acquisition.
useLockStriping(ISPN 6) striping (ISPN 7)	Boolean	false	If set to true, Infinispan will maintain a pool of shared locks to be shared by the entries that have to be locked. If set to false, a lock will be created under request, per entry in the cache. Lock striping can help to control the memory footprint of your cache, but may reduce concurrency.

Attribute	Type	Default	Description
writeSkewCheck (ISPN 6) write-skew (ISPN 7)	Boolean	false	This setting is only relevant when the isolation level is REPEATABLE_READ. If set to true, when Infinsipan identifies a version conflict (write skew check), it will raise an exception. Otherwise, if during the commit phase, the writer thread discovers that the working entry is different to the underlying entry, Infinispan will overwrite the underlying entry with the working entry.

Infinispan provides the `LockManager` component to deal with all aspects of acquiring and releasing locks for cache entries.

LockManager makes use of the `org.infinispan.util.concurrent.locks.containers LockContainer` class to acquire a lock for a given key, to get and release a lock. `LockContainer` has two implementations, one with support for lock striping and support for one lock for each entry.

Lock striping is a technique used in the implementation of `ConcurrentHashMap` in Java 6 to increase concurrency. The basic idea is that you can break up a cache to different segments (or stripes) and write to these segments concurrently.

Lock striping provides a highly scalable locking mechanism and helps control memory footprint, but you may reduce concurrency in the system and run the risk of blocking irrelevant entries in the same lock.

Lock striping is disabled as a default in Infinispan; to enable lock striping, set the `useLockStriping` attribute to `true` in the config file, and you can tune the size of a segment used by lock striping using the `concurrencyLevel` attribute of the locking configuration element.

For Infinispan 6 the configuration is as follows:

```
<namedCache name="transactionCacheWithLocking">
  <jmxStatistics enabled="true"/>
  <transaction transactionManagerLookupClass=
    "org.infinispan.transaction.lookup.
      JBossStandaloneJTAManagerLookup"
        transactionMode="TRANSACTIONAL"
          lockingMode="PESSIMISTIC" />
  <locking isolationLevel="READ_COMMITTED"
    writeSkewCheck="false" concurrencyLevel="5000"
      useLockStriping="true" />
</namedCache>
```

The way you configure locking in Infinispan 7 is quite similar to the earlier version:

```
<local-cache name="transactionCacheWithLocking">
  <transaction transaction-manager-lookup=
    "org.infinispan.transaction.lookup.
      JBossStandaloneJTAManagerLookup" mode="NON_XA"
        locking="PESSIMISTIC" />
  <locking isolation="READ_COMMITTED" write-skew="false"
    concurrency-level="5000" striping="true" />
</local-cache>
```

If the lock striping attribute is disabled, a lock will be generated based on the hash code of the entry's key, created per entry in the cache, which can increase memory usage, and so on.

Previously, in Infinispan 4.*x* lock striping was enabled by default. From Infinispan 5.0, due to potential deadlocks, this mechanism is disabled by default.

Implicit and explicit locking

Infinispan provides two lock mechanisms for managing and controlling concurrent access to objects in the grid. These mechanisms can be used as an alternative solution in situations where MVCC does not provide the expected behavior.

Infinispan, by default, uses lazy remote locking, which reduces traffic. Locks are acquired on the local node that is running the transaction while other nodes try during the two-phase commit phase to lock cache entries involved in a transaction. However, since you are working with Infinispan 6, you can configure your cache to (explicitly or implicitly) eagerly lock cache entries.

 This feature was removed from the current version of Infinispan (7.*).

The Infinispan cache interface includes basic locking methods, which allows cache users to use these methods during a transaction, to lock the cache entries eagerly.

On lock calls, Infinispan will attempt to lock the requested cache keys across the cluster nodes of the grid and at the commit (or rollback) phase, Infinispan will release all locks held by the transaction, regardless of success or failure.

A cache object can be locked explicitly by the lock method:

```
tx.begin()
cache.lock(K1)      // acquire cluster wide lock on K1
cache.put(K1,VX)    // guaranteed to succeed
tx.commit()         // releases locks
```

Implicit locking obtains access rights to cache entries, as they are needed by an application. In general, the implicit locking offered by Infinispan provides a level of concurrency that is sufficient for most applications.

Infinispan will implicitly obtain the appropriate locks for your application at the point at which they are needed, as cache entries are accessed for write operations.

In the following sample transaction, we can see one transaction running in one of the cache nodes:

```
tx.begin()
cache.put(K1,V1)    // acquire cluster wide lock on K1
cache.put(K2,V2)    // acquire cluster wide lock on K2
```

```
cache.put(K1,VX)      // no-op, we already own cluster wide lock for
   K1
tx.commit()           // releases locks
```

In a nutshell, for implicit eager locking, Infinispan will check for each modification whether the cache entry is locked locally. If the entry is locked, it means that the entry is also locked in the grid, otherwise, if the entry is not locked Infinispan will send a cluster wide lock request to acquire the lock.

You can also lock a single remote node; however, this configuration is only applied on distributed mode, and would make the number of remote locks acquired to be 1 always, regardless of the configured number of owners.

 Infinispan guarantees data consistency in front of a single node lock. The lock for a given key is always deterministically acquired on the same node of the cluster, regardless of where the transaction originates.

Lock timeouts

Once you have a lock, you can hold it to execute your required operations, and then, when you finish your tasks you can release the lock for another process to use. You can define the limit of time a cache client can spend waiting to acquire a lock; if a lock request does not return before the specified timeout limit, one of the transactions will rollback, allowing the other to continue working.

You can define a **lock acquisition timeout (LAT)**, to a higher threshold (default is 10 seconds), in the <locking> element of your default or named cache configuration.

The following example sets the lock acquisition timeout to 20 seconds:

To set the LAT to 20 seconds in Infinispan 6, add the following code:

```
<locking lockAcquisitionTimeout="20000"/>
```

To set the LAT to 20 seconds in Infinispan 7, add the following code:

```
<locking acquire-timeout="20000"/>
```

Deadlock detection

One risk that might come out with the use of explicit lock is the occurrence of deadlocks, which can occur when concurrent users (two or more) are waiting for an object that has been locked by themselves.

The following situation illustrates a deadlock, imagine we have two transactions and each transaction has a lock on the entry it attempts to update; and the two transactions (in parallel) proceed without committing the transaction. However, each transaction tries to update the cache entry held by the other transaction. As a consequence, both of them will be blocked, because both transactions will not be able to retrieve the entry they need in order to proceed or terminate the transaction.

The following diagram depicts the scenario where two simple transactions, both trying to lock two of the same entries, can get into a deadlock situation:

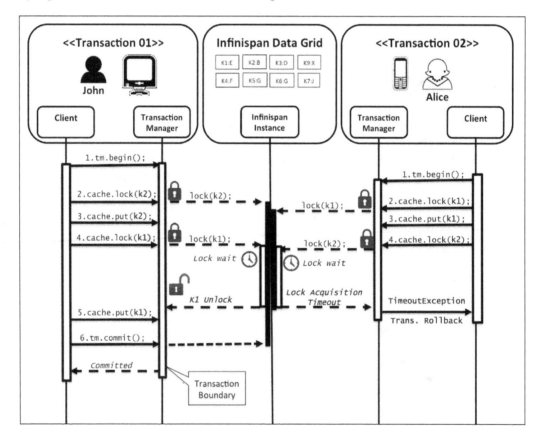

Transaction 01 started off by successfully acquiring the lock on entry key **K2**, with the intent to change it later. Likewise, **Transaction 02** successfully acquired the lock on entry key **K1**.

Now, in order to continue its processing, **Transaction 01** tries to acquire the lock on **K1** as well. But now, **Transaction 02** already locks **K1**. **Transaction 01** has to wait until **Transaction 02** finishes.

In this scenario, **Transaction 01** patiently waits for **Transaction 02** to finish and to release **K1** eventually. But at the same time, **Transaction 02** holds **K1**, it tries to acquire **K2**, and cannot get it. This is the most common and simplest scenario of a deadlock, where we have two or more clients (threads) waiting forever because of a locking dependency in all the threads.

User experience may be affected because in all of the following, request(s) to the cache entry will freeze during the deadlock period, which might extend up to LAT.

Neither transaction can obtain the desired key they need in order to proceed or terminate the transaction. The only way out from the deadlock is to break some of the locks by sacrificing at least one transaction, so that another transaction can complete successfully. Also there's a chance that both **Transaction 01** and **Transaction 02** rollback by timing out.

By default, deadlock detection is disabled, but in Infinispan 6, you can enable it for individual caches, under the `namedCache` configuration element, by adding the following:

```
<deadlockDetection enabled="true" spinDuration="1000"/>
```

In Infinispan 7, you can enable deadlock detection by specifying the `deadlock-detection-spin` attribute, which defines the time period allowed that an instance can wait to acquire a particular lock:

```
<local-cache deadlock-detection-spin="1000"/>
```

An indication that you may need to enable deadlock detection is when you start to see a large number of transactions rolling back and the `TimeoutException` messages. In fact, `TimeoutException` might be caused by other factors too; however, during deadlocks Infinispan will always throw a `TimeoutException`.

Another situation where you should consider using deadlock detection is when you have a high contention on a set of keys, also there are other ways to analyze where deadlock detection is appropriate, but the best method is to monitor and benchmark the server from outside. You can use JMX to monitor and get statistical information such as the number of deadlocks detected, using the `DeadlockDetectingLockManager` MBean. We will see monitoring and management aspects in details in the next chapter.

Note: The deadlock detection process only works per cache basis, for other cases, deadlock spread over multiple caches won't be detected.

Data versioning

To configure an efficient write skew check, you can also configure your Infinispan cache to enable versioning and write skew check explicitly using the `<versioning>` section in your configuration file. Versioning allows concurrency to be managed through MVCC.

The `<versioning>` element defines only two attributes. The enable attribute determines if versioning is enabled as by default it is disabled, while the `versioningScheme` attribute defines the versioning scheme Infinispan should use. The possible values are `SIMPLE` or `NONE`, the default value is `NONE`.

When Infinispan is operating in local mode, it's possible to make a more adequate and reliable write skew check using Java object references to compare differences; however, this technique is useless in a distributed environment and a more reliable form of versioning is necessary to provide reliable write skew checks.

The `org.infinispan.container.versioning.SimpleClusteredVersion` class is an implementation of the proposed `org.infinispan.container.versioning.EntryVersion` interface, which provides a simple cluster-aware versioning schema, backed by a long version attribute that is incremented each time the cache entry is updated.

 By default, versioning is disabled, so pay attention if you are using transactions with write skew checks and `REPEATABLE_READ` as an isolation level, because it is not reliable if you are using it in a cluster.

To enable versioning in Infinispan 6, add the following code:

```
<versioning enabled="true" versioningScheme="SIMPLE" />
```

To enable versioning in Infinispan 7, add the following code:

```
<versioning scheme="SIMPLE" />
```

Otherwise, if you want, you can create versioning programmatically by adding the following code:

```
Configuration config = new ConfigurationBuilder()
    .versioning()
    .enable()
    .scheme(VersioningScheme.SIMPLE)
    .transaction()
    .transactionMode(
    TransactionMode.TRANSACTIONAL)
    .transactionManagerLookup(
    new GenericTransactionManagerLookup())
    .autoCommit(true)
    .build();
```

Summary

In this chapter, we looked at how Infinispan deals with transactions, but first we had an introduction to transaction fundamentals, a glimpse of JTA integration, and how to design your application to use different transactional models, optimistic and pessimistic.

In the second part of the chapter, we had a deeper look on concurrency control mechanisms to ensure data integrity, such as Multi-Version Concurrency Control (MVCC), isolation level, and locking control.

Now that you know how to configure different transaction strategies for your cache, it's time to learn how to monitor problems in production and how to manage your cache instances.

8

Managing and Monitoring Infinispan

This chapter is about using different tools to manage and monitor your Infinispan caches and their underlying JVM environment. You will learn about **Java Management Extensions (JMX)** and how Infinispan uses this technology to interact with a local or remote cache, to provide statistical information and control important events that might occur in your data grid. You will also learn how to use JMX and the Infinispan API to create and register your own MBean to expose any information you want.

In the following sections, we will analyze the following topics:

- JMX Technology and MBeans
- Interacting with Infinispan via JMX
- JMX clients such as JConsole and Visual VM
- The RHQ project

An overview of monitoring and managing with Java

The Java SE platform provides several mechanisms for monitoring and managing capabilities to access the Java Virtual Machine (JVM) both remotely and locally, which can be categorized as follows:

- Instrumentation for the JVM, such as the **Simple Network Management Protocol (SNMP)**, a protocol for managing devices on IP networks, such as routers, servers, switches, and more.

- The Monitoring and Management APIs Java SE provides many APIs, such as `java.lang.management`, which provide a number of interfaces for monitoring and management of the the JVM (locally and remotely) and other components. These interfaces provide access to many types of information, such as the `ClassLoadingMXBean` interface for the class loading system, `GarbageCollectorMXBean` for the garbage collector, `MemoryManagerMXBean` for memory manager, `PlatformLoggingMXBean` for logging, and many more.

- Monitoring and Management Tools, such as JConsole a graphical JMX-compliant tool that you can use to monitor how your Infinispan grid behaves and **Java Mission Control (JMC)** includes tools for profiling and diagnosis for JVM environments. There are also other tools that JavaSE makes available out of the box to monitor and collect performance statics, such as **jps (JVM Process Status Tool)**, **jstat (JVM Statistics Monitoring Tool)**, and **jstatd (JVM jstat Daemon)**.

- The Java Management Extensions (JMX) technology represents an open Java technology, which allows you to monitor and manage your applications and services. Infinispan adopted this technology to expose management or statistical information.

Monitoring and managing Java applications with JMX

The JMX technology, which started as **JSR 160 (Java Management Extensions Remote API)** and **JSR 3 (Java Management Extensions Instrumentation and Agent Specification)**, was added as part of the Java SE platform in the 5.0 release. The specification defines the APIs, best practices, architecture, and services for managing and monitoring the Java Virtual Machine and their resources as they are created.

JMX is commonly used for a variety of Java applications, including the JVM itself, the JBoss server and the container; for instance, having an architecture completely based on components and JMX for a long time (until JBoss AS 6.0) was the only way for developers to interact with the container, making this technology essential to manage JBoss AS components.

With JMX, it's possible to retrieve general information about classes, threads, log level control, CPU usage, and also detect low memory conditions and deadlocks.

In order to provide this level of control and all this information, a developer must first instrument the resources he wants to make available for users to manage. To do so, the developer must wrap the code using Java objects knows as MBeans or Managed Beans.

An MBean is a simple Java object that satisfies some standard design patterns, and implements one of the standard MBean interfaces, to expose all the information needed to manage and control a given resource.

The JMX specification also defines a JMX agent technology included in the JDK, which consists of an MBean server, a set of services, and standard connectors and adaptors that will provide the means to control resources, and make them available for remote access.

For each MBean you want to create, you must register it in an MBean Server, which is one the most important components of a JMX architecture responsible to manage the MBeans. JMX provides the MBeanServer interface, which contains methods to manipulate the registered MBeans, as well as the methods to create, register, and remove them.

The MBean instance does not change the management interface. You can also use MBeans (in the instrumentation level) to propagate notifications when some events occur.

Given that short introduction, we can divide the JMX Architecture into three levels:

- Instrumentation
- JMX agent
- Remote management

The following figure presents a graphical representation of the JMX architecture:

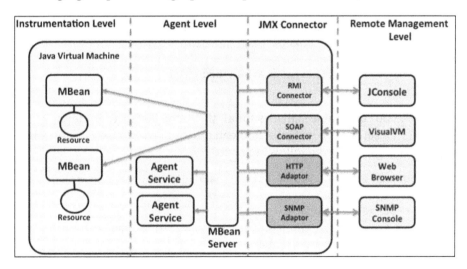

Infinispan runs on top of this architecture, exposing statistical information about the cache instances, as we will see in the next section.

Interacting with Infinispan via JMX

Infinispan has a broad support for JMX in order to provide external access to monitor statistical information and control the cache data of each Infinispan instance, and it also provides two different levels of information, CacheManager and Cache.

The CacheManager level

By default, both levels are disabled. In the CacheManager level, you can extract global statistics for all cache instances managed from a given CacheManager object, as we could see earlier; CacheManager is the mechanism from which you can retrieve new cache instances.

If you are an Infinispan 6 user and you want to configure it declaratively, you can enable the monitoring characteristics of the CacheManager level using the `<globalJMXStatistics>` tag, under a `<global>` tag to define the global JMX settings, which will be shared with existing cache instances under the domain of a single CacheManager.

The following example shows a global JMX configuration. In order to enable global JMX statistics in Infinispan 6, we set the attribute enable to `true`:

```
<global>
  ...
  <globalJmxStatistics
    enabled="true"
      jmxDomain="com.packt.erp"
        cacheManagerName="WMSCacheManager"
          mBeanServerLookup="org.infinispan.jmx.
JBossMBeanServerLookup"
            allowDuplicateDomains="true" />
</global>
```

In Infinispan 7, you can enable statistics for all the cache instances under a CacheManager by setting the statistics Boolean attribute within the `cache-container` element, which is shown in the following code:

```
<cache-container statistics="true" name="WMSCacheManager">
<jmx domain="com.packt.erp"
    mbean-server-lookup=
      "org.infinispan.jmx.PlatformMBeanServerLookup"
        duplicate-domains="true" />
</cache-container>
```

Otherwise, you can enable and configure JMX statistics programmatically as well:

```
GlobalConfiguration globalConfig = new GlobalConfigurationBuilder()
    .globalJmxStatistics().
        enable().
        jmxDomain("com.packt.erp").
        cacheManagerName("WMSCacheManager").
        mBeanServerLookup(new JBossMBeanServerLookup()).
        allowDuplicateDomains(true)
    .build();
```

In our previous example, for both versions, we used the `jmxDomain(ISPN 6)` / `domain(ISPN 7)` attribute, as we have seen in *Chapter 3, Using the APIs*, which covered details about CacheManager, we can have Caches created by different cache managers under the same Virtual Machine. If this is your scenario then you could use the `jmxDomain(ISPN 6)/domain(ISPN 7)` attribute to identify which objects belong to which cache manager.

The `cacheManagerName(ISPN 6)` / `name(ISPN 7)` attribute allows you to define a friendly name for the cache manager, which will be used by Infinispan for all public JMX objects that belong to the cache manager.

We also have the possibility to define the class responsible for locating a JMX MBean server to bind to. To do so, you can have your own version implementing the `org.infinispan.jmx.MBeanServerLookup` interface, which only has the `getMBeanServer()` method that is used to return the `MBeanServer`, Infinispan will register its MBeans, as you can see in the following code:

```
public interface MBeanServerLookup {
  MBeanServer getMBeanServer(Properties properties);
}
```

If omitted, the default MBeanServer lookup class `org.infinispan.jmx.PlatformMBeanServerLookup` is used and will return a reference to the standard MBean server platform. In Infinispan, we have the `org.infinispan.jmx.JBossMBeanServerLookup` class, a specific implementation to locate the MBean Server inside JBoss. However, you can register Infinispan MBeans in a different `MBeanServer` instance. For example, here is the `JBossMBeanServerLookup` implementation of the `getMBeanServer()` operation:

```
public class JBossMBeanServerLookup implements MBeanServerLookup {
  @Override
  public MBeanServer getMBeanServer(Properties properties) {
    Class<?> mbsLocator =
      Util.loadClass("org.jboss.mx.util.MBeanServerLocator",
        null);
```

```
    try {
      return (MBeanServer)
        mbsLocator.getMethod("locateJBoss").invoke(null);
    } catch (Exception e) {
      throw new CacheException("Unable to locate JBoss MBean
        server", e);
    }
  }
}
```

Internally, Infinispan will call the `Class.forName()` object causing the `org.jboss.mx.util.MBeanServerLocator` class to be dynamically loaded and initialized, and it will invoke the `locateJBoss()` method, which will return the main JBoss MBeanServer.

 MBeanServerLocator is a helper class inside JBoss used to locate an MBeanServer.

If you'd like to register Infinispan MBeans in a different MBean Server, modify the source code to implement your own version of the `getMBeanServer()` method and you'll be in business. With your implementation in hand, just inform the fully qualified name of your class in the `mBeanServerLookup` (ISPN 6) / `mbean-server-lookup` (ISPN 7) attribute.

At last, the `allowDuplicateDomains` (ISPN 6) / `duplicate-domain` (ISPN 7) attribute allows one JMX domain to be responsible for multiple cache manager instances.

The cache level

At this level, as you can probably imagine, you will receive more specific information about individual cache instances, which means that you can enable JMX statistics for specific named caches or enable it in the default element.

You can enable the cache to report statistical data using JMX, which is disabled by default, adding the XML configuration. To enable JMX statistics with Infinispan 6, use the following code:

```
<jmxStatistics enabled="true"/>
```

The `jmxStatistics` element has only the enabled attributes, and can be placed under the `<default>` element for the default cache instance or under the `<namedCache>` element for specific caches.

In Infinispan 7, you can also enable statistics for individual cache instances, as you can see in the following example:

```
<local-cache statistics="true"/>
```

Otherwise, you can configure programmatically as well, using the Fluent API:

```
new ConfigurationBuilder().
    jmxStatistics().enable().
        build();
```

You could also use the setter method `setExposeJmxStatistics()`:

```
Configuration c = c.setExposeJmxStatistics(true);
```

Monitoring Infinispan with JConsole

To take advantage of this entire infrastructure, the JDK provides a monitoring tool named JConsole, which complies with the JMX specification. The JConsole graphical user interface enables you to monitor the JVM and analyze the performance and memory consumption of local applications, as well as remote applications.

If your path is correctly set, in the command line type the following command to start JConsole:

```
$ jconsole
```

The initial screen will be displayed and will present all Java applications (with the PID number), which the JConsole can connect to:

If you know the application's process ID (PID), then you can start JConsole by connecting directly to your application by typing the following command, where {PID} is the application's process ID:

```
$ jconsole {PID}
```

The second option is to connect JConsole with the **Remote Process** option, where you will obtain a connector stub to connect a remote application. This requires that you provide an address known as the JMX service URL, and a **Username** and **Password**, if required. The JMX service URL has the following syntax:

```
service:jmx:rmi://[host[:port]][urlPath]
```

Otherwise, you can connect directly to a remote application using the command line. For instance use the following command:

```
jconsole service:jmx:rmi://78.84.14.115:1099/infinispan
```

It's also possible to connect JConsole to a remote process. By providing the hostname of the server running the java application and the port number, specified for the JMX agent during JVM initialization.

```
$ jconsole hostName:portNum
```

 You can find more details on how to use JConsole at the following link:

http://docs.oracle.com/javase/7/docs/
technotes/guides/management/toc.html

If everything goes right, you should see the following screen:

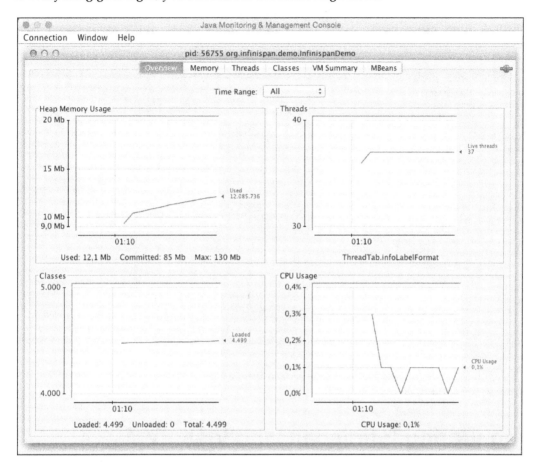

You can see that the main page presents six tabs that display information about the JVM running the Infinispan application, such as memory consumption of both heap and non-heap memory, thread activity, loaded classes and CPU utilization.

 You can also connect to multiple JMX agents simultaneously; just create a new connection and repeat the steps to connect to another running Infinispan node.

Finally, JConsole includes the **MBeans** tab (the tab that interests us), which displays a tree view that lists all MBeans registered in the MBean Server, which is shown in the following screenshot:

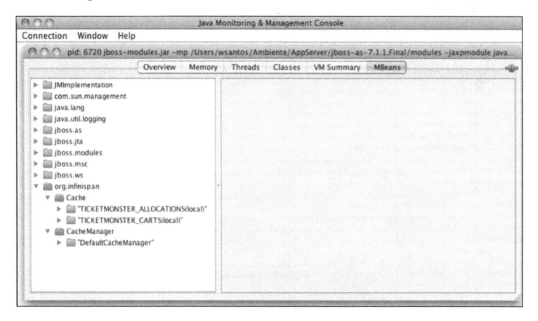

We will come back later to the MBeans tab, but first you will learn and take a look at how to set up the VisualVM.

Monitoring Infinispan with VisualVM

VisualVM is a tool that provides information about different Java applications running on a given JVM. It's built on the NetBeans platform, which provides an extensible architecture through plugins and modules that allow developers to add or remove components. VisualVM integrates many command line JDK tools and utilities such as jmap, jstack, jstat, and JConsole. With VisualVM, you can perform CPU profiling, generate and analyze heap dumps and memory leaks, and monitor garbage collection.

To start VisualVM, in the command line, type the following command:

```
$ jvisualvm
```

Similar to JConsole, an initial screen will be displayed and will present all java applications and PID numbers that are running locally in the same JVM available for connection.

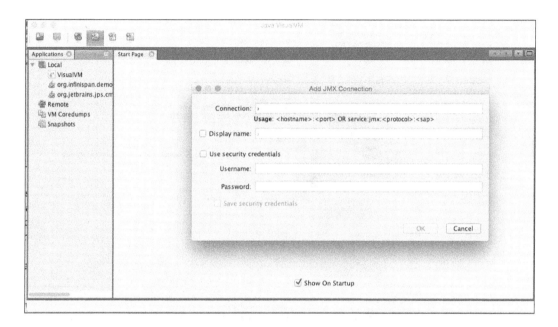

When you select the desired application, the main page will be displayed and will allow Java application developers to monitor the JVM, improve the application's performance, and troubleshoot applications. By default, MBeans is not enabled, but you can install an optional plug-in that adds JMX monitoring to VisualVM. The plugin creates an MBean tab, which allows you to access and manage the MBeans that are present in the JVM.

In order to install the MBeans tab plug-in, you will have to install the **VisualVM-MBeans** plugin, by selecting **Tools** and then **Plugins** in the **VisualVM** menu. The following screen will be displayed. Check the **VisualVM-Beans** plugin and click on **Install**:

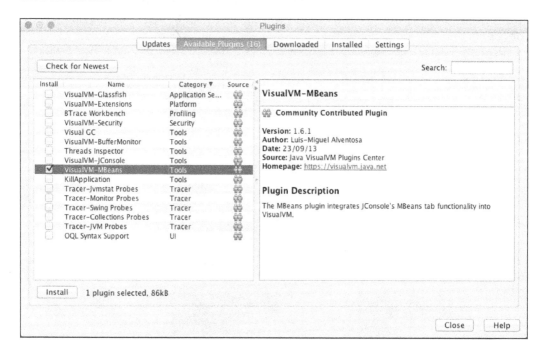

Now, if you open a running application, you will notice a new **MBeans** tab in VisualVM's right-hand window. Click on it; the **MBeans** tab will open and display data about the MBeans registered within the platform MBean server, as you can see in the following screenshot:

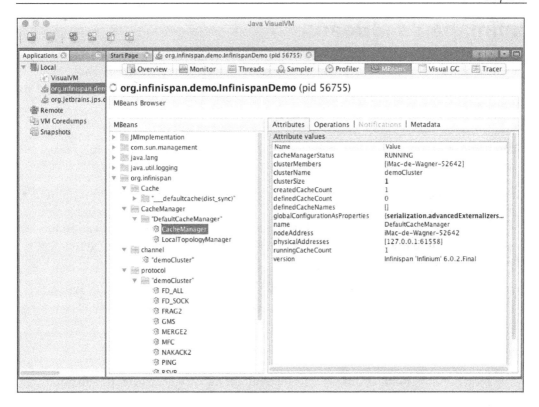

All the platform MBeans and their attributes, operations, notifications, and metadata are accessible on different tabs in the MBeans Browser.

Now that we have been introduced to JMX and the available out-of-the-box monitoring tools such as JConsole and VisualVM, we are going to inspect now the available MBeans registered by Infinispan.

Infinispan's MBeans

Once you have turned on the JMX statistics gathering at either the CacheManager or Cache level, you should be able to connect with a JMX client like JConsole or VisualVM (after installing the VisualVM MBeans plugin) in order to manage the Infinispan MBeans it exposes.

If you enabled the CacheManager level or the Cache level JMX statistics, you will have a folder named `org.infinispan` in the **MBeans** tab. Under this table, you should see a folder for each corresponding level you have enabled.

In the CacheManager level, you will find a folder with the same name you defined in `cacheManagerName` in the configuration file. If not defined, the folder will be named `DefaultCacheName`. If you have multiple cache managers in your application, it's recommended to name your cache managers for a better display and organization that follows the JMX best practices.

In the `DefaultCacheName` folder, you will see the CacheManager node. By expanding this node, you can access the MBean attributes and operations. The following table presents the available information:

Attribute	Description
cacheManagerStatus	This presents the status of the cache manager instance.
clusterMembers	This attribute lists all cluster members.
clusterName	This is the name of the cluster.
clusterSize	This is the number of nodes that form a cluster.
createdCacheCount	This is the total number of caches that are running in the grid, including the default cache.
definedCacheCount	This is the total number of caches defined in the application, excluding the default cache.
definedCacheNames	This presents the defined cache names and their statuses (created or not created). The default cache is not included in this representation.
Name	This is the name of the Cache Manager you are using.
nodeAddress	This is the network address associated with this instance.
physicalAddresses	This is the physical network addresses associated with this instance
runningCacheCount	These are the total number of running caches, including the default cache.
Version	This is the Infinispan version.

The available operation in the CacheManager level is `startCache`, which starts the default cache associated with this CacheManager, and `startCache(cacheName)`, a specific method that is based on the input parameter, and starts a named cache from this CacheManager.

In the Cache Level, you will find MBeans that provide information related to cache instances that belong to the cluster. Depending on the settings you have set up on your cache, you may see different MBeans.

In fact, all these MBeans are Infinispan classes annotated by `@MBeans`, which means that all classes annotated with this will be exposed as MBean. But this annotation is not enough to provide statistical information, you will need to annotate the methods with `@ManagedAttribute`, which indicates that a public method or a field in an MBean annotated class defines an MBean Attribute.

Finally, for MBean operations, you have the `@ManagedOperation` annotation. The following example is an extract of the `org.infinispan.CacheImpl` class, with some attributes and operations defined:

```
@MBean(objectName = CacheImpl.OBJECT_NAME, description =
  "Component that represents an individual cache instance.")
public class CacheImpl<K, V> implements AdvancedCache<K, V> {
   public static final String OBJECT_NAME = "Cache";
   @ManagedOperation(
     description = "Clears the cache",
     displayName = "Clears the cache", name = "clear"
   )
   public final void clearOperation() {
       //if we have a TM then this cache is transactional.
       // We shouldn't rely on the auto-commit option as it might be
disabled, so always start a tm.
       if (transactionManager != null) {
          try {
             transactionManager.begin();
             clear(null, null);
             transactionManager.commit();
          } catch (Throwable e) {
             throw new CacheException(e);
          }
       } else {
          clear(null, null);
       }
   }
   @ManagedOperation(
       description = "Starts the cache.",
```

```
            displayName = "Starts cache."
    )
    public void start() {
        componentRegistry.start();
        defaultMetadata = new EmbeddedMetadata.Builder()
                .lifespan(config.expiration().lifespan())
                .maxIdle(config.expiration().maxIdle())
                .build();
        // Context only needs to ship ClassLoader if marshalling will be
required
        isClassLoaderInContext = config.clustering().cacheMode().
isClustered()
                || config.persistence().usingStores()
                || config.storeAsBinary().enabled();

        if (log.isDebugEnabled()) log.debugf("Started cache %s on %s",
getName(), getCacheManager().getAddress());
    }


    @Override
    @ManagedOperation(
            description = "Stops the cache.",
            displayName = "Stops cache."
    )
    public void stop() {
        stop(null);
    }


    @ManagedAttribute(
            description = "Returns the cache status",
            displayName = "Cache status",
            dataType = DataType.TRAIT,
            displayType = DisplayType.SUMMARY
    )
    public String getCacheStatus() {
        return getStatus().toString();
    }


    @ManagedAttribute(
            description = "Returns the cache name",
            displayName = "Cache name",
            dataType = DataType.TRAIT,
            displayType = DisplayType.SUMMARY
    )
```

```
    public String getCacheName() {
        String name = getName().equals(CacheContainer.DEFAULT_CACHE_
NAME) ? "Default Cache" : getName();
        return name + "(" + getCacheConfiguration().clustering().
cacheMode().toString().toLowerCase() + ")";
    }
@ManagedAttribute(
        description = "Returns the cache configuration as XML
string",
        displayName = "Cache configuration (XML)",
        dataType = DataType.TRAIT,
        displayType = DisplayType.SUMMARY
    )
    @Override
    public String getVersion() {
        return Version.VERSION;
    }
    ...
}
```

As you can see in the previous source code, you are able to create and register your own custom MBean to provide business information using JMX. This is just a regular annotation that will expose our annotated class to JMX. The following screenshot presents the MBean created for the `CacheImpl` class, exposed on JConsole:

The MBean annotation has two elements **ObjectName** and **Description**. Notice in the preceding image that the **ObjectName** element has the following format:

```
org.infinispan:type=Cache,name="<name-of-cache>(<cache-
mode>)",manager="<name-of-cache-manager>",component=<component-
name>
```

Where `<name-of-cache>` is the name of the actual cache name. In the screenshot, our cache name is ___defaultCache because it represents the default cache and `<cache-mode>` represents the cache mode of the cache; in our example, our cache is configured with synchronous distribution, so it's replaced by `dist_sync`.

The `<name-of-cache-manager>` parameter is replaced by the name of the cache manager to which this cache belongs, which you defined in the `cacheManagerName` attribute value in the `globalJmxStatistics` element.

Other management tools

JConsole and Visual VM are wonderful management tools, but they cannot fit into all customer needs. Besides all the support you have with JConsole or VisualVM, JBoss recommends the RHQ tool; if you want a more professional monitoring tool to manage all Infinispan instances spread across the grid, you should use RHQ.

Introducing RHQ

RHQ is an open source management and monitoring tool that provides administration capabilities for JBoss Application Server, or other application servers like Tomcat. RHQ has Server/Agent architecture with an extensible plugin-based system that delivers automatic discovery and inventory of managed resources, configurable alerting, real-time graphing, administration, and monitoring for different products and platforms.

RHQ is composed of a number of components, which are outlined below:

- **RHQ Server**: The RHQ Server is the central component where the RHQ Agents will send monitoring information and statistics.
- **RHQ Agent(s)**: The RHQ Agent is a standalone Java application that we will install and execute in each server that we would like to monitor.
- **RHQ Storage Node**: The RHQ Storage Node is a customized Cassandra instance that RHQ uses to keep configuration information and all the data gathered.
- **Database**: In order to run, RHQ requires that an external database be created. The supported databases are Oracle and Database.

MySQL support is planned for future versions. At the time of writing, there is a MySQL plugin available and some features do not function correctly.

- **RHQ CLI**: RHQ Command Line Interface (CLI) is a command line shell that you can use to interact with the RHQ server. It does not require an installation and should run out of the box.

- **Web Interface**: A web-based interface is provided for easy access to RHQ. The interface is part of the RHQ server. It usually runs on the same machine that the RHQ Server is running on.

- **RHQ Rest API**: RHQ provides a REST API with many services available to manage RHQ such as platforms, groups, alerts, status, and others.

- **Remote API**: RHQ also provides an API for developers to develop specific integration with remote clients of the RHQ Server. A good example of the usage of this API is RHQ CLI, which makes use of the remote API.

- **Plugins**: A plugin is provided to the RHQ Platform as a means to integrate specific software packages, such as the Infinispan Plugin. The plugin describes which features and operations the RHQ platform can use.

Basically, for each node you have in your cluster that you want to manage, you will have to install a standalone agent, so, for each Infinispan instance that is participating in the Datagrid you will have to install a RHQ Agent, as displayed in the following diagram depicting a common architecture of a RHQ solution:

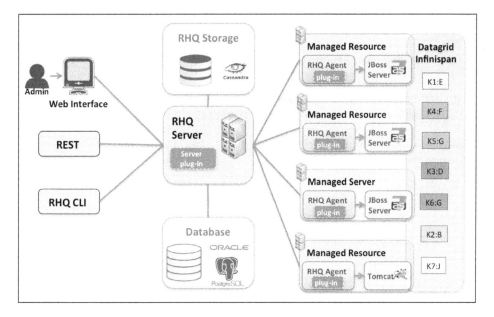

A RHQ Agent provides autodiscovery capabilities, and can easily monitor multiple instances across a cluster.

Installing and configuring RHQ

The RHQ installation process comes in two phases, the RHQ Server and RHQ Agent(s) installations.

The next section will provide the basic steps needed to install and set up the RHQ Server, Agent, and Storage. For a more detailed installation guide, you can go to the RHQ installation guide, which can be located at `https://docs.jboss.org/author/display/RHQ/Installation`.

Installing RHQ Server

First, you have to download the latest stable RHQ release from the official website at `https://docs.jboss.org/author/display/RHQ/Download+RHQ`.

You are going to be redirected to a Sourceforge page to download it, on the Sourceforge page you can also download the Rest API documentation. Download the `rhq-server-<version number>.zip` file and unzip it in your preferred location.

Currently, the RHQ Server supports either a Windows, Mac OSX, Linux, or UNIX operating system on x86_64, i686, and ia64 architectures. RHQ requires Java 6 or higher to run both RHQ Server and RHQ Agents.

> It's important to note that the operating system clocks on RHQ Servers, Storage Nodes, and Agents need to be accurate and synchronized.
>
> To keep them synchronized, a Network Time Synchronization tool is highly recommended.

The RHQ Server is a customized JBossAS Server; when you start the RHQ Server, you are actually starting up a custom JBoss AS Server with the RHQ application deployed.

The basic installation steps you need to perform after unzipping the distribution is to customize the server's configuration file.

Load the configuration file `<RHQ-HOME>/bin/rhq-server.properties` in a text editor and edit the configuration settings. First, configure the database settings for your chosen database, which can be Oracle 11g or PostgreSQL Versions 8.3.*x* through 9.3.*x*. The following sample shows how to access a PostgreSQL database:

```
# PostgreSQL database
rhq.server.database.connection-url=jdbc:postgresql://127.0.0.1:5432/
rhqdb
rhq.server.database.user-name=rhqadmin
rhq.server.database.password=1eeb2f255e832171df8592078de921bc
rhq.server.database.type-mapping=PostgreSQL
rhq.server.database.server-name=127.0.0.1
rhq.server.database.port=5432
rhq.server.database.db-name=rhqdb
hibernate.dialect=org.hibernate.dialect.PostgreSQLDialect
rhq.server.quartz.driverDelegateClass=org.quartz.impl.
    jdbcjobstore.PostgreSQLDelegate
```

If you choose the PostgreSQL database for the target database platform, as we used in our example, you have to comment out the Oracle settings. Next, change all the settings to match the needs of your environment such as the SMTP settings, high-availability, and SSL.

> Storing a plaintext password in the `rhq.server.database.password` property allows anyone to see the password. But instead, you can encode the password using the `rhq-installer.sh` script, as follows:
>
> `rhq-installer.sh(.bat) --dbpassword=<your password>`

In the next step, let's review the properties of the RHQ Storage; it is not required to edit any storage properties but it's recommended to review the default options. So load the `<RHQ-HOME>/bin/rhq-storage.properties` file in a text editor and change all the settings to suit your environment.

Once your database is prepared and you finish reviewing all the properties, you can finally install the RHQ Server.

There is more than one way to install RHQ. Navigate to `<RHQ-HOME>/bin` and execute the following command to start the server:

./rhq-server.sh (Linux) or rhq-server.bat (Windows)

This command will start the JBoss Application Server and once your server is up and running, you can navigate to the admin page by directly following the URL: `https://localhost:7890`.

To validate whether your settings are correct, you can execute the following command to perform some validation before installing RHQ:

```
./rhq-installer.sh --test (Linux) or rhq-installer.bat --test
  (Windows)
```

If everything is well, you can install the RHQ services (which refers specifically to one of the RHQ Server, RHQ Agent, or RHQ Storage nodes) using RHQ Control Script (rhqctl) from the bin directory:

```
./rhqctl install (Linux) or rhqctl.bat install (Windows)
```

> Running the rhqctl.bat install command in Windows will install the RHQ Server as a Windows service.

Alternatively, you can install the RHQ services one by one to install the RHQ Server and the RHQ Storage will do the following:

```
./rhqctl install --storage [options]
./rhqctl install --server
```

Now, start the RHQ services by running the following command:

```
./rhqctl start  (Linux) or rhqctl.bat install (Windows)
```

> To prevent memory leaks or OutOfMemoryErrors errors you can increase the memory requirements of the RHQ Server by adjusting the following VM settings:
>
> -Xms, -Xmx, -XX:PermSize, -XX:MaxPermSize.

You can check the status of the RHQ services by executing the following code:

```
./rhqctl status (Linux) or rhqctl.bat status (Windows)
```

After executing this command, you should see the following output:

```
MacBook-Pro-de-Wagner:bin wsantos$ ./rhqctl status
16:02:52,991 INFO  [org.jboss.modules] JBoss Modules version 1.2.0.CR1
RHQ Storage Node              (pid 8372   ) IS running
RHQ Agent                     (pid 8399   ) IS running
RHQ Server                    (pid 8274   ) IS running
JBossAS Java VM child process (pid 8274   ) IS running
```

Installing the Infinispan plugin

By now, you should have an RHQ server running, so it's time to install the Infinispan plugin; if you downloaded one of the binary distributions (`*-bin.zip` or `*-all.zip` should do), it already comes with the Infinispan plugin name `infinispan-rhq-plugin.jar`. This is located under the `<Infinispan-home>/modules/rhq-plugin` directory.

Open the RHQ Web console and provide the default username and password as required (default `rhqadmin`).

 It's recommended that after the first access you change the default password from `rhqadmin`.

Navigate to **Administration** | **Configuration** | **Agent Plugins**, you should see the following screen:

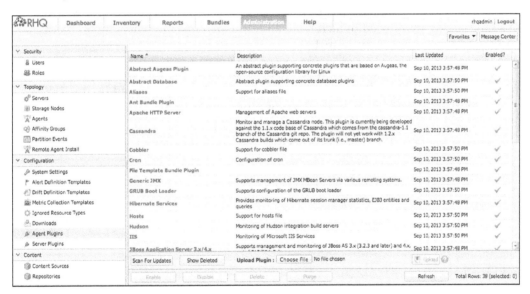

Press the **Choose File** button in the **Upload Plugin** option and select the **infinispan-rhq-plugin.jar** file, then press the **Upload** button.

Now you have to wait for the server to autodetect the Infinispan plugin. When the RHQ Server detects the plugin, it will appear in the plugin list as you see in the following screenshot:

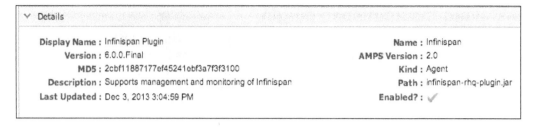

 You can force the RHQ Server to detect the plugin immediately by pressing the **Scan for Updates** button.

Now, we only have to install and configure the RHQ agent on all machines that have an Infinispan instance that you want to manage.

Installing the RHQ Agent

The last step in the installation procedure is to install a fresh agent on each of the machines being monitored, which have an Infinispan instance running on them. Perform the following steps to install a fresh agent:

1. You will need the RHQ Agent Update Binary jar file, whose purpose is to install an agent on a machine that has not been monitored by the RHQ Server, or update an existent agent plugin.

2. You can get the RHQ Agent plugin inside the RHQ Server, you can download it by navigating to **Administration | Configuration | Downloads**.

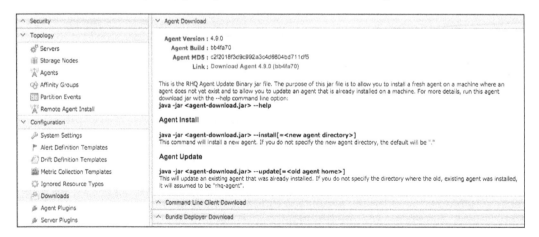

3. On this page, you will find all the information needed to download and execute the RHQ Agent and other utilities available for download such as the Command Line Client (CLI), the Bundle Deployer Tool, Connectors, and Script Modules.

 You can also download the RHQ Agent Binary jar file directly from http://< server-hostname>:<server-port >/ agentupdate/download\.

4. Now that you've downloaded the JAR file, you need to install a single agent on each machine you want to monitor, which can be either a Unix or Windows platform.

5. In order to install the agent in the target machine, run the command as follows. If you do not specify the directory, the default directory will be the directory from which you have launched. To install the agent, run the following command:

```
java -jar rhq-enterprise-agent-<version>.jar
  --install[=<directory>]
```

To update an existing agent, we will have to use the option update:

```
java -jar rhq-enterprise-agent-<version>.jar --update[=<old
  agent home>]
```

This command will tell the agent update binary to extract the RHQ Agent and install a copy of it in the directory you specified. If you do not specify the directory where the old agent was installed, it will be assumed as rhq-agent.

 Before you run the agent, you can preconfigure the agent with your own preference by editing the agent-configuration.xml file in the conf folder located in any agent's directory.

If you do not change the XML file when you run the agent for the first time, you'll need to provide the correct IP/hostname and Port to connect the RHQ Server, so that the agent plugin works correctly.

6. After installing the agent, go to the <AGENT-HOME>/bin directory and execute the rhq-agent.sh (or bat) script and follow the prompts (if you have not configured it before).

```
MacBook-Pro-de-Wagner:bin wsantos$ ./rhq-agent.sh
RHQ 4.9.0 [bb4fa70] (Tue Sep 10 17:05:44 BRT 2013)
Answer the following questions to setup this RHQ Agent instance.
- After each prompt, a default value will appear in square brackets.
  If you press the ENTER key without providing any value,
  the new preference value will be set to that default value.
- If you wish to rely on the system internal default value and
  not define any preference value, enter '!*'.
- If you wish to stop before finishing all the questions but still
  retain those preferences you already set, enter '!+'.
- If you wish to cancel before finishing all the questions and revert
  all preferences back to their original values, enter '!-'.
- If you need help for a particular preference, enter '!?'.

Agent Name [192.168.0.111] :
Agent Hostname or IP Address [!*] : localhost
Agent Port [16163] :
RHQ Server Hostname or IP Address [192.168.0.111] :
RHQ Server Port [7080] :
The setup has been completed for the preferences at node [/rhq-agent/default].
!!! This agent is registering under the loopback address [socket://localhost:16163/?rhq.communications.connector.rh
qtype=agent&numAcceptThreads=1&maxPoolSize=303&clientMaxPoolSize=304&socketTimeout=60000&enableTcpNoDelay=true&back
log=200] - this should only be done for testing or demo purposes - this agent will only be able to interact with a
server running on the same host as this agent
```

7. At this point, the RHQ agent will automatically detect Infinispan instances that are running on the machine.

Monitoring Infinispan

Before you start to monitor your Infinispan instances, you may have to set some system properties, to make sure that the RHQ agents are able to discover the Infinispan Instances. The following is the code for setting up system properties:

```
-Dcom.sun.management.jmxremote.port=6996
-Dcom.sun.management.jmxremote.ssl=false
-Dcom.sun.management.jmxremote.authenticate=false
```

You have to set these properties in the JVM used to run Infinispan. To monitor an Infinispan instance embedded into JBoss AS 7, you have to add the following properties to the `<JBOSS-HOME>/standalone/configuration/standalone.xml` file for the Standalone mode and the `domain.xml` file for the Domain mode.

In order to monitor multiple Infinispan instances in a single machine, you have to provide a different JMX port, otherwise, the RHQ Agent will not be able to discover the Infinispan instances.

In the standalone mode, consider setting these properties into the `<system-properties>` element after the `<extensions>` element:

```
</extensions>
  <system-properties>
    <property name="com.sun.management.jmxremote.port" value="6996"/>
    <property name="com.sun.management.jmxremote.ssl" value="false"/>
```

```
        <property name="com.sun.management.jmxremote.authenticate" value=
    "false" />
    </system-properties>
```

The next step is to discover available Infinispan instances using the RHQ Administration console and open `http://<RHQ-Server>:7080` (assuming you're using the default port).

Once you login, navigate to **Inventory | Discovery Queue**, you should see a new resource. Select the available Infinispan resources and press the **Import** button.

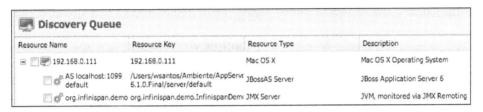

You can optionally have multiple Infinispan instances running on the same machine, but you will have to provide different JMX ports and import them manually into the RHQ server.

To add a resource manually, navigate to **Inventory | Platforms** and select the IP or the hostname of the target platform; then click on the **Inventory** tab and you will see a list under **Child Resources**. At the bottom of the page, there's a toolbar, press the **Import** button, which will display a drop down list containing a list of resources that you can manually import, which is shown in the following screenshot:

On the list, select **JMX Server**. A new page will be displayed asking you to select a **Connection Settings Template**; these templates provide information specific to the environment you are working in, such as Weblogic 9 and WebSphere.

For simplicity, let's choose the **JDK 5** template and press the **Next** button; this will lead to a page where you will need to enter the JMX connector address of the Infinispan instance you're trying to monitor, for instance:

```
service:jmx:rmi:///jndi/rmi://localhost:6996/jmxrmi
```

If everything goes right, a new entry called **JMX Servers** will be added to the platform list.

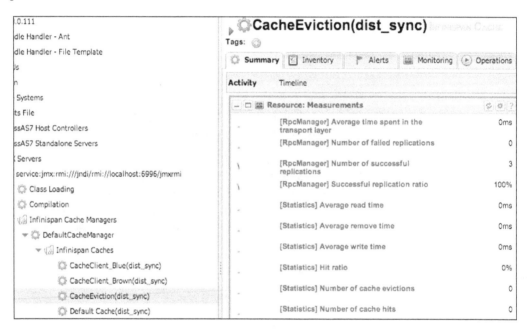

Now you can use this information to monitor your Infinispan caches and instances.

Planning and scheduling operations

RHQ includes multiple features in a single package devoted to different aspects of systems management.

One of the most interesting features is the **Operations** tab, where you can configure RHQ to execute remote operations provided by the MBean on different resources on your inventory.

You can have operations that change the state of a resource, such as to start or stop the cache, or operations to provide basic information like the Infinispan version and the cache status.

To see how it works, let's create a schedule. First navigate to the **Infinispan Cache** you want to create the schedule in. Select the **Operations** tab and press the **New** button.

In the **Operations** list, you can select any operation available on the MBeans. In the following figure, we selected the **showInDoubtTransactions()** operation from the **RecoveryAdmin** MBean in a cache with transaction support:

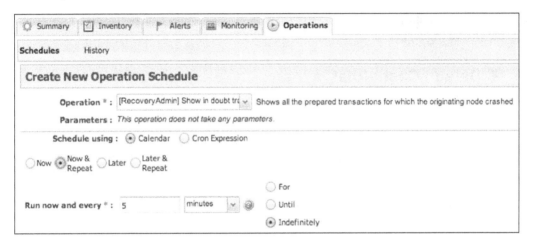

Every operation exposed through RHQ has a wide array of options for execution. You can configure your operation to be executed only once and immediately select the **Now** option, or you can also schedule your operation to execute periodically. If an operation is set to execute periodically, RHQ allows you to schedule operations using a Calendar or a Cron Expression.

Note that in the **History** view, all results are recorded within log tables that provide audit trails or the history. It records the name of the user who requested the operation, the date of execution, and the status (success, failure, in progress, and canceled).

Creating alerts

RHQ includes a powerful alert system that enables you to customize alerts and take proactive action to suit your organizational objectives. You can, for instance, create an alert to notify an administrator when an event or predefined condition is met, such as when a cache goes down or when an operation is being executed on the monitored resource. For all triggered alerts on any condition defined by you, RHQ provides an audit trail.

When the information flows into the RHQ alert system, it processes the information received and takes an action, which can either correlate with data from other parts of the system, transform, or filter the data.

Let's take a look at a simple example, we will repeat the same steps as we did to create a schedule; navigate to the **Infinispan Cache** you want to create an alert on. Select the **Alerts** tab and then, the **Definitions** options.

Each resource in the inventory (in this example, the resource is our cache) might have zero, one, or many alert definitions.

We could, for instance, create an alert that triggers when the cache stops, as shown in the following figure:

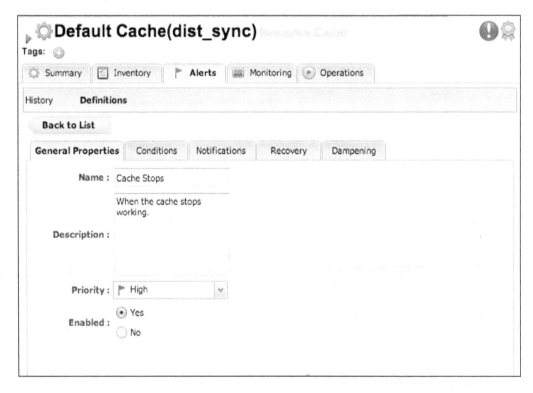

Now we have to define the conditions that should fire the alert; we can define multiple conditions and configure it to fire an alarm when an ANY condition evaluates to true. The following figure shows a simple condition that will be displayed when someone executes the operation to stop the cache:

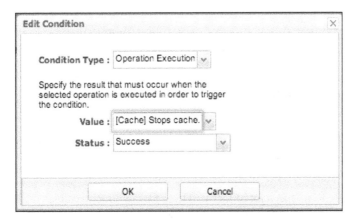

When an alert is fired, you can optionally have one or more notifications sent. You do this by assigning alert notifications in the **Notification** tab. Press the **Add** button to assign a notification to your alert definition.

 To send alert emails, the SMTP settings must be configured in the e-mail settings section of the rhq-server.properties file.

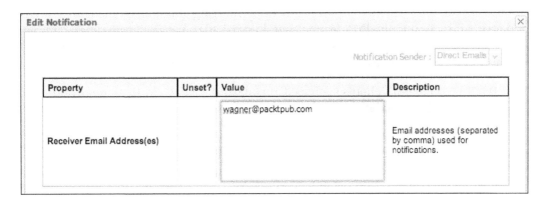

There are several types of notifications that you can assign to your alert definitions. We can send e-mails to all the RHQ users that belong to a particular set of roles using the **System Roles Notification** option, or to a specific RHQ user (System Users Notification) using the **Direct Email** option to enable notification by e-mail.

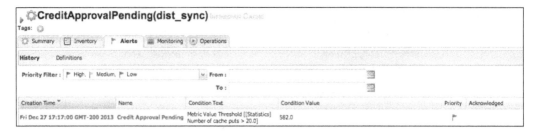

Using the **Recovery** tab, we can configure a second alert definition to automatically re-enable the first alert definition when the problems/conditions are cleared up or fixed.

Using the **Dampening** tab, we can define whether or not any dampening should take place to limit the number of fired alerts.

> RHQ has a lot of features that, for obvious reasons, we are not covering here, so it is recommended that you read more about it at https://docs.jboss.org/author/display/ RHQ49/User+Documentation.

In the dashboard, you can see the recent alerts and operations. Customize it to include the information you want and what is important and relevant to you.

Summary

In this chapter, we presented an overview of monitoring and management with Java and an introduction to the JMX technology. In particular, we went into detail on how Infinispan provide different statistical information about the cache and operations to manage the grid and its resources, through the use of MBeans.

We saw how to use JMX clients such as JConsole and Visual VM to manage and analyze your Infinispan data grid.

There are a variety of other monitoring tools that are more professional; during this chapter, we have seen how to install and work with RHQ to manage all your Infinispan instances in detail. Another powerful monitoring tool that your organization should consider using is Hawt.io (see http://hawt.io/), which has a lightweight and modular HTML 5 web console with a nice Infinispan plugin, which adds support to visualize your caches.

In the next chapter, you will learn about the Infinispan Modules in depth.

Server Modules

9

Until this chapter, for all the scenarios and code samples we have used Infinispan bundled as a library embedded into your application code.

In this chapter, we will examine Infinispan in another perspective. We will analyze Infinispan server modules, which are modules deployed in an Application server that provide Infinispan as a service, and get some clients to consume the data provided by the cache service.

There are several modules available:

- Client/Server access
- Introduction to server modules
- Infinispan REST server
- Using Hot Rod server
- Infinispan Memcached server
- Infinispan WebSocket server
- Introducing the command line interface.

You will also see how to deploy and configure each server module and how to use the command line interface provided by Infinispan to access the data grid.

Client/Server access

In *Chapter 3, Using the APIs*, we presented two ways to interact with Infinispan, the Embedded mode and Client-Server mode. The architecture of a software system using Infinispan is not limited to the embedded mode.

You can create a combination of a client-server architectural style to make your system complete. There are some situations in which accessing Infinispan in a client-server mode might make more sense than accessing it via **Peer-to-Peer** (**P2P**).

As the name suggests, the client-server mode describes the relationship between the data grid system with one or more servers responsible to control the state of the objects and a client that initiates one or more requests, waits, and processes the replies on receipt.

Consider using the client-server model if you are creating services for other applications to consume or you will be supporting many clients. As you should know by now, Infinispan is written in Java, so in this scenario, we could have clients written in the Java language as well other languages such as C++, Ruby, or Python.

In addition to these benefits, in the client-server mode, you can get a higher security, since the data is stored on the server (in the data grid), which offers a better control of security, and provides an easier maintenance procedure if you have to make a repair or upgrade the server.

Considering the limitations of this model, in contrast to the benefits, the client-server mode still has disadvantages over P2P. One common problem related to client-server architecture is related to network traffic blocking, when you have multiple client requests to the server, increasing the server latency. Depending on the number of requests, the server can become overloaded.

Introduction to server modules

Infinispan provides a separate package to install the server endpoints, for those who are interested in implementing Infinispan in a client-server mode.

To install Infinispan server modules, you have to download a ZIP file from the official website `http://infinispan.org/download/`, which contains a JBoss AS 7.2 standalone server that exposes the grid to clients over a variety of protocols.

All these server modules follow the same pattern; the server backend creates an embedded Infinispan instance and if you start multiple instances, they can form a cluster and share data in accordance with the settings provided.

Here's a brief summary of the available server endpoints:

- The Hot Rod server module provides cache access through the Hot Rod protocol
- The REST Server module exposes the cache data via REST services

- The Memcached Server module provides Memcached access to the cache
- The WebSocket Server module provides WebSocket access

Starting the server

To start the Infinispan server, open the Command Prompt, navigate to the Infinispan home folder, and run the `standalone.sh` (or `.bat` depending on your platform) or `clustered.sh` (`.bat`) scripts in the same way as you start a JBoss Application Server. To run it through Command Prompt, run the following command:

```
./bin/standalone.sh
```

After starting the server by running the above command from the command line, you should see the following log output in the JBoss server console. Portions of the output have been lightly edited for better comprehension:

```
Coyote HTTP/1.1 starting on: http-/127.0.0.1:8080
REST starting
REST mapped to /rest
[org.jboss.as.remoting] Listening on 127.0.0.1:4447
[org.jboss.as.remoting] Listening on 127.0.0.1:9999
HotRodServer listening on 127.0.0.1:11222
WebSocketServer listening on 127.0.0.1:8181
MemcachedServer listening on 127.0.0.1:11211
Http management interface listening on http://127.0.0.1:9990/management
Admin console listening on http://127.0.0.1:9990
```

Notice that now you should be able to connect to your Infinispan cache using one of these available protocols and the HTTP management interface.

If you want to use the Infinispan server in a clustered environment to get high availability and communication among the nodes, you will have to start the servers by using the `clustered.sh` (`.bat`) script and the `standalone/configuration/clustered.xml` configuration file.

When in clustered mode, they should communicate amongst themselves via UDP multicast and form a cluster.

> To start multiple nodes on the same host, you need to provide a unique node name with `jboss.node.name` and specify a port offset on which node would be running using the `jboss.socket.binding.port-offset` system property:
>
> ```
> ./bin/clustered.sh -Djboss.socket.binding.
>   port-offset=100 -Djboss.node.name=nodeX
> ```

If you prefer, you can change Infinispan to use TCP discovery, but you will have to change the JGroups subsystem declaration, as we will see in *Chapter 11, An Introduction to JGroups*.

Configuration

The configuration in JBoss AS7 is quite different from earlier versions; the new configuration file is composed of a list of subsystems (for example, the servlet subsystem, the datasource subsystem, and the messaging subsystem, among others) where each service represents a subsystem, which in turn contains the functionalities that can be used by the application server.

In the configuration file, you also have a special subsystem for Infinispan called Infinispan subsystem configuration that is responsible for keeping the session data synchronized across its members and provides high availability, and the endpoint subsystem responsible for exposing the container over a specified connector protocol.

Customizing the endpoint and Infinispan subsystem

The available connectors are defined in the endpoint subsystem section of the XML file. This allows you to bind the listening port to a specific protocol.

Here's a complete sample subsystem declaration, which enables the available servers:

```
<subsystem xmlns="urn:infinispan:server:endpoint:6.0">
  <hotrod-connector socket-binding="hotrod"
    cache-container="clustered">
    <topology-state-transfer lazy-retrieval="false"
      lock-timeout="1000" replication-timeout="5000"/>
  </hotrod-connector>
  <memcached-connector socket-binding="memcached"
    cache-container="clustered"/>
    <rest-connector virtual-server="default-host"
      cache-container="clustered" security-domain="other"
        auth-method="BASIC"/>
    <websocket-connector socket-binding="websocket"
      cache-container="clustered"/>
</subsystem>
```

The hotrod-connector, memcached-connector and websocket-connector elements contain a socket-binding attribute, where you can define how to bind the relationship between network ports to a network interface. Actually, you define the port numbers in the <socket-binding-group> section of the configuration file.

> Because REST uses the HTTP protocol, changes to socket binding, timeout, and other settings must be performed on the web subsystem.

In the configuration file, the `<socket-binding-group>` references a network interface through the default-interface attribute. If you prefer, you can change the port attribute where services are bound:

```
<socket-binding-group name="standard-sockets"
  default-interface="public"
    port-offset="${jboss.socket.binding.port-offset:0}">
    <socket-binding name="hotrod" port="11222"/>
    <socket-binding name="memcached" port="11211"/>
    <socket-binding name="websocket" port="8181"/>
</socket-binding-group>
```

The Infinispan subsystem configures the cache containers; the configuration of these subsystems is slightly different from the traditional Infinispan configuration, since it uses a specific JBoss AS configuration schema.

You can create or customize your own configuration file and initialize the server with the file you want; to do so, you have to copy the configuration file to the `standalone/configuration` directory and start the server. For example, if you create a file called `clustered-topology.xml` and include it in the `configuration` folder, you can start the server and use this file using the following syntax:

.bin/standalone.sh -c clustered-topology.xml

> You can find several files with examples of configurations and different scenarios in the following directory:
> `/<infinispan-server-home>/docs/examples/configs`

The following XML structure is the backbone of the Infinispan configuration:

```
<subsystem xmlns="urn:infinispan:server:core:5.3"
  default-cache-container="clustered">
    <cache-container name="clustered" default-cache="default">
    <transport executor="infinispan-transport"
      lock-timeout="60000"/>
    <distributed-cache name="default" mode="SYNC"
      segments="20" owners="2" remote-timeout="30000"
        start="EAGER">
      <locking isolation="READ_COMMITTED"
        acquire-timeout="30000" concurrency-level="1000"
          striping="false"/>
```

```
          <transaction mode="NONE"/>
        </distributed-cache>
      <invalidation-cache name="entity" mode="SYNC">
        <transaction mode="NON_XA"/>
        <expiration max-idle="100000"/>
        <eviction strategy="LRU" max-entries="10000"/>
      </invalidation-cache>
    </cache-container>
      <cache-container name="security"/>
  </subsystem>
```

The `<cache-container>` element allows you to declare multiple caches, as you could see in the last example. In this model, we don't have implicit default cache, and we can use the `default-cache` attribute to specify any named cache we want as the default.

To create a cache, we have four different elements for each type of cache: local cache, distributed cache, replicated cache, and invalidation cache. In our previous example, we defined a distributed and an invalidation cache.

For the default cache, we declared it as distributed and added the `<locking>` element to change the locking configuration of the cache, set up the isolation level as `READ_COMMITED`, and changed the timeout, concurrency level, and striping settings.

Further in the cache entity, we declared it as an invalidation cache and added the following elements:

- The `<expiration/>` element defines the maximum idle time a cache entry will live in the cache.
- The `<eviction/>` element configures the eviction mechanism with a **Least Recently Used (LRU)** pattern and maximum number of entries.
- The `<transaction>` element sets the transaction cache mode as `NON_XA`. Possible values are `NONE`, `NON_XA`, `NON_DURABLE_XA`, and `FULL_XA`.

Next, we have an example of a replicated cache with asynchronous replication and a file-based cache store:

```
<replicated-cache name="repl" mode="ASYNC" batching="true">
  <file-store/>
</replicated-cache>
```

A local cache with a start attribute that defines the cache will be started during server startup. The nested tag `remote-stores` is used to define a remote cache store, which must be a cluster of the Infinispan Hot Rod servers. Nested properties will be treated as Hot Rod client properties.

The `<remote-server/>` tag and the `outbound-socket-binding` element are used to define and bind the remote server that is running the Infinispan Hot Rod server, which is as follows:

```
<local-cache name="myLocalCache" start="EAGER">
  <remote-store cache="namedCache" socket-timeout="60000"
    tcp-no-delay="true" passivation="false">
    <remote-server outbound-socket-binding=
      "remote-store-hotrod-server"/>
  </remote-store>
</local-cache>
```

When you connect to a remote Hot Rod store, you'll also need to add an `<outbound-socket-binding>` element to the `<socket-binding-group>` element:

```
<socket-binding-group name="standard-sockets"
  default-interface="public" port-offset=
    "${jboss.socket.binding.port-offset:0}">
    <outbound-socket-binding name="remote-store-hotrod-server">
      <remote-destination host="remote-host" port="11222"/>
    </outbound-socket-binding>
    <outbound-socket-binding name="remote-store-rest-server">
      <remote-destination host="remote-host" port="8080"/>
    </outbound-socket-binding>
</socket-binding-group>
```

Enabling protocol interoperability

By default, the Infinispan server does not allow you to access the same cache and data from multiple protocols. If you want to provide external access to the grid for more than one protocol, you will have to enable the compatibility mode by adding the `<compatibility/>` element on every cache you want. But it's important to note that all endpoints are configured with the same cache manager and communicate to the same cache. To enable compatibility, add the following code:

```
<replicated-cache name="repl" mode="ASYNC" batching="true">
    <compatibility enabled="true"/>
</replicated-cache>
```

Infinispan REST server

If you are using a fresh version of Infinispan, follow the steps to start and configure the Infinispan REST server.

If you started the server properly, then to access the REST module, just point your browser to the Infinispan REST Server located at `http://localhost:8080/ infinispan`, and you will see a welcome page with general instructions on how to use his module.

Before we go into the details, let's make an overview of some REST concepts.

Introduction to REST services

In 2000, one of the authors of the HTTP specification, the scientist Roy Fielding, presented in his doctoral thesis a new way of integrating distributed hypermedia systems called **Representational State Transfer** (**REST**). It was based on the same architectural principles behind the **World Wide Web** (**WWW**), thus attracting great attention.

According to *Roy Fielding* and the Wikipedia definition:

> *"REST is a style of software architecture for distributed hypermedia systems such as the World Wide Web."*

Generally, we use a web browser to access resources that we want, usually an HTML page or an XML document providing the address (an URL) to such resources. REST dictates how you should use the HTTP protocol correctly by providing guidelines and best practices to create a scalable and distributed hypermedia system.

Still in his thesis, Fielding says the REST architecture style is an abstraction of the architectural elements within a distributed multimedia system, defined as follows:

- **Data elements**: These are classified as resources, the metadata of these resources, their identifiers (URIs), and their representations, which can be represented as an HTML file, an XML document, an image, and so on.

- **Connectors**: These are the various types of connectors that REST uses to encapsulate the activities of accessing resources and transferring a representation of a resource. We can classify connectors as clients, servers, caches, resolvers, and tunnels.

- **Components**: These are classified by their roles in an overall application action; the REST components are classified as origin servers, gateways, proxies, and user agents.

REST uses HTTP, a stateless protocol, usually used on client-server architecture, which is considered a lightweight alternative to **Remote Procedure Calls (RPC)** and Web Services SOAP.

When applying REST principles in the development of a web application, we explored the use of HTTP and URIs in a natural way, which makes it the most simple, lightweight, and high-performance application.

Configuring the Infinispan REST Server on earlier versions

In earlier versions, Infinispan came with a WAR file that provides RESTful HTTP access, ready to deploy in a servlet container with as many instances as you need.

By default, the REST Server will create a default cache on the LOCAL mode; if you want to create your own cache, you will have to provide your own configuration file.

 It's not possible to create named caches on the fly in the Infinispan REST Server.

If that's your case and you're working with a legacy version of the Infinispan REST Server. First, will need to unzip the REST WAR file in the Infinispan folder and deploy it. If the deployment completes successfully, point your browser to the Infinispan REST Server located at `http://<yourhost>:<port number>/infinispan`. It will open a welcome page with some information, as follows:

Now, create an Infinispan configuration file and place it wherever you want.

Edit the `web.xml` file located at `infinispan-server-rest.war/WEB-INF/web.xml` and change the `infinispan.config init-param` element to include the full path to your Infinispan configuration file:

```
<web-app>
    <display-name>Infinispan cache REST server</display-name>
    <context-param>
        <param-name>resteasy.resources</param-name>
        <param-value>org.infinispan.rest.Server</param-value>
    </context-param>
    <!-- Specify your cache configuration file -->
    <context-param>
        <param-name>infinispan.config</param-name>
        <param-value>config-samples/sample.xml</param-value>
    </context-param>
</web-app>
```

Finally, restart the web server and you will be done!

Introducing the REST API

The REST API provides access to the entities in the cache via **uniform resource identifiers** (**URI**) to exchange information between client applications and the REST Server module.

Fortunately, it is relatively easy to work with HTTP requests and responses, and the most popular programming languages provide an API to handle HTTP requests, such as **urllib2** and **httplib** in Python, **libcurl** in PHP, **HttpWebRequest** in C #, **open-uri** in Ruby, **java.net.* package**, and the **Apache HttpClient** project in Java, among others.

However, for any language, if the request is made to a REST service, we have to go through some steps:

1. Come up with all necessary data that will go into the HTTP request, such as the URI, HTTP header (if any), the desired HTTP method, and any content that you want to include in the request's entity-body.
2. Format the data as an HTTP request and send it to a valid HTTP server.
3. Parse the response data (XML, JSON, and so on) to the data structures that your application needs.

The supported HTTP methods in the REST API for entities are as follows:

- HEAD: This retrieves a cache entry, but you'll receive exactly the same content that you have stored, which means that if you have stored a binary object, you will need to deserialize the content yourself
- GET: This retrieves a cache entry or a list of keys
- POST: This creates a new cache entry
- PUT: This updates a cache entry
- DELETE: This deletes an entry

The REST API provides the following methods:

HTTP Verb	URI	Action
HEAD	/{cacheName}/{cacheKey}	A HEAD request works exactly like the GET method, but it will not return content in the response body, only the header fields.
GET	/{cacheName}	A GET request will return a list of keys present in the cache as the response body.
GET	/{cacheName}/{cacheKey}	A GET request will retrieve a representation of the cache entry from the given cache.
POST	/{cacheName}/{cacheKey}	A POST request will create a new cache entry in the given cache, with the given key. If an entry already exists for the given key, the content will not be updated and the server will return a HTTP 409 CONFLICT status.
PUT	/{cacheName}/{cacheKey}	A PUT request will insert or update a cache entry in the given cache, with the given key.
DELETE	/{cacheName}	A DELETE request will remove all the entries from the given cache
DELETE	/{cacheName}/{cacheKey}	A DELETE request will remove a cache entry from the given cache, with the given key.

HTTP GET and HEAD are similar methods and can be used to read data from the cache. The HTTP GET method is used to retrieve a cache entry. If the cache entry exists, the GET will return a representation of the data that was stored in the cache and a response code of 200 (OK). Otherwise, if the requested cache key does not exist, it will return a 404 (NOT FOUND) or 400 (BAD REQUEST) response code.

Since the release of Infinispan 5.3, you can obtain additional information for a given cache key by appending the extended parameter on the query string, as follows:

GET /cacheName/cacheKey?extended

This GET operation will return the following custom headers:

- **Cluster-Primary-Owner**: This is the name of the node that is the primary owner of the key
- **Cluster-Node-Name**: This is the name of the node that handled the request in JGroups
- **Cluster-Physical-Address**: This is the physical address of the JGroups cluster that handled the request

The HTTP methods POST and PUT are used to store and modify data in the cache, and cannot be compared to CRUD's create and update operations. The key point here is to identify whether you're making an idempotent change to your cache entry or not. An operation is considered idempotent if more than one call to the same operation in the cache entry results in the resource state.

According to the HTTP 1.1 specification, the following HTTP methods are idempotent:

- GET
- HEAD
- PUT
- DELETE

The POST method is not considered idempotent, which means that two different POST requests are considered as different operations, even if you're using an identical resource, whereas a sequence of several PUT requests to the same URL will result in the same resource state as a single operation.

So, use the POST method when you want to create a new cache entry. If you try to create an entry with a key that already exists, the content will not be updated and you will get an HTTP 409 CONFLICT status.

Use PUT when you want to change a new cache entry, the method will place the cache entry in your cache with the provided key.

It's valid in some occasions to use POST to create resources with the cache name and key within the URL and send data enclosed in the body of the request, which can be anything you want. You have to set the content header to the corresponding format you want.

You can also add other headers to control the cache settings and behavior.

Using HTTP request headers for GET and HEAD operations

For GET and HEAD operations, you can use the accept attribute. You can find more details in the next section:

Accept

Defines the expected MIME type of the response as part of content negotiation mechanism defined in the HTTP specification, which can be:

- **Supported Values**: This is useful for the GET /{cacheName} method, which returns a list of keys present in the cache. This header is used to specify the response type you want the server to send. Infinispan currently accepts the following MIME types:
    - application/xml: This will render the list of keys in an XML representation
    - application/json: This will render the list of keys in a JSON representation
    - text/html: This will render the list of keys in an HTML representation
    - text/plain: This will render the list of keys (one key per line) in plain text format

- **Required**: The Accept attribute is optional.

Using HTTP request headers for POST and PUT operations

Now, let's take a look at HTTP request headers. They will allow you to customize the request's behavior. For every REST call you make, there is a set of required HTTP headers that you must include in your request and also others you can optionally include.

Content-Type

This element defines the MIME type of the response body, which can be:

- **Supported Values**: These can be any valid MIME type defined by the IANA
- **Required**: The Content-Type attribute is optional

 The official list of MIME type, as defined by IANA can be found here http://www.iana.org/assignments/media-types/media-types.xhtml.

performAsync

If defined, performAsync will perform asynchronous requests and the operation will return without waiting for data replication.

- **Supported Values**: This attribute supports only true and false boolean values
- **Required**: The performAsync attribute is optional

timeToLiveSeconds

timeToLiveSeconds is the number of seconds before this entry is automatically deleted. You can change the following characteristics of the timeToLiveSeconds attribute:

- **Supported Values**: This attribute supports only number values. If omitted, Infinispan assumes -1 as the default value and the cache entry will not expire.
- **Required**: The timeToLiveSeconds attribute is optional

maxIdleTimeSeconds

maxIdleTimeSeconds is the number of seconds between the last usage of this entry and the time it will automatically be deleted. Similar to timeToLiveSeconds attribute, you can change only the following characteristics:

- **Supported Values**: This attribute supports only number values. If omitted, Infinispan assumes -1 as the default value and the cache entry will not expire as a result of idle time.
- **Required**: The "maxIdleTimeSeconds" attribute is optional.

Passing 0 as the parameter for `timeToLiveSeconds` or `maxIdleTimeSeconds`.

If both `timeToLiveSeconds` and `maxIdleTimeSeconds` are 0, the cache will use the default lifespan and the `maxIdle` values, as defined declaratively in the XML file or programmatically using the Configuration API.

If only `maxIdleTimeSeconds` is 0, it uses the `timeToLiveSeconds` value passed as the parameter (or `-1`, if not present) and the maxIdle attribute defined declaratively or programmatically in the cache configuration.

If only `timeToLiveSeconds` is 0, it uses 0 as `timeToLiveSeconds` meaning that it will expire immediately.

Client side code

As we said at the beginning of this chapter, we have many options available to work with HTTP requests and responses. In the following sections, we will see some options to test and consume the REST services.

cURL

If your goal is just to test the REST services, the simplest option is to use existing tools, such as the cURL library, which is a well known command line tool developed for transferring files using a URL syntax, and it supports protocols such as **HTTP**, **HTTPS**, **FTP**, and **FTPS**, among others.

The following are some cURL commands to produce simple HTTP requests:

- POSTing an XML document into a given cache:

```
curl -X POST -i -H "Content-type:application/xml" -d "<person
   doc="123456789"><name>Wagner</name><age>33</age>
      <maritalStatus>Married</ maritalStatus></person>"
         http://localhost:8080/infinispan/rest/
            CreditApprovalPending/456233
```

- Using GET to retrieve the XML document for the key 456233:

```
curl -i -H "Accept:application/xml"
   http://localhost:8080/infinispan/rest/
      CreditApprovalPending/456233
```

- PUT to update the data for the key `456233`:

```
curl -i -X PUT -H "Content-type:application/xml" --data
  "<person doc="123456789"><name>Wagner</name><age>34</age>
    <maritalStatus>Married</maritalStatus ></person>"
      http://localhost:8080/infinispan/rest/
        CreditApprovalPending/456233
```

- DELETE to remove the entry from the given cache:

```
curl -i -X DELETE
  http://localhost:8080/infinispan/rest/
    CreditApprovalPending/456233
```

Options

cURL comes with many options. In our previous examples, we have seen some of them in action. There are various flags, which are as follows:

- `-i`: This displays the response header in the output
- `-H`: We can send custom request headers to pass to the server and this option can be used several times to perform any operation (that is, add/update/remove) on different headers
- `-X`: This is used to specify a a HTTP method to communicate with the server
- `-d`: This is used to specify the data you want to send or parameters enclosed in quotes

To post binary data, you can use the `--data-binary` or `--data-urlencode` option to encode the payload or the URL respectively, before sending it to the Infinispan REST Server.

 Check out this link to see all available options: `http://curl.haxx.se/docs/manpage.html`

Testing REST services with RESTClient

If you are looking for a graphical tool to easily send HTTP messages, you should try RESTClient. As the name suggests, RESTClient is a Swing application, designed to assist in the testing of RESTful services.

First, download the JAR file `restclient-ui-XXXX-jar-with-dependencies.jar` (with dependencies) from `https://code.google.com/p/rest-client/`, and execute it with the following command:

```
java -jar restclient-ui-3.2.2-jar-with-dependencies.jar
```

The following screen will be displayed:

From the graphical user interface, we can easily deduce how to use it. Type in the **URL** field, the desired URI, select the HTTP method in the **Method** tab, and press the **>>** button to execute it.

In the **Header** tab, you can include the request headers and the **Body** tab allows you to specify the data you want to send with the PUT or POST request.

Consuming RESTful web services with Java

There are many options available if you want to create a REST client with Java, you could use the Apache HttpClient, RESTEasy Client API, or JAX-RS Client API if you're using Java EE 7, or even the java.net.* package to create a simple Java client to consume a REST web service.

The following code sample presents a simple application with JAXB and two REST Java clients using the standard `java.net` package and another one with `Apache HttpClient`.

Java Architecture for XML Binding (JAXB) provides the necessary tools and compilers to bind XML documents to Java representations and vice versa. We can unmarshal an incoming XML file from different sources to Java **Plain Old Java Object (POJO)**.

We can also access, modify, and validate the XML against a schema, and finally, marshal a Java object into XML.

The following diagram presents a high-level overview of the JAXB architecture:

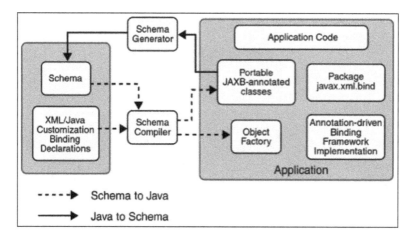

Extracted from the Java tutorial: `https://docs.oracle.com/javase/tutorial/jaxb/intro/arch.html`

JAXB provides two ways to customize an XML schema, which can be either inline annotations or as declarations in an external binding customization file. The JAXB annotations that are defined in the `javax.xml.bind.annotation` package can be used to customize elements of your code to XML Mapping schema, such as `@XmlSchema` and `@XmlSchemaType` for Java packages, `@XmlType` and `@XmlRootElement` for Java classes, and `@XmlElement` and `@XmlAttribute` for properties and fields, among others.

 To learn more about JAXB, visit the link `http://docs.oracle.com/javase/tutorial/jaxb/intro/index.html`.

Here's an example in which the JAXB class presents some of these annotations in action:

```
@XmlRootElement(name = "person")
@XmlType(name = "", propOrder = { "name", "age",
  "maritalStatus", "credit" })
public class Customer {
  // Setters and toString() are omitted for brevity
  private String name;
  private int age;
  private String maritalStatus;
  private String doc;
  private double credit;

  @XmlElement
    public String getName() {
      return name;
    }
  @XmlElement
  public int getAge() {
    return age;
  }
  @XmlAttribute(name = "doc")
  public String getDoc() {
    return doc;
  }
  @XmlElement
  public String getMaritalStatus() {
    return maritalStatus;
  }
  @XmlElement
  public double getCredit() {
    return credit;
  }
}
```

Next, we will see a JAXB marshalling example, an utilitary class with two methods to convert an XML into a `Customer` object and `Customer` to XML. The `m.marshal()` method is overloaded and can accept other arguments; find one that suits your needs. The code is as follows:

```
public static final Customer convertXMLtoJava(String xmlData)
  throws JAXBException {
    JAXBContext context = JAXBContext.newInstance(Customer.class);
    Unmarshaller unmarshaller = context.createUnmarshaller();
```

```
     Customer cust = (Customer) unmarshaller.unmarshal(new
        StringReader(xmlData));
     return cust;
}
public static final String convertJavaToXML(Customer customer)
  throws JAXBException {
     JAXBContext context = JAXBContext.newInstance(Customer.class);
     StringWriter writer = new StringWriter();
     Marshaller m = context.createMarshaller();
     m.marshal(customer, writer);
     return writer.getBuffer().toString();
}
```

Java.net

Now, we will create a client code with the `java.net.*` classes to make an HTTP request. First, we will make an HTTP POST request to the REST service to create a new entry in the cache and an HTTP GET request to query customer information. The code is as follows:

```
public final void executeHTTPOperationsWithJavaNet(String URL,
   String key, Customer cust) throws IOException, JAXBException {
     System.out.println("Execution with java.net");
// Open Connection
     URL url = new URL(URI_CREDIT_PENDING+key);
     HttpURLConnection conn = (HttpURLConnection)
        url.openConnection();
     conn.setDoOutput(true);
     conn.setRequestMethod("POST");
     conn.setRequestProperty("Content-Type", "application/xml");
     String xmlData = CustomerConverter.convertJavaToXML(cust);
// Send POST request
     OutputStream os = conn.getOutputStream();
     os.write(xmlData.getBytes());
     os.flush();
     validateResponseCode(conn);
     conn.disconnect();
// Reopen connection to send GET request
     conn = (HttpURLConnection) url.openConnection();
// Define a HttpGet request
     conn.setRequestMethod("GET");
// Set the MIMe type in HTTP header
     conn.setRequestProperty("accept", "application/xml");
     validateResponseCode(conn);
```

```
    BufferedReader in = new BufferedReader
      (new InputStreamReader(conn.getInputStream()));
    String line;
    StringBuffer output = new StringBuffer();
    while ((line = in.readLine()) != null) {
      output.append(line);
    }
    in.close();
    conn.disconnect();
    cust = CustomerConverter.convertXMLtoJava(output.toString());
    System.out.println("\nJAXB Customer");
    System.out.println(cust);
  }


public void validateResponseCode(HttpURLConnection conn) throws
  IOException{
// Verify the status code of the response
    System.out.printf(conn.getRequestMethod()+
      " Request >> HTTP Status %d : %s \n",
    conn.getResponseCode(), conn.getResponseMessage());
    if (conn.getResponseCode() != HttpURLConnection.HTTP_OK) {
      throw new RuntimeException("Error: HTTP Message>> "
        + conn.getResponseMessage());
    }
  }
```

Next, we will present a Java method that calls the same services, but this time, we will use the Apache `HttpClient` library.

`HttpClient` supports all HTTP methods and there is a specific class for each method type. In the following example, we are using the `HttpGet` and `HttpPut` methods:

```
public void executeHTTPOperations(String URL, String key,
  Customer cust) throws IOException, JAXBException {
  CloseableHttpClient httpclient = HttpClients.createDefault();
  try {
    HttpPut put = new HttpPut(URI_CREDIT_PENDING + key);
    String xmlData = CustomerConverter.convertJavaToXML(cust);
    StringEntity xmlEntity = new StringEntity(xmlData);
    put.setEntity(xmlEntity);
    CloseableHttpResponse response = httpclient.execute(put);
    // Verify the status code of the response
    StatusLine status = response.getStatusLine();
    if (response.getStatusLine().getStatusCode() >= 300) {
```

```
  throw new HttpResponseException(status.getStatusCode(),
    status.getReasonPhrase());
  }
  System.out.printf("PUT Request >> HTTP Status %d : %s \n",
    status.getStatusCode(), status.getReasonPhrase());
// Define a HttpGet request
  HttpGet get = new HttpGet(URI_CREDIT_PENDING + key);
// Set the MIMe type in HTTP header
  get.addHeader("accept", "application/xml");
// Creating a custom ResponseHandler to handle responses
  ResponseHandler<String> responseHandler = new
    ResponseHandler<String>() {
  public String handleResponse(final HttpResponse response)
    throws ClientProtocolException, IOException {
   // Checking the status code again for errors
  StatusLine status = response.getStatusLine();
  if (response.getStatusLine().getStatusCode() >= 300) {
  throw new HttpResponseException(status.getStatusCode(),
    status.getReasonPhrase());
  }
  System.out.printf("GET Request >> HTTP Status %d : %s \n",
    status.getStatusCode(), status.getReasonPhrase());
  System.out.println("\nResponse Header");
  System.out.println("========================");
  for (Header header : response.getAllHeaders()) {
    System.out.printf("%s : %s \n", header.getName(),
      header.getValue());
  }
  HttpEntity entity = response.getEntity();
  return entity != null ? EntityUtils.toString(entity) : null;
  }
  };
// Send the request; It will return the response
  xmlData = httpclient.execute(get, responseHandler);
  System.out.println("\nResponse Body");
  System.out.println("========================");
  System.out.println(xmlData);

  cust = CustomerConverter.convertXMLtoJava(xmlData);
  System.out.println("\nJAXB Customer");
  System.out.println(cust);
```

```
    } finally {
      httpclient.close();
    }
  }
}
```

Using the Hot Rod server

The Infinispan server module provides a module that implements a custom binary protocol designed for smart clients called Hot Rod, a custom TCP client-server protocol that was designed specifically for Infinispan and is considered the fastest way to interface a client application to an Infinispan server instance.

This protocol enables faster and cheaper client and server interactions in comparison to other client/server protocols, such as **Memcached**.

This module allows you to create remote applications and perform the standard operations in the cache, such as store, retrieve, change, and remove data from the cache, using the Hot Rod protocol.

> For more information, refer to the Hot Rod protocol documentation at `http://infinispan.org/docs/7.0.x/user_guide/` `user_guide.html#_hot_rod_protocol`.

Infinispan Hot Rod uses a well-documented consistent hash mechanism to assign keys to each peer. When using the Hot Rod protocol to interact with Infinispan, cache entries must be sent as arrays of bytes to ensure platform neutral behavior, which can allow other developers to calculate the hash-codes of the byte array keys to implement their own (non-java) client, if needed.

On the server side, Hot Rod provides built-in connection pooling mechanism and also automatic load balancing and failover capabilities by routing client requests smartly across the grid to the node that owns the data.

In order to achieve this, Hot Rod uses the same hash algorithm to provide information about cluster topology changes to clients and allows clients to determine the partition of a key to let clients send a command directly to the server that owns the key.

The following image shows an overview of the Hot Rot architecture:

Hot Rod clients

Hot Rod has a reference client that is written in Java that ships with Infinispan, but there are a number of open source clients for many programming languages such as Ruby, Python, C++, and .NET, written as conveniences by third-party developers.

You can easily embed any of these native clients in your application.

> Visit the following site to download one of these client libraries:
> http://infinispan.org/hotrod-clients/

In the next section, we will see how to use the Hot Rod Java Client.

Using the Hot Rod Java Client

To start using the Hot Rot Java Client, create a Java project, and add the Infinispan libraries you need on your build path. If you are using Maven, in addition to `infinispan-core`, you will have to include the `infinispan-client-hotrod` dependency in the `pom.xml` file, in order to compile, add the following code:

```
<dependency>
  <groupId>org.infinispan</groupId>
  <artifactId>infinispan-core</artifactId>
  <version>7.0.0.Beta1</version>
</dependency>
<dependency>
  <groupId>org.infinispan</groupId>
  <artifactId>infinispan-client-hotrod</artifactId>
  <version>7.0.0.Beta1</version>
</dependency>
```

Starting a RemoteCacheManager

To connect the Hot Rod Server module, you will need a `RemoteCacheManager` object, which is responsible for instantiating the connection to the Hot Rod server, similar to the `CacheManager` interface, it represents a factory for the `RemoteCache` instances.

Once connected, you can call the `getCache()` method to retrieve the default cache or the `getCache(String cacheName)` method to retrieve a named cache from the remote Hot Rod Server.

The easiest way to start `RemoteCacheManager` is to create an instance calling the default constructor or supplying the `Configuration`. If you want to decide the time to start it, there are two other constructors that you can pass a Boolean start parameter that will define whether it will start the manager or not on return from the constructor.

After construction, you can start the `RemoteCacheManager` object by calling the `start()` method.

Starting from release 5.0, Infinispan allows using SSL certificates for a secure connection between the client and the server network.

The following example shows how to create a `Configuration` object by adding two different servers, enabling SSL support, and specifying connection-pooling setting to start a `RemoteCacheManager`.

There are many available options to configure the connection pooling. In the next example, we use the following attributes:

- `maxActive`: This controls the maximum number of connections that can be allocated for each server.

- `maxIdle` and `minIdle`: These control the maximum and minimum number of idle persistent connections for each server.

- `maxTotal`: This defines the total number of connections that can be active for the whole grid.

- `exhaustedAction`: This defines what action Infinispan should take when there are no more available connections in the server's pool. The available options are: CREATE_NEW, EXCEPTION, or WAIT.

- `timeBetweenEvictionRuns`: This defines the time (in milliseconds) an eviction thread should sleep before looking for idle connections.

- `minEvictableIdleTime`: This specifies the minimum amount of time an active connection can be idle before being eligible for eviction.

The preceding attributes are added in the code, which is as follows:

```
public class HotRodClient {
  private static final String KEY = "k01";
  public static void main(String[] args) {
    HotRodClient client = new HotRodClient();
    // Create a JAXB Customer
    Customer cust = new Customer();
    cust.setName("Wagner");
    cust.setAge(33);
    cust.setCredit(15000d);
    cust.setDoc("212.333.111");
    cust.setMaritalStatus("Married");

    // Get the ClassLoader to load a KeyStore resource
    ClassLoader cl =
      Thread.currentThread().getContextClassLoader();
    ConfigurationBuilder builder = new ConfigurationBuilder();
    // Add two HotRod Remote Servers
    builder.addServer().
        host("192.168.10.1").
        port(11222).
        marshaller(new ProtoStreamMarshaller()).
      addServer().
        host("192.168.10.2").
```

```
            port(11223).
      // Enable SSL support and specifies the filename and the
        password needed to open the keystore (keystore.jks)
        ssl().
            enable().
            keyStoreFileName(cl.getResource("keystore.jks").getPath()).
            keyStorePassword("myPasswprd".toCharArray()).
            trustStoreFileName(cl.getResource("keystore.jks").getPath()).
            trustStorePassword("myPassword".toCharArray()).
      // Specify Connection pooling properties
        connectionPool().
            lifo(true).maxActive(10).maxIdle(10).
            maxTotal(20).exhaustedAction(ExhaustedAction.CREATE_NEW).
            timeBetweenEvictionRuns(120000).minEvictableIdleTime(1800000).
            minIdle(1);
      // Build the RemoteCacheManager using our previous configuration
        RemoteCacheManager rcm = new
            RemoteCacheManager(builder.build());
        client.executeHotRodOperations(rcm, cust);
    }
}
```

Note that in the end of our last example, we call the executeHotRodOperations method, whose definition follows.

 It's also possible to make queries in the Hot Rod, we will see this feature in detail in *Chapter 12, Advanced Topics*.

In this method, we will perform some basic operations in the cache:

```
public void executeHotRodOperations(RemoteCacheManager rcm,
    Customer cust){
    RemoteCache<String, Customer> rc = rcm.getCache();
    System.out.printf("Using the %s.\n", rc.getProtocolVersion());
    // Add a Customer in the Cache
    System.out.println("Added customer: \n"+cust);
    rc.put(KEY, cust);
    // Retrieve the Customer
    Customer custFromCache = rc.get(KEY);
    assert cust.equals(custFromCache) : "Customer must be the same";
    // Remove the Customer
    rc.remove(KEY);
    custFromCache = rc.get(KEY);
    assert custFromCache == null : "Customer should be removed!";
```

```
// Printing Server Statistics
System.out.println("*** Server Statistics ***");
for(Entry<String, String> entry :
    rc.stats().getStatsMap().entrySet()){
    System.out.println("\t"+entry);
}
// Stopping the Remote Cache Manager
rcm.stop();
}
```

Configuring authentication for your Hot Rod application

As you could see in our last example, Hot Rod supports secure communication with your cache using SSL/TLS encryption. And now, since Infinispan 7.0, Hot Rod supports authentication using the SASL mechanism. It extends the SASL by allowing Hot Rod to authenticate any valid user via several mechanisms. With this solution, a remote Hot Rod client can authenticate to the Infinispan server and once the client is authenticated, the Infinispan server can give access to the cache data based on the role of the user.

Introducing the SASL framework

The acronym **SASL** stands for **Simple Authentication and Security Layer**. It's an IETF standard and defines a framework for authentication and data security to be used in web applications. Currently, there are several standard SASL mechanisms that are defined and approved by the Internet community for different security levels and scenarios.

It provides a well-defined interface that provides an abstraction security layer between protocols, such as LDAP, SMTP, and authentication mechanisms. And now, from Infinispan 7.0, SASL was integrated into the framework to implement Hot Rod authentication. By using SASL, the Infinispan server can automatically support a number of authentication mechanisms. The following image shows the relation between the Hot Rod protocol and the authentication mechanisms:

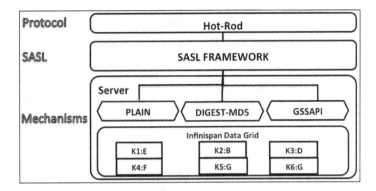

Supported SASL mechanisms

The Infinispan server currently supports the several SASL mechanisms that are supported by JDK. Each of these mechanisms relies on a challenge-response system, where the Infinispan server issues a challenge based upon these mechanisms and the Hot Rod client will handle the challenge from the server. But, in order to work, the client will need to implement the `CallbackHandler` interface that will be used by the mechanism drive.

Infinispan supports the following mechanisms:

- **PLAIN**: This is the simplest authentication mechanism, where the Hot Rod client sends the credentials without any encryption to the Infinispan server.

- **DIGEST-MD5**: This is a mechanism based on the HTTP Digest authentication, described by the RFC 2831, and offers better security than the PLAIN mechanism. This mechanism provides the a Hot Rod client with the ability to authenticate to an Infinispan server without necessarily sending the actual password. Instead, the client hashes the credentials with a randomly generated code that is provided by the server.

- **GSSAPI**: This mechanism provides the ability for Hot Rod clients to authenticate to the Infinispan server using Kerberos tokens.

- **EXTERNAL**: This mechanism uses an external channel, external to SASL, to obtain authentication information. By using this mechanism, you don't need to supply your credentials; you can use a client-certificate identity of the underlying transport as the credentials.

 Please note that you can introduce more SASL mechanisms in your project by using the **Java Cryptography Architecture (JCA)**.

Configuring authorization policies

The Infinispan server security is based on permissions and roles, where Infinispan uses application roles to manage user permissions to a cache manager or a cache. These permissions allow individual Hot Rod clients to perform specific actions; if a user has EXEC permission on the cache, he will be able to execute a MapReduce task on a cache.

The following diagram illustrates the relationship between User, Role, Permission, and the CacheManager cache:

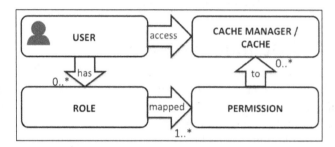

The following table shows the possible values for permission in the `standalone.xml` file:

Type	Permission	Description
Cache Manager / Cache	`ALL`	This permission gives the user all permissions.
Cache Manager / Cache	`LISTEN`	This allows the grantee permission to register listeners on cache objects and receive notifications when events take place.
Cache Manager / Cache	`LIFECYCLE`	This grants the user permission to control the lifecycle of the cache (`Lifecycle.start()` / `stop()`).
Cache	`ALL_READ`	This grants the user all read permissions.
Cache	`ALL_WRITE`	This grants the user all write permission.
Cache	`READ`	This grants the user permission to retrieve entries (`get()` / `containsKey()`) from the cache.
Cache	`WRITE`	This grants the user permission to write (`put()`) data to a cache.

Type	Permission	Description
Cache	EXEC	This allows the grantee permission to execute map/reduce and distributed executors tasks. Please note that to work properly, this permission needs to be combined with READ or WRITE permission.
Cache	BULK_READ	This grants the user permission to perform bulk read operations.
Cache	BULK_WRITE	This grants the user permission to perform bulk write operations.
Cache	ADMIN	This grants the user permission to perform administrative operations on the cache.
Cache	NONE	No privileges are granted to cache users.

Realm configuration

In order to configure Infinispan Server to use the security system, you need to configure a security realm. A security realm consists of an abstract set of users, groups, and roles and certain mechanisms to authenticate users and authorize access to the management interfaces.

You can configure the security realm in the `standalone.xml` file. Depending on your needs, you can configure one or more different security realms within the `<security-realms>` element. For each realm that you create, you will need to define the `<authentication>` element to configure the authentication mechanism in the server side.

The following example is taken from the standalone configuration with the default configuration; it enables two security realms `ManagementRealm` and `ApplicationRealm`.

In `ManagementRealm`, we use a local mechanism and enable an authentication based on username/password. This realm will authenticate users loaded from the `mgmt-users.properties` file:

```
<security-realms>
  <security-realm name="ManagementRealm">
    <authentication>
      <local default-user="$local" skip-group-loading="true"/>
      <properties path="mgmt-users.properties"
        relative-to="jboss.server.config.dir"/>
    </authentication>
      <authorization map-groups-to-roles="false">
```

```
        <properties path="mgmt-groups.properties"
          relative-to="jboss.server.config.dir"/>
      </authorization>
   </security-realm>
     <security-realm name="ApplicationRealm">
       <authentication>
       <local default-user="$local" allowed-users="*"
         skip-group-loading="true"/>
       <properties path="application-users.properties"
         relative-to="jboss.server.config.dir"/>
       </authentication>
       <authorization>
         <properties path="application-roles.properties"
           relative-to="jboss.server.config.dir"/>
       </authorization>
     </security-realm>
   </security-realms>
```

After a realm has been defined, you will need to associate it with a management interface. The following example shows how to use the `security-realm` attribute to associate `ManagementRealm` to an `http-interface`:

```
<management-interfaces>
  <http-interface security-realm="ManagementRealm"
    http-upgrade-enabled="true">
  <socket-binding http="management-http"/>
  </http-interface>
</management-interfaces>
```

 The `security-realm` attribute is optional, so if it's omitted from the interface definition, the access will be open to any user.

Authorization configuration

To secure a cache container, we have to include the `<security>` element within the cache container that we want to protect from unauthorized access and define the roles that can use the cache. The next example shows how to map roles to permissions:

```
<subsystem xmlns="urn:infinispan:server:core:7.0"
  default-cache-container="local">
  <cache-container name="local" default-cache="default">
    <security>
      <authorization>
      <identity-role-mapper/>
```

```
          <role name="manage" permissions="ADMIN EXEC"/>
          <role name="view" permissions="READ"/>
          <role name="edit" permissions="WRITE"/>
          <role name="super" permissions="ALL"/>
        </authorization>
      </security>
      <local-cache name="default" start="EAGER">
        <locking acquire-timeout="30000" concurrency-level="1000"
          striping="false"/>
      </local-cache>
      <local-cache name="secured">
        <security>
          <authorization roles="manage view edit super"/>
        </security>
      </local-cache>
    </cache-container>
    <cache-container name="security"/>
  </subsystem>
```

As part of the authorization decision, users and roles are mapped to a set of roles used for authorization in runtime. The Infinispan server makes use of `PrincipalRoleMapper`, which is responsible for the mapping process.

In our last example, we used the `<identity-role-mapper>` element that will convert principal names into role names.

By default, Infinispan ships with three mappers, if they are not enough, you can create your own custom role mapper by implementing the `PrincipalRoleMapper` interface, as shown in the following table:

Mapper	XML Element	Description
IdentityRoleMapper	`<identity-role-mapper />`	The identity role mapper will convert principal names (as-is) to role names.
CommonNameRoleMapper	`<common-name-role-mapper />`	This mapper handles a string representation of a **Distinguished Name (DN)** following the LDAP standard. The common name role mapper will extract the **Common Name (CN)** to use it as a role.

Mapper	XML Element	Description
`ClusterRoleMapper`	`<cluster-role-mapper />`	The cluster role mapper uses `ClusterRegistry`, a common object that is used for all nodes to share metadata, to store the role mapping information.
`Custom Role Mapper`	`<custom-role-mapper>`	You can use it to specify a custom role mapper.

Next, we have to enable the SASL authentication for the server in the Hot Rod connector. In the following example, for didactic purposes, we use the DIGEST-MD5 mechanism:

```
<subsystem xmlns="urn:infinispan:server:endpoint:7.0">
  <hotrod-connector socket-binding="hotrod"
    cache-container="local">
  <topology-state-transfer lock-timeout="1000"
    replication-timeout="5000"/>
  <authentication security-realm="ApplicationRealm">
    <sasl server-name="localhost" mechanisms="DIGEST-MD5"/>
  </authentication>
  </hotrod-connector>
</subsystem>
```

To enable the PLAIN mechanism, you have to follow the exact same steps, and replace only the DIGEST-MD5 mechanism with PLAIN.

Client configuration

Since our SASL DIGEST-MD5 mechanism requires an input from the client, we will need to create a client to authenticate it in our application realm, and also we will need to implement the `javax.security.auth.callback.CallbackHandler` interface. The client will pass the implementation to the SASL security service, and when it requires input, the server will invoke the `handle()` method, in order to supply a list of callbacks that it needs to get that input.

In the next example, we create the `AuthenticatedHotRodClient` class, which contains the static class `SimpleCallbackHandler` that implements the `CallbackHandler` interface. Our example handles `NameCallback` (to retrieve name information), `PasswordCallback` (to retrieve password information), and `RealmCallback` (to retrieve Realm information, required by the DIGEST-MD5 mechanism) by reading the credentials from the manual input via the constructor.

The code for which is as follows:

```
import javax.security.sasl.Sasl;
import org.infinispan.client.hotrod.RemoteCache;
import org.infinispan.client.hotrod.RemoteCacheManager;
import
  org.infinispan.client.hotrod.configuration.ConfigurationBuilder;
  public class AuthenticatedHotRodClient {
  public static void main(String[] args) {
    ConfigurationBuilder builder = new ConfigurationBuilder();
    builder
      .connectionPool()
      .maxTotal(1)
      .security()
      .authentication()
      .enable()
      .serverName("localhost")
      .saslMechanism("PLAIN")
      .callbackHandler(new TestCallbackHandler("user",
        "ApplicationRealm", "qwer1234!".toCharArray()));
    RemoteCacheManager rcm = new
      RemoteCacheManager(builder.build());
    RemoteCache<String, String> cache = rcm.getCache("secured");
    cache.getVersion();
    cache.put("key", "value");
    cache.get(key);
    rcm.stop();
  }

  public static class SimpleCallbackHandler implements
    CallbackHandler {
    final private String username;
    final private char[] password;
    final private String realm;
    public TestCallbackHandler(String username, String realm,
      char[] password) {
      this.username = username;
      this.password = password;
      this.realm = realm;
    }
    @Override
    public void handle(Callback[] callbacks) throws IOException,
      UnsupportedCallbackException {
    for (Callback callback : callbacks) {
```

```
        if (callback instanceof NameCallback) {
          NameCallback nameCallback = (NameCallback) callback;
          nameCallback.setName(username);
          } else if (callback instanceof PasswordCallback) {
            PasswordCallback passwordCallback = (PasswordCallback)
              callback;
          passwordCallback.setPassword(password);
            } else if (callback instanceof AuthorizeCallback) {
              AuthorizeCallback authorizeCallback =
                (AuthorizeCallback) callback;
                authorizeCallback.setAuthorized(authorizeCallback.
                  getAuthenticationID().equals
                    (authorizeCallback.getAuthorizationID()));
              } else if (callback instanceof RealmCallback) {
              RealmCallback realmCallback = (RealmCallback)
                callback;
              realmCallback.setText(realm);
              } else {
                throw new UnsupportedCallbackException(callback);
              }
          }
        }
      }
    }
```

To test if our configuration is working, let's create a user named wsantos with the password test123 and assign a super role, by using the add-user.sh (.bat for Windows users) script.

The user data will be stored in the application-users.properties file using the following command:

```
./add-user.sh -a -u wsantos -p "test123" -ro super
```

Let's add a simple unit test to validate our secure Infinispan cache:

```
public class HotRodSecurityClientTest {
  private RemoteCache<String, Customer> rc;
  private static final String KEY = "k01";
  private Customer customer;
  private RemoteCacheManager rcm;
  private static final Log logger =
    LogFactory.getLog(HotRodClientTest.class);
  private static final String REALM = "ApplicationRealm";
  @Before
  public void setUp() throws Exception {
```

```
customer = new Customer();
customer.setName("Wagner");
customer.setAge(33);
customer.setCredit(15000d);
customer.setDoc("212.333.111");
customer.setMaritalStatus("Married");
ConfigurationBuilder builder = new ConfigurationBuilder();
builder.addServer(). -
  host("localhost").
  port(11222).
  connectionPool().
  lifo(true).
  maxActive(10).
  maxIdle(10).
  maxTotal(20).
  exhaustedAction(ExhaustedAction.CREATE_NEW).
  timeBetweenEvictionRuns(120000).
  minEvictableIdleTime(1800000).
  minIdle(1).
    security().
      authentication().
        enable().
        serverName("localhost").
        saslMechanism("DIGEST-MD5").
        callbackHandler(new SecurityCallbackHandler("wsantos",
          "test123", REALM));;
  rcm = new RemoteCacheManager(builder.build());
  rc = rcm.getCache("securedCache");
}
@Test
public void executeHotRodOperations() {
  logger.infof("Using the %s.", rc.getProtocolVersion());
  logger.infof("Add a Customer %s in the
    Cache:",customer.getName());
  rc.put(KEY, customer);

  logger.info("Retrieving customer from remote cache");
  Customer customerFromCache = rc.get(KEY);
    assertEquals("Customer must be the same", customer,
      customerFromCache);

  logger.infof("Removing customer from remote cache");
  rc.remove(KEY);
  customer = rc.get(KEY);
```

```
        assertNull( "Customer should be removed!", customer);
    }

    @After
    public void closeRemoteCM(){
        rc.stop();
        rcm.stop();
    }
}
```

Infinispan memcached server

Memcached is a simple, highly scalable distributed memory key-based store developed by Danga Interactive to reduce the database load for LiveJournal, storing data and objects on the RAM memory instead of a disk. But nowadays, it is used by many other websites to speed up database-driven websites by caching objects in the memory to reduce read operations to an external data source.

If you are using memcached, you might have faced some of the following issues:

- **Cold cache**: This happens when the memcached node goes down; then we can overload the database and slowdown or collapse data

- **Loss of performance**: This happens when adding or removing memcached nodes

- **Lack of L1 cache**: To overcome this, there are some memcached clients that can cache locally

- **Data loss**: This happens due to server crash

Furthermore, cache entries are not relocated to a different node during a shutdown.

Clients of memcached can communicate with a running memcached server using a text-based protocol, known as the memcached protocol.

The memcached server operates through a standard TCP/IP network connection and listens on a specific configurable port where the client can obtain new connections, send commands, read and parse responses, and close the connection.

For clustered system architectures that use the memcached protocol and are looking to replace it with a new solution, Infinispan offers a memcached server that implements the memcached protocol, allowing you to replace it with Infinispan transparently. You have to point your application to the Infinispan memcached server and only use it as if you were using memcached.

The memcached protocol

The Infinispan server module implements the memcached text protocol, which makes it simpler for clients to talk to one or multiple Infinispan memcached instances. The communication can be achieved through a standard TCP/IP connection and by default, operates over port 11211; no authorization is needed to open a new connection.

 Due to limitations in the memcached protocol, which limits the usage of the Infinispan API, you can expose only one cache by a connector, and Infinispan does not allow specifying a cache to use. To expose another cache, you will have to declare additional memcached connectors on different socket bindings.

For reference, a list of commands supported by the memcached text protocol and their syntax and a short description is provided in the following table:

Command	Syntax	Description
set	set key value flags exptime bytes	The set command adds a new entry (key/value pair) into the cache. If the entry key already exists, Infinispan will overwrite it.
add	add key flags exptime bytes	The add command adds a new entry (key/value pair) into the cache. It only works for new entries keys; otherwise, the command will fail.
replace	replace key flags exptime bytes	This replaces an existing cache entry with a new value.
append	append key flags exptime bytes	This appends the given value (after) to an existing cache entry.
prepend	prepend key bytes	This prepends the given value (before) to an existing cache entry.
cas	cas key flags exptime bytes casunique	**Compare And Swap (CAS)** the cache entry with the provided CAS (cas unique) key. It's used to ensure no one else has updated it.
get	get key	This is a retrieval command that gets a cache entry from a given key.
gets	gets key	This gets the cache value from a given key along with a CAS token. It should be used when issuing CAS updates.

Command	Syntax	Description
delete	delete key	The delete command deletes a cache entry associated with the given key.
incr	incr key valueToInc	The incr command increments the cache value associated with the key. It only works for cache entries that already exist.
decr	decr key valueToDec	The decr command decrements the cache value associated with the key. It only works for cache entries that already exist.

As you can see in the table of commands, the memcached text protocol provides many arguments to meet your needs. They are as follows:

- key: This is the key of the cache entry
- value: This is the cache entry value
- flags: This can be used as a bit field; it creates a 16-bit unsigned integer that will be stored in the server and can be retrieved when the cache entry is retrieved
- expiry: This is the expiration time in seconds; 0 means no delay
- bytes: This is the length of the value in bytes
- valueToInc: This is the amount value required to increase the item
- valueToDec: This is the amount value required to decrease the item
- casunique: This is the unique 64-bit value of an existing entry to use with the cas command

You can test some of these memcached commands using a telnet connection. To begin, start a telnet session connecting to the memcached server providing the IP address and port number, which is as follows:

If everything went right, you should be able to execute the memcached commands.

Let's first add a new cache entry for the key **k01**. Remember that the syntax to submit a set command is as follows:

```
set key value flags exptime bytes
```

The output of the following command will be as follows:

Our set command returned a STORED message, which indicates the command was successful. The command might also return other messages indicating the status of the request, as follows:

- **NON_STORED**: This message is returned for add or replace commands
- **EXISTS**: If you are trying to store something using the CAS option that has been modified since you last fetched it
- **NOT_FOUND**: This indicates the cache entry if the given key does not exist

Now, we will retrieve the **k01** value issuing a get command, which is shown in the following screenshot;

In the next example, we will prepend and append the **k01** value, as follows:

We can increase or decrease a numeric value using the incr and decr commands, as follows:

```
● ○ ○              ⌂ wrsantos — telnet — 80×24
set k02 0 0 5
12345
STORED
incr k02 5
12350
decr k02 10005
2345
```

To delete a cache entry, use the delete command:

```
● ○ ○              ⌂ wrsantos — telnet — 80×24
delete k02
DELETED
```

Finally, you case use the stats command to extract statistics and information about your cache instance. The following figure shows the output of stats command:

```
● ○ ○              ⌂ wrsantos — telnet — 100×35
stats
STAT pid 0
STAT uptime 8303
STAT uptime 8303
STAT time 1391544808
STAT version 6.0.0.Final
STAT pointer_size 0
STAT rusage_user 0
STAT rusage_system 0
STAT curr_items 1
STAT total_items 18
STAT bytes 0
STAT curr_connections 0
STAT total_connections 0
STAT connection_structures 0
STAT cmd_get 27
STAT cmd_set 18
STAT get_hits 24
STAT get_misses 3
```

There are some statistical information provided by the STATS command that is not supported by the Infinispan memcached server implementation and they will always return 0, they are: auth_cmds, auth_errors, bytes, connection_structures, conn_yields, curr_connections, limit_maxbytes, pid, pointer_size, reclaimed, rusage_user, rusage_system, threads, and total_connections.

> For a full list of all available statistics, please check the *Statistics* section in the memcached text protocol documentation at `https://github.com/memcached/memcached/blob/master/doc/protocol.txt#L424`.

Connecting the Infinispan memcached server by using a Java Client

There are many Java memcached clients available; in this section, we will present an example with XMemcached, a memcached client based on Java NIO, which is very efficient in highly concurrent environments.

XMemcached supports the binary protocol and text protocol of memcached, provides MBeans for JMX monitoring, integrates with spring framework, and you can dynamically add or remove new servers.

The following example presents a simple method that receives a `MemcachedClient` instance and a JAXB customer to execute some operations (set, get, and delete) in the Infinispan memcached server:

```java
public void executeMemcachedOperations(MemcachedClient client,
  Customer cust) throws Exception{
  try {
    System.out.printf("Execution with XMemcached. Using the %s
      Protocol.\n", client.getProtocol());
  // Add a Customer in the Cache
    System.out.println("Add customer \n"+cust);
    client.set(KEY, 0, cust);
  // Send a get
    Customer xml = client.get(KEY);
    System.out.println("Retrieve customer >> "+ cust);
  // Delete entry
    client.delete(KEY);
    xml = client.get(KEY);
    System.out.println("Customer after delete >>>" + xml);
  }catch (MemcachedException e) {
    System.err.printf("Memcached Error. Exception >> %s",
      e.getMessage());
  } finally{
    try {
      client.shutdown();
    } catch (Exception e) {
```

```
        System.err.printf("Memcached Shutdown Error. Exception >> %s
          ", e.getMessage());
      }
    }
  }
```

To test this method, you can create a `main` method to build a `MemcachedClient` and a `Customer` object. XMemcached provides a `Builder` class called `XMemcachedClientBuilder` to help build MemcachedClient. If your Infinispan memcached server is up and running, you can use the `Builder` class to establish a connection with a single Infinispan Memcached Server providing the IP address (or host name) and the service port, or send a list of memcached servers in one single string in the following format:

```
host1:port1 host2:port2 …
```

In this way, the `AddrUtil.getAddresses` method will be able to extract the IP addresses after parse it.

The `Builder` class also provides many options to customize your memcached client. The code for `Builder` class is as follows:

```
public static void main(String[] args) throws Exception {
  XMemcachedClient xclient = new XMemcachedClient();
  Customer cust = new Customer();
  cust.setName("Wagner");
  cust.setAge(33);
  cust.setCredit(15000d);
  cust.setDoc("212.333.111");
  cust.setMaritalStatus("Married");

  MemcachedClient memcachedClient = new XMemcachedClientBuilder(
    AddrUtil.getAddresses("localhost:11211")).build();
  if (memcachedClient == null) {
    throw new NullPointerException(
      "Null MemcachedClient,please check memcached has been
        started");
  }
  xclient.executeMemcachedOperations(memcachedClient, cust);
}
```

The Infinispan WebSocket server

The Infinispan Server exposes access to the grid via a WebSocket interface, which means that Infinispan allows you to access the data grid though the WebSocket protocol. If you prefer, you can use a JavaScript Cache API provided by Infinispan.

Before we get into the details, let's make an overview of some WebSocket concepts.

Introducing WebSocket

There are situations where we need bidirectional communication between our remote server and a client application, such as in an instant messaging or gaming application. Remember that HTTP is a stateless protocol and in traditional web applications, to implement this kind of solution, we need to use a technology such as Comet, HTTP Server Push, or Ajax Push and perform many HTTP requests to poll in the server several updates.

Another problem is that HTTP is also half duplex, which means that the traffic flows in one direction in the same channel at a time (request/response), which can be inefficient in certain domains (such as a multiuser platform with simultaneous and parallel interaction, online games, and so on).

By now, you probably have realized why we need something new and WebSocket is the answer to all these questions. WebSocket is an application protocol that uses a single TCP channel to support full-duplex and two-way communication between the client and the server. It was standardized by the **Internet Engineering Task Force (IETF)** as RFC 6455, and is designed to replace existing technologies that enable the server to send data to the client such as Ajax Push, Comet for bidirectional messaging over the web with HTTP. In this memo, the reason and motivation behind the creation of WebSocket and all the technical details about its operation are described.

The WebSocket protocol is designed to operate over ports 80 and 443, just like HTTP proxies and other components. The intent of WebSocket is to provide a simple protocol over TCP that can coexist with the HTTP protocol.

One of the benefits of WebSocket is that it does not require several headers as with the HTTP requests and responses of the HTTP protocol. There is only an additional cost of two bytes per message.

To establish a WebSocket connection, the first step is an opening handshake, with the client sending an HTTP handshake request to the server, via a special header called **Upgrade**. Once established, the client can upgrade the connection to the WebSocket protocol.

The following figure illustrates the HTTP request to upgrade WebSocket and compares a polling scenario with a WebSocket scenario:

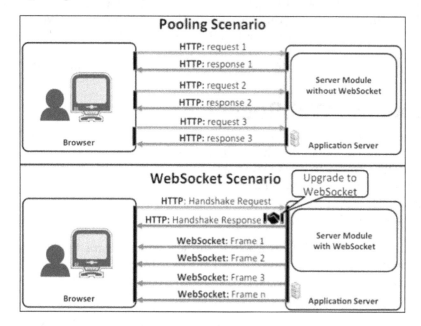

Overview of the WebSocket API

The WebSocket API specification under development consortium W3C, allows web pages to make use of the WebSocket protocol defined by IETF RFC 6455. Therefore, web developers can take advantage of the resources provided by this protocol.

Developers may be confused between the API and protocol, since both have the same name (WebSocket). However, both are developed and controlled by different parties, IETF controls the standards for the protocol and W3C for the API. The latter complements the specifications by adding WebSocket features to browsers, along with other features provided by HTML5.

Currently, the WebSocket API is supported by most of the modern web browsers, which include methods and attributes to create bidirectional and full duplex WebSocket connections.

However, we must remember that WebSocket is still a new technology and not fully supported in all browsers. The following figure is extracted from the site Can I use? (`http://caniuse.com/websockets`) and presents a list of browsers and their respective versions that support WebSockets:

						Usage stats:		Global		
						Support:		69.73%		
# Web Sockets - Candidate Recommendation						Partial support:		2.21%		
Bidirectional communication technology for web apps						Total:		71.94%		

Show all versions	IE	Firefox	Chrome	Safari	Opera	iOS Safari	Opera Mini	Android Browser	Blackberry Browser	IE Mobile
								2.1		
						3.2		2.2		
						4.0-4.1		2.3		
						4.2-4.3		3.0		
	8.0					5.0-5.1		4.0		
	9.0					6.0-6.1		4.1	7.0	
	10.0	25.0	31.0							
Current	11.0	26.0	32.0	7.0	18.0	7.0	5.0-7.0	4.2-4.3	10.0	10.0
Near future		27.0	33.0		19.0			4.4		
Farther future		28.0	34.0		20.0					
3 versions ahead		29.0	35.0							

Notes   Known issues (1)   Resources (6)   Feedback   Edit on GitHub

Partial support refers to the websockets implementation using an older version of the protocol and/or the implementation being disabled by default (due to security issues with the older protocol).

WebSocket in Java

In Java, the JSR 356 is the specification that describes the Java API for WebSocket and defines the features for creating WebSocket applications.

This JSR targets the Java EE 7 platform, released in June 2013, and one of the main changes is the addition of HTML 5 support, for example, the Java API for JSON Processing 1.0, major updates on JAX-RS 2.0, and the Java API for WebSocket.

The API allows developers to create, configure, and provide WebSocket endpoints in web applications by playing the role of a server or allowing Java clients to communicate with WebSocket servers, as in a chat.

Using the Infinispan JavaScript API

The Infinispan JavaScript API allows developers to create their own script files that can access caches and manipulate the cache data.

To use the JavaScript API, you need to include the `infinispan-ws.js` script in your page by adding a `<script>` tag in your web page, as follows:

```
<script type="text/javascript"
    src="http://localhost:8080/infinispan-ws.js"></script>
```

The Infinispan JS API is now installed in your application and ready to use.

The script provides the client-side interface cache, a JavaScript object that we can use to access the server-side Infinispan cache.

The following HTML and JavaScript code present a very simple example of how to use the script that comes with the Infinispan server distribution. The rest of the work will be done inside `infinispan-ws.js`, as follows:

```html
<script type="text/javascript"
  src="http://localhost:8888/infinispan-ws.js"> </script>
<script type="text/javascript">
  var cache = new Cache("namedCache", "ws://localhost:8181"); //
  var curKey;
  cache.registerCallback(cacheCallback);
  function cacheCallback(key, value) {
    if(key == curKey) {
      var node = document.getElementById("val");
      node.value = value;
    }
  }
  function keyChange(newKey) {
    // turn off notification for old key...
    cache.unnotify(curKey);
    // turn on notification of new key...
    cache.notify(newKey);
    // record the new curkey so we can turn off notification on
      next keychange
    curKey = newKey;

  }
</script>
</head>
<body>
  <form onsubmit="return false;">
  Key:
    <input type="text" id="key"
      onchange="keyChange(this.form.key.value)"/>
  Value:
    <input type="text" id="val" /><br/>
    <input type="button" value="Put"
      onClick="cache.put(this.form.key.value,
        this.form.val.value)" />
    <input type="button" value="Get"
      onclick="cache.get(this.form.key.value)" />
    <input type="button" value="Remove"
      onclick="cache.remove(this.form.key.value)" />
  </form>
</body>
</html>
```

In our example, we created a cache object instance that was associated with the WebSocket server address ws://localhost:8181 and the cache namedCache. Then, we performed a couple of operations in the cache object such as get, put, remove, notify, and unnotify.

The get and notify operations require a callback function to be registered with the cache object instance via the registerCallback function. This callback function asynchronously has two parameters: key and value, relating to the cache key and value, and receives the results of the get method invocation and also receives notifications for the methods add, put, and remove on any cache entries for which the notify function was invoked.

We can see also a sample HTML form in the preceding code, which makes use of the WebSocket server. Note that the input buttons (**Put**, **Get**, and **Remove**) in the form directly trigger the cache methods.

> You can find this sample code in the Infinispan source tree.

Introducing the command line interface (CLI)

In combination with the server module, Infinispan provides a command line interface (CLI), convenient for performing many of the functions that are available in the standard API. Using the command line interface, you can issue many commands such as start caches under a specific CacheManager to manipulate data within, put, remove and evict data, manipulate transactions, cross site backups, and stop caches.

The CLI is based on **Another Extendable SHell (Æsh)**, a java library that provides an API to developers to create their own command-based console and handle console input. It also offers additional features, such as tab completion for all commands, argument values and options, keyboard shortcuts to navigate, Emacs and VI editing mode, undo and redo, and search the history of commands.

Starting the command line interface

Before you execute the command line interface, make sure you have the Infinispan server installation up and running, or if you are running a local Infinispan server node, then be sure it has been correctly configured before invoking the CLI.

 For a future release, CLI will support other communication protocols such as Hot Rod.

Currently, you can connect CLI to the server in two different ways using the JMX protocol, as follows:

- JMX over RMI, using the template `jmx://[username[:password]]@host:port[/container[/cache]]`

- JMX over JBoss Remoting, using the template `remoting://[username[:password]]@host:port[/container[/cache]]`

 JBoss Remoting is a framework for symmetric and asymmetric communication over a network that is used by JBoss AS 5 and 6 to provide remote services such as JMX MBeans and remoting EJBs.

If you are ready to begin, navigate to the `bin` directory in the Infinispan server installation directory and execute the `ispn-cli.sh` script (or `.bat` on Windows) using the `help` option, in order to see all the available options, as follows:

./ispn-cli.sh --help

If successful, you will see the following output:

```
Usage: ispn-cli [OPTION]...
Command-line interface for interacting with a running instance of Infinispan

Options:
  -c, --connect=URL     connects to a running instance of Infinispan.
                        JMX over RMI jmx://[username[:password]]@host:port[/container[/cache]]
                        JMX over JBoss remoting remoting://[username[:password]]@host:port[/container[/cache]]
  -f, --file=FILE       reads input from the specified file instead of using
                        interactive mode. If FILE is '-', then commands will be read
                        from stdin
  -h, --help            shows this help page
  -v, --version         shows version information
```

As you can see, the `ispn-cli` script takes an option parameter, which can be a URL for a running instance of Infinispan or you can use the `--f` option with the full path to a text file, that should contain a list of operations (one per line) that will be executed by the `ispn-cli` in a noninteractive mode, like a batch script.

In the following example, we are connecting the CLI to an Infinispan server instance on localhost to the local CacheManager:

```
./ispn-cli.sh -c remoting://localhost:9999/local/
```

The CLI prompt will start and display some information related to the current connection, such as data and hour of connection, URL, and the selected CacheManager. If connected to a CacheManager, you can see the list of active cache by typing the command cache and pressing the *Tab* key, as shown in the following screenshot:

```
[remoting://localhost:9999/local/]> cache
___defaultcache  default             memcachedCache   namedCache
```

Using Infinispan CLI commands

To see all available commands, you can use the `help` command or press *Tab* on an empty line:

```
[remoting://localhost:9999/local/]>
abort        container   evict     put       site
begin        create      get       quit      start
cache        disconnect  help      remove    stats
clear        encoding    info      replace   upgrade
commit       end         locate    rollback  version
```

You can also use the `help <command>` element to see more detailed information about a specific command, as shown in the following screenshot:

```
[remoting://localhost:9999/local/]> help cache

SYNOPSIS
    cache [ cachename ]

DESCRIPTION
    Shows the currently selected cache or selects a cache to be used as
    default for CLI operations

ARGUMENTS
    cachename
        (optional) the name of the cache to set as default for the
        following operations
```

Defining data types and time values

When executing commands in CLI, you can use a special format to define a specific data type. The following table shows the data types supported by CLI:

Data Type	Explanation	Example
String	This must be enclosed between single (') or double (") quotes.	put k01 "stringValue"
int	An integer data type is identified by a sequence of decimal digits.	put k01 1234
long	A long is identified by a sequence of decimal digits that end with the letter L or l.	put k01 123332L
double	A double precision number is identified by a floating-point number and can optionally end with the letter D or d.	put k01 1.233332D
float	A single precision number is identified by a floating-point number that ends with the letter F or f.	put k01 3.422F
boolean	A Boolean is represented either by the keywords true or false.	put k01 true
UUID	A **Universally Unique IDentifier (UUID)** is represented by 32 hexadecimal digits.	put k01 550e8400-e29b-41d4-a716-446655440000
JSON	Serialized Java classes can be represented by using the JSON notation. Please note that the specified class must be available to the CacheManager's class loader.	put k01 {"com.packtpub.Customer": {"name":Wagner, "age":33, "maritalStatus":"Married", "doc"="212.333.111", "credit":15000}}

A time value is an integer number that is followed by a time unit suffix, as follows:

- Days (d)
- Hours (h)

- Minutes (m)
- Seconds (s)
- Milliseconds (ms)

The following section provides a complete list of Infinispan CLI commands.

Basic commands

Some of the basic commands and their synopsis are mentioned here:

connect

Synopsis: `protocol ://[ user [: password ]@] host ][: port ][/ container [/ cache ]]`

Connect to an Infinispan cache using the JMX or the JBoss Remoting protocol for an interactive session. You have to supply the host and port of the given server and optionally, the required credentials.

disconnect

Synopsis: `disconnect`

The `disconnect` command closes the connection between the CLI and the Infinispan instance. To disconnect an active connection, enter `disconnect` in the Command Prompt and press *Enter*.

cache

Synopsis: `cache [ cache ]`

This command, when executed with the optional `cache` parameter, defines the cache that will be used for all the following operations. If invoked without the `cache` parameter, it will display a list of the available caches.

container

Synopsis: `container [ containername ]`

This command when executed with the optional `containername` parameter, selects a container that will be used for all the following operations. If invoked without the `containername` parameter, it will display a list of the available caches.

quit

Synopsis: `quit`

This command quits the CLI and returns to the prompt.

Manipulating caches

The commands for manipulating caches are as follows:

get

Synopsis: `get [--codec=codec] [ cache. ] key`

Use this command within Infinispan CLI to retrieve a particular value associated with the specified key and cache; if the name of cache is omitted, the selected cache will be used. This command will print a string representation of the value in the console.

put

Synopsis: `put [ --codec=codec ] [ --ifabsent ] [ cache. ] key value [expires expiration [maxidle idletime ]]`

Use the `put` command to insert a new entry in the cache associated with the specified key. If the key already exists, the old value is replaced by the new value.

The value argument will be stored in the cache associated with the key. You can enter it in conjunction with the `--codec=codec` option to encode to a specific structure such as Hot Rod or Memcached; otherwise, the default session codec will be used.

You can also use the optional `expires` and `maxidle` parameters; both must follow the time notation. For example, create a cache entry that will expire in 5 minutes and maximum idle time of only 1 minute, as follows:

```
> put default.k1 myValue expires 5m maxidle 1m
```

clear

Synopsis: `clear [ cache ]`

Clear all the content from the cache. If the optional cache name argument is omitted, the selected cache will be used.

evict

Synopsis: `evict [ cache. ] key`

This command evicts the entry at a specific key.

remove

Synopsis: `remove [ cache. ] key`

This command removes the entry at a specific key.

replace

Synopsis: `replace [ --codec=codec ] [ cache. ] key value`
`  [expires expiration [maxidle idletime ]]`

`replace [ cache. ] key old_value new_value [expires expiration`
`  [maxidle idletime ]]`

This command replaces the cache entry for a key only if currently mapped to any other value.

The following figure displays some of the commands presented in this section:

```
[remoting://localhost:9999/local/default]> put hello world
[remoting://localhost:9999/local/default]> get hello
world
[remoting://localhost:9999/local/default]> put default.k1 myValue expires 5s
[remoting://localhost:9999/local/default]> get default.k1
myValue
[remoting://localhost:9999/local/default]> get default.k1
null
[remoting://localhost:9999/local/default]> remove hello
[remoting://localhost:9999/local/default]> get hello
null
[remoting://localhost:9999/local/default]> put hello world
[remoting://localhost:9999/local/default]> replace hello wagner
[remoting://localhost:9999/local/default]> get hello
wagner
[remoting://localhost:9999/local/default]> evict hello
[remoting://localhost:9999/local/default]> get hello
null
```

Managing caches

The commands to manage caches are as mentioned here:

upgrade

Synopsis: `upgrade [ --dumpkeys | --synchronize=migrator |`
`  --disconnectsource=migrator ] [ cache | --all ]`

This command performs many operations during an upgrade procedure.

For a detailed description of the upgrade procedure without a service shutdown, see the instructions on the following link:
`http://infinispan.org/docs/6.0.x/user_guide/`
`user_guide.html#_rolling_upgrades`

Arguments

You can use the following arguments with the upgrade command:

- `--dumpkeys`: This performs a dump of the keys in the cache on a target cluster
- `--synchronize=migrator`: This synchronizes all the data from the source cluster to the target cluster using a specific migrator, which can be either Hot Rod or the REST migrator
- `--disconnectsource=migrator`: This disconnects the target cluster from the source cluster
- `--all`: This indicates that the requested operation will be performed on all caches

create

Synopsis: `create [ cache ] [ like existingCache ]`

This command creates a new cache based on an existing cache and it's configuration.

encoding

Synopsis: `encoding [ --list | codec ]`

This command sets a default codec to encode/decode the data entries from/to a cache. If executed without arguments, it displays the selected codec. To see all the available options, use the `--list` argument.

Managing transactions

The commands for managing transactions are as follows:

begin

Synopsis: `begin [ cache ]`

The `begin` command will start a transaction in a transactional cache. The optional cache parameter indicates the name of the cache the transaction will start.

commit

Synopsis: `commit`

This command commits the existing transaction.

rollback

Synopsis: `rollback [ cache ]`

The `rollback` command will roll back the existing transactions.

The following figure displays some of the transaction commands presented in this section:

```
[remoting://localhost:9999/local/default]> begin
[remoting://localhost:9999/local/default]> put k1 v1
[remoting://localhost:9999/local/default]> put k2 v2
[remoting://localhost:9999/local/default]> commit
[remoting://localhost:9999/local/default]>
[remoting://localhost:9999/local/default]> begin
[remoting://localhost:9999/local/default]> put k3 v3
[remoting://localhost:9999/local/default]> put k4 v3
[remoting://localhost:9999/local/default]> rollback
```

 The current version of the Infinispan server does not provide support for transactions for any available protocol.

Batching

The batching commands are as follows:

start

Synopsis: `start [ cache ]`

This command starts a batch process, in order to provide the ability to batch multiple cache operations.

end

Synopsis: `end [ cache ]`

This command executes all batched operations and ends the batch process.

abort

Synopsis: abort [cache]

This command aborts a running batch process.

The following figure displays some of the commands presented in this section:

```
[remoting://localhost:9999/local/default]> start
[remoting://localhost:9999/local/default]> put k1 v1
[remoting://localhost:9999/local/default]> put k2 v2
[remoting://localhost:9999/local/default]> put k3 v3
[remoting://localhost:9999/local/default]> end
[remoting://localhost:9999/local/default]>
[remoting://localhost:9999/local/default]> start
[remoting://localhost:9999/local/default]> put k4 v5
[remoting://localhost:9999/local/default]> put k5 v6
[remoting://localhost:9999/local/default]> abort
[remoting://localhost:9999/local/default]> stop
Command stop unknown or not available
```

Our last example shows that if we abort an ongoing batch process, we have to start it again.

Getting statistics and system information

The commands to obtain the statistics and system information are as follows:

locate

Synopsis: locate [--codec=codec] [cache.] key

locate is a command made exclusively for distributed caches. It locates and displays the addresses of the cache instances in the cluster that own the entry associated with the specified key.

site

Synopsis: site [--status | --online | --offline] [cache.sitename]

A special command to manage data grids with cross-site replication, you can use site to retrieve information about the current status of a given site and change the status to online or offline by using the --online and --offline parameters.

stats

Synopsis: `stats [ --container | cache ]`

Use the `stats` command to display statistics about the specified cache or about the active cache manager. You can use the `--container` option to display information about the specified container.

version

Synopsis: `version`

The `version` command displays the current version of the client running on the system.

info

Synopsis: `info [ cache ]`

The `info` command displays information about the cache configuration and attributes of the active CacheManager.

Summary

In this chapter, we looked at the ways in which you can connect to the Infinispan remote server. There are many server modules available such as the Memcached, Hot Rod, REST, and WebSocket server module, each with its own strengths and limitations.

We analyzed how to install and configure each server module, customize the Infinispan subsystem, and saw some examples of how to use them; finally, we also examined a command line interface (CLI) provided by Infinispan, which is convenient for performing many of the functions that are available in the standard API.

In the next chapter, we are going to cover Hibernate OGM, an interesting framework that provides support for JPA, Infinispan, and NoSQL data stores such as MongoDB.

10
Getting Started with Hibernate OGM

So far, you have learned how to access data in the Infinispan cache using standard API and also remotely with Hot Rod or other client/server modules.

In this chapter, you will learn a different way to access your cache data, which may be a more familiar way than you think.

You will learn about the Hibernate **Object/Grid Mapper** (**OGM**), a very ambitious project that aims to provide **Java Persistence API** (**JPA**) support for NoSQL data stores.

In this chapter, we will discuss the following topics:

- An overview of Hibernate OGM
- The Hibernate OGM architecture
- Configuring Hibernate OGM and controlling transactions
- Creating a sample application with OGM

Introducing Hibernate OGM

If you are a Java developer with some experience, you might know that Hibernate is an **Object/Relational Mapping** (**ORM**) framework. For those who don't know what Hibernate is, it is a powerful tool that lets you map a traditional **Plain Old Java Object** (**POJO**) to a traditional database table.

When we say traditional database, we are referring, in particular, to relational databases like Oracle, MySQL, and SQL Server. Because of the great popularity of Hibernate, the **Java Community Process (JCP)** created the JPA specification as part of the JSR 220 for Enterprise JavaBeans 3.0, totally inspired by the Hibernate framework. The following figure depicts the main components of the JPA architecture:

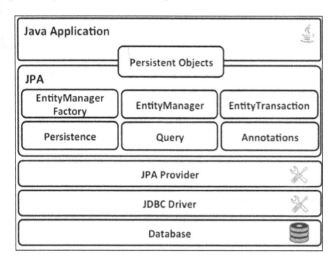

With the emergence of NoSQL solutions and its new paradigm for databases, many developers took advantage of this solution in their applications.

There are a number of NoSQL stores, which can be classified as follows:

- **Key-value stores**: Key-value stores are considered the simplest model, where every database item is stored under a key, which is used to identify a value in a bucket. In this model, we have Riak and Voldermort databases. In this model, the data store has no knowledge of the internals of the values. It simply stores the value, as opposed to document databases, where the store has insight into the contents of the value.

- **Document databases**: Similar to key-value stores, these databases store a key with a complex data structure (a JSON document, for instance). MongoDB and CouchDB are good examples.

- **Column family stores**: These store columns of related data under the same key, similar to a relational database. In this category, we have the Apache Cassandra and HBase.

- **Graph databases**: These are designed to store data structures whose relations are represented as a graph with nodes, edges, and properties. There are several graph databases such as Neo4j and HyperGraphDB.

Within this context, Hibernate launched the Object/Grid Mapper (OGM), a framework that has the ambitious goal of bringing JPA support to the NoSQL store, which can be good for developers who want to port their applications to NoSQL or for developers who don't have too much experience with NoSQL databases, since it provides a well-known JPA interface for Java developers.

Hibernate OGM features

At the time of writing, the latest Hibernate OGM distribution is `4.1.2 Final`, which already provides a JPA interface for different NoSQL backends. Hibernate OGM provides rapid scaling of a data store up or down and many ways to retrieve entities.

Hibernate OGM also supports basic CRUD operations for JPA entities, JPA unidirectional and bidirectional associations (`@ManyToOne`, `@OneToOne`, `@OneToMany`, and `@ManyToMany`), collections, embeddable objects (JPA classes annotated with `@Embeddable` or `@ElementCollection`), specific native queries, and full-text queries (via Hibernate Search as indexing engine).

Hibernate OGM has planned several features, including polyglot persistence, map/reduce on queries, various queries improvements, and so on.

Polyglot Persistence is a term coined by Neal Ford, and refers to the idea that developers should create applications using a mix of languages to take advantage of them for tackling specific problems where a language best suits.

Map/Reduce is a programming model introduced by Google that allows for massive scalability across hundreds or thousands of servers in a data grid.

You can read more about Map/Reduce in *Chapter 12, Advanced Topics*.

Hibernate OGM architecture

Hibernate OGM is based on the Hibernate ORM and reuses and extends some components by adding new characteristics. Basically, OGM reuses the Hibernate ORM for:

- JPA support
- The Lucene and Hibernate Search to build indexes
- The Teiid query engine to implement complex features (for instance, joins between entities and aggregations)
- The NoSQL drivers to connect and interact with the datastore
- Infinispan's Lucene Directory to store indexes

You can see them integrated in the following figure:

The `Persist` and `Loader` interfaces from Hibernate ORM were rewritten to support persistence and load operations in different NoSQL stores.

Another important change in the OGM architecture is that the JDBC drivers that connect to databases are not needed anymore. They were replaced by two new elements `DatastoreProvider` and `GridDialect`, which work like a JDBC layer for the NoSQL store.

While `DatastoreProvider` provides native access to the underlying NoSQL data store, the `GridDialect` interface abstracts OGM from the grid implementation, which includes the data format and associations.

Currently, Hibernate OGM implements the following datastore providers:

- `InfinispanDatastoreProvider`: This class provides access to an Infinispan CacheManager.

- `EhcacheDatastoreProvider`: This class provides access to EhCache.

- `MapDatastoreProvider`: This class represents a data store example class, created for testing purposes. It implements only the basic interface needed by OGM and does not support clustering and transaction features.

- `MongoDBDatastoreProvider`: This class provides access to the MongoDB document database.

- `Neo4jDatastoreProvider`: This class provides access to the Neo4J graph database.

- `CouchDBDatastoreProvider`: This class provides access to a fully configured instance of CouchDB.

Once connected to one of these data stores, you will be able to perform standard query operations using **Java Persistence Query Language (JPQL)**. To support JPQL queries, OGM provides a sophisticated query engine that converts JPQL queries into a native query.

However, if the query is complex for the native query capabilities of the NoSQL store, OGM will use the Teiid query engine to parse the query in order to validate syntax and rewrite the query to simplify expressions, joins, and criteria.

 Teiid is a data virtualization system that is composed of several tools, components, and services that allows applications, web services, and reports to use data from multiple data stores.

For more information, visit `http://www.jboss.org/teiid/`.

We may have some cases where the NoSQL solution does not have query support; in these situations, Hibernate OGM relies on the Hibernate Search as an external query engine.

Understanding how the mappings work

In JPA, the challenge of object-relational mapping relies on the differences between an object-oriented domain model and a relational database model because there is no logical equivalence between the concepts of both models, which can become quite complex to map when the database table and a class differ in representation, especially when the database model already exists, and where we have to adapt the domain model to the database schema structure.

Hibernate OGM is no different, since we have four different models for a NoSQL stores. As we said, OGM tries to reuse most of the Hibernate ORM, so the idea is still the same, that is, to create an abstraction between both the application object and the persistent data model and also to continue to use a primary key to address an entity and a foreign key to link two entities.

An entity in Hibernate OGM is represented by a `Map<String, Object>` structure stored as tuples of values by Hibernate OGM, where the key to the Map is represented by the `EntityKey` class, which is basically composed of the table name and the primary key column (annotated with `@Id`), `name`, and `value`, as you can see in the following figure:

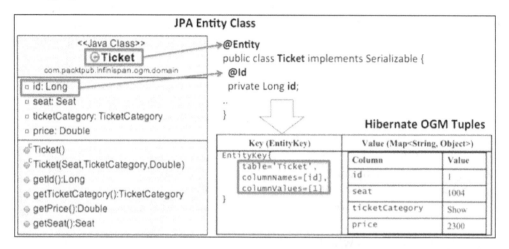

As you can see, a tuple is `Map<String, Object>` object that is used to represent an entity instance, by mapping the column names to column values, where the string is the type of key that represents the column name and the object represents the column type. Hibernate OGM will use the specific `GridDialect` object to convert the Map to the standards of the NoSQL data store you target. It will use the column name as the key and will try to use, whenever possible, basic types (for instance string and number objects) to represent the value of an entity attribute, in order to increase portability across different platforms and specific types of the chosen NoSQL data store. This structure is stored in an Infinispan-named cache called **ENTITIES**.

In the last example, we saw how OGM represents a single entity, but we have to consider that those objects rarely exist in isolation. Just like in a traditional database, it's common that a domain class depends on another class, or a domain class that is associated with other domain classes. Consider the previous `Ticket` class; now let's introduce the `TicketCategory` domain class, for which a `Ticket` class might have, at most, one instance of `TicketCategory` associated with it, while `TicketCategory` might have zero or many instances of `Ticket` associated with it. In this case, we say that `Ticket` has a many-to-one relationship with `TicketCategory`, represented by the notation **0..1** (multiplicity) in the **Unified Modeling Language (UML)**. The following figure demonstrates this relationship:

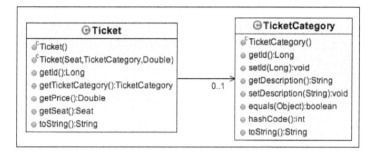

In this example, a `TicketCategory` instance does not hold onto the `Ticket` instance that owns it, however, the `Ticket` instance must hold a reference to the `TicketCategory` class.

In such cases, Hibernate OGM does not serialize associations to Blob objects. OGM stores the associations between entities as a set of tuples of `Map<String, Object>` and all information necessary to navigate from an entity to another, where the key to the `Map` is represented by the `AssociationKey` class.

For instance, in a many-to-many association, each entity of the relation is associated with a collection of the other entity. In this scenario, each tuple stores a pair of foreign keys, which can bring some level of duplication. This is because the navigational information has to be stored for both sides of the association.

The following diagram shows a simple example of a many-to-many relationship between **User** and **UserGroup**, where a user could belong to many groups and a group could contain many users:

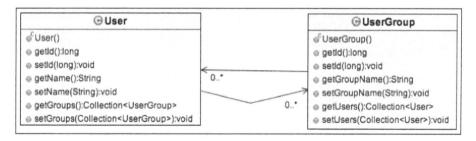

These associations follow the same approach for entities, but the key is composed of the table name, the foreign key column name, and the column value of the referenced entity. In a `@ManyToMany` association, as we said, Hibernate OGM allows some level of duplication to store both sides of the association, in order to ensure that the association data can be obtained through a simple key lookup from any of the two sides, which is good, because it doesn't require a more expensive operation, like reading all the entries from the cache.

When using Infinispan as a data store, OGM stores the associations into a named cache called **Associations**. To visualize how this process works in general terms, the following code example persists two instances of the entity User associated with two different UserGroups:

```
tm.begin();
EntityManager em = emf.createEntityManager();

User wagner = new User();
wagner.setId(1711);
wagner.setName("Wagner");

User thiago = new User();
thiago.setId(1721);
thiago.setName("Thiago");

UserGroup java = new UserGroup();
java.setId(12);
java.setName("Java User Group");

UserGroup dotNet = new UserGroup();
dotNet.setId(141);
dotNet.setName("Dot Net User Group");

List<UserGroup> groupList = new ArrayList<UserGroup>();
groupList.add(java);
groupList.add(dotNet);

List<User> userList = new ArrayList<User>();
userList.add(wagner);
userList.add(thiago);

wagner.setGroups(groupList);
thiago.setGroups(groupList);

java.setUsers(userList);
dotNet.setUsers(userList);

em.persist(java);
em.persist(dotNet);

em.persist( wagner );
em.persist(thiago);
```

```
em.flush();
em.close();
tm.commit();
```

To understand how this works, the following figure shows how Hibernate OGM stores the associations and entities presented in the preceding code:

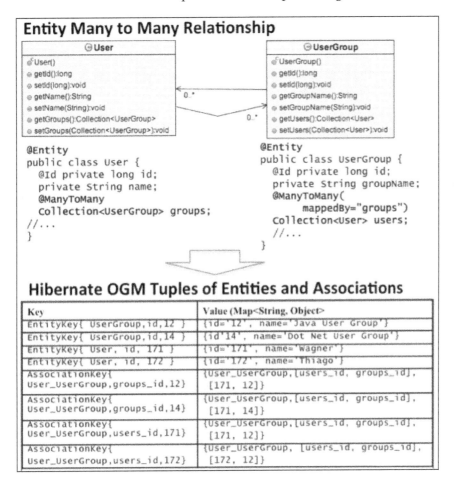

The table presented in the preceding figure shows how Hibernate OGM stores the entities and associations. The first four lines represent the **User** and **UserGroups** instances we created in the code, and the rest of the lines show how Hibernate OGM stores the associations.

In the next section, we will create a sample Hibernate OGM application, connect this to an Infinispan data store to explain the different parts of OGM.

Installing and using Hibernate OGM

I know it's quite ambitious to provide a set of tools that can match each individual's needs, so we will focus on a simple reference case study, which will help us to demonstrate the basic steps of how Java developers start using Hibernate OGM. So, for this tutorial, we will need the following tools:

- Java Development Kit (JDK) Version 1.6 or later
- Apache Maven 3.*x*
- An IDE such as Eclipse Kepler or JUNO along with JBoss AS tools, IntelliJ IDEA 14.*, or Netbeans 7.2.* or 7.3
- JBoss AS 7
- JBoss JTA 4.16.4 Final
- Hibernate OGM 4.1.2.Final

In order to install Hibernate OGM, you need to download the latest release from the Hibernate OGM website. At the time of writing, the last distribution was `4.1.2.Final`. The easiest way to do so is to download the corresponding ZIP file with the binaries, documentation, sources, and dependencies by following the link from the main Hibernate OGM page located at `http://hibernate.org/ogm/`.

Once you unzip it, you should have a folder that contains the following content:

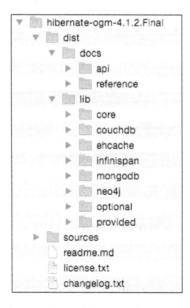

The dist folder contains two subfolders named lib and doc. The lib folder contains the main library hibernate-ogm-core-4.1.2.Final.jar inside the core folder, along with the libraries that need to be on your class path, and a folder for each supported datastore, including Infinispan.

The doc folder contains the Javadocs API documentation and the reference guide for Hibernate OGM; and finally, the source folder that contains the source code as a distinct Maven project for each module.

To use it in your project, include a copy of the OGM library and all the dependencies from the dist folder to the classpath of your application.

Creating a Hibernate OGM project using Maven

Like a usual Java application, OGM does not require running an installer. You will need to add the dependencies to classpath before you start to use it.

Hibernate OGM builds are also published to the JBoss Maven repository, so you have to add the Maven repository to your Maven settings, located in your .m2 directory.

Note: *Chapter 1, Getting Started* shows how to configure the JBoss Maven repository.

Once you have a JBoss Maven repository configured, you need to include Hibernate OGM and Hibernate OGM, for Infinispan dependencies, to your Maven project; open the pom.xml file of your recently created project in your editor and add the following dependencies:

```xml
<dependencies>
  <!-- Hibernate OGM dependency -->
  <dependency>
    <groupId>org.hibernate.ogm</groupId>
    <artifactId>hibernate-ogm-core</artifactId>
    <version>4.1.2.Final</version>
  </dependency>
  <!-- Hibernate OGM to persist objects in Infinispan -->
  <dependency>
    <groupId>org.hibernate.ogm</groupId>
    <artifactId>hibernate-ogm-infinispan</artifactId>
    <version>4.1.2.Final</version>
  </dependency>
  <!-- Infinispan JDBC CacheStore module -->
  <dependency>
    <groupId>org.infinispan</groupId>
    <artifactId>infinispan-cachestore-jdbc</artifactId>
```

```
    <version>6.0.1.Final</version>
</dependency>
<!-- standard APIs dependencies -->
<dependency>
    <groupId>org.hibernate.javax.persistence</groupId>
    <artifactId>hibernate-jpa-2.0-api</artifactId>
    <version>1.0.1.Final</version>
</dependency>
<!-- JBoss Transaction Service -->
<dependency>
    <groupId>org.jboss.jbossts</groupId>
    <artifactId>jbossjta</artifactId>
    <version>4.16.6.Final</version>
</dependency>
<!-- Beans Validation API for our sample code -->
<dependency>
<groupId>javax.validation</groupId>
<artifactId>validation-api</artifactId>
<version>1.1.0.Final</version>
</dependency>
<!-- C3P0 -JDBC Connection pooling for Standalone applications -->
<dependency>
<groupId>c3p0</groupId>
<artifactId>c3p0</artifactId>
<version>0.9.1.2</version>
</dependency>
</dependencies>
```

 We included the dependency `org.jboss.jbossts` in our `pom.xml` file because we are going to run our examples in a non-JTA environment, which we'll discuss in the *Transaction Management* section.

Build your Maven project and if successful, at the end, you should see the Hibernate OGM distribution and its dependencies.

Now, let's create a Hibernate OGM application; if you're using Eclipse, perform the following steps:

1. Click on the Start button and select menu **File | New | Project** and click on **Next**.

2. In the new Maven project screen, select the checkbox **Create a simple project (skip archetype selection)** and click on **Next**.

3. Enter `com.packtpub.infinispan.guide` for the **Group ID** and `chapter10` for **Artifact ID** and click on **Finish**.

4. To provide JPA support, you need to add a JPA facet to your project. In the **Project Explorer** view, right-click the project and then select **Properties**.

5. Select **Project Facets** and click on **Convert to faceted form**.

6. Select the **JPA** option and click the **Apply** button and then, click on **OK**.

If everything goes well, Eclipse will create a `persistence.xml` file for you in the `META-INF` folder.

Configuring the persistence unit

In this section, we will discuss how to configure the persistence configuration file.

Like any JPA application, we have to define one named persistence unit in an XML file called `persistence.xml`, but in Hibernate OGM the configuration is much easier than a traditional JPA application. In general terms, JPA will use Hibernate OGM as a persistence provider, so you have to explicitly include the persistence provider you want in your file. In Hibernate OGM, we have a specific JPA `PersistenceProvider` implementation called `HibernateOgmPersistence`, which you can use in your configuration.

In the next sample, we create a `persistence.xml` file, with a persistence unit named `ogm-infinispan-guide`, and since we are using JPA in a standalone application we have to set the transaction type attribute to JTA. In this example, we will use JBoss Transaction with Hibernate OGM, which is as follows:

```
<persistence xmlns="http://java.sun.com/xml/ns/persistence"
  xmlns:xsi="http://www.w3.org/2001/XMLSchema-instance"
    xsi:schemaLocation="http://java.sun.com/xml/ns/persistence
      http://java.sun.com/xml/ns/persistence/persistence_2_0.xsd"
        version="2.0">
  <persistence-unit name="ogm-infinispan-guide"
    transaction-type="JTA">
  <!-- A Hibernate OGM provider specific to OGM -->
  <provider>org.hibernate.ogm.jpa.HibernateOgmPersistence
  </provider>
  <properties>
    <!-- Configure Hibernate OGM to work with Infinispan. -->
    <property name="hibernate.ogm.datastore.provider"
      value="org.hibernate.ogm.datastore.infinispan.impl.
        InfinispanDatastoreProvider" />
    <!-- Point to a custom Infinispan configuration file -->
```

```
        <property
          name="hibernate.ogm.infinispan.configuration_resource_name"
            value="META-INF/config.xml" />
        <!-- defines which JTA Transaction we plan to use -->
        <property name="hibernate.transaction.jta.platform"
          value="org.hibernate.service.jta.platform.internal.
          JBossStandAloneJtaPlatform" />
    </properties>
    </persistence-unit>
  </persistence>
```

Now, we are going to discuss the details of this configuration.

Transaction management

When we talk about transaction management, we are referring to how the lifecycle of entities in an application are managed. JPA supports two types of transaction management, which are, RESOURCE_LOCAL transactions or JTA transactions. We generally use RESOURCE_LOCAL to execute a JPA application in a nonmanaged environment, such as a Swing application and JPA transaction to execute our application in a managed JEE environment, which provides container-managed transactions. Hibernate OGM supports both options and can run in many environments. However, our sample application in this chapter is not running in a Java EE environment.

Running Hibernate OGM in the Java EE environment

When running a Hibernate OGM application in the Java EE container such as JBoss AS, you have to specify a couple of settings in the persistence.xml file, which are as follows:

- Set the transaction-type attribute to JTA to indicate the persistence unit to use JTA transactions.

- Set the hibernate.transaction.jta.platform attribute to define the right Java EE container. It will help how Hibernate OGM will interact with the JTA services on the given platform.

- Set the jta-data-source attribute to indicate a JTA data source.

 Hibernate OGM will ignore the jta-data-source attribute, but it's necessary because the JPA specification requires this setting.

The next sample shows the relevant part of the `persistence.xml` file for this example:

```xml
<?xml version="1.0"?>
<persistence xmlns="http://java.sun.com/xml/ns/persistence"
  xmlns:xsi="http://www.w3.org/2001/XMLSchema-instance"
    xsi:schemaLocation="http://java.sun.com/xml/ns/persistence
      http://java.sun.com/xml/ns/persistence/persistence_2_0.xsd"
        version="2.0">
  <persistence-unit name="ogm-infinispan-guide"
    transaction-type="JTA">
  <!-- A Hibernate OGM provider specific to OGM -->
<provider>org.hibernate.ogm.jpa.HibernateOgmPersistence</provider>
  <jta-data-source>java:/DefaultDS</jta-data-source>
  <properties>
    <property name="hibernate.transaction.jta.platform"
      value="org.hibernate.service.jta.platform.internal.
        JBossAppServerJtaPlatform" />
    <property name="hibernate.ogm.datastore.provider"
      value="infinispan" />
  </properties>
  </persistence-unit>
</persistence>
```

Running Hibernate OGM in a standalone JTA environment

To create our sample application, we created a simple Maven project, which is going to be executed in a standalone JTA environment. To use Hibernate OGM in such an environment, we have to define some specific settings in our `persistence.xml` file, which are as follows:

- Set the transaction-type attribute to JTA to indicate the persistence unit to use JTA transactions
- Set the `hibernate.transaction.jta.platform` attribute to `org.hibernate.service.jta.platform.internal.JBossStandAloneJtaPlatform`

The persistence file we created for the sample application will follow all these rules.

Running Hibernate OGM without JTA

Without JTA, you will have to demarcate your transaction boundaries yourself using the `EntityTransaction` API. However, despite this it works; it's not recommended to work without a JTA transaction in a production environment, because there is no guarantee that the operations will be performed as an atomic unit within the current transaction, so rollback operations may not work properly.

In the future, it will change, but today, Hibernate OGM does not ensure that transactions will work properly and it cannot rollback your transaction.

In our sample application, we are running Hibernate OGM without JTA and we also have a (commented) version to execute in a standalone JTA environment, just for demo purposes.

Configuration properties

The Hibernate OGM standard properties fall into the data store category, but you can use most of the options available in the Hibernate ORM and Hibernate Search, except the following list of properties that do not apply to Hibernate OGM:

- `hibernate.connection.*`
- `hibernate.dialect`
- `hibernate.show_sql`
- `hibernate.format_sql`
- `hibernate.default_schema`
- `hibernate.default_catalog`
- `hibernate.use_sql_comments`
- `hibernate.jdbc.*`
- `hibernate.hbm2ddl.auto`
- `hibernate.hbm2ddl.import_file`

Next, the following table outlines the properties available for Infinispan that can be specified in the `<properties>` tag of the `persistence.xml` descriptor:

Property Name	Description
`hibernate.ogm.datastore.grid_dialect`	You can override this setting to manually define the grid dialect you want to use. By default, the data store provider chooses the grid dialect.
`hibernate.ogm.datastore.provider`	This is the property used to define the data store provider. As mentioned earlier, Hibernate OGM has four implementations of data store providers. For obvious reasons, in our sample application, we are using `InfinispanDatastoreProvider` to provide access to Infinispan's CacheManager.
`hibernate.ogm.infinispan.cachemanager_jndi_name`	Use this setting to define the JNDI name of the cache manager. But first, you have to register an `EmbeddedCacheManager` object in the JNDI.

Property Name	Description
`hibernate.ogm.infinispan. configuration_resource_ name`	If you're not using JNDI, you can use this property to point to a custom configuration file for Infinispan. In our sample example, we are pointing to the `META-INF/config.xml` file.
	The default value points to `org/hibernate/ogm/ datastore/infinispan/default-config.xml`

Configuring Infinispan caches for Hibernate OGM

In the Hibernate OGM architecture section of this chapter, you learned how the mapping works and that entities and associations are represented by a `Map<String, Object>` structure, which are to be stored as tuples of values by Hibernate OGM.

When Infinispan is in use as a data store, Hibernate OGM will use three different named caches in Infinispan to store these different structures, which are as follows:

- `ENTITIES`: This cache is used to store the tuples of values of the application entities
- `ASSOCIATIONS`: This cache is used to store the tuples of values related to the association information between the application entities
- `IDENTIFIER_STORE`: This cache is used to store the internal metadata related to ID generation specified by the `@GeneratedValue` annotation in JPA

The XML configuration that is used by Hibernate OGM complies with the Infinispan schema, so you can define your own eviction and expiration strategy and persistence settings. The most simplest structure of an Infinispan configuration file must have three different named caches, as we can see in the following code:

```
<namedCache name="ENTITIES">
</namedCache>
<namedCache name="ASSOCIATIONS">
</namedCache>
<namedCache name="IDENTIFIERS">
</namedCache>
```

- For our sample application, the named caches `ENTITIES` and ASSOCIATIONS will be using a JDBC-based cache store to store the JPA entities and associations.

 Please note that we are going to use the JDBC-based cache store in our example only as a cache store entity; associations and the identifier information will be stored normally in the Infinispan cache.

- To do so, you have to link the `infinispan-cachestore-jdbc-config-6.0.xsd` schema to the configuration file. The next example shows how to do this:

```
<infinispan xmlns:xsi="http://www.w3.org/2001/
  XMLSchema-instance"
    xsi:schemaLocation="urn:infinispan:config:6.0
      http://www.infinispan.org/schemas/
        infinispan-config-6.0.xsd
          urn:infinispan:config:jdbc:6.0
            http://www.infinispan.org/schemas/
              infinispan-cachestore-jdbc-config-6.0.xsd"
                xmlns="urn:infinispan:config:6.0"
                  xmlns:jdbc="urn:infinispan:config:jdbc:6.0">
```

- In the `<global>` section, we will just enable the JMX statistics, but you could also change the transport characteristics used for network communications across the cluster.

- For the `<default>` tag, we will enable the distribution mode, the L1 cache and the synchronous replication as the default behavior for all named caches that belong to this cache manager.

- To allow Infinispan to talk to a JTA transaction manager, we will set the `transactionMode` attribute to define our cache as transactional, and configure the JBoss Standalone `TransactionManager` lookup class:

```
<global>
  <globalJmxStatistics enabled="true"></global>
</global>
<default>
  <clustering mode="distribution">
    <sync replTimeout="25000" />
    <l1 enabled="true" />
  </clustering>
  <transaction transactionMode="TRANSACTIONAL"
    transactionManagerLookupClass="org.infinispan.
      transaction.lookup.JBossStandaloneJTAManagerLookup">
  </transaction>
</default>
```

- Finally, for the named caches ENTITIES and ASSOCIATIONS, we will be using a JDBC-based CacheStore to store the JPA entities and associations. In the named cache IDENTIFIERS, we are defining the directory for SingleFileStore:

```
<namedCache name="ENTITIES">
  <eviction strategy="LIRS" maxEntries="10" />
  <persistence>
    <binaryKeyedJdbcStore
      xmlns="urn:infinispan:config:jdbc:6.0"
        fetchPersistentState="false"
          ignoreModifications="false"
            purgeOnStartup="false">
    <connectionPool
      connectionUrl="jdbc:mysql://localhost:3306/Infinispan"
        username="infinispan" password="infinispan"
          driverClass="com.mysql.jdbc.Driver" />
      <binaryKeyedTable prefix="ISPN_GRID_OGM_BIN"
        createOnStart="true">
      <idColumn name="ID_ENT_TICKET" type="VARCHAR(255)" />
      <dataColumn name="DATA_ENT_TICKET" type="BLOB" />
      <timestampColumn name="TIMESTAMP_ENT"
        type="BIGINT" />
      </binaryKeyedTable>
    </binaryKeyedJdbcStore>
  </persistence>
</namedCache>
```

Now that you have enabled JMX monitoring, you can connect to it from any JMX client, such as JConsole, as you can see in the following image:

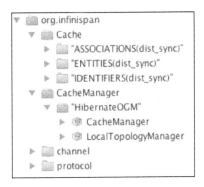

Creating the domain model

Often, the first step to developing an application is based on the business domain. We can create a domain model, which is defining the entities in the domain and the relationships between them. For this simple use case, we'll explore the Ticket Monster application domain again in order to extract a subset of JPA entities with their attributes, relationships, and cardinality. To keep things simple, we assume for our domain model, the Ticket Monster entities are `TicketCategory`, `Ticket`, `Seat`, `Section`, and `Venue`, as you can see in the following model:

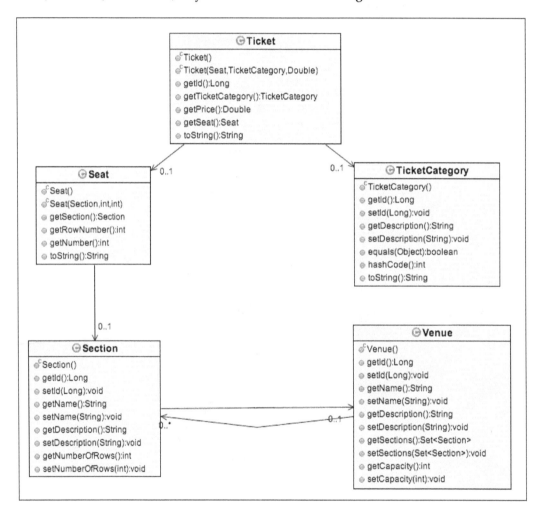

Now, we can recreate the entities following the given model or copy the entities from the Ticket Monster project, making some adjustments.

The source code for this book is publicly available and can be found on GitHub.

Mapping JPA entities in Hibernate OGM is quite simple, since you can use standard JPA annotations such as @Entity to indicate to the persistence engine that the class is an entity, @Id to identify the field that represents the key, and other common annotations such as @Column and @Table. But due to the dynamic nature of a NoSQL schema, not all features and annotations are supported by Hibernate OGM, such as secondary tables (@SecondaryTables, @SecondaryTable), named queries and native queries (@NamedQueries, @NamedQuery, @NamedNativeQuery), and other annotations such as @Inheritance and @DiscrimatorColumn, which could throw unexpected exceptions or just be ignored by Hibernate OGM.

Now, you will need to define the attributes and implement the operations of the domain model classes. In the case of the TicketCategory entity, we have to define an id attribute annotated with @Id and apply the @GeneratedValue annotation to generate the values of primary keys automatically, which is shown in the following code:

```
@Entity
@Indexed
public class TicketCategory implements Serializable {
    @Id
    @GeneratedValue(strategy = IDENTITY)
    @DocumentId
    private Long id;

    @Column(unique = true)
    @NotNull
    private String description;

    /* Getters, Setters, toString(), equals() and hashCode() methods
       are omitted*/
}
```

You probably notice that in the implementation of the domain classes, we are also including constraints on our domain objects using the Bean Validations API annotation @NotNull. We are using the same strategy in the Ticket entity that has a @ManyToOne association to the TicketCategory entity.

Another important aspect in this class is the usage of Hibernate Search annotations such as @Indexed, which marks an entity class as searchable through Hibernate Search. Hibernate Search will not index entities that are not annotated with @Indexed.

If you try to search an entity without the annotation, Hibernate Search will throw an `IllegalArgumentException` exception, stating that the entity is not an indexed entity.

The second thing to notice is that we have annotated the `id` property with `@DocumentId`, which will make the Hibernate Search index the property in the Lucene document, as shown in the following code:

```
@Entity
@Indexed
public class Ticket implements Serializable {
  @Id
  @GeneratedValue(strategy = IDENTITY)
  @DocumentId
  private Long id;

  @NotNull
  private Seat seat;

  @ManyToOne
  @NotNull
  @IndexedEmbedded
  private TicketCategory ticketCategory;

  private Double price;
  /* Contructors, Getters, Setters, toString(), equals() and
     hashCode() methods are omitted*/
}
```

The `Seat` entity is annotated with `@Embeddable` because it's a part of the `Ticket` entity and also has a `@ManyToOne` association to the `Venue` entity. The `rowNumber` and `number` attributes are annotated with `@Min` of the Bean Validation API to ensure that the values of these fields are an integer value equal to or greater than 1:

```
@Embeddable
public class Seat {
  @Min(1)
  private int rowNumber;
  @Min(1)
  private int number;
  @ManyToOne
  private Section section;
```

```
    /* Constructors, Getters, Setters, toString(), equals() and
hashCode() methods are omitted*/
    }
```

The next code listing shows the Section entity class that has a @ManyToOne association to the Venue entity:

```
@Entity
@Table(uniqueConstraints=@UniqueConstraint(columnNames={"name",
    "venue_id"}))
public class Section implements Serializable {
    @Id
    @GeneratedValue(strategy = IDENTITY)
    private Long id;

    @NotNull
    private String name;

    @NotNull
    private String description;

    @ManyToOne
    @NotNull
    private Venue venue;

    private int numberOfRows;
    private int rowCapacity;

    /* Constructors, getters, setters, toString(), equals()
       and hashCode() methods are omitted*/
    }
```

Lastly, the Venue entity has a Set<Sections> attribute, which establishes a bidirectional relationship with the Section entity:

```
@Entity
public class Venue implements Serializable {

    @Id
    @GeneratedValue(strategy = IDENTITY)
    private Long id;

    @Column(unique = true)
    @NotNull
    private String name;
```

```
    private String description;

    @OneToMany(cascade = ALL, fetch = EAGER, mappedBy = "venue")
    private Set<Section> sections = new HashSet<Section>();

    private int capacity;
    /* Constructors, getters, setters, toString(), equals()
       and hashCode() methods are omitted*/
}
```

Next, we create a JUnit Test Case to generate a couple of tickets and retrieve them. The following code sample demonstrates a simplified version of the method:

```
@Test
public void generateTicketDataWithoutJTASimplified() {
    EntityManager em = getEntityManager();
    em.getTransaction().begin();
    TicketCategory theatre = new TicketCategory();
    theatre.setDescription("Theatre");

    em.persist(theatre);

    Section a1 = new Section();
    a1.setName("A1");
    a1.setNumberOfRows(1);
    a1.setRowCapacity(50);

    Seat seat101 = new Seat(a1, 1, 10);
    Set<Section> theatreSections = new HashSet<Section>();
    theatreSections.add(a1);

    Ticket ticket101 = new Ticket(seat101, theatre, 2950d);

    Venue opera = new Venue();
    opera.setName("Opera Garnier");
    opera.setCapacity(1979);
    opera.setSections(theatreSections);
```

```
    em.persist(opera);
    a1.setVenue(opera);
    em.persist(a1);
    em.persist(ticket101);

    ticketNumber = ticket101.getId();
    assertNotNull(ticketNumber);

    em.flush();
    em.getTransaction().commit();
    em.close();

    em = getEntityManager();
    em.getTransaction().begin();
    Ticket returnedTicket101 = em.find(Ticket.class, ticketNumber);
    em.flush();
    assertNotNull(returnedTicket101);
    assertEquals(ticket101.getId(), returnedTicket101.getId());
    em.close();
    em.getTransaction().commit();
}
```

In the next and final test, we show a Hibernate Search query example, which we wrap into an `org.hibernate.Query` class, which is as follows:

```
@Test
public void queryTicketWithHQL() {
    EntityManager em = getEntityManager();
    em.getTransaction().begin();

    Session session = em.unwrap(Session.class);
    Query q = session
        .createQuery("from Ticket t where t.id = :ticketNumber");
    q.setLong("ticketNumber", ticketNumber);
    Ticket retrievedTicket = (Ticket) q.uniqueResult();
    assertEquals(retrievedTicket.getId(), ticketNumber);
    em.getTransaction().commit();
    em.close();
}
```

Summary

In this chapter, we looked at how to get started with Hibernate OGM; we learned the concepts behind it, the main features and gained an overview of its architecture. We also learned how to create and configure a `persistence xml` file, the available properties in Hibernate OGM, and how to integrate it with Infinispan.

To better understand the concepts, we created a sample application using Maven and Eclipse, for porting part of the domain model from the Ticket Monster application. At last, we created some unit tests to perform some basic operations and querying information about tickets.

In the next chapter, we are going to cover JGroups, one of the most important pieces of Infinispan. JGroups is a toolkit for reliable group communication, and you will learn about the JGroups architecture and how it integrates with Infinispan.

11
An Introduction to JGroups

In this chapter, we'll examine several aspects of Infinispan communication, it makes use of JGroups, a group communication framework, which implements a paradigm that eases the development of distributed applications, ranging from application servers, distributed caching systems (Infinispan, JCS), Fault-Tolerant CORBA specification (GroupPac), just to name a few.

We will introduce the basic concepts of JGroups, the supported protocols, and how it is integrated to Infinispan via the configuration file, and discuss the following topics:

* Introduction to group communication and JGroups
* The JGroups architecture
* Integrating JGroups and Infinispan
* An overview of protocols used by JGroups

So, let's get started.

Introduction to group communication

Distributed object technology has been used intensely and became an essential part of several solutions, such as middlewares, CMS's, distributed caches, and data grid platforms like Infinispan.

As you saw in detail in *Chapter 2, Barriers to Scaling Data*, the basic idea behind these platforms is no matter how many nodes are connected through a **local area network** (**LAN**). When you interact with a client / server application, the application should provide the same experience that you would expect interacting with a local application with one single node.

No matter the number of nodes in your cluster, the user perceives the system as a single and integrated application.

In this field, we have popular solutions for distributed communication such as **Remote Method Invocation (RMI)**, CORBA, and Web Services (SOAP). These solutions enable distributed objects to interact using protocols adapted for object-oriented systems, where remote clients can access the services provided by server component by invoking them using remote methods.

Although the hardware for distributed systems nowadays is advanced, a bad decision to choose a software layer or a communication protocol can result in many problems. For instance, we can have situations where point-to-point communication is enough, but we can have other situations that require point-to-multipoint communication.

A well-known example of point-to-point communication is the Java RMI application, where you have unicast communication, a process that provides a communication point between exactly one sender to exactly one receiver. In this scenario, generally we have a stub/skeleton layer, where clients can invoke methods in a local interface through a stub object, which will act as a proxy of a remote object. All invocations of methods on the stub are routed to the remote system containing the remote object. The client is completely unaware that the method call actually resulted in a remote method invocation, which is shown in the following figure:

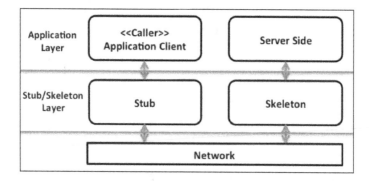

On the other side, point-to-multipoint communication, also known as group communication, is a very important tool in distributed applications, and requires a hardware that provides multicast to send the same message to a group of hosts running applications that want to participate in the multicast group. It is not addressed to all hosts (as in broadcasting), nor does it go to a single host (as in unicasting).

In practical terms, it creates a multicast address that is shared between a group of hosts called a multicast group. Any information sent to a multicast address will be relayed to all host members of the group.

It sounds very good for distributed computing; however, there is a tradeoff with the **User Datagram Protocol (UDP)**, the communication protocol generally used in multicast communication. Although UDP is three times faster than TCP, it's not a reliable protocol because it doesn't require that the hosts of a multicast group acknowledge that they have received packets; so it's difficult to guarantee the delivery of a message stream. So, if you are building a data grid platform like Infinispan, you can imagine how difficult it can be to ensure the data integrity of a distributed cache system.

Under this context, we have the JGroups framework, which is a bundle of group communication services that are fully written in Java that can facilitate the development of reliable distributed systems. In group communication, we have two important elements — **Groups** and **Members**.

A group is a cluster that consists of a collection of nodes or members. A group can have one or more nodes (LAN or across a WAN) belonging to it and members are able to participate in the communication between members of the same group. A member also can be part of more than one group.

Understanding the JGroups project

JGroups is a very mature project (it exists since 1999) authored by Bela Ban. It continues to have a very good support from the development community. It serves as a foundation for several projects such as JBoss application server and related components such as Jetty Http Session Replication, Tomcat HTTP session replication, among others.

JGroups has many useful features, but the most important is the reliability. It takes the standard protocol such as TCP and UDP and includes additional features to improve reliability and failure detection. The features are:

- Point-to-point and point-to-multipoint communication
- Node discovery
- Cluster management (creation and deletion)
- Failure detection and removal of crashed members

The JGroups architecture

As we said, JGroups is a toolkit for reliable group communication. It's possible to configure JGroups to use UDP with IP multicast for point-to-multipoint communication, or use JGroups with TCP for a point-to-point reliable communication, where group members are interconnected by TCP point-to-point connections, as you can see in the following figure:

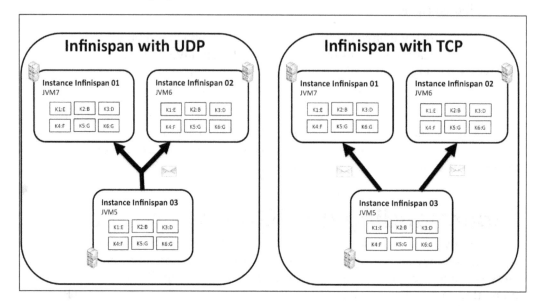

As you can see in the diagram, for large clusters, it's more efficient to use UDP, because with UDP only one message is sent, and all the members of the group can receive it.

In the Infinispan with TCP example, JGroups will have to send one message for each node you have in the cluster, which can decrease performance.

 A Message (org.jgroups.Message) is how data is exchanged, that is, how data is sent and received from one member to a single member, or can be sent by a member to all members of the group.

To interact with the group, JGroups provides the Channel API for clients. The client (for instance, Infinispan or a JEE Server) will use the JChannel API to create a Channel and connect to it using the group name.

A Channel class has a unique address and allows one client to be connected at a time and can be considered an abstraction of a group communication socket. A client requires a channel to join or leave a group. Once connected to channel, clients can send messages to the other cluster nodes over the channel, which will be received by all members connected to the same group. If you have multiple groups, you will have to create one Channel with the same group name for each group in order to connect them.

> Channels know all the members that take part of the group by the of list of member addresses called the View (via getView() method from the JChannel class).
>
> For each group, we have a coordinator, which is the first member of the view responsible to emit new views whenever the membership changes.
>
> A process can get an address from the current view's list and send a message to a specific destination address, or if the address is omitted, the message will be sent to all the current group members.

On top of the channels, we also have another layer called **Building Blocks**, a more sophisticated higher-level API available on top of Channel, to help developers communicate with the cluster without having to write recurring code. Anyway, if the building block is not enough, a client can access the channel directly.

When your application sends a message, the message passes through the protocol stack. A protocol stack is composed of multiple layers, where each layer is defined by a protocol and its required properties.

Messages go up and down the protocol stack, where they will be able to modify the message such as encrypt, reorder, pass, drop, or add a header to the message, or fragment a large message into a smaller one.

The architecture of JGroups is shown in the following figure:

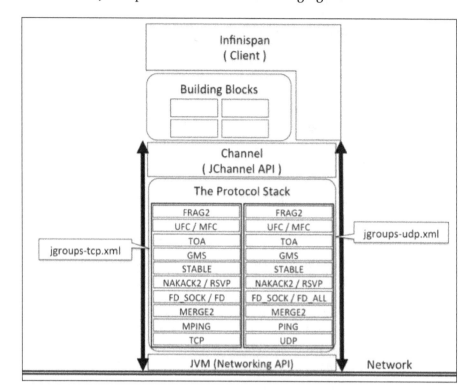

JGroups provides the ability to developers to create their own protocol or extend an existing one, and use it in their applications by editing a simple XML file.

A developer can include many characteristics such as fragmentation, encryption and authentication, compression, among others, in the protocol, which we will understand in the upcoming sections.

Customizing JGroups settings on Infinispan

In clustered mode, Infinispan uses JGroups to enable intermachine communication between nodes within a cluster. It is also used for discovery of new members, departing members, state transfer, failure detection, and reliable delivery.

JGroups provides a declarative way to manage the protocols by using a configuration XML file that will be used to determine the behavior and characteristics of each protocol in JGroups.

To start using Infinispan, you're not required to create or provide a configuration file because, by default, Infinispan uses a configuration file called `jgroups-udp.xml` bundled in the `infinispan-core.jar` file. Additionally, you have two other built-in configuration files that you can use within `infinispan-core.jar`, which are as follows:

- `jgroups-tcp.xml`: This file defines a configuration based on TCP as transport (tag `<TCP>`) and IP multicast address for discovery (tag `<MPING>` with the `mcast_addr` attribute). This option is recommended for smaller clusters; also note that you will have to list all hosts in the JGroups configuration file.

- `jgroups-ec2.xml`: This file defines a configuration based on TCP as transport and the `S3_PING` (tag `<S3_PING>`) protocol to discover the initial members.

- `jgroups-udp.xml`: This is the default option. This file uses UDP as transport and defines an UDP multicast for discovery. It's recommended to use UDP configuration for large clusters with many nodes, or when you are using your cache in replication or invalidation mode.

If you want to change the default configuration for cluster multicast from the UDP protocol to TCP or EC2, you need to change the `configurationFile` property in the `transport` section of the Infinispan configuration file, by including a `properties` attribute that points to a JGroups properties file you want to use:

```
<transport
  clusterName=" Infinispancluster10203"
  distributedSyncTimeout="50000">
  <properties>
    <property name="configurationFile" value="jgroups-tcp.xml" />
  </properties>
</transport>
```

The transport element defines the transport configuration for network inter-communications between nodes on the same cluster.

If you do not wish to use an XML configuration file, you can change the transport settings using the `GlobalConfiguration` API. Remember that we use the `GlobalConfigurationBuilder` class to define global settings, which will be shared among all cache instances, as shown in the following code:

```
GlobalConfiguration globalConfig = new GlobalConfigurationBuilder()
  .globalJmxStatistics()
  .transport()
    .clusterName("Infinispancluster10203")
```

```
    .distributedSyncTimeout(500001)
  .addProperty("configurationFile", "jgroups-udp.xml")
  .build();
```

As said, these bundled configuration files are for default configuration; however, if you need to make changes to fine-tune your JGroups stack or include new protocols, you can provide your own configuration file.

If you wish to make your own JGroups configuration file, Infinispan provides other configuration sample files that ship with the distribution.

See the samples that are available in the {INFINISPAN-HOME}/etc/config-samples directory, you can change the Infinispan configuration file to use your own configuration file and not the default one.

JGroups specifies an expression that allows you to override some information such as the Unicast address and port (if using UDP) or the TCP address and port in runtime, as shown in the following example:

```
<UDP mcast_addr="${jgroups.udp.mcast_addr:228.6.7.8}"
  mcast_port="${jgroups.udp.mcast_port:46655}"
   ip_ttl="${jgroups.udp.ip_ttl:2}"/>
```

 Note that you can edit your XML configuration file and specify your own expressions.

Now, you are able to override the corresponding values defined in the XML configuration by providing these values as system properties to the JVM at startup, and doesn't matter if you are running Infinispan in embedded or client/server mode. JGroups will ignore the correspondent value in the configuration file if it finds that system property.

In the next example, we are overriding the default multicast address and port, which can be done if you are executing it using a command line:

```
java -cp $CLASSPATH -Djava.net.preferIPv4Stack=true -
  Djgroups.udp.mcast_addr=239.42.42.42  -Djgroups.udp.mcast_port=7500
    -Djgroups.udp.ip_ttl=32 MyInfinispanClass
```

 JGroups supports several system properties that you can override. You can find more about these system properties on the following page:

https://developer.jboss.org/docs/12352

An Overview of protocols used by JGroups

JGroups includes a variety of protocols for different purposes.

For ease of use, the protocols are divided into several categories, such as for Transportation (UDP and TCP), Membership discovery (PING, TCPPING, S3_PING, and so on), and Failure Detection (FD, FD_PING), among others. The protocols can be enabled or disabled, and you can modify the XML file that describes the protocols to be used and the parameters associated with each protocol.

Furthermore, you can create or customize your own protocols. Protocols are used to handle messages that are sent and received over the channel.

As a minimum, however, it's important to understand the semantics of each protocol and some knowledge about the available layers, because JGroups allows you to configure the protocol stack to arrange them in any order and even include the same protocol multiple times.

This section provides a general overview of the available protocols in each category.

 For all the available protocols and its attributes, visit the link
http://www.jgroups.org/manual/html/protlist.html.

Transportation

The transport protocol is responsible for packet handling — to send and receive messages over the network.

Currently, in version 3.4.3, JGroups messages can run over three transport protocols, which are TCP, UDP, and TUNNEL. It's important to note that these transport protocols are mutually exclusive, which means you can have only one transport protocol per configuration file.

The following table lists the available transport protocols:

Protocol	Description
UDP	The UDP transport protocol opens a unicast socket to send and receive unicast messages (UDP datagrams) from/to individual members of a group and a multicast socket to send and receive multicast messages.
TCP	The TCP protocol will make the cluster members open TCP connections between each other, in order to send messages between members of a group.

Protocol	Description
TUNNEL	The TUNNEL protocol is a tunneling protocol used to provide a communication through a firewall, which enables the encapsulation of any protocol within the datagram of a different protocol.
	It requires a GossipRouter (a router for TCP-based group communication) to be present outside the firewall with at least one TCP port enabled.

The following code is an extract from the jgroups-tcp.xml file that defines a configuration based on TCP as transport:

```
<TCP
    bind_addr="${jgroups.tcp.address:127.0.0.1}"
    bind_port="${jgroups.tcp.port:7800}"
    loopback="true"
    port_range="30"
    recv_buf_size="20m"
    send_buf_size="640k"
    max_bundle_size="31k"
    ...

    thread_pool.enabled="true"
    thread_pool.min_threads="2"
    thread_pool.max_threads="30"
    thread_pool.keep_alive_time="60000"
    thread_pool.queue_enabled="true"
    thread_pool.queue_max_size="100"
    thread_pool.rejection_policy="Discard"
/>
```

Listed here are some of the attributes available in the TCP element:

- The bind_address and bind_port defines the address and port, which the transport binds. You could also define a range of TCP ports the server should bind to. We are also using the port_range attribute, which defines a range of ports, from bind_port to end_port.

- The loopback attribute specifies whether to loop outgoing messages back immediately to the source, which is useful for testing the transmission of the message or the transportation infrastructure.

- The recv_buf_size and send_buf_size attributes define the senders and receivers buffer size respectively. It's quite useful when you have big messages, because a higher buffer can avoid packet loss during the sending or receiving events.

- The `max_bundle_size` defines the maximum number of bytes the messages can be queued up for before they are sent.

- The `use_send_queues` attribute creates a separated send queue for each connection.

- We also have many `thread_pool` attributes to manage or change the pool of threads used to deliver incoming messages up the stack. In our earlier example, we enabled a thread pool with a minimum of two threads (`min_threads`) and a maximum of 30 threads (`max_threads`).

  - The `keep_alive_time` attribute defines how long a thread will wait (in our example, 60,000 milliseconds) in the thread before being removed.

  - The `queue_enabled` attribute enables a queue and `queue_max_size` limits the number of incoming messages.

  - The `max_size` attribute defines the maximum number of elements in the queue. This only works if the queue is enabled.

  - The `rejection_policy` attribute defines the policy of rejection when the thread pool reaches the maximum size (the `max_size` attribute). The possible values are `Abort` (an exception will be thrown), `Discard` (discards the message), `DiscardOldest` (discards the oldest message), and `Run` (the default value, which is to run on the caller's thread).

Now, let's see an extract from the `jgroups-udp.xml` file, that defines a configuration based on UDP as the transport layer:

```
<UDP
    mcast_addr="${jgroups.udp.mcast_addr:228.6.7.8}"
    mcast_port="${jgroups.udp.mcast_port:46655}"
    tos="8"
    ucast_recv_buf_size="20m"
    ucast_send_buf_size="640k"
    mcast_recv_buf_size="25m"
    mcast_send_buf_size="640k"
    loopback="true"
    max_bundle_size="31k"
    ip_ttl="${jgroups.udp.ip_ttl:2}"
    ...
    />
```

Listed here are some of the attributes available in the TCP element:

- The `mcast_addr` and `mcast_port` attribute defines the multicast address and port for joining a group.

- The `tos` attribute sets a traffic class in the IP datagram header for sending unicast and multicast datagrams. It receives an integer value, which is a bitset created by bitwise values that can be `IPTOS_LOWCOST` (02), `IPTOS_RELIABILITY` (04), `IPTOS_THROUGHPUT` (08), and `IPTOS_LOWDELAY` (16).

- The `ucast_recv_buf_size` and `ucast_send_buf_size` attributes define the receiver buffer size and the sender buffer size of the unicast datagram socket, respectively.

- The `mcast_recv_buf_size` and `mcast_send_buf_size` attributes define the receiver buffer size and the sender buffer size of the multicast datagram socket, respectively.

- The `ip_ttl` attribute specifies the default **time-to-live** (TTL) for IP multicast packets.

Finally, a sample code of a `TUNNEL` configuration is as follows:

```
<TUNNEL
  gossip_router_hosts="${jgroups.tunnel.gossip_router_hosts:
    localhost[12001]}"/>
```

We are using the `gossip_router_hosts` attribute to define a comma-separated list of `GossipRouter` hosts, for instance, `192.168.1.5[8012]` and `192.168.23.64[8013]`.

Membership discovery

This protocol is responsible to discover initial membership to determine the current coordinator by sending a ping request. It can send a unicast or multicast discovery request, depending on the selected protocol. It sends a ping request and waits for the response, and when it finds the current coordinator, the joiner sends a `JOIN` request and initiates a `MERGE` (see *Merging*) process.

For large clusters, it can be a problem if JGroups sends a multicast discovery request to a large cluster. With, for instance, 500 nodes, we may run the risk that all nodes reply with a discovery response and create a bottleneck.

In these cases, consult the `udp-largecluster.xml` file, which is shipped in the JGroups distribution, specially designed for large clusters.

The following table describes the available protocols under the membership discovery category:

Protocol	Description
PING	The PING discovery protocol employs dynamic discovery by sending out PING packets to an IP multicast address to find the group coordinator. Once found, it sends a JOIN request to join the cluster. If there are no answers, it will become the coordinator.
TCPPING	The TCPPING protocol works on top of TCP and is based on a static list of known members; it will ping the given address for discovery.
MPING	The MPING protocol uses IP multicast to discover the initial membership and it is used generally in conjunction with TCP transport.
TCPGOSSIP	The TCPGOSSIP is a protocol that works on top of UDP and TCP transport protocols. To work properly, this protocol requires a GossipRouter. It is recommended in cases where you usually have firewalls that can block the TCP traffic between the cluster nodes.
FILE_PING	This protocol uses a shared directory (via NFS or SMB) between all members of the group where they write their addresses. The new members can access the addresses from this directory. If a member leaves the group, it deletes its corresponding file.
JDBC_PING	This protocol is similar to FILE_PING, but it uses a shared database between all members of the group where they write their addresses.
BPING	BPING stands for Broadcast Ping and this protocol uses UDP broadcasts to discover initial membership. Before using it, you have to replace the default address with a subnet specific broadcast. The default address is 255.255.255.255.
RACKSPACE_PING	This protocol uses the Rackspace cloud files storage to discover the initial members. Each member of the group uses a Rackspace container to write their addresses. If a member leaves the group, it deletes its corresponding object.
S3_PING	This protocol can be used only for members running on Amazon EC2, and uses an Amazon S3 bucket, which is shared between all members of the group, where they write their addresses. If a member leaves the group, it deletes its corresponding file. Note that Amazon EC2 does not allow the use of MPING (multicast) or PING.

Protocol	Description
SWIFT_PING	This protocol is based on Openstack Swift, an object/blob store used to store lots of data. SWIFT_PING uses this service to discover the initial members. Each member of the group uses a shared Openstack Swift store to write their addresses. If a member leaves the group, it deletes its corresponding object.
AWS_PING	This protocol was written by a software company called Meltmedia. It proposes a replacement for the TCPPING protocol, because it provides autodiscovery for other cluster members on AWS, removing the need for a static list of members.
PDC	The **Persistent Discovery Cache** (PDC) provides a cache to store the results of the discovery process.

The jgroups-tcp.xml file combines a configuration based on TCP as transport and UDP Multicast for discovery (MPING), as you can see in the following code extracted from the configuration file:

```
<TCP
    ... />
    <MPING bind_addr="${jgroups.bind_addr:127.0.0.1}"
      break_on_coord_rsp="true"
        mcast_addr="${jgroups.mping.mcast_addr:228.2.4.6}"
        mcast_port="${jgroups.mping.mcast_port:43366}"
        ip_ttl="${jgroups.udp.ip_ttl:2}"
        num_initial_members="3"/>
```

Let's see another code snippet from the jgroups-udp.xml file:

```
<UDP
    ... />
        <PING timeout="3000" num_initial_members="3"/>
```

This follows a different strategy, combining UDP as a transport layer and UDP multicast for discovery, by using the PING protocol.

Now, let's analyze how JGroups use the S3_PING protocol layer to connect an Amazon S3 bucket to discover initial members. Each member uploads a file that will be available for all other members of the group for read. You can configure S3_PING to access either a public or a private bucket.

In the next example, extracted from the `jgroups-ec2.xml` file, you have to provide the Amazon AWS credentials (both access key and secret access key) to access the private bucket and provide the absolute path of the shared file, as shown in the following code:

```
<UDP
   ...  />
    <S3_PING secret_access_key="${jgroups.s3.secret_access_key}"
      access_key="${jgroups.s3.access_key}"
        location="${jgroups.s3.bucket:jgroups}" />
```

Remember that in Amazon EC2 it does not allow multicast between EC2 instances.

JBoss AS 7.0 users have many options to set system properties, such as the `standalone.xml` file if using JBoss in the standalone mode, or the `domain.xml` file in the domain mode, as shown in the following code:

```
<server xmlns="urn:jboss:domain:1.2">
  <system-properties>
    <property name="jgroups.s3.secret_access_key"
      value="+qieMeV63xQ63iFFe+O9qnmpgaEkkLEITh3raA9k"/>
    <property name="jgroups.s3.access_key"
      value="IEL2SSR4POODE9RIXI3A"/>
    <property name="jgroups.s3.bucket" value=
      "prd-infinispan-farm01"/>
  </system-properties>
```

If you don't want to provide your Amazon credentials every time you write to the bucket, you can pass presigned URLs for `put` and `delete` operations, as shown in the following configuration example:

```
<S3_PING
   pre_signed_put_url="http://s3.amazonaws.com/my_bucket/
      DemoCluster/node1?AWSAccessKeyId=AKIAIOSFODNN7&
        Expires=1141889120&Signature=vjbyPxybdZaNmGa%2ByT272YEAiv4%3D"
          pre_signed_delete_url="http://s3.amazonaws.com/my_bucket/
            DemoCluster/node1?AWSAccessKeyId=
              AKIAIOSFODNN7&Expires=1416216200&Signature=
                NpgCjnDzrM%2BWFzoENXmpNDUsSn8%3D&"
                  timeout="2000" num_initial_members="3"/>
```

Merging

This category defines merge protocols, which provides an innovative way to discover subgroups that were split for some reason (for instance, due to a network partition) and merge them back into one.

 You can see how Infinispan behaves during a network partition in *Chapter 2, Barriers to Scaling Data.*

The coordinator of the group (or subgroup) sends periodically, in multicast, a message containing information about its presence and view information to the other peers. If another group coordinator in the same cluster receives the message, it's going to start a merge process.

In this category, we have the protocols MERGE2 and MERGE3, which are used to discover subgroups (that is, it could be created because of a network partition). In situations where we have multiple merges running at once, the MERGE2 protocol can lead to merge collisions. This happens when we have more than one merge leader trying to start a merge process at the same time, which was eliminated in the MERGE3 protocol by performing one merge in the cluster at any time.

The three built-in configuration files available within `infinispan-core.jar` use the MERGE2 protocol to discover subgroups, as shown in the following code:

```
<UDP
    ...   />
  <MERGE2 max_interval="30000" min_interval="10000"/>
```

The `min_interval` and `max_interval` attributes specify the minimum and maximum number (in milliseconds) to send out a `MERGE` message.

Failure detection

In a distributed system, failure detection is a fundamental issue for fault-tolerance. In JGroups, we have several protocols that can be used to detect when one of the group member crashes. If the protocol suspects a node is down, it will initiate a verification phase, where a `SUSPECT` message will be sent to all members of the group.

If the node member is still unresponsive, the member will be considered dead and another group membership protocol called GMS will be responsible to change the view so that other members avoid the member that is down or not responding. This is done in order to save queue space, CPU, and bandwidth.

JGroups supports the following failure detection protocols:

Protocol	Description
FD / FD_ALL / FD_ALL2	This protocol provides failure detection by using simple heartbeat messages. When a member is not reachable, the protocol will send a multicast SUSPECT message to the cluster and eventually get excluded by GMS. It's recommended to use it with the TCP transport protocol.
FD_SOCK	This failure detection is based on a ring of sockets. Each cluster member connects to another cluster member (a neighbor) via a TCP server socket connection, forming a ring between the members.
FD_PING	Internally, this protocol performs a default ping request to a host to validate whether the host responds to the ping or not. It uses an executable script with the ping command (it uses /sbin/ping or ping.exe on Windows), which can be replaced for a user provided file.
VERIFY_SUSPECT	It makes a last validation by pinging a suspected member before removing it. If it receives a positive answer, it drops the suspect message from the cluster member.

The following code uses the FD_ALL, FD_SOCK, and VERIFY_SUSPECT protocols to detect the failed nodes. As you can see in the following example, you will be able to use more than one protocol at the same time:

```
<UDP
    ... />
...
<FD_SOCK/>
<FD_ALL timeout="15000" interval="3000"/>
<VERIFY_SUSPECT timeout="1500"/>
...>
```

It's using the timeout attribute to define the amount of time in milliseconds, it will wait for the response from the members whose message was sent. It will use the interval attribute to define the interval at which JGroups will send periodic HEARTBEAT messages to the cluster.

Reliable transmission

This protocol ensures that a message sent will not be lost. It's important to note that the UDP is not reliable by nature, so it's JGroups' job to ensure that the message is properly delivered to the target recipient.

JGroups has the following protocols to achieve a reliable transmission:

Protocol	Description
NAKACK	This provides reliability for message transmission by controlling that a message will be received, otherwise, it will request for a retransmission. This protocol also implements a FIFO (First In First Out) algorithm to guarantee that the messages are received in the order they were sent by the sender.
NAKACK2	This is a more performant successor of the NAKACK; it uses less memory and has the same properties as the first version.
UNICAST	This provides reliability for unicast message transmission (point-to-point communication) by using an ACK mechanism to make sure that the message is received; otherwise, it will request for a retransmission. This protocol also provides FIFO capabilities for the messages.
UNICAST2	This is the opposite of the UNICAST protocol. It provides reliability for unicast message transmission by using a negative ACK mechanism, which generates less traffic because it's not required to send an acknowledgment for every message.
UNICAST3	UNICAST3 is the successor of UNICAST2 and uses a more performatic positive acknowledge mechanism.
RSVP	The RSVP protocol cannot be considered to be a reliable protocol, but for synchronous messages, it flags messages and blocks reception until all the cluster members have acknowledged reception. It should be placed somewhere above other reliable transmission protocols such as NAKACK or UNICAST.

An example of using the reliable transmission protocols pbcast.NAKACK2, UNICAST3, and RSVP extracted from the jgroups-udp.xml configuration file is shown in the following code:

```
<UDP
    ...  />
<pbcast.NAKACK2
        xmit_interval="1000"
        xmit_table_num_rows="100"
        xmit_table_msgs_per_row="10000"
        xmit_table_max_compaction_time="10000"
```

```
            max_msg_batch_size="100"/>
    <UNICAST3
            xmit_interval="500"
            xmit_table_num_rows="20"
            xmit_table_msgs_per_row="10000"
            xmit_table_max_compaction_time="10000"
            max_msg_batch_size="100"
            conn_expiry_timeout="0"/>
        <RSVP timeout="60000" resend_interval="500"
          ack_on_delivery="false" />
```

The following are the list of some of the attributes available in the protocols `pbcast.NAKACK2` and `UNICAST3`:

- The `xmit_interval` attribute sets the timing interval in milliseconds; a sent message is resent.

- JGroups creates a matrix to transmit the messages, where the capacity is defined by the attributes `xmit_table_num_rows` that defines the number of rows and `xmit_table_msgs_per_row` that defines the number of elements per row (`xmit_table_num_rows * xmit_table_msgs_per_row`).

- The `xmit_table_max_compaction_time` defines the maximum number of time the matrix can be compacted.

- The `max_msg_batch_size` attribute defines how many messages will be removed from the retransmission window.

- The `conn_expiry_timeout` attribute sets the amount of time (in milliseconds) JGroups will wait before close an idle connection. If set to `0`, the timeout will be disabled.

Fragmentation of large messages

Depending on the network configuration, it may not handle messages that exceed the default size limit. In these cases, for messages larger than the limit, the fragmentation protocol will automatically fragment them into several smaller messages before they can be sent across the network and reassemble these packets back to the original message.

The `FRAG` and `FRAG2` protocols work for both unicast and multicast messages. The difference between these two protocols is that `FRAG` serializes each message (including headers) to calculate message's size before fragmentation; whereas, `FRAG2` does not serialize it, it fragments only the payload, excluding the headers.

The next code example presents another snippet from the `jgroups-udp.xml` file that uses the `FRAG2` protocol, which will fragment a large message in chunks of `30k`, defined by the `frag_size` attribute.

```
<UDP
   ...  />
   <FRAG2 frag_size="30k"  />
```

Ordering protocols

As the name suggests, ordering protocols ensure that messages are actually delivered in the specified order to the destination node. Since UDP cannot guarantee that the packet/datagrams will be received in the same order that they were sent. JGroups needs to implement its own ordering protocols to ensure that the messages are received in the same order that they are sent. The JGroups protocols are as follows:

Protocol	Description
SEQUENCER	This protocol implements total order using a sequencer and requires NAKACK and UNICAST.
TOA	This protocol implements **Total Order Anycast (TOA)** based on Skeen's algorithm for total ordering.

The total-order-based protocol is a fundamental part of JGroups and relies on a concept that all cluster members can update the available data. However, when a node is responsible to deliver a set of messages, it must deliver them in the correct order.

In the case of the TOA protocol, as we will see in the following example, the protocol intercepts messages using an `AnycastMessage` attribute before sending those messages to a list of addresses in total order.

The following example shows the TOA protocol in action. It's present in all configuration files provided by Infinispan; note that it is not using any attribute:

```
<UDP
   ...  />
   <tom.TOA/>
```

Group membership

This protocol tracks all the members in a given group and notifies the application when members join or leave the cluster, and it is also responsible to handle SUSPECT messages emitted by failure detection protocols, which is as follows:

- `pbcast.GMS`: This is a group membership protocol.

The following code extracted from the `jgroups-udp.xml` configuration file uses the `pbcast.GMS` protocol for group membership:

```
<UDP
   ...  />
     <pbcast.GMS print_local_addr="false" join_timeout="3000"
        view_bundling="true"/>
```

It uses the `print_local_addr` attribute that will print (or not) the local address of this member after connection. The `join_timeout` attribute defines how long it will wait for a new node to join after a JOIN request. Also, `view_bundling` enables JGroups to handle multiple JOIN or LEAVE requests at the same time.

State transfer

This protocol is responsible to keep the data integrity of the cluster by making sure that the shared application state is transferred correctly to a joining member.

The state protocols are as follows:

Protocol	Description
pbcast.STATE	The STATE protocol streams the state from an existing node in chunks to a newly joining node. For each chunk, it sends a unicast message. It's recommended for large state transfers.
pbcast.STATE_TRANSFER	The STATE_TRANSFER protocol streams the state from an existing node to a new node using a ByteArray. It is recommended for small state transfers.
STATE_SOCK	This is similar to STATE protocol, but uses a TCP socket connection to send one single message over the socket. It is recommended for large state transfers.
BARRIER	This is a protocol used to support other state transfer protocols. It creates a barrier that will lock a thread until all messages have completed. The BARRIER protocol is only useful if another state protocol is present.

The configuration files provided by Infinispan don't make use of state transfer protocols.

Security

JGroups provide protocols to encrypt messages (ENCRYPT) that are sent between group members in order to prevent network sniffing (also known as Man-in-the-middle attack) and eavesdropping attacks, and to make sure that only authorized members can join a cluster (AUTH), as shown in the following table:

Protocol	Description
ENCRYPT	The ENCRYPT protocol adds a layer to encrypt and decrypt messages.
AUTH	The AUTH protocol adds a layer to prevent unauthorized cluster nodes from joining a group.

The configuration files provided by Infinispan don't make use of any security protocols. To show how it can be configured, the upcoming example shows how ENCRYPT protocol is configured to encrypt only the message body and not the header (via encrypt_entire_message), but doesn't encrypt message headers.

The asym_init and sym_init attributes define, respectively, the initial length of the asymmetric public and private keys and the initial key length for matching symmetric algorithm. The asym_algorithm and sym_algorithm attributes specify the asymmetric and symmetric algorithm that will be used for key exchange and encrypting data. The code for that is as follows:

```
<UDP
    ...  />
<PING/>
<MERGE2/>
<FD/>
<VERIFY_SUSPECT/>
<pbcast.NAKACK2/>
<UNICAST3/>
<pbcast.STABLE/>
<FRAG2/>
<ENCRYPT encrypt_entire_message="false" sym_init="128"
   sym_algorithm="AES/ECB/PKCS5Padding" asym_init="512"
     asym_algorithm="RSA"/>
```

Note that the order of the protocols will define how much of the message will be encrypted, which can decrease performance if you insert ENCRYPT too low in the stack.

Flow control

Flow control provides the protocols responsible to measure the cluster member's responsiveness during a message transmission. It's an important mechanism to prevent out-of-memory exceptions and avoid a cluster member from being flooded with messages.

The protocol attempts to balance the process of sending and receiving data by using a credit-based system, where each sender has an amount of credits and decrements them whenever a message is sent.

When the credit falls below a threshold (defined by the `min_threshold` or `min_bytes` attributes), the sender stops sending messages, and will only resume sending messages after receiving a replenishment message from other receivers.

All receivers keep and manage a table of credits for each sender and will decrement sender's balance whenever receive a new message.

The Flow Control protocol was separated into **Multicast Flow Control (MFC)** and **Unicast Flow Control (UFC)**.

All built-in configuration files available within `infinispan-embedded.jar` use the UFC and MFC protocols with the `max_credits` and `min_threshold` attributes, which define, respectively, the number of credits a cluster member can send before receiving an acknowledgment and the percentage value of the threshold at which a receiver sends more credits to a sender. The code is as follows:

```
<UDP
    ... />
    <UFC max_credits="2m" min_threshold="0.40"/>
    <MFC max_credits="2m" min_threshold="0.40"/>
```

Message stability

This protocol gives the ability to cluster nodes to ensure periodically that sent messages have been received by all members are purged to allow a distributed garbage collection.

The `STABLE` protocol provides message stability. This protocol, as stated earlier, removes the read messages that have been seen by all the nodes, but have not been removed.

The configuration files provided by Infinispan use the `pbcast.STABLE` protocol defining the `stability_delay` attribute that specifies a delay time before a `STABLE` message is sent.

The `desired_avg_gossip` attribute defines the average time taken by JGroups to send a STABLE message and `max_bytes` specifies the total amount of bytes the cluster members can receive before JGroups sends a STABLE message. The code is as follows:

```
<UDP
    ...   />
    <pbcast.STABLE stability_delay="500"
        desired_avg_gossip="5000" max_bytes="1m"/>
```

Summary

In this chapter, we focused on how Infinispan uses JGroups to communicate with a group of machines that are interested in receiving the message. We also saw how to customize the JGroups configuration file to specify different protocols or change the behavior of a protocol by using a variety of settings in the configuration file that can help us do this.

There are several isolated settings for each specific category group (for instance, Transportation, Membership Discovery, Merging, and so on) that you can update in JGroup's configuration file, although the defaults are often appropriate. You can use one of the configuration files that ships with Infinispan and then tune it appropriately.

In the next chapter, we will take a look at how to configure cross-site replication, Infinispan and CDI, how to improve the serialization process with the Externalizer API and will take a closer look at the Map/Reduce API.

12
Advanced Topics

In this chapter, we will look at some advanced concepts to improve your experience with Infinispan, or to improve the performance and scalability of your cache applications, through code as well as server architecture. We will explore the Map Reduce API to run an Infinispan application in multi-node server clusters.

You will also learn how to integrate Infinispan with the **Contexts and Dependency Injection** (**CDI**) to inject CacheManager and Cache in your application and finally, how to implement Cross-site replication to replicate cache data to cache managers asynchronously, to one or multiple data centers.

In this chapter, we will discuss the following topics:

- Cross-site replication
- Infinispan and CDI
- Creating externalizers
- Using the Map/Reduce API

Cross-site replication

Depending on the business requirements, you may have an application with Infinispan that requires high availability and operates on a 7 x 24 x 365 basis, located in two or more disparate geographic locations.

There are many reasons you may want to replicate data across multiple domains, for instance, reduce latency to bring the cache data closer to the client, or to provide fault tolerance. While replication or distribution within a cluster helps with single server failures, it does not prevent your application from catastrophic failures, such as loss of power or a natural disaster. And replicating data across multiple sites is an easy way to maintain data integrity across all sites; once local modifications are made to the cache they are sent to remote nodes, reducing latency by keeping data closer to users.

The next diagram shows a simple example of cross-site replication between two sites, where each site has a different clustering mode (**Site 01** uses replication and **Site 02** uses distribution):

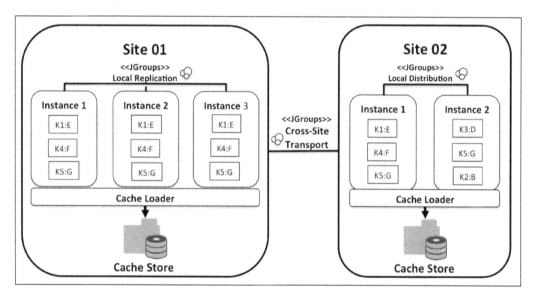

As you can see in the diagram, to provide cross-site functionality, Infinispan uses an additional transport to connect sites together.

Configuring cross-site replication

For cross replication, Infinispan relies on JGroups' RELAY2 protocol, responsible for providing clustering between different sites, and needs to be added to the JGroups protocol stack in the `jgroups` configuration file. In Infinispan 6 distribution, Infinispan provides some sample configuration files available in the `{$INFINISPAN_HOME}`/etc/ `config-samples` directory. You can see a sample configuration of the RELAY2 in the file called `relay2.xml`.

If you open this file, you will see the following content:

```
<global>
    <transport clusterName="demoCluster2">
        <properties>
            <property name="configurationFile" value="config-samples/
jgroups-relay2.xml" />
        </properties>
    </transport>
    <globalJmxStatistics enabled="true"/>
</global>

<default>
    <jmxStatistics enabled="true"/>
    <clustering mode="distribution">
        <l1 enabled="false" lifespan="10000"/>
        <hash numOwners="2" />
        <async/>
    </clustering>
</default>
```

Note that the transport element points to the JGroups configuration file `jgroups-relay2.xml` available in the same directory. The following code is an extract from the `tcp.xml` file that defines a configuration based on RELAY:

```
<relay.RELAY2 site="__site_name__"
              config="config-samples/jgroups-tcp.xml"
              relay_multicasts="false"
              async_relay_creation="false"/>
```

The RELAY2 protocol can exchange data between multiple sites and can be configured to use either unicast or multicast requests.

Infinispan data grids in different sites can be of different sizes, and Infinispan supports geographic data partitioning and can replicate data synchronously or asynchronously to one or multiple sites.

You can see more about Infinispan and network partitions in *Chapter 2, Barriers to Scaling Data*.

The following diagram presents a possible setup of replicated sites:

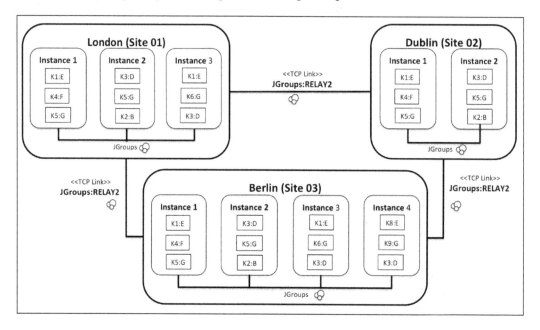

In the preceding diagram, we have three data centers, **London** with three physical nodes, **Dublin** with two nodes, and a site in **Berlin** with four nodes.

All of them update the same named cache, but each city operates on its own cache data, which in turn, can replicate data to the other sites as well.

The named cache commonly used by all applications can have different configurations from each other, which provide users the flexibility to create several complex topologies. For example, in the preceding diagram, we can configure the **London** site with a distributed strategy with numOwners=3, the **Berlin** site with a distributed strategy with numOwners=2, and the **Dublin** with a replication strategy.

It is also possible to define different replication mechanisms between sites. For instance, you could configure **Berlin** to backup data synchronously to **Dublin** and asynchronously to **London**.

You have to configure the local site in the global configuration section and the backup policy for each individual cache in the `infinispan.xml` file. The local site is the site where the node using this configuration file resides, which you can see in the next example:

The code in Infinispan 6 is as follows:

```
<global>
  <site local="Berlin"/>
  <transport clusterName="infinispan-cluster"
    distributedSyncTimeout="50000" nodeName="nd101"
      machineId="m1"
  rackId="r1" siteId="s1">
    <properties>
      <property name="configurationFile"
        value="jgroups-udp.xml"/>
    </properties>
  </transport>
</global>

<default>
  <locking concurrencyLevel="100"
    lockAcquisitionTimeout="1000"/>
    <sites>
      <backups>
        <backup site="London" strategy="SYNC"
          backupFailurePolicy="WARN" timeout="10000">
      </backup>
      <backups>
        <backupFor remoteCache="aCache" remoteSite="Dublin"/>
      </backups>
    </sites>
      <jmxStatistics enabled="false"/>
</default>

<namedCache name="backedUpCache">
  <sites>
    <backups>
      <backup site="London" strategy="SYNC"
        backupFailurePolicy="WARN" timeout="12000"/>
      <backup site="Dublin" strategy="ASYNC"
        backupFailurePolicy="WARN" timeout="12000"/>
    </backups>
  <backupFor/>
  </sites>
  </namedCache>
```

The same example can be written in Infinispan 7 as follows:

```
<jgroups>
  <stack-file name="udp" path="jgroups-udp.xml"/>
</jgroups>

<cache-container name="BerlinCacheManager" statistics="true"
  default-cache="berlinCache" shutdown-hook="DEFAULT">
  <transport stack="udp" cluster="infinispan-cluster"
    node-name="nd101" machine="m1" rack="r1" site="s1" />

<distributed-cache name="berlinDefaultCache">
  <backups>
    <backup site="London" strategy="SYNC" failure-policy="WARN"
      timeout="12000"/>
  </backups>
    <backupFor cache="someCache" site="Dublin"/>
  </distributed-cache>

<distributed-cache name="backedUpCache">
  <backups>
    <backup site="London" strategy="SYNC"
      failure-policy="WARN" timeout="12000"/>
    <backup site="Dublin" strategy="ASYNC"
      failure-policy="WARN" timeout="12000"/>
  </backups>
    <backupFor/>
  </distributed-cache>
</cache-container>
```

The name of the site is case sensitive and should match the name of a site as defined within JGroups' RELAY2 protocol configuration file. Besides the global configuration, each cache specifies its backup policy in the `<site>` element.

In the previous example, the `backedUpCache` is configured to back up data to London and Dublin.

The following table reviews the configuration attributes you can specify for each site's `<backup>` element, with a short description for each:

Element	Description
site (ISPN 6 and 7)	This is the name of the remote site where this cache backs up data.
strategy (ISPN 6 and 7)	This is the strategy used to back up data to SYNC or ASYNC. It defaults to ASYNC.

Element	Description
`backupFailurePolicy` (ISPN 6) `failure-policy` (ISPN 7)	This decides what the system should do in case of a failure during backup. It defaults to `FAIL`. The possible values are: • `IGNORE`: This allows the local operation/ transaction to succeed • `WARN`: This is the same as `IGNORE` but also logs a warning message • `FAIL`: This is only in effect if the strategy is `SYNC`; it fails the local cluster operation/ transaction by throwing an exception to the user • `CUSTOM`: This defines a user-provided backup failure policy
`failurePolicyClass` (ISPN 6) `failure-policy-class` (ISPN 7)	If the `backupFailurePolicy` value is set to `CUSTOM` then this attribute is required, and it should contain the fully qualified name of a class implementing `org. infinispan.xsite.CustomFailurePolicy`.
`timeout` (ISPN 6 and 7)	This is the timeout in milliseconds and is to be used when backing up data remotely. It defaults to `10` seconds.
`useTwoPhaseCommit` (ISPN 6) `two-phase-commit` (ISPN 7)	For synchronous (`SYNC`) backups, Infinispan will use a two-phase commit cycle. It defaults to `false`. Note: This is only for `SYNC` backup strategies.
`enabled` (ISPN 6 and 7)	This property defines the cache under configuration as a backup for a remote cache.

Cross-site replication and transactions

Data replication on different geographic locations differ in transactional caches, but in both caches, the replication requests from one remote grid to another are performed in parallel, while Infinispan replicates (depending on the cache mode) the affected data to the other member nodes of the same cluster.

This means that in our example, if you change the data in one of the nodes of the Dublin site, then Infinispan will replicate the new data to the other local node, and in parallel, will start the replication process from Dublin to the London and Berlin sites.

Cross-site replication with non-transactional caches

If you are working with a non-transactional cache, the replication process described above will be performed for each operation, which depending on the case; can lead to performance problems due to the latency.

Another important thing to note in non-cache transactions with cross-site replication may result in data inconsistencies. Since the replication process for local nodes and remote sites are different, it is possible that remote replication fails, while the local replication succeeds (or vice versa).

Cross-site replication with transactional caches

For transaction caches with cross-site replication, the cache behavior will be slightly different if your cache is synchronous or asynchronous.

For synchronous caches with async backup configuration, Infinispan will make use of the two-phase commit protocol to lock the affected data during the prepare phase (1st phase) and commit the changes in the commit phase (2nd phase). During the second phase, Infinispan will start the async backup, which means that if the first phase fails, Infinispan will not start the remote backup.

If you have decided to use an asynchronous backup strategy, Infinispan will perform one additional call during the prepare phase containing the state of the transaction. If the remote backup cache is not transactional, Infinispan will apply the changes remotely.

Otherwise, Infinispan will start a new transaction in the remote node and reproduce the same changes within the new transaction during the prepare phase (without committing the changes). The back up site will be waiting for a commit/rollback message from the same remote site to commit or rollback the transaction.

On asynchronous caches, Infinispan uses the notion of one-phase transaction; where the data is sent asynchronously from one site to another during the transaction commit to the owners of data. In both cases, it's irrelevant whether you're using a pessimistic or optimistic transaction.

If the backup call fails, Infinispan will raise an exception. You can decide what Infinispan has to do in case of a failure during the backup process, by changing the `failure-policy` option on Infinispan 7 (or `backupFailurePolicy` on Infinispan 6); see the previous table for more details.

Taking a site offline and online again

To prevent the system from performing a data backup of an offline site, you can configure Infinispan to mark a site offline after the backing up operation fails for a certain number of times during a time interval. Once the site is marked as offline, the local site won't try to back up data to it anymore.

In order to bring the application online again, a system administrator will have to use the JMX Console in order to take the site online again, invoking the `bringSiteOnline(siteName)` method on the `XSiteAdmin` managed bean.

Integrating Infinispan with CDI

Infinispan provides a module that integrates with CDI in the Java EE environment and can be used to inject Infinispan components, such as CacheManager and Cache into your CDI application and also provides (partial) support for JCache caching annotations.

An introduction to CDI

CDI is an important and foundational aspect of the Java EE 6 stack. To understand the importance of this specification and understand its programming model, we have to look back at early versions of Java EE and the introduction of the concept of **Inversion of Control** (**IoC**), where the container was always responsible for creating and managing the lifecycle of managed components.

Before Java EE 5, to enable an enterprise Java application to use external resources (like a DataSource), you had to explicitly specify the dependencies in the deployment descriptor file and obtain a reference to these declared resources by performing a JNDI lookup.

From Java EE 5, it included a simplified programming model to resource access using **Dependency Injection** (**DI**), where instead of using JNDI lookups, you can simply annotate a resource reference with a CDI annotation and have it injected automatically.

The following diagram compares both approaches:

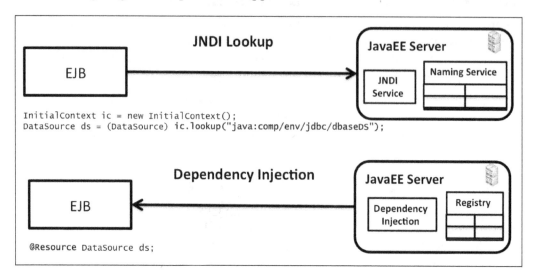

So basically, the CDI specification is the dependency injection standard for Java EE, based on frameworks such as Spring, Seam 2, and Google Guice, and the specification extracts the best ideas of all these frameworks.

CDI is based around the philosophy of loose coupling and strong typing, which means that CDI provides a way to decouple non-functional and other technical concerns regarding object creation from the code. Nearly any Java EE component can be injectable, and it's possible to inject these beans into objects that are not managed by the container.

Furthermore, CDI provides other services such as the `typesafe` dependency injection using annotations, a contextual lifecycle management for `stateful` objects, interceptors, decorators, and an event-notification facility.

Setting up CDI support in your Maven POM

If you are using a dependency management system like Maven, the recommended way to get started using the `infinispan-cdi` module in your project is by adding the following dependency to your Maven `pom.xml`:

```
<dependency>
  <groupId>org.infinispan</groupId>
  <artifactId>infinispan-cdi</artifactId>
  <version>7.1.1.Final</version>
</dependency>
```

If you are not using Maven as your build system, then you can add the `infinispan-cdi-VERSION.jar` or `infinispan-cli-client-VERSION.jar` and `infinispan-cli-server-VERSION.jar` (for remote access) libraries under the `{INFINISPAN_HOME}/lib` directory of your classpath.

Injecting an Infinispan cache into your Beans

According to the CDI 1.1 specification (JSR-346), a CDI Bean can be any kind of POJO class that follows certain conditions, as follows:

- It must be a concrete class or be annotated with `@Decorator`
- It must expose at least one public constructor or contain a constructor whose declaration is annotated with `@Inject`
- It can't be a non-static inner class

Using CDI, you can inject a CacheManager or a Cache object into your beans, which can be called directly from the Java code via injection, or you can invoke it using **Expression Language (EL)** from a JSF page.

Let's look at the following example; we have to create an EJB web service that provides weather information for a given country and city. We are going to use the `OpenWeatherInfo` API—a service that provides free weather data and forecast, suitable for any cartographic application. Infinispan will be used to cache the results of the web service calls.

The following diagram depicts the proposed scenario:

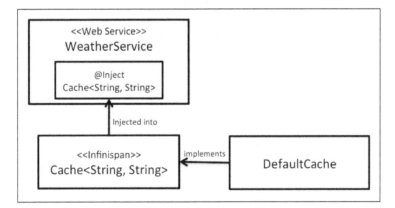

In this simple scenario, we can take advantage of the @Inject annotation to demonstrate how we can inject an Infinispan Cache into other beans:

```java
@Stateless
@WebService
public class WeatherService {
  @Inject
  private Cache<String, String> openWeatherCache;

  @WebMethod
  public String openWeatherTo(String country, String city)
    throws MalformedURLException, IOException {
    String weather = "";
    if (!openWeatherCache.containsKey(getKey(country, city))){
      RESTClient client = new RESTClient();
      weather =
        client.executeRESTOperation(String.format(getURL(),
          country, city));
      openWeatherCache.put(getKey(country, city), weather, 121,
        TimeUnit.HOURS);
    } else {
      weather = openWeatherCache.get(getKey(country, city));
    }
    return weather;
  }
}
```

We created a web service that returns weather information; we first verify that we have the weather information for the given country and city in the cache, otherwise, we will request for the information from the online API and store the results in the cache.

As you can see from the previous code sample and diagram, assuming that our application will have only one cache, the CDI container will be able to inject the cache by only using @Inject on it. Using the @Inject annotation you don't need to construct dependencies by hand. It creates an injection point and you can leave the Java EE container to inject a reference to cache for you in the openWeatherCache property.

Customizing the default configuration

Let's suppose that we have more than one weather service available, and you want to introduce a different cache in your application. To avoid an ambiguous dependency (for two named caches), you will have to provide a cache configuration and a cache qualifier for the cache you want. A qualifier is a user-defined annotation that defines the kind of CDI bean the annotated class or field is.

To demonstrate the need for a qualifier in our application, let's change our current implementation and create two qualifiers and add a named cache for our options, `openweather-cache` and `wunderground-cache`. The next diagram presents the scenario we want to implement:

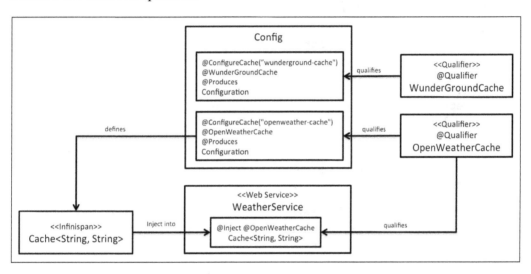

In our application, we will provide users with two named caches, where `OpenWeatherCache` will be the default cache. So, we have to provide the configuration for both caches and write our own qualifier for both caches, as follows;

```
@Qualifier
@Target({ElementType.FIELD, ElementType.PARAMETER, ElementType.
METHOD})
@Retention(RetentionPolicy.RUNTIME)
@Documented
public @interface OpenWeatherCache {
}
```

A qualifier for `WunderGroundCache` is as follows:

```
@Qualifier
@Target({ElementType.FIELD, ElementType.PARAMETER, ElementType.
METHOD})
@Retention(RetentionPolicy.RUNTIME)
@Documented
public @interface WunderGroundCache {
}
```

Now that we have defined the qualifiers for both caches, we have to define the configuration for each cache and apply the qualifiers on the appropriate implementation, as you can see in the following example:

```
public class Config{
  @ConfigureCache("openweather-cache")
  @OpenWeatherCache
  @Produces
  public Configuration openWeatherConfiguration() {
    return new ConfigurationBuilder().expiration()
      .lifespan(121, TimeUnit.HOURS).build();
  }

  @ConfigureCache("wunderground-cache")
  @WunderGroundCache
  @Produces
  public Configuration wunderGroundConfiguration() {
    return new ConfigurationBuilder().expiration()
      .lifespan(121, TimeUnit.HOURS).build();

  }
}
```

If you declare an injection point without specifying a qualifier, as we did in our first example, the container will explicitly assume the qualifier `@Default`. We can use the `@Default` qualifier to override the default cache configuration; to do so, we have to define a configuration method with the `@Produces` and `@Default` qualifiers, as shown in the following example:

```
@Produces
@Default
public Configuration defaultEmbeddedConfiguration() {
  return new ConfigurationBuilder().expiration()
    .lifespan(31, TimeUnit.HOURS).build();

}
```

Remote cache integration

The infinispan-cdi module provides support to integrate a RemoteCache or a RemoteCacheManager Hot Rod, as we did in the preceding examples with embedded caches. The following example shows how to override the default remote cache manager. Note that the new default cache manager must include the @ApplicationScope scope to prevent each injection operation to the cache being associated with a new cache manager instance:

```
@Produces
@ApplicationScoped
public RemoteCacheManager defaultRemoteCacheManager() {
  ConfigurationBuilder builder = new ConfigurationBuilder();
    builder.addServer().
    host("localhost").
    port(11222).
    connectionPool().
    lifo(true).
    maxActive(10).
    maxIdle(10).
    maxTotal(20).
    exhaustedAction(ExhaustedAction.CREATE_NEW).
    timeBetweenEvictionRuns(120000).
    minEvictableIdleTime(1800000).
    minIdle(1);
  return new RemoteCacheManager(builder.build());

  }
```

To inject the new default RemoteCacheManager, you've only to provide the @Inject annotation:

```
@Inject
private RemoteCacheManager remoteCacheManager;
```

You can do the same to inject RemoteCache:

```
@Inject
private RemoteCache<String, String> defaultRemoteCache;
```

JBoss AS7 configured Cache

If you're using JBoss AS 7, it provides an Infinispan subsystem, which provides caching support for High Availability services in the form of Infinispan caches and allows you to define your own configuration of named cache containers and caches in the server configuration file `standalone.xml` or `domain.xml`, so that they will be available upon server startup.

This allows you to refer to the Infinispan cache manager defined in the JBoss naming service using the JNDI lookup; normally you only need to annotate with the `@Resource` annotation for the default cache manager.

The following example shows an XML configuration of a custom Infinispan subsystem:

```
<subsystem xmlns="urn:jboss:domain:infinispan:1.2">
  <cache-container name="packt_container"
    default-cache="weatherCache" start="EAGER">
  <local-cache name="weatherCache">
    <transaction mode="NON_XA"/>
    <eviction strategy="LRU" max-entries="10000"/>
    <expiration max-idle="100000"/>
  </local-cache>
  </cache-container>
...
</subsystem>
```

Once you restart your JBoss server, you can check the JNDI binding in the JBoss Management Console, as shown in the following screenshot:

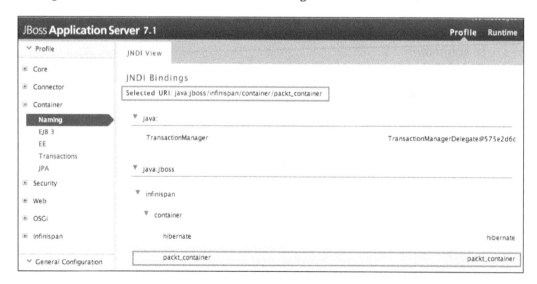

Now, you have only to annotate the producer with `@Resource` to use the JBoss Cache Manager:

```
@Produces
@Resource(lookup="java:jboss/packt/book-container")
private EmbeddedCacheManager jbossCacheManager;
```

An important thing to note is that you have to include the following code in your `MANIFEST.MF` or `pom.xml` file, if using Maven, then use the JBoss Dependencies:

```
Manifest-Version: 1.0
Dependencies: org.infinispan:main services
```

Change your `pom.xml` file using the following code snippet:

```
<archive>
  <manifestEntries>
    <Dependencies>org.infinispan export</Dependencies>
  </manifestEntries>
</archive>
```

Integrating with JCache annotations

The `infinispan-cdi` module provides a partial implementation of JCache caching annotations from JSR-107. These annotations provide a wrapper around an Infinispan cache to handle common use cases. The `infinispan-cdi` module provides the following standard method caching annotations that let you include caching capabilities effortlessly, just by annotating your methods:

- `@CacheResult` caches the result of a method call
- `@CachePut` caches a method parameter
- `@CacheRemoveEntry` removes an entry from a cache
- `@CacheRemoveAll` removes all entries from a cache

The following example presents a simple usage of JCache annotations, a class to expose cache information, and methods to manipulate the `openweather` cache:

```
@Named
@ApplicationScoped
public class OpenWeatherCacheInfo {

  private static Map<String, String> WeatherInfo = new
    HashMap<String, String>();

  @Inject
```

```
   @OpenWeatherCache
   private Cache<String, String> cache;

   public String getCacheName() {
     return cache.getName();
   }

   public int getNumberOfEntries() {
     return cache.size();
   }

   public EvictionStrategy getEvictionStrategy() {
     return cache.getCacheConfiguration().eviction().strategy();
   }

   public int getEvictionMaxEntries() {
     return cache.getCacheConfiguration().eviction().maxEntries();
   }

   public long getExpirationLifespan() {
     return cache.getCacheConfiguration().expiration().lifespan();
   }

   public String getCacheMode() {
     return cache.getCacheConfiguration().clustering().
cacheModeString();
   }

   public boolean isJMXEnabled() {
     return cache.getCacheConfiguration().jmxStatistics().enabled();
   }

   @CachePut(cacheName = "openweather-cache")
   public void createEntry(@CacheKey String key,
   @CacheValue String jsonWeather) {
   }

   @CacheResult(cacheName = "openweather-cache")
   public String getWeatherFor(@CacheKey String key){
     return WeatherInfo.get(key);
   }

   @CacheRemoveAll(cacheName = "openweather-cache")
   public void clearCache() {
   }
}
```

Note that the `getWeatherFor` method annotated with `@CacheResult` receives a parameter key annotated with `@CacheKey`, which can be used to retrieve weather information from the cache you want.

The `createEntry` method annotated with `@CachePut` will be used to create a new entry in the cache. We have to annotate one of the arguments (`jsonWeather`) with `@CacheValue`, to specify the parameter to be cached.

Finally, the `@CacheRemoveAll` is used to mark the `clearCache` method, which results in all cache entries being removed.

The next code snippet outlines a simple usage of the `OpenWeatherCacheInfo` class; we created a new simple web service to execute JCache operations:

```
@Inject
private OpenWeatherCacheInfo openWeatherInfo;

@WebMethod
public void jcacheOperations(String country, String city,
  String weather){
  printOpenWeatherCacheInfo();
  logger.infof("*** Get weather using JCache annotations ***");
  logger.infof("Looking the weather for %s = %s", getKey(country,
city), openWeatherInfo.getWeatherFor(getKey(country, city)));
    openWeatherInfo.createEntry(getKey(country, city),
      "The weather is good!!!!");
    logger.infof("Looking the weather again for %s = %s",
      getKey(country, city),
        openWeatherInfo.getWeatherFor(getKey(country, city)));
    openWeatherInfo.clearCache();
    logger.infof("Looking the weather after clean the
      cache s %s", getKey(country, city),
        openWeatherInfo.getWeatherFor(getKey(country, city)));
}
private void printOpenWeatherCacheInfo(){
  logger.info("Printing Open Weather ..........");
  logger.infof("Name: %s", openWeatherInfo.getCacheName());
  logger.infof("Cache Mode %s ", openWeatherInfo.getCacheMode());
  logger.infof("Number of entries: %d",
    openWeatherInfo.getNumberOfEntries());
  logger.infof("Eviction Strategy: %s",
    openWeatherInfo.getEvictionStrategy());
  logger.infof("Eviction Max Entries: %d ",
    openWeatherInfo.getEvictionMaxEntries());
  logger.infof("Expiration Lifespan: %d",
    openWeatherInfo.getExpirationLifespan());
```

```
    logger.infof("Is JMX Enabled? %s ",
        openWeatherInfo.isJMXEnabled());
}
```

If you call the above web service `jcacheOperations`, you should see the following output:

```
> Printing Open Weather ..........
> Name: openweather-cache
> Cache Mode LOCAL
> Number of entries: 1
> Eviction Strategy: NONE
> Eviction Max Entries: -1
> Expiration Lifespan: 43200000
> Is JMX Enabled? False
```

Using the Map/Reduce API

According to Gartner, from now on in-memory data grids and in-memory computing will be racing towards mainstream adoption and the market for this kind of technology is going to reach 1 billion by 2016. Thinking along these lines, Infinispan already provides a MapReduce API for distributed computing, which means that we can use Infinispan cache to process all the data stored in heap memory across all Infinispan instances in parallel.

If you're new to MapReduce, don't worry, we're going to describe it in the next section in a way that gets you up to speed quickly.

An introduction to Map/Reduce

MapReduce is a programming model introduced by Google, which allows for massive scalability across hundreds or thousands of servers in a data grid. It's a simple concept to understand for those who are familiar with distributed computing and clustered environments for data processing solutions.

 You can find the paper about MapReduce in the following link:
`http://research.google.com/archive/mapreduce.html`

The MapReduce has two distinct computational phases; as the name states, the phases are **map** and **reduce**:

- In the map phase, a function called `Map` is executed, which is designed to take a set of data in a given cache and simultaneously perform filtering, sorting operations, and outputs another set of data on all nodes.

- In the reduce phase, a function called `Reduce` is executed, which is designed to reduce the final form of the results of the map phase in one output. The reduce function is always performed after the map phase.

Map/Reduce in the Infinispan platform

The Infinispan MapReduce model is an adaptation of the Google original MapReduce model. There are four main components in each map reduce task, they are as follows:

- `MapReduceTask`: This is a distributed task allowing a large-scale computation to be transparently parallelized across Infinispan cluster nodes. This class provides a constructor that takes a cache whose data will be used as the input for this task. The `MapReduceTask` orchestrates the execution of the Mapper and Reducer seamlessly across Infinispan nodes.

- `Mapper`: A `Mapper` is used to process each input cache entry `K,V`. A Mapper is invoked by `MapReduceTask` and is migrated to an Infinispan node, to transform the K,V input pair into intermediate keys before emitting them to a Collector.

- `Reducer`: A `Reducer` is used to process a set of intermediate key results from the map phase. Each execution node will invoke one instance of `Reducer` and each instance of the `Reducer` only reduces intermediate keys results that are locally stored on the execution node.

- `Collator`: This collates results from reducers executed on the Infinispan cluster and assembles a final result returned to an invoker of `MapReduceTask`.

The following image shows that in a distributed environment, an Infinispan `MapReduceTask` is responsible for starting the process for a given cache, unless you specify an `onKeys(Object...)` filter, all available key/value pairs of the cache will be used as input data for the map reduce task:

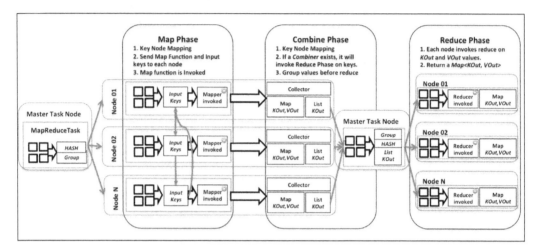

In the preceding image, the Map/Reduce processes are performing the following steps:

1. The `MapReduceTask` in the **Master Task Node** will start the **Map Phase** by hashing the task input keys and grouping them by the execution node they belong to and then, the Infinispan master node will send a map function and input keys to each node. In each destination, the map will be locally loaded with the corresponding value using the given keys.

2. The map function is executed on each node, resulting in a `map< KOut, VOut >` object on each node.

3. The **Combine Phase** is initiated when all results are collected, if a combiner is specified (via `combineWith(Reducer<KOut, VOut> combiner)` method), the combiner will extract the **KOut** keys and invoke the reduce phase on keys.

4. Before starting the **Reduce Phase**, Infinispan will execute an intermediate migration phase, where all intermediate keys and values are grouped.

5. At the end of the **Combine Phase**, a list of **KOut** keys are returned to the initial **Master Task Node**. At this stage, values (**VOut**) are not returned, because they are not needed in the master node.

6. At this point, Infinispan is ready to start the **Reduce Phase**; the **Master Task Node** will group **KOut** keys by the execution node and send a reduce command to each node where keys are hashed.

7. The reducer is invoked and for each **KOut** key, the reducer will grab a list of **VOut** values from a temporary cache belonging to `MapReduceTask`, wraps it with an iterator, and invokes the reduce method on it.

8. Each reducer will return one map with the **KOut/VOut** result values. The `reduce` command will return to the **Master Task Node**, which in turn will combine all resulting maps into one single map and return it as a result of `MapReduceTask`.

Sample application – find a destination

Now that we have seen what map and reduce are, and how the Infinispan model works, let's create a `Find Destination` application that illustrates the concepts we have discussed.

To demonstrate how CDI works, in the last section, we created a web service that provides weather information. Now, based on this same weather information service, let's create a map/reduce engine for the best destination based on simple business rules, such as destination type (sun destination, golf, skiing, and so on).

So, the first step is to create the `WeatherInfo` cache object that will hold information about the weather:

```java
public class WeatherInfo implements Serializable {

  private static final long serialVersionUID =
    -3479816816724167384L;

  private String country;
  private String city;
  private Date day;
  private Double temp;
  private Double tempMax;
  private Double tempMin;

  public WeatherInfo(String country, String city, Date day,
    Double temp) {
      this(country, city, day, temp, temp + 5, temp - 5);
  }

  public WeatherInfo(String country, String city, Date day,
    Double temp,
    Double tempMax, Double tempMin) {
    super();
```

```
            this.country = country;
            this.city = city;
            this.day = day;
            this.temperature = temp;
            this.temperatureMax = tempMax;
            this.temperatureMin = tempMin;
        }

    // Getters and Setters ommitted

        @Override
        public String toString() {
            return "{WeatherInfo:{ country:" + country + ", city:" +
                city + ", day:" + day + ", temperature:" + temperature + ",
                    temperatureMax:" + temperatureMax + ", temperatureMin:" +
                        temperatureMin + "}";
        }
    }
```

Now, let's create an `enum` object to define the type of destination a user can select and the rules associated with each destination. To keep it simple, we are going to have only two destinations, sun and skiing.

The `temperature` value will be used to evaluate if the destination can be considered the corresponding type:

```
    public enum DestinationTypeEnum {
        SUN(18d, "Sun Destination"), SKIING(-5d, "Skiing Destination");

        private Double temperature;
        private String description;

        DestinationTypeEnum(Double temperature, String description) {
            this.temperature = temperature;
            this.description = description;
        }

        public Double getTemperature() {
            return temperature;
        }

        public String getDescription() {
            return description;
        }
    }
```

Now it's time to create the `Mapper` class—this class is going to be responsible for validating whether each cache entry fits the destination requirements. To define the `DestinationMapper` class, just extend the `Mapper<KIn, VIn, KOut, VOut>` interface and implement your algorithm in the `map` method;

```
public class DestinationMapper implements
  Mapper<String, WeatherInfo, DestinationTypeEnum, WeatherInfo> {

  private static final long serialVersionUID =
    -3418976303227050166L;

  public void map(String key, WeatherInfo weather,
    Collector<DestinationTypeEnum, WeatherInfo> c) {
    if (weather.getTemperature() >= SUN.getTemperature()){
      c.emit(SUN, weather);
    }
    else if (weather.getTemperature() <=
      SKIING.getTemperature()) {
      c.emit(SKIING, weather);
    }
  }
}
```

The role of the `Reducer` class in our application is to return the best destination among all destinations, based on the highest temperature for sun destinations and the lowest temperature for skiing destinations, returned by the mapping phase. To implement the `Reducer` class, you'll need to implement the `Reducer<KOut, VOut>` interface:

```
public class DestinationReducer implements
Reducer<DestinationTypeEnum, WeatherInfo> {

  private static final long serialVersionUID = 7711240429951976280L;

  public WeatherInfo reduce(DestinationTypeEnum key,
Iterator<WeatherInfo> it) {
    WeatherInfo bestPlace = null;
    if (key.equals(SUN)) {
      while (it.hasNext()) {
        WeatherInfo w = it.next();
        if (bestPlace == null || w.getTemp() >
          bestPlace.getTemp()) {
          bestPlace = w;
        }
      }
```

```
        } else { /// Best for skiing
          while (it.hasNext()) {
            WeatherInfo w = it.next();
            if (bestPlace == null || w.getTemp() <
              bestPlace.getTemp()) {
              bestPlace = w;
            }
          }
        }

      return bestPlace;
    }
}
```

Finally, to execute our sample application, we can create a JUnit test case with the `MapReduceTask`. But first, we have to create a couple of cache entries before executing the task, which we are doing in the `setUp()` method:

```
public class WeatherInfoReduceTest {

  private static final Log logger =
    LogFactory.getLog(WeatherInfoReduceTest.class);

  private Cache<String, WeatherInfo> weatherCache;

  @Before
  public void setUp() throws Exception {
    Date today = new Date();
      EmbeddedCacheManager manager = new DefaultCacheManager();
      Configuration config = new ConfigurationBuilder()
      .clustering().cacheMode(CacheMode.LOCAL)
      .build();

      manager.defineConfiguration("weatherCache", config);
      weatherCache = manager.getCache("weatherCache");
      WeatherInfo
      weatherCache.put("1", new WeatherInfo("Germany", "Berlin",
        today, 12d));
      weatherCache.put("2", new WeatherInfo("Germany",
        "Stuttgart", today, 11d));
      weatherCache.put("3", new WeatherInfo("England", "London",
        today, 8d));
      weatherCache.put("4", new WeatherInfo("England",
        "Manchester", today, 6d));
```

```
        weatherCache.put("5", new WeatherInfo("Italy", "Rome",
          today, 17d));
        weatherCache.put("6", new WeatherInfo("Italy", "Napoli",
          today, 18d));
        weatherCache.put("7", new WeatherInfo("Ireland", "Belfast",
          today, 9d));
        weatherCache.put("8", new WeatherInfo("Ireland", "Dublin",
          today, 7d));
        weatherCache.put("9", new WeatherInfo("Spain", "Madrid",
          today, 19d));
        weatherCache.put("10", new WeatherInfo("Spain", "Barcelona",
          today, 21d));
        weatherCache.put("11", new WeatherInfo("France", "Paris",
          today, 11d));
        weatherCache.put("12", new WeatherInfo("France",
          "Marseille", today, -8d));
        weatherCache.put("13", new WeatherInfo("Netherlands",
          "Amsterdam", today, 11d));
        weatherCache.put("14", new WeatherInfo("Portugal", "Lisbon",
          today, 13d));
        weatherCache.put("15", new WeatherInfo("Switzerland",
          "Zurich", today, -12d));
    }


    @Test
    public void execute() {
        MapReduceTask<String, WeatherInfo, DestinationTypeEnum,
          WeatherInfo> task = new MapReduceTask<String, WeatherInfo,
            DestinationTypeEnum, WeatherInfo>(weatherCache);
        task.mappedWith(new DestinationMapper()).reducedWith(new
          DestinationReducer());
        Map<DestinationTypeEnum, WeatherInfo> destination =
          task.execute();
        assertNotNull(destination);
        assertEquals(destination.keySet().size(), 2);
        logger.info("********* PRINTING RESULTS FOR WEATHER CACHE
          *************");
        for (DestinationTypeEnum destinationType :
          destination.keySet()){
          logger.infof("%s - Best Place: %s
            \n",destinationType.getDescription(),
              destination.get(destinationType));
        }
      }
    }
```

When we execute the application, you should expect to see the following output:

```
INFO: Skiing Destination
Best Place: {WeatherInfo:{ country:Switzerland, city:Zurich,
  day:Mon Jun 02 19:42:22 IST 2014, temp:-12.0, tempMax:-7.0,
    tempMin:-17.0}
INFO: Sun Destination
Best Place: {WeatherInfo:{ country:Spain, city:Barcelona, day:Mon
  Jun 02 19:42:22 IST 2014, temp:21.0, tempMax:26.0, tempMin:16.0}
```

Improving the serialization process using externalizers

If something is clear at this point of the book, it is that when you put some object in the cache, the object will be serialized into a stream of bytes to be sent across the network into the target node, and then replicated between peers of the grid. And when you get an object from the grid, the cache entry needs to be deserialized back into a live object.

The process of serializing and deserializing an object can be time consuming; in normal configurations, this process can take around 20 percent of the time (it's important to note that Infinispan doesn't use the standard serialization mechanism due to performance reasons). Throughout the default Java serialization process, several reflection calls must be made to discover all the information needed about the class, and along the description of the class itself.

All the class description information is included in the stream, such as the serializable superclasses, field values, and all the instance data associated with the specific instance of the class, producing a large amount of (unnecessary) data.

To overcome some of these issues, Infinispan uses externalizers, which are part of a project called JBoss Marshalling framework, that contain a different serialization process based on magic numbers for known types; this improves the serialization/ deserialization process providing a more compact sequence of bytes.

For each known type, Infinispan registers an externalizer associated with a magic number, which replaces the reflective call for complete control of the marshalling and unmarshalling process.

However, if Infinispan cannot determine the object type of the cache entry, then it will rely on the default Java serialization process, which can dramatically decrease the performance of your application.

Introducing the Infinispan externalizer API

Infinispan provides an externalizable API to overcome the drawbacks of default serialization or to at least mitigate some of these performance problems.

The API contains the `Externalizer<T>` interface that lets you specify how specific object types are serialized. In fact, externalization is nothing but serialization (the externalizer interface extends Serializable), but it gives you complete control of the serialization process, which means that it's up to you to define how the class will marshall and unmarshall the contents of its instance.

 Marshalling is the process of converting Java POJOs into a data format that can be written and transferred over the wire. Unmarshalling is the reverse process whereby data read from a wire format can be transformed back into Java POJOs.

Making use of the externalizer interface can provide a great improvement in performance, but it will require some manual work.

You can use a customized externalizer in Infinispan by using the externalizer interface or using an advanced externalizer.

If you are familiar with the externalizer interface or the standard Java serialization, the implementation of the externalizer will not be difficult. As a developer, you will need to implement the `readObject(ObjectInput input)` method to read an instance from the stream and `writeObject(Object input, T object)` to write the object reference to the stream.

The following example shows a simple externalizer implementation for the `WeatherInfo` object used in our Map/Reduce code:

```
import org.infinispan.commons.marshall.Externalizer;

public class WeatherInfoExternalizer implements
  Externalizer<WeatherInfo>, Serializable{

  private static final long serialVersionUID =
    -2846683889209865017L;

  public void writeObject(ObjectOutput output, WeatherInfo
    WeatherInfo) throws IOException {
    output.writeObject(WeatherInfo.getCountry());
    output.writeObject(WeatherInfo.getCity());
    output.writeObject(WeatherInfo.getDay());
```

```
            output.writeDouble(WeatherInfo.getTemp());
            output.writeDouble(WeatherInfo.getTempMax());
            output.writeDouble(WeatherInfo.getTempMin());
    }

    public WeatherInfo readObject(ObjectInput input) throws
        IOException, ClassNotFoundException {
        WeatherInfo wm = new WeatherInfo(((String)
            input.readObject()),
            ((String) input.readObject()),
            ((Date) input.readObject()),
            input.readDouble(),
            input.readDouble(),
            input.readDouble());
        return wm;
    }
}
```

Now, in order to use the `WeatherInfoExternalizer` class, we will need to annotate the marshalled class, in this case, the `WeatherInfo` object with the `@SerializeWith` annotation, to indicate that our externalizer class should be used to serialize/unserialize it:

```
import org.infinispan.commons.marshall.SerializeWith;


@SerializeWith(WeatherInfoExternalizer.class)
public class WeatherInfo{

    private String country;
    private String city;
    private Date day;
    private Double temp;
    private Double tempMax;
    private Double tempMin;
    ...
}
```

It's quite easy and friendly to define externalizers in this way; however, it has some disadvantages.

First, this method is not so efficient if you have to support different versions of the same class, because of some constraints in the model.

Another issue, depending on the architectural style you choose for your application, such as **Domain Driven Design** (DDD), it might not be a good idea to couple the externalizer to your cache object, because by using the `@SerializeWith` annotation you might expose lower lever details, in this case, the `externalizer` class.

One last and generally worse problem occurs when you need to provide an externalizer for a class whose source is not available to you.

To overcome these limitations/disadvantages, Infinispan provides advanced externalizers.

Creating advanced externalizers

Since Infinispan 5.0, Infinispan provides an `AdvanceExternalizer` interface, an alternative solution for marshalling/unmarshalling defined classes. The good part is that it doesn't require any interface or annotations, so if the source code of the class you want to serialize or deserialize is not available or you cannot modify it, then that's definitely the way to go.

The following is an example of an `AdvancedExternalizer` interface, where we have to define and implement the `readObject()` and `writeObject()` methods again:

```
import org.infinispan.commons.marshall.AdvancedExternalizer;
import org.infinispan.commons.util.Util;

public class WeatherInfoAdvancedExternalizer implements
  AdvancedExternalizer<WeatherInfo>{

  public WeatherInfo readObject(ObjectInput input) throws
    IOException, ClassNotFoundException {
    return new WeatherInfo((String) input.readObject(), (String)
      input.readObject(), (Date) input.readObject(),
        input.readDouble());
  }

  public void writeObject(ObjectOutput output, WeatherInfo
    WeatherInfo) throws IOException {
    output.writeObject(WeatherInfo.getCountry());
    output.writeObject(WeatherInfo.getCity());
    output.writeObject(WeatherInfo.getDay());
    output.writeDouble(WeatherInfo.getTemp());
    output.writeDouble(WeatherInfo.getTempMax());
    output.writeDouble(WeatherInfo.getTempMin());
  }
```

```
      public Integer getId() {
        return 3252;
      }


      public Set<Class<? extends WeatherInfo>> getTypeClasses() {
        return Util.<Class<? extends
          WeatherInfo>>asSet(WeatherInfo.class);
      }
    }
```

Although we practically follow the same steps of the simple approach and implement the readObject() and writeObject() methods, the trick in the advanced externalizer lies with the implementation of the getTypeClasses() method.

This method is responsible for making the link between the externalizer and a collection of classes that the externalizer can marshall/unmarshall.

In our last example, getTypeClasses() returns only the WeatherInfo class, but if you have a externalizer responsible for more that one class, you can return all classes separated by comma, as shown in the following example:

```
      public Set<Class<? extends BaseClass>> getTypeClasses() {
        return Util.asSet(ConcreteClass01.class, ConcreteClass02.class);
      }
```

These examples may cover most of the scenarios, but you may face scenarios where the class you want to externalize is private, which makes the last solution impossible, since you cannot reference the class instance.

In these cases, it's possible to reference the private class by providing the fully qualified class name.

In the next example, you can see a new version of the WeatherInfoAdvancedExternalizer class, where the getTypeClasses() loads the WeatherInfo$PrivateWeatherInfo private class:

```
    public class WeatherInfoAdvancedExternalizer implements
      AdvancedExternalizer<Object>{

      public WeatherInfo readObject(ObjectInput input) throws
        IOException, ClassNotFoundException {
        return new WeatherInfo((String) input.readObject(), (String)
          input.readObject(), (Date) input.readObject(),
            input.readDouble());
      }
```

```
public void writeObject(ObjectOutput output, Object WeatherInfo)
  throws IOException {
  if (WeatherInfo instanceof WeatherInfo) {
    output.writeObject( ((WeatherInfo)
      WeatherInfo).getCountry());
    output.writeObject( ((WeatherInfo)
      WeatherInfo).getCity());
    output.writeObject( ((WeatherInfo) WeatherInfo).getDay());
    output.writeDouble( ((WeatherInfo) WeatherInfo).getTemp());
    output.writeDouble( ((WeatherInfo)
      WeatherInfo).getTempMax());
    output.writeDouble( ((WeatherInfo)
      WeatherInfo).getTempMin());
  }
}

public Integer getId() {
  return 3252;
}

public Set<Class<? extends Object>> getTypeClasses() {
  return Util.<Class<? extends Object>>asSet(
    Util.loadClass("com.packtpub.infinispan.chapter11.mr.domain.
      WeatherInfo",
        Thread.currentThread().getContextClassLoader()),
    Util.loadClass("com.packtpub.infinispan.chapter11.mr.domain.
      WeatherInfo$PrivateWeatherInfo",
        Thread.currentThread().getContextClassLoader()));
}
}
```

Another noticeable difference is the addition of the getId() method—this method returns a positive integer that is used in real time to identify the externalizer, which itself will be used to read the incoming buffer. An AdvancedExternalizer interface is required to be associated with an identifier, so this method should never return a negative number. You can return a null value, but you will need to define this number via declarative or programmatic configuration.

Before you start using it, you will need to register the advanced externalizer programmatically or via XML, as you can see in the following sample, where we are also registering the externalizer created in our last example and defining an identifier (optional).

The code in Infinispan 6 is as follows:

```
<global>
  <serialization
    marshallerClass="org.infinispan.marshall.
      VersionAwareMarshaller" version="1.0">
    <advancedExternalizers>
      <advancedExternalizer id="3252"
        externalizerClass="com.packtpub.infinispan.chapter11.
          mr.externalizer.WeatherInfoAdvancedExternalizer" />
    </advancedExternalizers>
  </serialization>
</global>
```

You can do this in Infinispan 7, with the following code:

```
<cache-container>
  <serialization
    marshaller="org.infinispan.marshall.core.
      VersionAwareMarshaller" version="1.0">
    <advanced-externalizer id="3252"
      class="com.packtpub.infinispan.chapter11.mr.
        externalizer.WeatherInfoAdvancedExternalizer" />
  </serialization>
</cache-container>
```

Otherwise, you can configure a transactional cache programmatically:

```
GlobalConfiguration gc = new GlobalConfigurationBuilder()
  .serialization()
    .addAdvancedExternalizer(3252, new
      WeatherInfoAdvancedExternalizer())
  .build();
```

Summary

In this chapter, we got an overview of cross-site replication, and how you can implement several cache topologies using the Infinispan technology.

You learned how to work with applications in modern distributed server architecture, using the Map Reduce API, and how it can abstract parallel programming into two simple primitives, the map and reduce methods. We have seen a sample use case Find Destination that demonstrated how use map reduce almost in real time.

We also discussed how you could make use of Infinispan's CDI module and some best practices to improve the quality of the code and the productivity. You learned how the CDI specification offers a standard, portable, and type safe support for dependency injection to Java EE. And you also learned how to create a simple application to start using CDI.

You also learned the differences between serialization and externalization and how to create advanced externalizers to define how to convert a cache object to bytes and improve the performance of your application.

This brings us to the end of our little adventure with Infinispan! We have covered a lot of critical concepts about in-memory data grids, scalability, NoSQL, patterns, monitoring, and other interesting topics. But that's not enough, there is always something new to learn, I invite you to read the online documentation at `http://infinispan.org/documentation/`, which is always updated with new content regarding the new features.

Index

Symbol

\<expiration\> element
  Lifespan attribute 94
  maxIdle attribute 95
  reaperEnabled attribute 95
  wakeUpInterval attribute 94

A

abort command 338
ACID
  about 40-43
  URL 46
Active/Passive configuration 49
addTicketRequest method 209
administrators use cases
  about 175-177
  administration UI, building with JBoss
    Forge 177
Another Extendable SHell (Æsh) 329
architecture, Infinispan 60
Arquillia
  about 164
  URL 164
Associations 348
asynchronous replication
  about 130, 131
  asynchronous marshalling 133
  asyncMarshalling attribute 132
  replication queue 134
  replQueueClass attribute 132
  replQueueInterval attribute 132
  useReplQueue attribute 133

authorization policies
  client configuration 314-316
  configuration 312-314
  configuring 310, 311
  Realm configuration 311, 312

B

Backbone Collections 189
Backbone Events 189
Backbone models 189
Backbone Views 189
Basic Available, Soft State, Eventual
    Consistency (BASE)
  about 45, 46
  URL 46
basic commands, CLI
  cache 333
  connect 333
  container 333
  disconnect 333
  quit 334
batching commands, CLI
  abort 338
  end 337
  start 337
batch mode 227, 228
begin command 336
Building Blocks 371
built-in configuration files
  jgroups-ec2.xml 373
  jgroups-tcp.xml 373
  jgroups-udp.xml 373

C

cache
  Read-Through mode 156-158
  Write-Through mode 156-158
cache API
  about 85-88
  evictions 88-91
  eviction, versus expiration 95
  expiration, configuring 92-94
  features 86
cache-aside programming pattern
  implementing 155, 156
cache command 333
CacheContainer class 77
cache-container element
  configuring 80-82
  default-cache attribute 80
  eviction-executor attribute 80
  listener-executor attribute 80
  name attribute 80
  persistence-executor attribute 81
  replication-queue-executor attribute 81
  shutdown-hook attribute 81
  statistics attribute 81
cache-level events
  annotations 107, 108
CAP theorem 43, 44
CDI
  about 391-400
  Infinispan, integrating with 399
  support, setting in Maven POM 400
CDI support, setting in Maven POM
  about 400
  default configuration, customizing 403, 404
  Infinispan cache, injecting into
      Beans 401, 402
  JBoss AS7 configured Cache 406, 407
  JCache annotations, integrating
      with 407-410
  remote cache integration 405
cleanUp() method 197
clear command 334
CLI
  about 329
  commands, using 331
  starting 330, 331

CLI commands
  basic commands 333
  batching commands 337
  data types, defining 332
  for cache management 335
  for cache manipulation 334
  for obtaining statistics and system
      information 338
  for transaction management 336
  rollback 337
  time values, defining 332
  using 331
CLI commands, for cache management
  arguments 336
  create 336
  encoding 336
  upgrade 335
CLI commands, for cache manipulation
  clear 334
  evict 334
  get 334
  put 334
  remove 335
  replace 335
CLI commands, for obtaining statistics
      and system information
  info 339
  locate 338
  site 338
  stats 339
  version 339
CLI commands, for transaction management
  begin 336
  commit 337
  rollback 337
client/server mode
  about 62, 281, 282
  Memcached 62
  REST HTTP protocol 62
  Server Modules REST 62
Client Session State
  about 190
  advantage 191
  disadvantage 191
clustering modes
  about 121, 122
  distribution mode 135

invalidation mode 124, 125
L1 caching 144
local mode 122, 123
replicated mode 126, 127
command line interface. *See* **CLI**
Comma Separated Values (CSV) 228
commit command 337
Compare And Swap (CAS) 319
components, Map/Reduce
Collator 411
Mapper 411
MapReduceTask 411
Reducer 411
concurrency control, issues
about 232-236
Dirty Reads 233
Lost Updates 234
Non-Repeatable Reads 233
Phantom Reads 234
READ COMMITTED 235
READ UNCOMMITTED 235
REPEATABLE READ 235
SERIALIZABLE 235
configuration settings
about 74-76
clustering element 75
compatibility element 75
customInterceptors element 74
dataContainer element 74
deadlockDetection element 75
eviction element 74
expiration element 75
indexing element 75
invocationBatching element 75
jmxStatistics element 75
locking element 74
persistence element 74
sites element 74
storeAsBinary element 75
transaction element 74
unsafe element 75
versioning element 75
connect command 333
container command 333
Contexts and Dependency Injection.
See **CDI**

createBookingFromCart method 209
create command 336
**Create, Read, Update, and Delete
(CRUD) 13**
cross site replication
about 392
and transactions 397
configuring 393-397
site offline, marking 399
site online, marking 399
using, with non-transactional caches 398
using, with transactional caches 398
cURL
about 295
options 296
URL 296

D

data
access patterns 149
versioning 246
database
clustering 49, 50
scaling out 47
**Database Management System
(DBMS) 39**
Database Session State
about 191
advantages 191
disadvantages 191
database scaling, options
about 47
Active/Passive configuration 49
Master-Slave replication 48, 49
database sharding
about 50, 51
horizontal partitioning 53
structure 53, 54
vertical partitioning 51, 52
data grid, Infinispan 2
data, persisting in Infinispan
about 96, 97
cache loader, configuring 98
filesystem-based cache loaders 98, 99
JDBC-based cache loaders 99
JDBC cache loader, selecting 102

JPA cache store 100, 101
passivation, using in application 103, 104
datastore providers, Hibernate OGM
CouchDBDatastoreProvider 345
EhcacheDatastoreProvider 344
InfinispanDatastoreProvider 344
MapDatastoreProvider 344
MongoDBDatastoreProvider 344
Neo4jDatastoreProvider 345
data types, CLI
boolean 332
double 332
float 332
int 332
JSON 332
long 332
String 332
Universally Unique IDentifier (UUID) 332
data types, second level cache
about 152
collections 152
entities 152
query results 152
timestamps 152
deadlock detection 244, 245
declarative configuration, on Infinispan 6.0.x
about 68
configuration settings 74-77
default element 69
global configuration (globalType) 70, 71
global element 68
namedCache element 69
declarative configuration, on Infinispan 7.0.x
about 77
cache-container element,
    configuring 77-82
JGroups element 78
threads subsystem, configuring 77-79
Dependency Injection (DI) 399
design tradeoffs 39
directory-based partitioning 53-55
disconnect command 333
distribution mode
about 135-143
capacityFactor attribute 138

factory attribute 137
hashFunctionClass attribute 137
implementations 143
numOwners attribute 137
numSegments attribute 137
Server Hinting mechanism 143
Domain Driven Design (DDD) 421

E

Eclipse
TicketMonster, project structure 167
encoding command 336
end command 337
ENTITIES 346
Errai
about 164
URL 164
event listeners
cache-level events, listening 107, 108
cache manager-level events,
    writing 111, 112
event listeners, registering 113
listener API 105
logging configuration, in Infinispan 114
registering 113, 114
writing 105
evict command 334
eviction policies
LIRS 88
LRU 88
NONE 89
UNORDERED 89
Expression Language (EL) 401
externalizers
advanced externalizers, creating 421-424
Infinispan externalizer API 419-421
used, for improving serialization
    process 418

F

failure detection protocol
about 383
and Infinispan 55
first-level caching 150

G

getCacheContainer() method 197
getCart method 209
get command 334
getId() method 423
global configuration (globalType)
  about 70
  asyncListenerExecutor element 70
  asyncTransportExecutor element 70
  evictionScheduledExecutor element 70
  modules element 71
  remoteCommandsExecutor element 70
  replicationQueueScheduledExecutor
    element 71
  serialization element 71
  site element 71
  sit element 71
  totalOrderExecutor element 71
group communication
  about 367-369
  Groups 369
  Members 369

H

hash partitioning 53
Hibernate Object/Grid Mapper
    (Hibernate OGM)
  about 341-343
  architecture 343-345
  creating, with Maven 351, 352
  domain model, creating 360-365
  features 343
  Infinispan caches, configuring 357-359
  installing 350, 351
  mapping, working 345-349
  persistence unit, configuring 353
  project, creating with Maven 351
  running, configuration properties 356, 357
  running, in Java EE environment 354
  running, in standalone JTA
    environment 355
  running, without JTA 355
  URL 350
  using 350, 351

high availability
  and Infinispan 58
high IRR (HIR) 89
horizontal partitioning 53
horizontal scalability 38
Hot Rod application
  authentication, configuring 308
  authorization policies, configuring 310, 311
  SASL framework 308
  supported SASL mechanisms 309
Hot Rod clients
  about 304
  Hot Rod Java Client, using 305
  URL 304
Hot Rod server
  RemoteCacheManager, starting 305-307
  using 303
HTTP request headers
  Accept 293
  Content-Type element 294
  maxIdleTimeSeconds 294
  performAsync 294
  timeToLiveSeconds 294
  using, for GET operations 293
  using, for HEAD operations 293
  using, for POST operations 293
  using, for PUT operations 294
HTTP requests
  Apache HttpClient 290
  httplib 290
  HttpWebRequest 290
  java.net.* package 290
  libcurl 290
  open-uri 290
  urllib2 290

I

Infinispan
  about 1, 46
  adding, to TicketMonster 193, 195
  advantages 2
  alerts, creating 277-280
  and high availability 58
  and networks partitions 55, 56
  and performance 35, 36
  architecture 60

building, from source 21, 22
caches, using for seat reservations 198-201
CLI commands 331
configuring, as hibernate second-level
    cache 152-154
contents, viewing 6-9
contribution, URL 26
data grid 2-4
data, persisting 96
DIGEST-MD5 mechanism 309
EXTERNAL mechanism 309
GSSAPI mechanism 309
importing, to IntelliJ IDE 22-24
infrastructure, configuring 196, 197
installing 6
integrating, with CDI 399
interacting, via JMX 252
isolation levels, configuring 236-241
JGroups settings, customizing 372-374
Maven, using 9-11
memcached server 318
monitoring 274-276
monitoring, with JConsole 255-258
monitoring, with VisualVM 258
operations, planning 276, 277
operations, scheduling 276, 277
PLAIN mechanism 309
project, creating 15-20
project, creating manually with
    Maven 20, 21
shopping carts, implementing 201-212
transaction 216
upgrades, URL 96
URL, for downloading 5
used, for improving performance 31, 32
using 5
WebSocket server 325

Infinispan APIs
  about 85
  cache API 85
  JCache API 86
  TreeCache API 85

Infinispan cache
  configuring 67, 68
  configuring, URL 85
  declarative configuration,
    on Infinispan 6.0.x 68

  declarative configuration,
    on Infinispan 7.0.x 77
  programmatic configuration 82-85

Infinispan clustered cache, anatomy
  about 60
  cache container 63
  client/server mode 62
  default cache 63, 64
  embedded (P2P) mode 61
  naming 64-67

Infinispan externalizer API 419-421

Infinispan interaction, via JMX
  about 252
  cache level 254
  CacheManager level 252-254
  JConsole, using 255-258
  MBeans 262
  monitoring, with VisualVM 258-261

info command 339

IntelliJ
  TicketMonster, project structure 168, 169

Internet Engineering Task Force (IETF) 325

Inter-Reference Recency (IRR) 88

invalidation mode 124, 125

Inversion of Control (IoC) 399

J

JAR file
  URL, for download 25

Java
  used, for management 249, 250
  used, for monitoring 249, 250

Java applications
  managing, with JMX 250, 251
  monitoring, with JMX 250, 251

Java Architecture for XML Binding (JAXB)
  about 298
  URL 298

Java Caching API (JSR-107)
  about 115-118
  Cache.Entry interface 116
  Cache interface 116
  CacheManager interface 116
  CachingProvider interface 116
  ExpiryPolicy interface 116

Java Client
   used, for creating Infinispan memcached
      server 323, 324
Java Community Process (JCP) 5, 342
Java Cryptography Architecture (JCA) 309
Java Management Extensions. *See* JMX
Java Mission Control (JMC) 250
Java Native Interface (JNI) 104
Java Persistence API (JPA) 100
Java Persistence Query Language
      (JPQL) 100, 345
Java Specification Request (JSR) 5
Java Temporary Caching API (JCACHE) 5
Java Transaction API (JTA) 217-220
JBoss developer framework. *See* JDF
JBoss Forge
   for Eclipse plugin 179-181
   installation 178
   setup 178
   URL, for download 178
   used, for building administration UI 177
JBoss.org Maven Repository 5
JCache annotations
   @CachePut 407
   @CacheRemoveAll 407
   @CacheRemoveEntry 407
   @CacheResult 407
   integrating with 407
JConsole
   URL 256
   used, for monitoring Infinispan 255-258
JDBC cache loaders
   JdbcBinaryCacheStore 99
   JdbcMixedCacheStore 100
   JdbcStringBasedCacheStore 100
JDF
   about 164
   components 164
   examples 164
   Quickstarts 164
JGroups
   about 369
   architecture 370-372
   features 369
   protocols 375
   settings, customizing on Infinispan 372-374
   URL 374

JGroups protocols
   failure detection 382
   flow control 389
   fragmentation of large messages 385, 386
   group membership 386, 387
   membership discovery 378-381
   merging category 382
   message stability 389
   ordering protocols 386
   overview 375
   reliable transmission 384, 385
   security 388
   state transfer 387
   transport protocol 375-378
   URL 375
JMX
   about 249
   Infinispan, interaction via 252
   used, for managing Java
      applications 250, 251
   used, for monitoring Java
      applications 250, 251
JPA caching 151

K

key-based partitioning 53
key k01 321

L

L1 caching
   about 144-146
   enabled attribute 145
   invalidationThreshold attribute 145
   lifespan attribute 145
   onRehash attribute 145
Least Recently Used (LRU) 286
listener API
   about 105
   cluster listeners, in Infinispan 7.0 106, 107
listener method 106
local area network (LAN) 367
local mode 122, 124
locate command 338
lock acquisition timeout (LAT) 243

lock mechanisms
   explicit locking 242
   implicit locking 242
lock() method 187
lock striping 240
lock timeouts 243
low IRR (LIR) 89

M

management tools
   about 266
   RHQ 266
Mapper class 415
map phase 411
Map/Reduce
   about 410
   in Infinispan platform 411-413
   sample application 413-418
   URL 410
Map/Reduce API
   using 410
marshalling process 419
Master-Slave replication 48, 49
Maven
   used, for creating Hibernate OGM
      project 351, 352
   using 9-11
Maven POM
   CDI support, setting up 400
MBeans 262-266
membership discovery category, JGroups
   about 378
   AWS_PING 380
   BPING 379
   FILE_PING 379
   JDBC_PING 379
   MPING 379
   Persistent Discovery Cache (PDC) 380
   PING 379
   RACKSPACE_PING 379
   S3_PING 379
   SWIFT_PING 380
   TCPGOSSIP 379
   TCPPING 379
memcached protocol
   about 319

add command 319
append command 319
cas command 319
decr command 320
delete command 320
get command 319
gets command 319
incr command 320
prepend command 319
replace command 319
set command 319
memcached server
   about 318
   connecting, Java Client used 323, 324
   issues 318
   memcached protocol 319-322
MIME type
   URL 294
Multicast Flow Control (MFC) 389
multiversion concurrency control
      (MVCC) 236

N

namedCache element 69
Network Attached Storage (NAS) 49
networks partitions
   and Infinispan 55
NoSQL stores
   column family stores 342
   document databases 342
   graph databases 342
   key-value stores 342
numVirtualNode method 142

O

Object/Relational Mapping
      (ORM) 98, 150, 341
openCart method 209
open source software (OSS) projects
   contribution 25, 26
ordering protocols, JGroups
   about 386
   SEQUENCER 386
   Total Order Anycast (TOA) 386

P

partition handling
  configuring 57
performance
  and Infinispan 35, 36
  and scalability 30, 31
  improving, Infinispan used 31, 32
  tuning 33-35
persistence unit, Hibernate OGM project
  configuring 353, 354
  transaction management 354
Persistent Discovery Cache (PDC)
    protocol 380
Plain Old Java Object (POJO) 341
PrincipalRoleMapper interface
  ClusterRoleMapper 314
  CommonNameRoleMapper 313
  Custom Role Mapper 314
  IdentityRoleMapper 313
Principles of Distributed Computing
    (PODC) 43
project structure, TicketMonster
  in Eclipse 167
  in IntelliJ 168, 169
put command 334

Q

query cache 151
quit command 334

R

range partitioning 53
Read-Through mode, cache 156-158
Recovery Manager 230
reduce phase 411
Reducer class 415
relational databases
  ACID 40-43
  distributed transactions 40-43
reliable transmission protocols, JGroups
  NAKACK 384
  NAKACK2 384
  RSVP 384
  UNICAST 384

UNICAST2 384
UNICAST3 384
Remote Method Invocation (RMI) 368
Remote Procedure Calls (RPC) 61, 289
remove command 335
replace command 335
replicated mode
  about 126
  asynchronous replication 127-132
  synchronous replication 127-129
Representational State Transfer (REST)
    services
  about 288
  components 288
  connectors 288
  data elements 288
  testing, with RESTClient 296, 297
REST API
  about 290, 292
  Client side code 295
  cURL 295
  DELETE method 291
  GET method 291
  HEAD method 291
  HTTP request headers, using for GET
    operation 293
  HTTP request headers, using for
    HEAD operation 293
  HTTP request headers, using for
    POST operation 293
  HTTP request headers, using for
    PUT operation 293
  POST method 291
  PUT method 291
  RESTful web services, consuming
    with Java 297
  supported HTTP methods 291
RESTful web services
  consuming, with Java 297-300
  Java.net 300, 301
REST server
  about 288
  configuring, on earlier versions 289, 290
  REST API 290
  REST services 288
RHQ
  about 266-268

components 266, 267
configuring 268
database 266
Infinispan, monitoring 274
Infinispan plugin, installing 271
installation guide, URL 268
installing 268
plugins 267
remote API 267
URL 280
web interface 267
RHQ Agent
installing 272, 273
RHQ Server
about 266
installing 268-270
URL 268
rollback command 337

S

sample application
running 11-15
scalability
and performance 30, 31
horizontal scalability 38
improving 36
vertical scalability 37
second-level cache
about 150, 151
configuring in Hibernate, Infinispan
used 150
data types 152
security protocols, JGroups
about 388
AUTH 388
ENCRYPT 388
serialization process
improving, with externalizers 418
server modules
about 282
configuration 284
server, starting 283
URL 282
server modules configuration
about 284
endpoint, customizing 284-287

Infinispan subsystem, customizing 284-287
protocol interoperability, enabling 287
Server Session State
about 191
advantage 191
disadvantage 191
implementing 192
**Simple Authentication and Security Layer
(SASL) 308**
**Simple Network Management Protocol
(SNMP) 249**
Site Backup 49
site command 338
Software as a Service (SaaS) 50, 65
start command 337
state transfer protocols, JGroups
about 387
BARRIER 387
pbcast.STATE 387
pbcast.STATE_TRANSFER 387
STATE_SOCK 387
stats command 339
Storage Area Network (SAN) 49
synchronous replication
about 128
awaitInitialTransfer attribute 130
chunkSize attribute 129
fetchInMemoryState attribute 129
timeout attribute 130

T

Teiid
URL 345
tenant 64
threads subsystem configuration
about 78
blocking-bounded-queue-thread-pool 80
blocking-bounded-queue-thread-pool
element 79
scheduled-thread-pool 80
TicketMonster
about 163
architecture 181-183
clustered Web servers, versus
stateful session 190

design 181-183
domain model 184, 185
Infinispan, adding 193-195
installing 165, 166
master data 192
operational data 192
pattern, selecting 192, 193
project structure 166
running 165
scaling 189
service layer 186-189
URL 165, 195
use cases 169
utility classes 185, 186
Total Order Anycast (TOA) protocol 386
transactional manager lookup classes
DummyTransactionManagerLookup 220
GenericTransactionManagerLookup 220
JBossStandaloneJTAManagerLookup 220
transactional modes
about 221
non-transactional data access 222
transactional models
about 222
optimistic transaction 223, 224
pessimistic transaction 225, 226
selecting 226
transaction recovery
enabling 229-231
integrating, with Transaction Manager 232
transactions per second (tps) 32
transport protocol, JGroups
about 375-378
TCP 375
TUNNEL 376
UDP 375
TreeCache API
URL 86

U

Unicast Flow Control (UFC) 389
Unified Modeling Language (UML) 346
uniform resource identifiers (URI) 290
Universally Unique IDentifier (UUID) 332

upgrade command
about 335
URL 336
use cases, TicketMonster
about 169
administrators use cases 175
book tickets 173
look for current events 170
look for venues 171
select shows 171, 172
view current bookings 174
User Datagram Protocol (UDP) 369
utility classes, TicketMonster
Base64.java 185
*CacheProducer.java 185
CircularBuffer.java 186
*DataDir.java 186
ForwardingMap.java 186
MultivaluedHashMap.java 186
Reflections.java 186
Resources.java 186

V

version command 339
vertical partitioning 51, 52
vertical scalability 37
VisualVM
used, for monitoring Infinispan 258-261

W

WebSocket
about 325
URL 326
WebSocket API
about 326
Infinispan JavaScript API, using 327-329
in Java 327
World Wide Web (WWW) 288
Write-behind cache
about 158, 159
advantage 158
Scheduled strategy 160
Unscheduled strategy 159
Write-Through mode, cache 157, 158

X

XA (eXtended Architecture) 218
XAResource interface 218

Thank you for buying
Infinispan Data Grid Platform Definitive Guide

About Packt Publishing

Packt, pronounced 'packed', published its first book, *Mastering phpMyAdmin for Effective MySQL Management*, in April 2004, and subsequently continued to specialize in publishing highly focused books on specific technologies and solutions.

Our books and publications share the experiences of your fellow IT professionals in adapting and customizing today's systems, applications, and frameworks. Our solution-based books give you the knowledge and power to customize the software and technologies you're using to get the job done. Packt books are more specific and less general than the IT books you have seen in the past. Our unique business model allows us to bring you more focused information, giving you more of what you need to know, and less of what you don't.

Packt is a modern yet unique publishing company that focuses on producing quality, cutting-edge books for communities of developers, administrators, and newbies alike. For more information, please visit our website at www.packtpub.com.

About Packt Open Source

In 2010, Packt launched two new brands, Packt Open Source and Packt Enterprise, in order to continue its focus on specialization. This book is part of the Packt Open Source brand, home to books published on software built around open source licenses, and offering information to anybody from advanced developers to budding web designers. The Open Source brand also runs Packt's Open Source Royalty Scheme, by which Packt gives a royalty to each open source project about whose software a book is sold.

Writing for Packt

We welcome all inquiries from people who are interested in authoring. Book proposals should be sent to author@packtpub.com. If your book idea is still at an early stage and you would like to discuss it first before writing a formal book proposal, then please contact us; one of our commissioning editors will get in touch with you.

We're not just looking for published authors; if you have strong technical skills but no writing experience, our experienced editors can help you develop a writing career, or simply get some additional reward for your expertise.

JBoss EAP6 High Availability

ISBN: 978-1-78328-243-2   Paperback: 166 pages

Leverage the power of JBoss EAP6 to successfully build high-availability clusters quickly and efficiently

1. A thorough introduction to the new domain mode provided by JBoss EAP6.

2. Use mod_jk and mod_cluster with JBoss EAP6.

3. Learn how to apply SSL in a clustering environment.

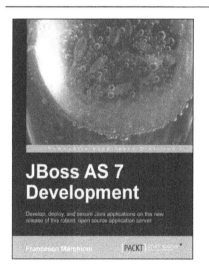

JBoss AS 7 Development

ISBN: 978-1-78216-134-9   Paperback: 326 pages

Develop, deploy, and secure Java applications on the new release of this robust, open source application server

1. A complete guide for JBoss developers covering everything from basic installation to creating, debugging, and securing Java EE applications on this popular, award-winning JBoss application server.

2. Master the most important areas of Java Enterprise programming including EJB 3.1, JPA, Contexts and Dependency Injection, web services, the security framework, and more.

3. Starts with the basics of JBoss AS 7 and moves on to cover important advanced topics with the help of easy-to-understand, practical examples.

Please check **www.PacktPub.com** for information on our titles